EMILY
BRONTË

Portrait of Emily Brontë, by Branwell Brontë

WINIFRED GÉRIN

EMILY
BRONTË

A BIOGRAPHY

OXFORD   NEW YORK   MELBOURNE
OXFORD UNIVERSITY PRESS
1978

Oxford University Press Walton Street, Oxford OX2 6DP

OXFORD   LONDON   GLASGOW
NEW YORK   TORONTO   MELBOURNE   WELLINGTON
KUALA LUMPUR   SINGAPORE   JAKARTA   HONG KONG   TOKYO
DELHI   BOMBAY   CALCUTTA   MADRAS   KARACHI
IBADAN   NAIROBI   DAR ES SALAAM   CAPE TOWN

ISBN 0 19 281251 3

© Oxford University Press 1971

First published 1971
Reprinted (with corrections) 1972
First issued as an Oxford Paperback 1978

MC81-0104

*Printed in Great Britain by
Fletcher & Son Ltd, Norwich*

FOR JOHN

PREFACE

EMILY BRONTË has been the subject of many books, even if few of them can be classed as biographies. The scarcity of direct evidence relating to her and the mystery that has been allowed to surround her life, while enhancing her appeal for writers, has tempted them to produce unauthenticated narratives and to invent where they could not record. This has been the chief cause of their failure.

Every writer on Emily Brontë finds himself handicapped from the outset by the same difficulty—the present biographer can claim no exception to the rule—that is, of the initial lack of material on which to base a biography. Whereas the writer on Charlotte, on Branwell, on their father, and, to a lesser extent, on Anne, has a wealth of documentation to work on that covers the whole range of their lives, for Emily no such material exists. Whether her early writings were prose or verse, good or bad, no one can now judge; they have disappeared, together with the whole body of her prose 'Gondal' chronicles. Whether the loss to literature be great can only be guessed; what is certain is that the loss to the biographer is incalculable.

Where personal statement is lacking as with Emily Brontë, of whom only three letters have been preserved, compared with the six or seven hundred of Charlotte, the want has to be supplied by the witness of others, with the effect that, however trustworthy they may be, Emily Brontë is heard through their medium, at second hand, seldom speaking in her own voice. When it is remembered how vital to a biography is the part played by the letters and reported speech of the protagonist, it can be judged how crippling are their absence to the would-be recorder of her life.

Her first memorialist, her devoted sister Charlotte, was so imbued with the tragedy of her loss that she could not speak of her without undertones of awe and pity. Her tributes are in the nature of apologias, not of biography. To her, through her confidences to Mrs. Gaskell, is mainly due the image of Emily propagated ever since, of a kind of Sibyl speaking in riddles, unapproachable to ordinary mortals, 'a remnant of the Titans', as Mrs. Gaskell reported of her, 'great-granddaughter of the giants'. In this respect, the witness of Ellen Nussey, who knew her when she was young and carefree, and of the parsonage servants who remembered her practical good sense and capable management, are useful correctives. Emily Brontë herself was not in the least portentous in writing about the circumstances of her life, as her objective, unselfconscious, contented diary-papers remain to show. The pity is that there are so few of them.

The effect of the mass–destruction of Emily's papers has been to leave the field wide open to speculation: on the one hand her life has been shown to be as romantic and emotionally charged as her own Gondal writings (of this school are Virginia Moore and Romer Wilson), at the other extreme are the scholars like Professor Ratchford of Texas University, who have sought to eliminate all biographical content from Emily Brontë's writings, to the extent even of denying the recognizable Haworth landmarks on the Gondal scene.

To seek the truth that lies between these two extremes, to correct the image of a girl who has been thought and spoken of as being always, at all ages, the woman she eventually became in the last three years of her life— a kind of Athena sprung complete from the head of Zeus—to show the degrees of her growth both as woman and visionary, the influences on her childhood, the causes for the major change in her last years, has been the present biographer's main excuse for attempting to write yet another book on the subject.

No one can claim to be qualified to write on Emily Brontë, though two or three writers have eminently succeeded in doing so (Jacques Blondel and Muriel Spark in particular), but a prerequisite to such an attempt must be to know not only Emily's work, but her home and the region that inspired her writings. This I have managed to do, living for ten consecutive years in Haworth, working throughout that time on the Brontë material preserved at the parsonage, and at all seasons and in all weathers walking Emily's moors.

While the record of her life is centred on Haworth, and a radius of ten miles from Haworth, Emily's manuscripts are scattered wide and far. The present location of some even that were once published, catalogued, and privately owned, is now again unknown. This is true, notably, of the important diary-papers of 1841 and 1845, and the letter dated 25 February 1846 once published by Shorter. But for the remainder, I have seen them all or received photostat copies of those in the United States. The manuscript of *Wuthering Heights* has long been lost; it was not the general practice of Victorian publishers to keep the manuscripts of novels once published.

When the remaining manuscripts are assessed, their value to the biographer, as to the literary expert, cannot be overrated. The reality of the person behind these writings—sometimes only a couple of lines of poetry—is compelling, however impersonal the theme she treats. It is the same with the few recorded utterances; they are consonant with the writer of *Wuthering Heights* and the poems, even did we not know her identity.

When every writer who has something to say on the subject has said it, Emily Brontë will still elude us; we can hardly wish it otherwise. It is a part of her fascination to elude definition, like the girl in Branwell's portrait whose eyes are not turned on us, but out of this world. Hers is a face which seen even in profile will haunt us for ever; it is more memorable than many a full-face portrait that meets us squarely.

It must be the dread of every restorer of paintings obscured by time and coats of varnish to spoil the original colour; so must the biographer feel who adds yet another volume to a known subject. Each one can only hope that the character of the portrait to emerge from his work may be seen both more freshly and more completely than before.

WINIFRED GÉRIN

Haworth, London,
1963–70

ACKNOWLEDGEMENTS

I WISH most gratefully to thank the following bodies for their kind permission to study Brontë MSS. in their keeping, and/or for supplying photostat copies of them:

The Department of MSS. of the British Museum.
The Brontë Parsonage Museum, Haworth, Yorks.
The Brotherton Library, University of Leeds.
Sheffield University Library.
Manchester University Library.
The Fitzwilliam Museum Library, Cambridge.
The Reference Department, Halifax Public Library, Yorks.
The Keeper of the The Berg Collection, New York Public Library.
The Keeper of MSS. of the J. Pierpont Morgan Library, New York.
The Librarian, Miriam Lutcher Stark Library, University of Texas.

I should also like to thank:

The Council of the Brontë Society for permission to reproduce portraits, drawings, and other documents in their keeping, and especially for permission to reproduce Emily's French devoirs published here for the first time.

The Trustees of the National Portrait Gallery, for permission to reproduce portraits in their collection.

Walter Cunliffe, Esq., for permission to reproduce his drawing by Emily Brontë.

The Governors of Casterton School for permission to quote from their Registers.

Finally, I thank my friends Elizabeth Jenkins and Joan Mott, who read the book in manuscript, for their expert comment and views, that have been most precious to me.

CONTENTS

LIST OF PLATES

ABBREVIATIONS

Biographical Notice	Biographical Notice of the authors, by Currer Bell, prefixed to the 1850 edition of *Wuthering Heights* and *Agnes Grey*
BM	British Museum
BPM	Brontë Parsonage Museum, Haworth
BST	*Brontë Society Transactions*
CB	Charlotte Brontë
Chadwick	Ellis Chadwick, *In the Footsteps of the Brontës*, 1914
Duclaux	Mary Robinson (Duclaux), *Emily Brontë*, 1883
Gaskell	Mrs. E. C. Gaskell, *The Life of Charlotte Brontë*, 1857 (Except where the 3rd edition [1857] is specified, references are to the Everyman reprint of the 1st edition)
Gaskell, *Letters*	*The Letters of Mrs. Gaskell*, edited by Chapple and Pollard, 1966
Hatfield	*The Complete Poems of Emily Jane Brontë*, edited from the MSS. by C. W. Hatfield, 1941
PBB	Patrick Branwell Brontë
Simpson	Simpson, C., *Emily Brontë*, 1929
SBC	Shorter, C. K., *The Brontës and their Circle*, 1914
SLL	Shorter, C. K., *The Brontës: Lives and Letters*, 1908
W & S	Wise, T. J. and Symington, J. A., *The Brontës: their Lives, Friendships and Correspondence*, 4 vols., 1932
WSW	William Smith Williams

'. . . whether we be young or old,
Our destiny, our being's heart and home,
Is with infinitude, and only there . . .'
WORDSWORTH, *The Prelude*, Bk. vi

CHAPTER I

'A DARLING CHILD . . .'[1]

EMILY JANE BRONTË was born at her father's parsonage at Thornton in the parish of Bradford on 30 July 1818. She was the fifth child in a family whose eldest was only four years and three months old. Close as the children were in ages, it proved a happy thing for Emily when yet another sister, Anne, was born on 17 January 1820, for Anne became her life-long confidante and friend, a boon to such an uncommunicative girl as Emily.

Only two facts are known about her infancy: apart from the date of her birth, noted in the diary of her parents' young friend, Elizabeth Firth, the one record concerning her is of her christening at her father's church, St. James's, Thornton, on 20 August 1818, when her godparents were her mother's aunt and uncle, Mr. and Mrs. John Fennell, and their daughter Jane, who was married to Mr. Brontë's best friend the Revd. William Morgan. From the Fennell ladies, both called Jane, Emily derived her middle name. Mr. Brontë's eldest sister, who died about the time of Emily's birth, was also called Jane.

The surviving servants, garrulous in old age about Emily's clever sister Charlotte, said nothing more of Emily than that she was 'the prettiest of the children'.[2]

The birth of Anne only shortly preceded their father's appointment to a new living eight miles away, to Haworth, where the family moved on 20 April 1820. While Haworth enjoyed considerable standing among evangelicals for the fame conferred on it by William Grimshaw in the previous century, the incumbency did not represent riches for Mr. Brontë. It was a 'perpetual curacy' in the parish of Bradford with no independent status of its own till after his death. It is therefore incorrect to speak of him, as is still repeatedly done, as the 'Vicar' or 'Rector' of Haworth; he was never either, and had throughout his long ministry to pay the church dues to Bradford, a bitter enough imposition on a poor clergyman with a large family.

Of all the influences on Emily's life, the landscape of her home at

Haworth had the greatest effect in quickening her mind and in shaping her character. Of human influences, there can be no doubt, her father's was the most lasting; a countryman born with a keen love of nature, he early opened her eyes to the natural world lying at her door. The things that had meant most to him in his lonely struggles after a better life, were not material possessions, but the companionship of nature, and the communion with living creatures. However lame were Mr. Brontë's attempts at describing the beauty that touched him, the feeling was there, unchecked, to be handed on to his children. Long before Ellis Bell was writing of

> The linnet in the rocky dells,
> The moor-lark in the air,
> The bee among the heather-bells,

Patrick Brontë was writing of these things.

> Ye feathered songsters of the grove,
> Sweet philomel and cooing dove,
> Goldfinch, and linnet gray,
> And mellow thrush, and blackbird loud,
> And lark, shrill warbler of the cloud,
> Where do ye pensive stray?
> The milk-white thorn, the leafy spray,
> The fragrant grove, and summer's day,
> Are seen by you no more;
> Ah! may you light on friendly sheds,
> To hide your drooping pensive heads,
> From winter's chilling roar.[1]

In the new parsonage garden there were lilac and currant bushes and a central grass plot, where small children could safely play, and in the court-yard behind the house there was a dovecot. The shining doves, as they flew to and fro, took on recognizable identities and would each, in turn, be given names: Rainbow, Diamond, Snowflake. Echoes of the little moorland birds, of the invisible larks, of the linnets chattering in the eaves of the houses, are a feature of that region; Emily grew up to the sound. The four elder children, already resolute walkers like their father, brought home trophies from their excursions on the unknown moors, a golden lapwing's plume, a coral spray of bilberry, a tuft of starry moss, a fistful of wool that the old ewes shed in the warm pastures. Such things

---

[1] From the poem 'Winter' in *The Rural Minstrel*, 1813; see the *Collected Works* of the Revd. Patrick Brontë, ed. J. Horsfall Turner, Bingley, 1898.

Emily loved. The attraction towards animals was instinctive in all Patrick Brontë's children. Recalling those early affinities, Anne wrote:

A little girl loves her bird—why? Because it lives and feels? because it is helpless and harmless? A toad likewise lives and feels, and is equally helpless and harmless; but though she would not hurt a toad, she cannot love it like the bird, with its graceful form, soft feathers and bright speaking eyes...[1]

Anne lay as yet in the wooden cradle that can still be seen in her old home, the rockers making a noise like shuttles on the wooden floors of the house. The sense of her helplessness wakened protective feelings in all her sisters, and prompted Charlotte, aged five, to rush into her father's study one day to say that there was an angel standing at Anne's head—and though disconcerted that the apparition did not wait for his coming, she stoutly declared it had indeed been there.

While material prosperity was never the prime consideration of that home (Ellen Nussey noticed it years later and said how completely it was replaced by the things of the mind) it is not true to say the children lacked the things that mattered to their happiness. They had love, they had security (the two kind servants from Thornton, Nancy and Sarah Garrs, followed them to Haworth), they had toys—dolls, marionnettes, ninepins, bricks (many of which were found in a cache under their nursery floorboards after their deaths); they had successive boxes of soldiers which in time fired their imagination to become adventurers, epic writers, chroniclers; above all, they had books, as they grew. Reading came to them like an epidemic; so soon as one could read, they were all infected.

As he walked and talked with the older, astoundingly perceptive children, treating them as equals with interests like his own, teaching them to watch the moods of nature, to see God everywhere, impatient to make them perfect as they promised to be, could Mr. Brontë be blamed for believing the auspices favourable?

He had been happy indeed in marrying an intrepid young woman with high ideals who regarded poverty as a positive advantage in the pursuit of perfection; a viewpoint that she had elaborated in a sprightly essay written before marriage [2]—and before she came to realize the burdens of maternity. Her courage was, unfortunately, not equalled by her health, and within

---

[1] *Agnes Grey*, ch. 17.
[2] 'The Advantages of Poverty in Religious Concerns'. The MS. was signed by an initial 'M', and endorsed by Mr. Brontë: 'The above was written by my dear wife and sent for insertion in one of the periodical publications—Keep as a memorial of her.' *SLL*, ii, Appendix I.

eighteen months of the family's settling at Haworth she died of cancer, aged only thirty-eight.

The life of her widower and orphans was profoundly, lastingly, affected by her loss. Though he subsequently made three efforts to replace her, Mr. Brontë's respectable poverty did not find the same response among the eligible young ladies of his circle as it had with Maria Branwell; not even Elizabeth Firth, whose diary betrays a strong inclination towards him, would take the risk. Mr. Brontë at the age of forty-four was left without a wife, to his lasting misery and increasing oddity, and the children were subjected to the authoritarian rule of a maiden aunt.

She was their mother's elder sister, Miss Elizabeth Branwell, who came north from Penzance to keep house for her brother-in-law and bring up his children. The arrangement, though a necessity, was unhappy for all including Miss Branwell herself, who never ceased regretting the refinements of Penzance.

The only tribute the girls were able to pay her in later life, was that she inculcated in them a sense of duty, order, and punctuality. Of love between them, there was never any question, though she had her preferences; these were for her nephew Branwell, and for her youngest niece, Anne. But as with so many other circumstances of family life, Emily remained unaffected, and her aunt appears to have had no influence on her at all.

During their mother's illness, the eldest children, Maria and Elizabeth, aged respectively seven and six, assumed the guardianship of their little sisters and brother. They were singularly tender and adroit for their age in teaching them to read, in singing them to sleep at night. Charlotte and Branwell in particular worshipped them. Their influence was not so deeply felt by Emily and Anne, who were the peculiar care of young Sarah Garrs; but their mother's death and the advent of their aunt brought all the children together in one common gesture of self-preservation. Their interdependence, which remained so characteristic of them in adult life and in their careers as authors, sprang from this double need for love and for union against a common 'menace'. What their aunt exacted from them, and what they passionately wanted to be and do could never be reconciled. While Charlotte was often driven to rebellious thoughts—if not to open rebellion (she told Mrs. Gaskell that Jane Eyre's aunt was very like her own)—and Anne to tears, Emily was simply driven in on herself. The profound secrecy of her manner, which had nothing whatever to do with duplicity, sprang from the vital need to preserve herself from interference of any kind. Years later she said that she wished to be 'as God made her', and she succeeded in a degree rare among men, and scarcely paralleled among women.

They may all have appeared secretive to their bewildered father when he came to consider them afresh after the loss of his wife. To test their knowledge and their real feelings on things he put those questions to them which he thought appropriate to their age, about which he told Mrs. Gaskell (the presence of Maria and Elizabeth places the incident before 1824 when they went to school), each of them standing behind a mask so that they might answer the more readily. After the metaphysical questions addressed to the three elder children, he put a wholly practical one to Emily: what to do with Branwell when he was naughty? Was this because Emily's practical good sense, so notable later, was already apparent, or a shot in the dark? Branwell's violent tempers were often a trial to his sisters in their nursery games, as Charlotte's early tales of him betray.[1] 'Reason with him,' was the laconic reply of Emily, aged six, 'and when he won't listen to reason, whip him.'[2]

The need to provide an education for his five daughters other than their aunt's rudimentary instructions, determined Mr. Brontë on sending them away to school. He wished keenly to give them the best education that his circumstances permitted, especially the brilliant Maria whose maturity amazed him even before she was ten. He sent them first to the famous and rather expensive Crofton House School at Wakefield where Miss Firth was educated (Miss Mangnall had been its first principal), and then to the Clergy Daughters' School opened in January 1824 at Cowan Bridge near Kirkby Lonsdale. There board and education was offered, under a charitable scheme for the daughters of poor clergy, for £14 per annum. The sum was not so derisory then as it appears today, the more so that the charitable funds available to the school were intended to supplement all the children's needs not covered by the fees.

The story is too well known to be repeated in detail here. Believing in the promises of the prospectus which offered an excellent education for girls, including languages and music, to fit them to earn their livings later as teachers and governesses, and swayed by the opinion of his colleagues, such as the Rector of Keighley, the Revd. Theodore Dury, who sent his daughter Isabella to the school, Mr. Brontë took his two eldest girls to Cowan Bridge on 1 July 1824. Charlotte followed them on 10 August. The whole family had had whooping cough that spring, so that Emily,

[1] See 'Tales of the Islanders'. Now in the Berg Coll., New York Public Library.
[2] Gaskell, 36.

whom he intended to benefit in due course like her sisters, was kept at home to recover fully before joining them there.

The delay allowed her to experience a natural phenomenon the impact of which, at that early age, had obvious effects on her response to nature. She was out on the moors with Branwell and Anne, in the care of Nancy and Sarah, at the moment of the Crow Hill bog burst of 2 September 1824, which, under the stress of the moment, Mr. Brontë and other local residents did not hesitate to call an earthquake. To Mr. Brontë, who had sent the children out, 'as they were indisposed and the day was fine . . . to take an airing on the moors . . .'[1] the ordeal was terrifying. He stood, as he subsequently described, at the back window of the house, alarmed at the absolute stillness, the sultry menace of storm clouds, at the gathering darkness; and literally saw the windowpane and the floor of the room in which he stood heave as the storm broke. The children had been got in to shelter, but he did not know it—there were more inhabited farms in those days on the moors. The violence of the storm, the palpable earth tremors, the lashing wind and rain, and the successive detonations as the peaty subsoil burst and roared down the hillside above Ponden, hurling boulders from the heights into the valleys, shook other adult witnesses besides Mr. Brontë. Mr. Heaton and his party from Ponden House who were out on the heights rushed home for shelter. But the spectacle appears simply to have delighted the six-year-old Emily, to judge by her subsequent addiction to storms. The author of *Wuthering Heights* never quite succeeded in hiding her contempt for those mortals who shrank before nature's fury.

Before following her sisters to school, Emily was also the first to be affected by a domestic change that was decided that autumn: Nancy Garrs left to be married (her first husband was an Irish builder called Pat Wainwright) and Sarah went with her, both of them the richer by a £10 gratuity from Mr. Brontë as a reward for their faithful service. The extent to which Miss Branwell's regime at the parsonage precipitated Nancy and Sarah into matrimony can only be surmised from the views they expressed of her later in life.

Paying tribute to Mrs. Brontë's kindness as a mistress, old Nancy commented:

Miss Branwell were another soart, she were so cross-like an' fault-finding an' so close, she ga'e us, Sarah an' me, but a gill o' beer a day, an' she gi'e it to us

---

[1] *A Sermon preached in Haworth Church on Sunday 12th September 1824, in Reference to an Earthquake*. Privately printed, Bradford, 1824.

hersel', did Miss Branwell, to our dinner, she wouldn't let us go to draw it oursel' in t'cellar. A pint a day, she gi'e us, that were half a pint for me an' half a pint for Sarah.[1]

In place of Nancy and Sarah Mr. Brontë engaged 'an elderly woman', as he confided to his banker, both as a measure of economy and because, with Emily's departure for school, there was no more need for two servants. The 'elderly woman' was Tabitha Aykroyd (the 'Tabby' immortalized in the Brontë saga), a widow of fifty-six and a 'joined Methodist' of many years standing.

The sharpness of her tongue, and her wholesale disciplinary methods were only equalled by her warm heart and generous nature. In her the children gained what no stepmother could ever have given them: disinterested devotion, which as years passed and she became a burden rather than an asset in the home, they returned tenfold. She became in the true primitive sense a member of the 'family', and left it only for the grave.

Though she took all the children to her heart in the ensuing years, Tabby appears to have harboured for Emily a special care and affection, for she was her first nursling and the one most in need of her love.

Mr. Brontë's letter to his bankers, withdrawing the sum needed for Emily's school fees, has been preserved; it is dated 10 November 1824, and reads:

DEAR SIR,

I take this opportunity to give you notice that in the course of a fortnight it is my intention to draw about twenty pounds out of your savings bank. I am going to send another of my little girls to school, which at the first will cost me some little—but in the end I shall not loose [sic]—as I now keep two servants but am only to keep one elderly woman now, who, when my other little girl is at school— will be able to wait I think on my remaining children and myself.[2]

On 25 November 1824 Emily joined her sisters at the Clergy Daughters' school. While the records remain of Mr. Brontë having taken the three elder ones there, the absence of such a record in Emily's case would suggest that she travelled, like Jane Eyre, in the charge of the guard of the coach from Keighley. She may have travelled with other children from the district in the care of their parents.

Emily was entered in the school registers as the forty-fourth pupil, and the sum of her accomplishments was recorded thus: 'Reads very prettily

[1] H. Arnold, 'The Reminiscences of Emma Cortazzo', *BST*, 1958.
[2] Mr. Brontë to Mr. Marriner, Worsted Manufacturer, Keighley; Lock and Dixon, *A Man of Sorrow*, (1965), p. 255.

and works a little.' Her age was, incorrectly, given as five years and nine months, whereas in reality she was six years and three months. She was, even so, the youngest child to enter the school. The girls' ages varied, indeed, considerably, the oldest being twenty-two. Altogether there were eleven girls in their teens, ten aged between ten and twelve, and only four girls under ten, of whom three were Brontës! Emily's extreme youth gave her a favoured position; on the later evidence of the Superintendent, Miss Evans, she was 'quite the pet nursling of the school'. Miss Evans's additional recollection, to the effect that Emily 'was a darling child',[1] explains no doubt Emily's happy isolation in the midst of the general misery. To this fact may be attributed her intellectual as well as her physical survival from the ordeal of Cowan Bridge, which hastened the deaths of her two eldest sisters, and marked Charlotte for life.

While the epidemic of the following April (1825)—designated by the school authorities as a 'low fever' and presumably typhoid—caused the deaths and the removal of several children, Charlotte and Emily remained immune from the general infection. Maria Brontë had already been sent home 'in a decline' on 14 February, and died there of tuberculosis on 6 May. Elizabeth, whose state of advanced consumption must have been nearly as bad, was sent home only on 31 May, where she died on 15 June. Her condition on arriving (in the care of a Mrs. Hardacre employed by the school) left Mr. Brontë in no doubt of his other daughters' peril, and he set out on the very next day, 1 June, to fetch them home. The school authorities had already taken the precaution of sending them to their holiday home on the coast, The Cove at Silverdale, where Mr. Brontë went on to find them. The next day he took them home. Contrary to his muddled recollections given to Mrs. Gaskell thirty years later, they never returned to the school; the registers confirm that they left on 1 June 1825 for good.

On the nine-year-old Charlotte the effect of her sisters' deaths was heightened by her sense of their extraordinary goodness and cleverness, and of the injustice with which they had been treated. The memory of what they had been remained indelible, and prompted the writing of *Jane Eyre* more than twenty years later. Recalling her own school experiences to her publisher then, she spoke with the complete self-effacement that any comparison with them always evoked: 'My career was a very quiet one. I was plodding and industrious, perhaps I was very grave, for I suffered to see my sisters perishing.'[2] She met the incredulity of the critics over the portrait of Maria in Helen Burns with quiet contempt:

[1] See Gaskell, 48.   [2] To WSW, 5 Nov. 1849. *SLL*, ii. 81–2.

'You are right,' she wrote to Mr. Williams after the appearance of *Jane Eyre*, 'in having faith in the reality of Helen Burns; she was real enough. I have exaggerated nothing there.'[1]

On Branwell, the effects of his sisters' deaths were as deep and lasting as on Charlotte. Much of his mental instability can be traced to the double shock of losing Maria, who had become a mother-figure to him, and of being present at her death and funeral. In the January issue of *Blackwood's* for 1828 appeared an article by 'Christopher North' (John Wilson) entitled 'Christmas Dreams', the theme of which was the death of a little sister:

. . . long, long, long ago the time when we danced along, hand in hand, with our golden-haired sister . . . long, long, long ago the day on which she died—the hour, so far more dismal than any hour that can now darken us on this earth, when she— her coffin—and that velvet pall descended—and descended—slowly, slowly into the horrid clay, and we were borne deathlike, and wishing to die, out of the churchyard, that, from that moment, we thought, we could enter never more! And oh! What a multitudinous being must ours have been, when, before our boyhood was gone, we could have forgotten her buried face!

Writing to *Blackwood's* several years later, in December 1835 when he himself was a budding author, Branwell evoked his early delight in the numbers of Blackwoods and recalled Professor Wilson's articles, which he 'read and re-read while a little child'. 'Passages like these, Sir (and when the last was written my sister died)—passages like these, read then and remembered now, afford feelings which, I repeat, I cannot describe.'[2]

The early deaths of her sisters had no comparable effect upon Emily. Nor do the teaching or the sufferings of Cowan Bridge appear to have left any mark on her. She was the only one of her family not to go through a religious crisis in adolescence—which was a secondary effect of the Calvinistic teaching of Carus Wilson in Charlotte's case, and of their aunt's influence in the case of Branwell and Anne. Emily's extreme youth would appear to have spared her not only the actual rigours of the school establishment, but the realization of their consequences for others. She appeared to come away from the six months' ordeal of institutional life unscathed in mind and body.

Yet, even to a child of six, the deaths of Maria and Elizabeth could not go unfelt, though the feeling might be suppressed. She heard the lamentations of her father and elder sister and brother too often, and for too long, not to know what it all meant. The impact might reach her in echoes only, but the echoes were vibrant.

Branwell, a strong new influence on the sisters just returned from school, with his ghoulish imaginings, declared characteristically that he heard Maria's voice crying outside the windows at night. Though Emily may have kept silent on the event, when she did speak twenty years later she showed she had not forgotten. The experience was transposed onto another level, but it was authentic enough. The voice of Catherine Earnshaw wailing at the window of Wuthering Heights: 'Let me in! Let me in!... It's twenty years, twenty years... I've been a waif for twenty years', would never have been so chilling but for the death all those years before of the family's darling, Maria.

CHAPTER II

EXPLORERS

THE image of the mature Emily Brontë, of the mystic poet, the baffling woman, the 'Sphinx of Literature' as her devotees have called her, has for so long been fixed in her readers' minds that they tend to overlook the stages of childhood, of the inarticulate years through which like any other growing creature she struggled before finding a voice. She is too often written and spoken about as though at all ages she had been what she became in the last crowded couple of years of her short life.[1] It is important for the biographer therefore to detect what went to the making of the personality she became, to trace those circumstances of childhood and youth from which emerged Ellis Bell. Happily, the records, though few, are definite, since the chroniclers were her sharp-eyed playfellows, Charlotte and Branwell. Thanks to them, Emily's likes and dislikes, her looks and gestures in childhood, her few decisive words, have been preserved.

In June 1826, when she was nearly eight, and Branwell received the momentous gift from his father of the wooden soldiers from Leeds, Emily was allowed her choice as were the others. Both Charlotte and Branwell recorded the incident. Their accounts differ. Charlotte's, written nearer the event, is the more detailed:

Papa bought Branwell some wooden soldiers at Leeds. When Papa came home it was night, and we were in bed, so next morning Branwell came to our door with a box of soldiers. Emily and I jumped out of bed, and I snatched up one and exclaimed: 'This is the Duke of Wellington! This shall be the Duke!' When I had said this Emily likewise took up one and said it should be hers; when Anne came down, she said one should be hers. Mine was the prettiest of the whole, and the tallest, and the most perfect in every part. Emily's was a grave-looking fellow, and we called him 'Gravey'. Anne's was a queer little thing, much like herself, and we called him 'Waiting-Boy'. Branwell chose his, and called him Buonaparte.[2]

---

[1] Muriel Spark has noticed the tendency. See Spark and Stanford, *Emily Brontë, her Life and Work*, 1953, p. 18.
[2] CB, 'History of the Year, 1829'. BPM.

In Branwell's report of the incident, the permission to choose a soldier was graciously given to his sisters 'to take care of them though they were to be mine and I to have the disposal of them as I would'—though he relented later and 'gave them to them as their own'.[1] Chosen for his stern features perhaps (Emily's devotees would say a characteristic choice) her soldier, according to Branwell, was not called 'Gravey' at first, but Parry, in deference to Emily's already established devotion to the arctic explorer Captain Edward Parry. Parry, whose name would appear repeatedly in the Brontë children's games, first as a hero-figure in their dramatized adventures and later as an actual pseudonym for Emily, was her tutelary Genius when the Arabian script of their plays demanded magical powers in the actors.[2] The mysterious and prolonged incidence of the name 'Parry', 'Parrysland', 'Parry's Glasstown', 'Chief Genius Parry' as personifications and pseudonyms for Emily in the Brontë juvenilia is thus explained, even if the springs that motivate hero-worship in the very young remain a mystery.

The intense intellectual activity of the older children, of Branwell and Charlotte at the time, has to be realized to explain something of the precocious interests of the little ones in subjects so far beyond their years. Their education was necessarily one-sided, as their father's lessons in history, geography, grammar, and scripture had to be constantly interrupted by his avocations as a busy parson with a far-flung parish, and supplemented by their own avid reading. Their sources of books were wide for children of their age: Mr. Brontë's own library was well-stocked with works of history, biography, and poetry (which included the complete works of Byron); and the children had access to the Keighley Mechanics' Institute Library, of which he was one of the founder members. Emily's early predilection for arctic regions (Monsieur Heger said of her years later that she should have been a navigator) sprang as much from Bewick's engravings as from Parry's voyages. Mr. Brontë's copy of Bewick's *British Birds* made a lasting impression on all his children, as their later comments show, but Emily was the one to copy, with great accuracy in the detail, his drawings of birds. Her copy of his 'Winchat' and 'Ring Ousel' (dated 1 March and 22 May 1829 respectively) were drawn long before her handwriting was even decipherable. To Bewick's haunting pictures of the arctic regions can be attributed the stirrings of imagination in young Emily for the men—Parry and Ross—who first explored them.

[1] Branwell Brontë, 'History of the Young Men', 1830. Ashley Libr., BM.
[2] Parry's *Voyages to the Arctic Region*, 1818–1827, was obtainable at Keighley Mechanics' Institute Library, where it figures as No. 216 in the first catalogue.

Like Jane Eyre sitting cross-legged in the window-seat at Gateshead Hall reading Bewick's descriptions of the 'vast sweep of the Arctic Zone and those forlorn regions of dreary space—that reservoir of frost and snow, where firm fields of ice, the accumulation of centuries of winters, glazed in Alpine heights above heights, surround the pole, and concentre the multiplied rigours of extreme cold', young Emily Brontë would form her own ideas of those 'death-white realms', and seek to know more of their accessibility to intrepid navigators.

As in the poems and novel to come, the natural setting for any human drama was all-important to Emily. While her imagination was not so pictorial as Charlotte's, her sense of nature as a presence and a power in human destiny was all-pervading, and for this she must have owed a good deal to Bewick's insistence on showing the natural habitats of his land and water creatures.

While Emily and Anne were capable of sharing in the games of their elder brother and sister, and sustaining their own parts in the developing drama of 'Glasstown', their inability to write fluently prevented them from contributing to the written chronicles. In kindness to her younger sister and bedfellow, Charlotte contributed a 'reportage' designed for the October 1830 number of the 'Young Men's Magazine' to please Emily and to supply the want of a contribution from 'Captain Parry' himself. She called her article 'A Day at Parry's Palace'. It is strikingly different in landscape and character from the Glasstown settings of most of her articles of the time. She was, obviously, accepting the idiom personal to Emily's (verbal) contributions to their serials. Emily did not dabble in magic; she preferred realism, factual settings, forceful dialogue, sober sense. (It is symptomatic perhaps that in the councils of the 'Twelves', as the soldiers came to be called, 'Gravey' occupied the role of sage, a very Nestor in curbing their foolhardy dreams of conquest.) In complete contrast to her own extravagant, luxurious, oriental type of settings, Charlotte placed her sister's story in the surroundings of Haworth. Of these, however, she did not scruple to make fun. The reporter, Lord Charles Wellesley himself (her pen-name for many years), was wryly aware of the altered circumstances of his present assignment:

I was immediately struck with the changed aspect of things; all the houses were ranged in formal rows they contained four rooms each with a little garden in front. No proud castle or splendid palace towers . . . over the cottages around. No high-born noble claimed allegiance of his vassals. every inch of ground was inclosed with stone walls . . . Here and there were some poplar trees, but no

heavy woods or nodding groves—rivers rushed out with foam and thunder
through meads and mountains Nasty factories with their tall black chimneys
breathing thick columns of almost tangible smoke discoloured not that sky of
dull hazy hue. Every woman wore a brown stuff gown with white cap and hand-
kerchief. Glossy satin rich velvet and costly silk or soft muslin broke not on the
fair uniformity ... Parry's palace was a square building surmounted by blue
slates and some round stone pumpkins, the garden around it was of moderate
dimensions laid out in round and oval flowerbeds rows of peas gooseberry bush
and black and white currant trees. Some few common flowering shrubs and a
grass plat to dry clothes on. All the convenient offices such as wash-house, back-
kitchen stable and coal-house were built in a line and backed by a row of trees.
In a paddock behind the house were feeding one cow to give milk for the family
and butter for the dairy and cheese for the table; one horse to draw the gig, carry
their majesties and bring home provisions from market, together with a calf and
foal as companions for both ... [Sir Edward and Lady Emily Parry come out to
welcome their guest] I was ushered into a small parlour tea was on the table and
they invited me to partake of it but before sitting down Parry took from the
cupboard a napkin which he directed me to pin before my clothes lest I should
dirty them, saying in a scarcely intelligible jargon 'that he supposed they were
the best as I had come on a visit and that perhaps my mama would be angry if
they got stained.'

Invidious as the suggestion must have appeared to the experienced
chronicler, Lord Charles, his readers would recognize in it one of the daily
habits of home. The article is crammed indeed with vignettes of parsonage
life. The chronicler continues:

I thanked them but politely declined the offer and during tea a complete
silence was preserved; not a word escaped the lips of my host and hostess ...
['Little Peter', their son, is sent for after the meal and appeared] in a dirty and
greasy pinafore of which Lady Emily stripped him and put on a clean one
muttering in a cross tone that she wondered how Anny could think of sending
the child into the parlour with such a filthy slip on. Parry now withdrew to his
study and Lady Emily to her work room. I was now left alone with Peter.

Peter's conduct provokes such exasperation in the guest that he 'beats
and kicks the brat' whose yells rouse the whole household. After Peter has
been removed, 'supper was brought in it consisted of coffee and a very
few slices of bread and butter—this meal like the former one was eaten in
silence ...' After supper, the household went straight to bed. Next
morning Lord Charles rose at 7 and after breakfast went for a walk through
the fields. 'In the yard I saw Peter surrounded by three cats 2 dogs five
rabbits and six pigs all of whom he was feeding.' On his return he meets

Captain Ross—who was Anne's hero—and converses with him in dialect.
Ross is elsewhere referred to as 'Ann' or 'Anny'.

Dinner was set on the table at precisely 12 o'clock, the dishes were roast beef
and yorkshire pudding; mashed potatoes Apple pie and preserved cucumbers.
Ross wore a white apron during dinner. I observed that he took not the smallest
notice of me though I must necessarily seem a different object from what he was
in the habit of seeing. All eat as if they had not seen a meal for three weeks. At the
desert each drank a single glass of wine not a drop more and eat a plateful of
strawberries with a few sweet cakes. I expected some blow-up after the surfeit
which Ross, if I might judge from his continued grunting and puffing had
evidently got and was not disappointed. An hour subsequent to dinner he was
taken extremely sick. No doctor being at hand Death was momentarily expected
and would certainly have ensued had not the *Genius Emily* arrived at a most
opportune period when the disorder was reaching its crisis. She cured with an
incantation and vanished.[1]

Magical powers, as daily displayed in 'making alive again' the casualties
among Branwell's soldiers, became the common attributes of the four
young *Genii* as their complex Glasstown chronicles evolved. They saw
themselves not circumscribed by the narrow limits of their home, but as
carrying within themselves powers that made them 'more than con-
querors'. This fact is essential to the true portrayal of their childhood; it
is essential also to their growth as artists. Delicate, motherless children as
they were, brought up in a home devoid of luxuries, it would be to falsify
the true picture to present them as merely so: it is how they saw themselves
that matters; and this, thanks to Charlotte's and Branwell's prolific pens,
we can follow almost uninterruptedly throughout their growing years.

It was not fortuitous that at about this time they began to call themselves
Kings and Queens. Carrying 'wands wreathed in ivy by virtue of which
we rule the hearts of men',[2] their activities by night and by day filled pages
of Charlotte's closely packed scripts. Branwell, as the only boy, naturally
and characteristically assumed the role of 'Little King'—his sisters serving
in his suite as his attendant Queens. Fortunately, their sense of justice and
of fun laid frequent checks on his inordinate claims, and his rule did not
go undisputed. Their vision of themselves—diminutive, quaint, all-
powerful—given in Charlotte's 'Tales of the Islanders', derived most
likely from the series of articles on 'Fairies, Devils, and Witches' by
James Hogg in *Blackwood's* from February to October 1828. In this new

---

[1] 'A Day at Parry's Palace', 'Young Men's Magazine', Oct. 1830. BPM.
[2] CB, 'Tales of the Islanders', Mar. 1829. Berg Coll.

guise, they assumed the characteristics of the mischievous 'Brownies', small and shrivelled, not above five spans high, 'much given to swift changes of shape, & sudden disappearances'; applying some humour indeed, to their physical limitations, as in the description of Branwell as 'A boy in form, and an antedeluvian in feature'. Equally felicitous is Charlotte's description of herself and her sisters as three old women spotted by Lord Charles Wellesley whom they have been following through a wood: 'He concluded they were fairies whom Little King had brought with him to this earth . . . he still felt an uneasy vague and by no means pleasant sensation when he looked at their little sharp faces and heard the shrill disagreeable tones of their voices.'[1]

The Brontë children were obviously acquainted with James Hogg's contributions on fairy lore to *Blackwood's*, but it would be more interesting to know whether the future author of *Wuthering Heights* also read his *Confessions of a Justified Sinner*, first published in 1824; the teasing coincidences of plot and character in the two books will be examined later.[2]

The honest Charlotte never attempted to gloss over the fierce disputes that raged between the *Genii*; the picture of their growing years is the more convincing. 'Little King' was not flattered by his chronicler; his role was chiefly confined to stirring up strife. When the 'three old women' were retained at Strathfieldsaye on a month's trial as 'washerwomen and laundry-maids', he instigated them to

quarrels among themselves often ending in furious fights where tooth nail feet and hands were employed with equal fury. In these fracas Little King was observed to be exceedingly active inciting them by every means in his power to maul and mangle each other in the most horrible way. This circumstance however was not much wondered at as his constant disposition to all kinds of mischief was well known and he was considered by every member of the house at Strathfieldsaye not excepting the Duke himself more as an evil brownie than a legitimate fairy.[3]

Long before Charlotte and Branwell could write well enough to chronicle the doings of their heroes, they acted them in 'plays' of their own devising. The violence and noise of these performances made it impossible at times to hide them from the elders of the family, and Francis Leyland (Branwell's later friend) recalled Mr. Brontë's evidence on the subject: 'When mere children, Charlotte and her brother and

---

[1] Ibid.   [2] See below, ch. xv, p. 217.
[3] CB, 'Tales of the Islanders', Berg Coll.

sisters used to invent and act little plays of their own in which the Duke of Wellington was sure to come off conqueror. When a dispute would not infrequently arise amongst them regarding the comparative merits of Bonaparte, Hannibal and Caesar.'[1]

Mr. Brontë's complacency in his young children's historical precocity was in no way shared by Tabby who was, at times, convinced that they were simply mad. Leyland recalled a further incident, which he received at first hand from Tabby's nephew, the village carpenter, William Wood, when Tabby was so much alarmed by them that she fled to his cottage out of breath, and cried: 'Willum! Ya mun gooa up to Mr. Bontë's, for aw'm sure yon childer's all goan mad, and aw darn't stop i' the house ony longer wi'en, an' aw'll stay till woll ya come back.'[2] The children were understandably gratified by the success of their acting, and greeted William Wood when he arrived at the parsonage 'with a great crack o' laughin'' at Tabby's expense.

Though behind them in writing, Emily equalled Charlotte and Branwell in deeds of daring. To Branwell's chagrin, she was already taller than he, and far more reckless. On a certain Oak Apple Day in those early years, a performance was decided on of Charles II's escape from Worcester, and Emily, because the tallest and darkest of that predominantly fair family, was chosen to play the chief part. Exiled monarchs were to feature conspicuously in her Gondal chronicles and she had no difficulty in identifying herself with such a harassed but heroic character. Outside Mr. Brontë's parlour window grew a double-cherry, quite his favourite tree in the garden, and in default of an oak in that sparse ground the cherry tree was fixed on for the exile's hiding place. The tree was in full blossom and afforded luxurious shelter for a hunted monarch. To Emily's long legs the ascent presented no problems, especially as the high branches were on a level with Papa's bedroom windows. Papa was obviously away for the day, on one of his long parochial tours, and it must also have coincided with one of Miss Branwell's rare absences from home on a round of calls. Heaven generally favoured the bold, the little Brontës had read, and they were prepared to sustain the roles of hunters and hunted all day, until the sinister sound of rending wood brought the branch on which Emily was sitting crashing to the ground. Her own agility saved her from harm, but there was an ugly gash in the tree-trunk necessitating a hurried consultation with Tabby. A bag of soot was fetched from across the lane at John Brown's stonemason's yard and

---

[1] Leyland, *The Brontë Family*, 1886, i. 63.   [2] Ibid.

applied to the gash; but though invention was strong in the children their
sense of truth was apparently stronger, and when Mr. Brontë came home
he was given a full account of what had happened.[1] What his reactions
were have remained unrecorded.

Images of the domestic scene are preserved side by side with the records
of feverish intellectual activity. Here are the children seen in their own
characters, divested for the time being of their adopted roles:

While I write this [recorded Charlotte in March 1829] I am in the kitchen of
the Parsonage, Haworth; Tabby, the servant, is washing up the breakfast things,
and Anne, my youngest sister (Maria was my eldest) is kneeling on a chair,
looking at some cakes which Tabby had been baking for us. Emily is in the
parlour, brushing the carpet. Papa and Branwell are gone to Keighley. Aunt is
upstairs in her room, and I am sitting by the table writing this in the kitchen.
Keighley is a small town four miles from here. Papa and Branwell are gone for
the newspaper the *Leeds Intelligencer*, a most Tory newspaper, edited by
Mr. Wood, and the proprietor, Mr. Henneman. We take two and see three
newspapers a week.[2]

By the time she was eleven Emily would appear already to have become
the most practically capable of the sisters. The household tasks, whether
sweeping carpets or making beds, need be no hindrance to learning poetry
by heart or even to composing it.

Her inventive share in the 'Plays' before she could put pen to paper is
also described by Charlotte in the same record of 1829 where the 'origins'
of the plays are set out in chronological order:

Emily's and my Bed Plays were established the 1st December 1827; the others
March 1828. Bed Plays mean secret plays; they are very nice ones. All our plays
are very strange ones. Their nature I need not write on paper, for I think I shall
always remember them.[3]

Emily's directing presence is often specifically stated by the young
scribe. She begins, 'A little while ago Emily and me one stormy night
were going through the wood which leads to Strathfieldsaye we saw by the
light of the moon the flashing of some bright substance . . . we heard a
well-known voice [Lord Charles's] say', and another adventure is under
way. What matters is that in such passages Emily's eye can be discerned
at work, the naturalist's eye, so soon to be the poet's.

. . . those trees listen there is a faint sound like the voice of a dying swan but now
a stronger breeze blows through it is rising hark how it swells what grace was in

[1] Leyland, *The Brontë Family*, i. 63–4; Chadwick, 87.
[2] CB, 'Tales of the Islanders', Mar. 1829.   [3] Ibid.

that wild note but the wind roars louder I heard the muttering of distant thunder it is drawing nearer and nearer and the tunes of the harp . . . the howling of the wind it peals with such awful wildness such unearthly grandeur that you are tempted to believe it is the Voice of spirits speaking in the Storm. [1]

The nocturnal adventures shared with Emily included visits to the Palace of Instruction, a college erected on a 'fictitious island' in the Atlantic, numbering one thousand pupils drawn from the 'elite of the land'. For naughty children there were cells 'dark and vaulted and arched and so far down in the earth that the loudest shriek could not be heard by any inhabitant of the upper world. In these as well as in the dungeons the most unjust torturing might go on without any fear of detection if it was not that I keep the key of the dungeons and Em'ly keeps the key of the cells.'[2] It is not very surprising that dungeons, vaults, and cells figured so largely in the Gondal poetry to come, or that jailers' steps and the clank of keys were an integral part of the theatrical set-up of the Gondal saga. For those who have descended into the vaulted stone cellars below the parsonage at Haworth, the origin of this preoccupation with dungeons is not far to seek. Determined children are not to be put off their play because of bad weather, and if 'the cold sleet and stormy fogs' of winter prevented the enactment of the latest serial in the garden, there were always the cellars at hand where the rebellious pupils of the Palace of Instruction could pursue their plotting.

From 'Tales of the Islanders' two features were later incorporated in Emily's Gondal Saga; the Island itself which became Gondal, and the Palace of Instruction. That Emily should 'lift' these set-pieces and integrate them into her own creation is proof enough that she considered them hers, even from the first. The strict code regulating the children's dealing in personal property—as Branwell's account of the sharing out of his soldiers shows—would not admit of predatory acts of appropriation between them. Moreover, it would not suit the artist in the growing Emily to be beholden even to Charlotte for any part of her personal creation; Gondal was her own and she shared it only with Anne.

Miss Branwell may on occasion have retaliated against riotous conduct by shutting her nieces up in a room (as commentators on the Red-room incident in *Jane Eyre* incline to think), but the cellars of Haworth parsonage exploited in play are far more likely to have provoked the long series of prison scenes in Emily's Gondal dramas.

Miss Branwell's task, it has to be admitted, was not always an easy one.

[1] Ibid.   [2] Ibid.

She confined her teaching to the rudiments of reading and ciphering when the children were tiny, and what she subsequently had to offer her nieces was plain sewing in every branch, enforced during long hours of practice. The girls' samplers remain, very indifferently executed in drab colours, to show with what little enthusiasm they responded to the practical needs of stitchery. The text of Emily's sampler, if chosen by herself, might be evidence of the trend of her tastes at the age of eleven: it is signed:

EMILY BRONTË finished this sampler March 1st 1829.
'Who hath ascended up into heaven, or descended? Who hath gathered the wind in his fist? who hath bound the waters in a garment? who hath established all the ends of the earth? What is his name, and what is his son's name, if thou canst tell. Every word of God is pure: he is a shield unto them that put their trust in him. Add thou not unto his words, lest he reprove thee, and thou be found a liar. Two things have I required of thee; deny me them not before I die: Remove far from me vanity and lies; give me neither poverty nor riches; feed me with food convenient for me; lest I be full, and deny thee, and say, Who is the Lord? or lest I be poor and steal, and take the name of my God in vain.' 30th of Proverbs, the first 9 Verses—.[1]

Learning to sew, though Charlotte later confessed that she was glad that she had mastered its mysteries, was a joyless exercise for the young Brontës. Mrs. Gaskell heard from Mary Taylor how the girls had reacted to their aunt's repressive rule.

She was a very precise person and looked very odd, because her dress, etc. was so utterly out of fashion. She corrected one of us once for using the word 'spit' or 'spitting' . . . She made her nieces sew with purpose or without, and as far as possible, discouraged any other culture. She used to keep them sewing charity clothes and maintained to me that it was not for the good of the recipients, but of the sewers. 'It was proper for them to do it,' she said.[2]

To such children, the only compensation afforded for the long sessions of sewing was when their father joined them in their aunt's room, and *Blackwood's Magazine* was read aloud. *Blackwood's*, which came out on the 20th of the month, was too expensive for Mr. Brontë to buy, but the family saw it through the kindness of the local doctor, and it was Branwell's agreeable mission to fetch the numbers from Dr. Driver. The copy then reverted to the eager boy who, long after the elders had read it, took it to bed and devoured it by candlelight.

From internal evidence it appears that the resumption of the 'Islanders', of which Charlotte had grown tired, in a second volume in October 1829,

[1] In fact verses 4–9   [2] Gaskell, 3rd ed., 100.

was due to an idea of Emily's. It shows her hero in action and, by its subject matter, looks forward to Gondal. Rebellion is the theme; the children at school in the Palace of Instruction have broken out in revolt and are encamped on the hills with two cannons; their ring leaders are newcomers to Emily's favour: 'little Johnny Lockhart', and the Princess Victoria. Walter Scott, Lockhart, and 'Johnny Lockhart' were her choice for 'cheif islanders' when the game of islands was first evolved round the kitchen fire. Asked to name her men Emily had unhesitatingly elected them. They were more than names to her, since Miss Branwell's new year's present of Scott's *Tales of a Grandfather* inscribed to her 'dear little Nephew and Nieces' in 1828 had introduced all Scotland into the Brontës' home. The gift had coincided with the January (1828) issue of *Blackwood's Magazine* which carried an article entitled 'Christmas Presents' describing a Christmas family party at which books were given to all—the choice judged most suitable for a little girl of the party being precisely the three volumes of the *Tales of a Grandfather*. The book was said to have been inscribed by the author to Hugh Littlejohn, and the commentary ran: 'Now, who do you think is the Grandfather—that tells these tales—and who is Hugh Littlejohn to whom they are told? Sir Walter Scott, Mary, is the Grandfather—and Hugh Littlejohn is no other than dear sweet clever Johnny Lockhart, whose health you and I and all of us shall drink by and by in a glass of cowslip wine.'[1]

When, at the height of her fame, Charlotte eventually visited Edinburgh, she said she had 'always liked the "idea" of Scotland'.[2] The 'idea' once implanted in the Brontë imagination was never eradicated; with Emily in particular it took root. The Scottish landscape, which she never saw, supplied those distinctive features of Gondal's lakes, inland creeks, and bays, that are not a part of the topography of Haworth. The contributions of James Hogg to *Blackwood's* on Scottish folklore, superstitions, customs, and beliefs, familiarized her to such a degree with the character of the highland landscape that she wrote of it almost as of home. The names of her Gondal heroes also—Douglas, Rodric Lesley, Gleneden, Alexander, Flora—were predominantly Scots.

The 'idea' of the Princess Victoria, early implanted, also bore fruit; if Emily broke away from the literary examples of Charlotte and Branwell and gave the major role in her Gondal Saga to a woman, this may well have been due, in the first place, to the 'idea' of the Princess; Victoria was the first 'symbol' of feminine power she came across. The position of

---

[1] *Blackwood's Magazine*, Jan. 1828.
[2] CB to WSW, 20 July 1850. W & S, iii. 125.

the Princess, as heir to the English throne, was bringing her into public notice as the expected death of George IV approached (he died in fact on 26 June 1830), by which time Princess Victoria had become one of the 'cheif' characters in the 'Tales of the Islanders'. (Emily later paid her the compliment of calling her tame geese after her and Queen Adelaide.)

Princess Victoria was close to Emily in age. Born on 24 May 1819, she was only nine months her junior. Her emergence on the political scene at this time coincided with the accession to the throne of her uncle and aunt, William IV and his consort Queen Adelaide, a childless pair, whom it was expected she would succeed. The presence of a new virtuous Queen at court, after the scandals attending the rejection of the last, was heralded with enthusiasm by the fashion designers and the editors of the Ladies' Annuals—whose issues found their way to Haworth parsonage. Queen Adelaide was a pleasant subject for the gossip columnists. A coronation was in preparation, a proper coronation it was hoped—exempt from the flagrant improprieties that had attended the last—and at this ceremony the Princess Victoria was for the first time to play a major role—so her kind aunt intended and her plotting mother, the Duchess of Kent, designed. In the press of the day the subject was discussed in detail during the early months of 1831, and the significance of a coronation [1]—eventually to be adapted to her own literary purposes by young Emily Brontë—made its impression.

No item of national news, read and debated by the elders of the Tory household at Haworth, ever escaped the curious attention of the Brontë children. The new king's coronation, and that of his consort, took place on 3 September 1831. Engravings of the sovereigns in their state robes were circulated in the press and the full splendour of the ceremonial at the Abbey related in detail. Princess Victoria's dramatic last-minute exclusion from the procession because of her arrogant mother's insistence that she should take precedence over the royal dukes, and her heartbroken confinement to Marlborough House throughout the day, was a titbit of news to set the country talking. Here was a potential heroine indeed, heiress to a great kingdom, who was immured in a 'little lobby' at the head of the stairs on a day of public rejoicing, and who, only through a slit in the curtain and her own tears, managed to get a glimpse of the procession as it passed down the Mall.

The subject evidently stimulated and excited the growing Emily, for to

[1] The coronation of Queen Victoria, 28 June 1838, is reflected in the Gondal chronicles, where Julius Brenzaida and his cousin Gerald Exina—joint heirs to the throne—are crowned in Mar. 1838. See Hatfield, 56.

it can be traced the pattern of her own emergence as a family scribe. While Charlotte applied all her talents to creating the Byronic 'Zamorna' and Branwell evolved the type of demagogue anti-hero in his 'Alexander Rogue', Emily chose a woman for her protagonist, an emancipated woman, a queen, and a rebel, round whose fatal destinies she raised a whole complex of plots that took her permanently outside the orbit of her sister's and brother's influence. When Emily called her heroine 'Augusta' she was not only asserting her regal status, but commenting on the known fact that the name had been refused the Princess Victoria at her baptism by her uncle George IV because it had sounded ominously imperious in his ears. Emily moreover gave the princess's first name, Alexandrina, to another of her Gondal heroines.

A final link binding Gondal to the childish scenario of the 'Tales of the Islanders', in which Emily was now to take a hand, can be found in the character of one of the 'young noblemen' studying at the Palace of Instruction, Jules de Polignac (a hangover from Branwell's pro-French-history days), whose name, anglicized to Julius, became that of Emily's hero in the unfolding drama of Gondal—Julius Brenzaida.

There was one character, belonging to the early stories of Charlotte and Branwell, who went right through the Glasstown chronicles and re-emerged in the literature of Angria (even as late as Branwell's novel of 1845, *And the Weary are at Rest*), whom Emily might be said also to have taken into her own work, and that was the Ashantee orphan, Quashia Quamina, son of the Ashantee chief killed at the battle of Coomassie by the invading forces under Branwell's original twelve wooden soldiers. Discovered by Wellington at his dying mother's side, and adopted as a companion for his own sons,[1] Quashia showed himself from the first as savage, ungrateful, and treacherous towards his benefactor,[2] no sooner grown up than heading a rebellion against him. The savagery of Quashia, together with his swarthy face, 'tusk-like teeth', and lust for revenge, find an echo not only in the enigmatic figure of the dark-haired orphan boy, of 'the iron man', the 'accursèd man' of the Gondal poems,[3] but pre-eminently in the conception of Heathcliff, the louring 'gypsy brat' whose origins, whether human or demonic, Emily deliberately left undefined.[4]

The creation of Gondal belongs to the year 1831. It was a declaration of independence, a first positive step from tutelage, which, at the age of thirteen, was perhaps the first indication Emily gave that she intended to direct her own life.

[1] CB, 'African Queen's Lament', Feb. 1833.   [2] CB, 'Green Dwarf', 1833.
[3] See Hatfield 11, 62, 64, 99, 111, 112.   [4] See below, pp. 219, 226.

CHAPTER III

THE STUFF OF GONDAL

In 1831 there were practical and domestic reasons that compelled Emily to emerge from childhood and find her own feet. In the new year Charlotte was sent away to school. Emily's dependence on her till then had been great. She had never lived without Charlotte, or slept a night without her since their infancy. Much as Emily loved Anne, and turned to her more and more, Anne slept with their aunt. The fact was not without its lasting effect on the girls' intellectual development; while Anne more than the others was subjected to their aunt's oppressive religious outlook, Emily remained free in spirit to pursue her own unorthodox purposes.

The very painfulness of her present situation made her react energetically. Branwell was no substitute for Charlotte either as companion or as playmate; he was completely absorbed in his own voluminous output and writing feverishly in every leisure moment. While studying under his father, and beginning Greek with him, he was left much to his own devices. He began to chronicle in orderly fashion the exploits of the preceding years, in a regular 'History of the Young Men', relating their conquests in Africa, and the erection of their Great Glasstown Confederacy. The work entailed so many statistics of population returns and military supplies, territorial demarcations, and government appointments, that it is hardly surprising Emily and Anne, left to his editorial direction, should grow bored.

Branwell's ability to counterfeit the production of a book, imprint, binding and all, the rate at which he worked, the intensity of his involvement in his subject matter, made him impatient of the younger girls. He was far in advance of them, in advance of Charlotte also, whose admiration of him at this stage was one of his chief incentives to excellence. It was probably the happiest period of his life when the expectations of all, father, aunt, and sisters, were centred upon him. But it was also time for Emily and Anne to break away from his domination and to choose a subject for their own 'Plays'.

When Charlotte went to school, she left Emily with the unfinished Island Story which she herself had grown weary of. At the conclusion of

'The North Wind'. Drawing by Emily Brontë

the section dealing with the children's rebellion Charlotte had noted: 'for a short time thereafter the school prospered as before but we becoming tired of it sent the children to their own homes and now only fairy's dwell in the Island of a dream.'[1]

This was sufficient for Emily and Anne to start to build up a new serial. The island was remote enough and big enough (fifty miles round) to permit of further exploration, and its natural beauties could be made to resemble their own moors which were beginning to take a major place in their lives. The need to have heroes and heroines of their own, above all the need to get away from Branwell and do something different, made them choose as their heroine from among the last characters in the Island Story the Princess Victoria, whose adventures were as yet all unsung.

The Gondal Chronicles deal predominantly with a feminine and royalist world. Its 'Emperors and Empresses', its 'young sovereigns', with their brothers and sisters, live in a state of perpetual crisis, as the rebel Republican armies harry, but never quite overcome them. The 'Princes & Princesses' are at times besieged within the Palace of Instruction, some are even taken prisoner and kept in vaulted dungeons; but their spirit is never broken, as the captive girls of Emily's mature poetry—the Rosinas and the Rochelles to come—eloquently prove in speech after speech of defiance thrown in their 'tyrants'' teeth.

While the origin of this ideal of young royalty may well be ascribed to Emily's early interest in the Princess Victoria, the independence and daring of her heroines was a reflex of her own nature, early observed by such strangers visiting the family as Ellen Nussey.[2]

On the top of a moor or in a deep glen Emily was a child in spirit for glee and enjoyment . . . A spell of mischief . . . lurked in her on occasions when out on the moors. She enjoyed leading Charlotte where she would not dare to go of her own free-will. Charlotte had a mortal dread of unknown animals, and it was Emily's pleasure to lead her into close vicinity, and then to tell her of how and of what she had done, laughing at her horror with great amusement.[3]

It was as Emily and Anne roamed the moors as growing girls, learning more each day about the natural life about them, that the feeling for Gondal was born. Gondal was more than a childish invention; it was a way of life, their life, which they shared in secret at each hour of every day. They were, as Ellen Nussey noted two years later, 'like twins, inseparable companions in the very closest sympathy, which never had any

[1] 'Tales of the Islanders', 6 Oct. 1829.   [2] SBC, 163.
[3] E. Nussey, 'Reminiscences of Charlotte Brontë', Scribner's Magazine, May 1871.

interruption'.[1] How close their paths ran to those of their Gondal characters can only be realized when the landscape of Gondal is compared with that around their home.

The poetry of Gondal, like Scott's and the Border Ballads before it, was an essentially outdoor creation, depending on landscape for its major effects. The more closely Emily and Anne grew to know the changing aspects of the moors in all seasons, the vegetation with its brilliant annual return of blushing bilberry leaves, hare-bells, heath, and bracken; to watch for and closely observe the swift changes of clouds and wind-directions which their position high up on a spur of the Pennines, between two nearby coasts, provoked; the more they identified themselves with the reckless actions of their outlaws and rebels fleeing from justice, or from pursuing armies, and sheltering in the hollows of rocks or down in the glens which were their secret haunts—the more Gondal grew. It was because they made Gondal such an integral part of their own lives, that it remained with them into adult life. 'Oh! happy life!' Anne apostrophized that Gondal world years later,

> Oh! happy life! To range the mountains wild,
> The waving woods, or ocean's heaving breast,
> With limbs unfettered, conscience undefiled,
> And choosing where to wander, where to rest.
> Hunted, opposed, but ever strong to cope
> With toils and perils; ever full of hope![2]

It might also be deduced that it was because the poetry of Gondal was so close a reflection of their way of life and their most personal aspirations towards liberty that the plots remained so essentially feminine. Contrary to the pattern set by Charlotte and Branwell in the Glasstown Chronicles, where the major roles were sustained by Master-men (Zamorna and Percy and a whole hierarchy of military and political characters below them, from whom the springs of action derive), the parts assigned to men in Emily's and Anne's stories—to Alexander Elbë, Lord Alfred, Fernando de Samara, etc.—were, with one notable exception, secondary roles, subservient to the leading female parts. The weakling character of most Gondal 'heroes' was well in the tradition of the Scott novels, where the 'juvenile leads'—Edward Waverley, Henry Moreton, Frank Osbaldistone, and Reuben Butler—appear as mere cyphers beside their female counterparts, notably Diana Vernon, Flora MacIvor, Jeanie Deans.

[1] Ibid.
[2] 'Come to the Banquet', 4 Sept. 1845. Poems, ed. Wise and Symington, p. 185.

Nourished on the sheer romance of Scott's novels and Byron's poetry, it was not surprising that Emily Brontë should find the prototype for her ideal of womanhood in the heroines of the former and recognize in them kindred spirits, parallel figures to her own, in their fight for an independent existence. Their adventurous destinies, that placed them at the heart of some desperate action, were the very 'compensation' Emily's ardent nature craved to overcome the dullness of her lot. It may well be questioned whether the very conception of the Gondal heroines, regal, dedicated girls, undaunted in some noble cause, beautiful and uncontrolled, would not have been different but for the inspiriting example of Diana Vernon, Flora MacIvor, and the others, close to hand. The Brontë girls had early and easy access to the whole range of the Waverley Novels, all forty-nine volumes of them, at the Keighley Mechanics' Institute Library. By 1834, when Charlotte told Ellen Nussey that 'all novels after Scott's are worthless', they had evidently read the lot. Diana Vernon and Flora MacIvor had qualities that may have evoked, but also closely resembled, the most characteristic qualities of the growing Emily. There is a *Zeitgeist* that dictates these fashions, and it is certainly not without relevance to Emily's development, that the real and the ideal girls (Diana Vernon in particular) were full contemporaries. *Rob Roy* was published on 31 December 1817, just six months before Emily's birth. Diana's qualities of independence and daring, her dedication to the lost cause of her exiled kings, her high manner, her scorn of meaner minds—her beauty and dash and wit and courage, laid an enchantment on her first readers, as reviews of the book attest, and stamped her image on the nascent heroines of Gondal.

What appeal for Emily Brontë lay in the description of Diana Vernon, 'the heathbell of Cheviot, the blossom of the Border', can only be reckoned by its reverberation throughout the Gondal scene.'She seemed a princess deserted by her subjects, and deprived of her power, yet still scorning those formal regulations of society which are created for persons of an inferior rank, and, amid her difficulties, relying boldly and confidently on the justice of Heaven, and the unshaken constancy of her own mind.'[1] What readers of Emily Brontë's poetry are not reminded of the life-long 'constancy of her own mind'?

> Riches I hold in light esteem
> And Love I laugh to scorn
> And lust of Fame was but a dream
> That vanished with the morn—

[1] *Rob Roy*, ch. 13.

And if I pray, the only prayer
That moves my lips for me
Is—'Leave the heart that now I bear
And give me liberty.'[1]

'Everything is possible', says Diana Vernon, 'for him who possesses courage and activity—to the timid and hesitating everything is impossible —because it seems so.' Such a philosophy finds an echo in Emily's lines:

Hope soothes me in the griefs I know,
She lulls my pain for others' woe,
And makes me strong to undergo
What I am born to bear . . .

The more unjust seems present fate
The more my spirit springs elate
Strong in thy strength, to anticipate
Rewarding Destiny![2]

The fact that none of the early Gondal MSS. survive may be some indication that Emily and Anne did not make a very good job of their writing. (At sixteen Emily's handwriting was still abominable.) Reviewing them some years later, when the full stream of invention was carrying the Gondal plot irresistibly forwards, they may well have been sufficiently dissatisfied with their early crude efforts to destroy them then and there. By the time they were in their late teens they knew every turn in the plot, every physical trait of each character, so that they did not need those early sketches to remind them of the origins of the Saga.[3]

Emily's earliest known poems have one point in common: they begin with a statement of nature's aspect, before the action or the *dramatis personae* are introduced. With her, the mood of a poem was everything, and the mood was dictated by nature. Many poems remain unfinished, because when the scene was set, she lost interest in the human situation. Typical of the early processes of composition, are such lines as:

High waving heather, 'neath stormy blasts bending,
Midnight and moonlight and bright shining stars;
Darkness and glory rejoicingly blending,
Earth rising to heaven and heaven descending,
Man's spirit away from its drear dungeon sending,
Bursting the fetters and breaking the bars . . .

[1] Hatfield, 146.   [2] Hatfield, 188
[3] For Anne's participation in Gondal see Appendix c.

Cold, clear, and blue, the morning heaven
Expands its arch on high;
Cold, clear, and blue, Lake Werna's water
Reflects that winter's sky.
The moon has set, but Venus shines
A silent, silvery star . . .

Woods, you need not frown on me;
Spectral trees, that so dolefully
Shake your heads in the dreary sky,
You need not mock so bitterly . . .

Redbreast, early in the morning
Dank and cold and cloudy grey,
Wildly tender is thy music,
Chasing angry thought away . . .

There shines the moon, at noon of night—
Vision of glory—Dream of light!
Holy as heaven—undimmed and pure,
Looking down on the lonely moor . . .

May flowers are opening
And leaves unfolding free;
There are bees in every blossom
And birds on every tree.[1]

At that early stage in the poet's development, delight was unbounded, springing from each day's discovery of the beauty at her door. Emily and Anne enjoyed exceptional liberty for girls of their time, with the limitless moors for their playground. Though there was a rule by which they had to be accompanied on their walks either by Branwell or Tabby, neither was a hindrance to them. Their aunt never set foot on the moors in all her years at Haworth, and Tabby was a local woman, well versed in the lore of the countryside, and her tales of bygone times were a further stimulus to the imagination.

Tabby was over fifty when she came to them, and had memories stretching back to the 1780s, a fact which was not without its influence on the author of *Wuthering Heights*, who set the main action of her tale in those times. Tabby remembered the days when the villagers believed in fairies, when, like her prototype Martha in *Shirley*, her own mother had come running home 'on the edge of dark', 'fleyed out of her wits', to say she had 'seen a fairish in the hollow'.[2] Tabby remembered the days when

[1] Hatfield, 5, 1, 6, 7, 9, 101.   [2] *Shirley*, ch. 37.

the wool packs were carried by pack horses with jingling bells across the moors from Lancashire; when the stone farms dotted about the hills— Elizabethan buildings most of them—were flourishing and their owners living in almost unchanged primitive conditions; a hard race submitting to no laws but their own. Tabby remembered hearing from her elders about the ministry of the good Mr. Grimshaw, who had died in 1763 of the plague epidemic because he would not desert his parish; of his charity and fearful language, quite as unbridled as that of his mostly unlettered flock, but whose goodness and fervour in trying to save their souls had become legendary. Into the attentive ears of her young ladies Tabby poured the tales of Mr. Grimshaw's charitable deeds, of the orphan children he adopted and took to live in his own poor parsonage (which was nothing like so comfortable as Mr. Brontë's), and how the wicked wild things played round his nose. If Catherine Earnshaw and Heathcliff had origins in any human story, they lay here, in Mr. Grimshaw's loft, which Emily could pass any day of the week, just up the lane beyond the church at nearby Sowdens.

Tabby knew at first hand the strong Methodist traditions of the district, where John and Charles Wesley had been rapturously welcomed on repeated visits, and where the enlightened Mr. Grimshaw had given them the platform of his pulpit from which to preach the gospel of repentance. Tabby did not pull her punches where her young charges were concerned, but spoke her mind in the forceful dialect they found so irresistibly funny; a sermon in her tongue was worth any comic book in the library.

So it was that Emily, in particular, grew up with a robust sense of humour, one far removed from the dainty standards of the young ladies in the south of England, her future readers. This has to be borne in mind when considering how *Wuthering Heights* was received.

With Tabby in attendance, or with Branwell, their walks across the moors had sometimes specific purposes such as carrying a note from Mr. Brontë to his church trustee, Mr. Heaton of Ponden House, to convene him to a Vestry meeting, or to return a book borrowed from his library and to borrow another. Ponden House was only a couple of miles away, on the further side of the moorland village of Stanbury. In spring and summer the young Brontës took the longer path across the moors, by Sladen Valley, where the falls of water into a turfed hollow ring of rocks became their secret hiding place and which, being well read in the Romantic poets, they called 'The Meeting of the Waters'. The lashing beck was stilled here in a reed-fringed pool set in turf and moss which formed a complete oasis of verdure in the midst of rocks and heather. Haworth villagers still relate that it was there that the young Brontës passed the summer days, reading, sketching, or writing.

Ponden House had been a Tudor manor, reconditioned in 1801 (a date that acquired significance for Emily, as the opening words of *Wuthering Heights* show) and had been owned uninterruptedly by the same family since 1513. The rambling stone edifice with its stone-pillared gates, square courtyard, and walled garden, narrow mullioned windows deepset and glazed with tiny leaded panes, was approached by an avenue of Spanish chestnuts, before the reservoir and the long road round were built in the twentieth century. It looked what it was, an uncompromising moorland homestead, despite the late attempt to give it the air of a gentleman's residence. From early in the seventeenth century the Heatons had, officially, ranked as 'gentlemen' and had been summoned for refusing a knighthood from Charles I and fined £10. The Robert Heaton of that time, besides purchasing the moor-rights from Alvery Copley of Batley, lord of the manor of nearby Oakworth, had acquired a First Folio edition of Shakespeare, which, together with the other volumes of his library, he bequeathed to his son 'to be kept *at Ponden* for the use of my son and his heirs'.[1] The 'gentlemanly' status of the Heatons of Ponden was further proclaimed by the presence of peacocks in the gardens, by the lavish funeral ceremonies in which they indulged at the deaths of members of their family, and by the unassailable possession of a family ghost, whose terrifying appearances in many and varying guises were testified to by many of the hill-folk thereabout. The Ponden ghost, said to be a certain Henry Cass, a parliamentary man of the time of the Civil Wars, was at times called 'The Headless Man', whose appearances were found to coincide with an impending death or disaster in the family; at other times he appeared like a flaming barrel which was seen to roll down the hillside and disappear through the garden wall. Branwell knew the tradition well and wrote of it in his unpublished story, 'Percy' (*c.* 1837), when he described it thus: 'The Darkwell Gytrash was known by its form of an old dwarfish and hideous man, as often seen without a head as with one and moving at dark along the naked fields which spread round the aged house.'[2]

Emily knew the interior of Ponden House intimately, the oak-beamed parlour and great bedroom above which ran the whole depth of the house with windows at either end; the high mantel-shelves, so high as almost to be beyond the reach of a woman of moderate height; the very large inglenook arches both in the parlour and the room above, in which she placed

[1] Heaton Papers, Cartwright Memorial Hall, Bradford.   [2] BPM.

the dying Catherine; the lattice windows with their uninterrupted outlook on the moors; the first-floor library with its close-ranged shelves of calf-bound volumes, the supports carved with Adam designs in the 1790s. She knew it all so well that when she wished to conjure up a civilized home for the Lintons in contrast to the dilapidated Heights, she took Ponden House for the model of her Thrushcross Grange.

The Heaton family consisted at that time of Robert Heaton the 7th and his wife, *née* Alice Midgley, of the Manor House, Haworth (Haworth Old Hall), who were only married on 31 May 1821, the year after Mr. Brontë's coming to Haworth. The Midgleys were another old local family, Alice's forbear, David Midgley of Withins, being the founder of a charitable trust in 1723 to clothe ten poor children annually, five boys and five girls. The provision specified that the children were 'to be clothed with good and convenient blue clothes', the boys to receive each 'a coat, waistcoat and breeches of blue cloth, a blue cap and a pair of stockings'. The girls were to have 'a blue jacket, two petticoats, a blue cap and a pair of blue stockings'.[1] The point of interest to the biographer of Emily Brontë is that David Midgley, the ancestor of Mrs. Heaton, lived at Withins, the Elizabethan farmhouse on the high crest of the moors, four miles above Ponden House, which Emily made the site of Wuthering Heights. She knew, moreover, of the family ties binding the households at Ponden and Withins, which she made the basic issue in her tale.

The Heatons' children were all boys. Their eldest son, Robert, born 4 May 1822, was followed by four others: William born 1 June 1825, John born 22 March 1827, and, after the birth and early death of an only girl, two more boys born in 1834 and 1836, Thomas and Michael. Mr. Brontë officiated, of course, at all these christenings. The Heaton boys were thus all younger than the Brontë children,[2] but the hospitable character of their parents, and their own privileged position, placed them in an advantageous position as regards the parson's children. It was they who lent them books; and if Branwell learnt to go out with the guns, which became one of his great pleasures, it was to the Heatons he owed it. The situation of Ponden House, almost at the head of three valleys, was topographically dominant; and, holding the moor rights as they did up to the Lancashire border, the Heatons were socially unchallenged in the district. With the Taylor family of nearby Stanbury, they were Mr. Brontë's most substantial parishioners.

[1] Parish Registers, Haworth Church.
[2] The fiction by Emily Heaton, called *White Windows*, which ascribed a love affair to Emily Brontë and Michael Heaton is unfounded. He was twelve when she died.

Branwell loved the moors as much as his sisters and when he was escort in place of Tabby, though it behoved him as the only son in a family of girls to appear contemptuous of them, he always preferred to extend their walks rather than curtail them. With Branwell they ranged far, over the top by Withins down into Walshaw Dene and across to Hardcastle Craggs, a good ten miles away; when Charlotte went with them they came home in a gig, but generally they relied on their own legs to complete the twenty-mile round.

In those early days Charlotte missed much of her sisters' happy care-free life. As the eldest of the family she felt her responsibility towards them oppressively, and worked furiously hard in her exile at the Miss Woolers' school at Roe Head, Mirfield Moor. Contrary to all her forebodings, she found it to be a very happy place; her teachers (there were five Miss Woolers to begin with) were both kind and practical, and in Mary and Martha Taylor and Ellen Nussey, girls of her own age, she found lasting friends. The ordeal which she had so greatly dreaded proved a permanent boon, as it developed her intellectual powers, gave her some self-assurance, and equipped her to teach her sisters, and later to earn her own living. She was only away three terms (a year and a half) but she got the most out of the experience; she left Roe Head with every available prize, and the goodwill of her teachers. It was not surprising that she wished Emily and Anne to share her advantages in due course, but her judgement where Emily was concerned was already at fault; Emily was developing on quite contrary lines to her sisters, and neither discipline nor coercion could benefit her.

At that stage Charlotte felt most acutely the separation from Branwell, her intellectual equal and the partner in all her early efforts at authorship, and it was to Branwell she addressed her weekly letters from school, and not to her sisters. She viewed them tenderly, in the light of helpless children, her 'petites sœurs', as she wrote of them on returning home after a first visit to her new friend Ellen Nussey. Ellen's home, Rydings, was the battlemented house at Birstall which she later took as model for Thornfield Hall in *Jane Eyre*. It had been decided with Ellen that they should correspond in French, and in the best French she could muster Charlotte wrote to Ellen on 18 October 1832:

J'arrivait a Haworth en parfaite sauveté sans le moindre accident ou malheur. Mes petites sœurs couraient hors de la maison pour me rencontrer aussitot que le voiture se fit voir, et elles m'embrassaient avec autant d'empressement et de plaisir comme si j'avais été absente pour plus d'un an . . . J'ai donné à mes sœurs les pommes que vous leur envoyiez avec tant de bonté; elles disent qu'elles sont sur que Mademoiselle Nussey est très aimable et bonne: l'une et l'autre sont extrémement impatientes de vous voir; j'espère que dans peu de mois elles auront ce plaisir.[1]

It is noticeable in this account that the eventually unsociable Emily is represented as every bit as friendly towards the strange Miss Nussey as her sisters.

How the 'petites sœurs' appeared to Ellen when she made her first visit to Haworth in the following summer (in 1833), when Emily was just fifteen, is interesting because it is the first evidence of an outsider to be preserved. It is evident that they struck Ellen, who was at least two years or more their senior, as very decided characters, remarkably self-reliant in their own setting on the moors, and markedly different from Charlotte in this. Their shyness was understandably more pronounced than Charlotte's, for they had never left home, but even Emily's taciturnity—which was becoming proverbial in the family—could be set aside when her sympathies were kindled, as they were on the moors.

Ellen Nussey had been warned by Charlotte of Emily's excessive reserve with strangers, and was prepared to meet an unfriendly girl; this was not what Ellen found. 'Emily', she said, 'could be vivacious in conversation and enjoy giving pleasure ... On the top of a moor or in a deep glen Emily was a child in spirit for glee and enjoyment or when thrown entirely on her own resources to do a kindness.'[2] Ellen later told Wemyss-Reid, Charlotte's second biographer, how

on one occasion whilst Charlotte's friend was visiting the parsonage, Charlotte herself was unable through illness to take walks with her. To the amazement of the household, Emily volunteered to accompany Miss Nussey on a ramble over the moors. They set off together, and the girl threw aside her reserve, and talked with freedom and vigour which gave evidence of the real strength of her character. Her companion was charmed with her intelligence and geniality. But on returning to the parsonage, Charlotte was found awaiting them ... she anxiously asked Miss Nussey: 'How did Emily behave?' ... It was the first time she had ever been known to invite the company of any one outside the narrow limits of the family circle. Her chief delight was to roam on the moors, followed by her dogs, to whom she would whistle in masculine fashion.[3]

Ellen further reported:

In fine and suitable weather, delightful rambles were made over the moors and down into the glens and ravines that here and there broke the monotony

---

[1] *SLL*, i. 98.   [2] *SBC*, 163.
[3] T. Wemyss-Reid, *Charlotte Brontë: A Monograph*, 42–3. The habit of whistling, transferred to the heroine of *Shirley*, was duly reprimanded by Shirley's governess.

Haworth Moor, looking towards Stanbury

'Meeting of the Waters', Haworth Moor

Sladen Beck, Haworth Moor

of the moorland... Emily, Anne and Branwell used to ford the streams, and sometimes placed stepping-stones for the other two; there was always a lingering delight in these spots—every moss, every flower, every tint and form, were noted and enjoyed. Emily especially had a gleesome delight in these nooks of beauty—her reserve for the time vanished. One long ramble made in these early days was far away over the moors to a spot familiar to Emily and Anne, which they called 'The Meeting of the Waters'. It was a small oasis of emerald green turf, broken here and there by small clear springs: a few large stones serving as resting-places; seated here, we were hidden from all the world, nothing appearing in view but miles and miles of heather, a glorious blue sky, and brightening sun. A fresh breeze wafted on us its exhilarating influence; we laughed and made mirth of each other, and settled we would call ourselves the quartette. Emily, half reclining on a slab of stone, played like a young child with the tadpoles in the water, making them swim about, and then fell to moralizing on the strong and the weak, the brave and the cowardly, as she chased them with her hand.[1]

Even on that first visit Ellen noticed two things about Emily which were essential to her character: her natural kindness when not constrained by shyness, and her gaiety on the moors. Nowhere else was she so much herself, nowhere else so free; nowhere else had she so many friends, wild animals living their own lives with whom she was in intense sympathetic communion. It was a region made to the measure of her mind, which already could endure no boundaries. Emily knew every height and hollow, every expanse of pasture, every clump of bilberry, every jutting rock, as landmarks in an otherwise trackless ocean of bracken and heather. She knew and loved the creatures nesting in the heather, and brought the injured ones home in her hands, as the servants remembered;[2] she had no fear of any of them.

Ellen also noted Emily's appearance:

Emily had by this time acquired a lithesome graceful figure. She was the tallest person in the house except her father. Her hair, which was naturally as beautiful as Charlotte's, was in the same unbecoming tight curl and frizz, and there was the same want of complexion. She had very beautiful eyes; but she did not often look at you; she was too reserved. Their colour might be said to be dark grey, at other times dark blue, they varied so. She talked very little ... she had now begun to have the disposal of her own time.[3]

In a further recollection of Emily, sent to Clement Shorter,[4] Ellen noted:

[1] Nussey, 'Reminiscences'.   [2] Duclaux, 49.
[3] Nussey, 'Reminiscences'.   [4] SBC, 162.

Her extreme reserve seemed impenetrable, yet she was intensely lovable; she invited confidence in her moral power. Few people have the gift of looking and smiling as she could look and smile. One of her rare expressive looks was something to remember through life, there was such a depth of soul and feeling, and yet such a shyness of revealing herself.

The judgement, both for that time and later, was most perceptive. The uncommunicativeness of Emily was not mere shyness, but a defence put up to safeguard her inner life. At fifteen this was acquiring complete dominion over her material existence.

CHAPTER IV

ERRATIC STUDIES

ELLEN NUSSEY, who spoke of Emily 'now having the free disposal of her own time', would have been surprised had she known how that freedom was spent. While fulfilling her household daily tasks (which she as often neglected with cheerful carelessness), her whole consciousness was absorbed by Gondal. As yet, her invention was not selective; every impression from without or within, was allowed to contribute to her creation. She relished intensely, as Ellen Nussey recalled, her father's stories of his parishioners which at times enlivened the breakfast table. Mr. Brontë's parishioners were for the most part sheep farmers living in isolated farmsteads on the hills, untouched as yet by any of the modern standards in manners and education spreading in the towns. They were highly original humorous folk whose coloured language was not modified because they were talking to 't'parson'; all they asked of him was to mind his own affairs and let them be. Mr. Brontë's sense of humour was equal to theirs (he was also born a peasant, and an Irish one at that) and he was capable of answering them on their own terms. Ellen, hearing and observing the hilarious effect of his racy tales on the children, whilst she herself was shocked by them, had to admit that it was to such sources as these that *Wuthering Heights* owed its being.

Mr. Brontë at times would relate strange stories 'which had been told to him by some of the oldest inhabitants of the parish, of the extraordinary lives and doings of people who had resided in far-off, out-of-the-way places, but in contiguity with Haworth—stories which made one shiver and shrink from hearing; but they were full of grim humour and interest to Mr. Brontë and his children, as revealing the characteristics of a class in the human race, and as such Emily Brontë has stereotyped them in her *Wuthering Heights*.[1]

Emily's early acquaintance with such types and incidents, her acceptance of their violence as a truth she held direct from her father, made her impatient of such shiverings and shrinkings as Ellen's. What is apparent

[1] Nussey, 'Reminiscences'.

even in that early period of poetic adolescence, when she was feeling her
way towards her first lyrical flights, is her acceptance of unvarnished
reality in the world about her. The records of that time are a strange mixture of fact, humorous observation, and of dream. Among her first verses
to be preserved are such lines as these, Blake-like in their deceptive
simplicity, but baffling as a riddle meant to confound.

> Tell me, tell me, smiling child,
> What the past is like to thee?
> 'An Autumn evening soft and mild
> With a wind that sighs mournfully.'
>
> Tell me, what is the present hour?
> 'A green and flowery spray
> Where a young bird sits gathering its power
> To mount and fly away.'
>
> And what is the future, happy one?
> 'A sea beneath a cloudless sun;
> A mighty, glorious, dazzling sea
> Stretching into infinity.' [1]

The diary-papers of Emily Brontë, which date from the year 1834,
which she wrote at four-yearly intervals in collaboration with Anne, and
in time made so peculiarly her own, were begun as ill-written, ill-spelt,
blotted, crumpled exercises to a pattern first suggested by Byron.[2] In
Moore's *Life* of the poet, read by the young Brontës in the 1833 edition
from Keighley Mechanics' Institute Library, he quoted from Byron's
domestic journals, whose form and content, as comparison will show, were
soon adopted by young Emily Brontë. At Harrow, Byron began the habit,
scribbling in a schoolbook the following note: 'George Gordon Byron
26th June 1805—3 quarters of an hour past 3 o'clock in the afternoon—
3rd school, Calvert Monitor—Tom Wildman on my left hand and Long
on my right.' Sixteen years later, at Ravenna, Byron's style for this kind
of record had not altered: 'January 5th 1821—Rose late—dull & droop-
ing—the weather dripping & dense—Snow on the ground & Sirocco in
the sky—Dined versus six o'clock—Fed the two cats, the hawk, & the
tame (but not tamed) crow.'

In time, Emily Brontë would also, in defiance of her aunt, domesticate
a Merlin Hawk and have tame geese in the house, and report on the ever-

[1] Hatfield, 3.
[2] This was first pointed out by John Hewish in his *Emily Brontë*, 1969, p. 39.

increasing domestic menagerie in laconic phrase just as Byron had done. The text of her first diary-paper reads:

> November the 24 1834 Monday
> Emily Jane Brontë
> Anne Brontë

I fed Rainbow, Diamond Snowflake Jasper phaesant (alias) this morning Branwell went down to Mr. Driver's and brought news that Sir Robert Peel was going to be invited to stand for Leeds   Anne and I have been peeling apples for Charlotte to make us an apple pudding and for Aunt nuts and apples   Charlotte said she made puddings perfectly and she was of a quick but limited intellect. Taby said just now Come Anne pilloputate (i.e. pill a potato)   Aunt has come into the kitchen just now and said where are your feet Anne   Anne answered On the floor[1] Aunt   papa opened the parlour door and gave Branwell a letter saying here Branwell read this and show it to your Aunt and Charlotte—The Gondals are discovering the interior of Gaaldine   Sally Mosley is washing in the back kitchen

It is past Twelve o'clock   Anne and I have not tidied ourselves, done our bed-work or done our lessons and we want to go out to play   we are going to have for Dinner Boiled Beef, Turnips, potatoes and applepudding. The Kitchin is in a very untidy state   Anne and I have not done our music exercise which consists of b major   Taby said on my putting a pen in her face Ya pitter pottering there instead of pilling a potate   I answered O Dear, O Dear, O dear I will directly with that I get up, take a knife and begin pilling (finished) pilling the potatoes) papa going to walk   Mr. Sunderland expected

Anne and I say I wonder what we shall be like and what we shall be and where we shall be if all goes on well in the year 1874—in which year I shall be in my 54th year   Anne will be going in her 55th year   Branwell will be going in his 58th year   And Charlotte in her 57th year   hoping we shall all be well at that time we close our paper

> Emily and Anne
> November the 24 1834[2]

The material life, sharply focused, is accurately transcribed—but as though at one remove. What aunt says or Tabby does are no more than the gestures of marionettes; they are funny, but not important; her aunt's admonitions made no impression on Emily. Life was carefree, and perhaps 1834 marked the peak of the family's happiness.

It was at this time that they all started studying music and art in a little flurry of extravagance in which Mr. Brontë indulged. The Mr. Sunderland

---

[1] Obviously Anne was still in the habit recorded years before by Charlotte of kneeling up on a chair.
[2] From the original MS. at the BPM.

expected in the diary-paper was the organist of Keighley Parish Church, Mr. Abraham Stansfield Sunderland, whose connection with the family began in the May of that year when a new organ was consecrated at Haworth Church. Mr. Brontë's notes convening his trustees and church-wardens to vestry meetings on the subject show that enthusiasm had been mounting since the previous year and that small benefactions towards the expense of an organ (including a £5 donation from Miss Branwell) had been coming in. The promised inauguration of the organ by Mr. Sunder-land, 'free gratis for nothing' as Mr. Brontë assured his trustees, was the culminating ceremony to months of planning. If an organ was secured for the church, Mr. Brontë assured his Parochial Church Council that a local organist would be found to play it on Sundays; the local organist was none other than Branwell himself, who, at that time, and for some few years after, was so absorbed in music that he rather neglected his professional studies in painting.

Being a piano teacher much in demand among local families, Mr. Sunderland was now engaged to teach the Misses Brontë, whose many preserved albums of music, inscribed and dated by their teacher, show they began to study seriously in that year. There was no piano at the parsonage at the time of Ellen Nussey's first visit in 1833, but she related that a little later 'there was the addition of a piano', and added that 'Emily, after some application, played with precision and brilliancy. Anne played also, but she preferred soft harmonies and vocal music. She sang a little; her voice was weak, but very sweet in tone.' Some years later, after Emily had studied under a first-class teacher in Brussels, Ellen recorded: 'The ability with which she took up music was amazing; the style, the touch, and the expression was that of a professor absorbed heart and soul in his theme.'[1] This was the time when the little upright piano was acquired (made by John Green of Soho Square) and placed in Mr. Brontë's study. Like all his children, he passionately loved music and, while the practising could take place during his long patrols of his far-flung parish, often taking him on a circuit of twenty miles, the finished performances could await his return. While the piano pieces studied by his daughters were based naturally on Czerny, Diabelli, and Cramer, they included the full reper-toire of contemporary operatic arias and bravura pieces by the fashionable Continental composers, Bellini, Auber, Meyerbeer, Weber. But the chief favourite of the whole family was Handel. His entire oratorios 'arranged for Two Performers' were gradually added to their repertoire. The

[1] *SBC*, 163.

majority of their pieces were arranged as Duets, inscribed with Emily's and Anne's names. Unhappily for Charlotte, who loved music as much as her sisters, her extreme shortsightedness prevented her from making any headway with her piano practice and she had to give it up.

In those days the performances of oratorios in churches were still a regular feature of parochial life. Mr. Brontë, eagerly seconded by Branwell, insisted on the maintenance of this tradition in his own church, even after the introduction of an organ. The opposition of the 'Singers' to this innovation is pardonable, since the performances had, from time immemorial, been in their hands. The 'Gimmerton band' described by Emily in *Wuthering Heights* (chapter 7) had its real equivalent at Haworth, where there was a strong musical tradition; the 'band', as she related, was fifteen strong and consisted of 'a trumpet, a trombone, clarionets, bassoons, French horns, and a bass viol, besides the singers'. This augmented 'band' furnished the Christmas and Easter Oratorios, and, as Emily described, went the rounds 'of all the respectable houses at Christmas' to perform carols and glees. At the weekly Sunday services the band consisted generally of a bugle, a horn and a bass viol to lead the singers. Mr. Brontë was not to be balked of a project so near his heart as the introduction of an organ, and countered the opposition of the singers by applying to 'the proper authorities', and finding that he himself, as the licensed minister, 'had full power to permit any performances of the kind in the Church', adding with a touch of celtic fire: 'it will not do for me to be dictated to by the singers'.[1]

The Heatons of Ponden House were also a family of gifted musicians, and as the sons grew up they formed their own family orchestra, which they maintained into old age. Emily's picture of the Earnshaws giving welcome to the Christmas Singers and setting them on to sing songs and glees in addition to the customary carols, gives a first-hand picture of scenes familiar to her in childhood and adolescence.

The high-spirited narrative written by Charlotte in October 1834 containing a skit on Branwell in the character of Patrick Benjamin Wiggins, tells of the inauguration of the organ at Haworth Church, and Branwell's raptures on the occasion (prompting him to stand on his head for fifteen minutes at a time). Mr. Sunderland, portrayed as Mr. Abe Sudbury Figgs, 'a Pianist by profession, accustomed to give music lessons to the various families in the neighbourhood', is described as performing 'And

---

[1] The Revd. Patrick Brontë to George Taylor, 6 June 1832. Lock and Dixon, *A Man of Sorrow*, 325.

the Glory of the Lord' at the new organ. A greater organist than he, come express from Leeds on the occasion, whose name Charlotte did not trouble to disguise—he was John Greenwood, a reputed organist of the day—then took his seat at the organ, 'placed his fingers on the keys, his feet on the Pedals, and proceeded to electrify us with "I know that my Redeemer Liveth". Branwell, unable to speak, breathe, or even look up as long as the music sounded, then cried: "this is a God and not a Man."' [1]

Branwell, indulged to the hilt at the time, with organ lessons on the one hand, and private painting lessons from the Leeds artist William Robinson on the other, could afford to look down on his sisters from the dizzy height of his fair prospects in his last year at home. In Charlotte's narrative about Wiggins, his contempt for them is lightheartedly portrayed. Wiggins, en route to making his fortune at the capital city of Verdopolis (the Great Glass Town rendered into Greek!) is encountered by Charlotte's alter ego, Lord Charles Wellesley, who questions him about his origins. Wiggins feels himself too much above any of his connections to avow them.

'In a way I may be said to have no relations. I can't tell who my father and mother were no more than that stone. I've some people who call themselves akin to me in the shape of three girls, not that they are honored by possessing me as a brother, but I deny that they're my sisters . . .'

'What are your sisters' names?'

'Charlotte Wiggins, Jane Wiggins, and Anne Wiggins.'

'Are they as queer as you?'

'Oh, they are miserable silly creatures not worth talking about. Charlotte's eighteen years old, a broad dumpy thing, whose head does not come higher than my elbow. Emily's sixteen, lean and scant, with a face about the size of a penny, and Anne is nothing, absolutely nothing.'

'What! Is she an idiot?'

'Next door to it.' . . .

'Humph, you're a pretty set, but pray Master Wiggins, what first induced you to leave Howard, and come to Verdopolis?'

'Why, you see Lord Charles, my mind was always looking above my station. I was not satisfied with being a sign-painter at Howard, as Charlotte and them things were with being semptresses . . .' [2]

Charlotte, as if not altogether unaffected by her brother's point of view, used an identical description of herself in a letter to Ellen Nussey of 4 July of that year: '. . . I am not grown a bit, but as short and dumpy as

---

[1] 'My Angria and the Angrians', MS. by CB. BPM.   [2] 'My Angria'.

ever.'[1] There was, in fact, much truth in her family caricatures, not the least excellent of which was the portrait of Patrick Benjamin Wiggins himself: 'a low, slightly built man attired in a black coat and raven grey trousers, his hat placed nearly at the back of his head, revealing a bush of carroty hair so arranged that at the sides it projected almost like two spread hands, a pair of spectacles placed across a prominent Roman nose'.

The subject of family-portraits was much in the air that year, with the commencement of art-lessons in earnest at the parsonage. According to F. B. Leyland (Branwell's later friend), it was after Mr. Brontë had taken Charlotte and Branwell to see the Annual Exhibition of the Northern Society for the Encouragement of the Fine Arts at Leeds in June 1834, when the enthusiasm of the whole family was roused by the work of the portrait painter William Robinson of Leeds, that Mr. Brontë then and there engaged him to give Branwell preliminary training in portrait painting. It was already confidently expected that Branwell would be admitted to the Academy Schools. Mr. Robinson was to visit the parsonage at a fee of two guineas a time, during which he was also to teach Branwell's sisters the rudiments of drawing. No arrangement could give more joy to the young people than this opportunity to put their lifelong passion into practice. For the girls, destined as they already were to become governesses when they grew up, drawing, like music, was a necessary qualification, even had they been devoid of talent—which they were not. Both Charlotte and Anne have left a great number of highly finished drawings, copies from the line-engravings published in the annuals and art magazines of the day. Charlotte would spend as much as six months of her scant leisure in copying minutely one engraving, and delight in the work, though she realized later how valueless it was.[2] The examples of Emily's drawings, though far fewer than her sisters', are equally good of their kind. She was the one in the family who was not satisfied with copying, and attempted drawing 'from the life'. She made a beginning on the household pets. In June 1834 Charlotte also attempted a portrait 'from the life', with a water-colour sketch of Anne, which she signed and dated '17th June 1834'. It confirms Ellen Nussey's description of Anne the year before: 'Her hair was a very pretty light brown, and fell on her neck in graceful curls. She had lovely violet-blue eyes, fine pencilled eyebrows, and clear, almost transparent complexion.' It also completely belies Branwell's alleged description of his youngest sister as 'nothing'.

Branwell's obligation to 'work from the life' in preparation for the

Academy Schools, and his dearth of models, forced him to turn to 'them things', his sisters, for the subjects of his portraits. According to Leyland, the family group, and the detail of Emily cut from another group, now preserved in the National Portrait Gallery, date from this time, 1834–5. Mrs. Gaskell, who saw them in 1853 when she visited Charlotte at Haworth, also attributed them to these years because of the girls' dresses: 'Charlotte in the womanly dress of that day of gigot sleeves and large collars . . . The two younger seemed hardly to have attained their full growth . . . they had cropped hair, and a more girlish dress . . . They were good likenesses however badly executed.'[1] The difference in Anne's hair-style, however, as well as the girls' more mature expressions, suggest that Branwell's portrait belongs to a later period—to 1838 when he once again concentrated on portrait painting after his first set-back. He never finished the portraits, and did not sign or date them; what alone matters is that, though he may have said of Emily that she was 'lean and scant', and had 'a face no bigger than a penny', when he came to paint her he was artist enough to perceive 'the hidden Ghost that had its home' in her.[2]

Among the few drawings by Emily to be preserved is a copy of Finden's engraving of the painting by Westall of Lady Charlotte Harley—the 'Ianthe' to whom Byron dedicated the opening Canto of *Childe Harold* in 1813. It was reproduced in the 1833 edition of Byron's *Collected Works*, which had its place on Mr. Brontë's shelves.

The influence of Byron on the young Brontës was an instant contagion that spread through everything they did and wrote during their formative years. It affected Charlotte and Branwell morally and mentally to such an extent that they lost contact with realities, and suffered acutely from the restrictions of their life. Their manuscripts from 1833, the year they first read the poems and Moore's *Life of Byron*, contain not only frequent allusions to Byronic characters, but introduce them into their plots, as *Manfred*, the 'all-wise magician', is introduced into Charlotte's story, 'The Foundling' (1833). On Emily, Byron's imprint may have been less immediate, but it was also more lasting. The poetry of Gondal was often indebted to him; the familiar figures of outlaws, bandits, exiles, and prisoners derive in part from her reading of him. So too the romantic settings of mountainous country, rocky shores by lake and sea, exotic islands. The courage and desperation of the Gondal characters in defying the rule of God and Man, was also a legacy from the author of *Cain*, *Manfred*, *Lara*, *Conrad*; but, though these foreshadow the lawlessness of

[1] Gaskell, p. 88.   [2] Hatfield, 190.

'Grasper' from life. Drawing by Emily Brontë

'Keeper' from life. Drawing by Emily Brontë

'The Whinchat'. Drawing by Emily Brontë

'Keeper, Flossie and Cat'. Drawing by Emily Brontë

the dwellers in Wuthering Heights, it was not until Emily created Heathcliff that the full measure of the Byronic impact on her could be judged.
Heathcliff is the Byronic hero *par excellence*. In him is embodied the sin of
pride to a Satanic degree. It is the sense of his own greatness, and of
Catherine's failure to recognize it, that makes him implacable. Frustrated
of his love, he becomes a devil. Yet never does he lose the consciousness
of his seraphic essence, and it is Heathcliff's daring that raises him to the
level of Lucifer, who proclaimed

> Nothing can
> Quench the mind, if the mind will be itself
> And centre of surrounding things—'tis made
> To sway.[1]

To make the mind its own centre, to shape one's own destiny, is power
supreme; so Lucifer taught. And so Emily Brontë understood it when she
left Heathcliff to direct his own end, allowing no intervention of man or
nature to bring about his death. Heathcliff was master of his fate; alone,
he makes his escape from this tormenting life.

Something like twelve years elapsed between Emily's first reading of
Byron and the writing of *Wuthering Heights*. There can be no suggestion
that she consciously adapted the work of the one in shaping the creation of
the other; but it is the measure of the impression Byron made on her
youthful mind that the resemblance exists.

There was an incident related by Moore in his *Life of Byron* which left
a recognizable trace in Emily's work; this was connected with the poet's
early love for Mary Chaworth. At the height of Byron's infatuation for
her, when he visited her daily and believed she returned his love, he over-
heard her saying to her maid one evening: 'Do you think I could care for
that lame boy?'—a speech which Byron himself described as hitting him
'like a shot through the heart'.[2] Newstead Abbey and Mary's home,
Annesley Park, were neighbouring properties, sóme three miles apart;
though it was late at night, Moore relates that Byron 'instantly darted out
of the house scarcely knowing whither he ran, and never stopped till he
found himself at Newstead'.[3] Mary's rejection, induced by a physical
repulsion, was not merely a heart-break to Byron, but a humiliation, and
according to Moore, it embittered him for ever. The relevance of this
incident to the scene in *Wuthering Heights*, in which Heathcliff overhears
Catherine telling Nellie Dean that it would degrade her to marry him,

[1] *Cain*, I. i.   [2] Moore, *Life of Byron*, i. 83.   [3] Ibid.

whereupon he runs away and is not heard of for three years, need not be stressed.

In Byron, Emily found the champion of unsociable man. His ill-fated lovers attracted her equally because of their contempt for conventional society and their boldness in defying their unpropitious stars. The mystery of their origins was another source of romantic inspiration to her; there was *Lara*, whose origins, like Heathcliff's after him, no man knew:

> He stood a stranger in this breathing world,
> An erring spirit from another hurl'd . . .
> What had he been? What was he, thus unknown,
> Who walked their world, his lineage all unknown?
> (*Lara*, I. xviii)

There was the defiance of *Cain*; the fatal love of Manfred; all these Byronic attributes were bestowed in time on the emerging Gondal heroes, and were finally justified in the protagonist of *Wuthering Heights*.

Emily Brontë was no plagiarist; few novelists were so original as she. What she took from Byron she took because the seed lay in her. The voice of Heathcliff is no less authentic when he cries to the dead Catherine 'Haunt me then! Be with me always!' because Manfred cried with equal passion years before to Astarte:

> 'Yet speak to me! . . .
> Speak to me! though it be in wrath!—but say—
> I reck not what—but let me hear thee once—
> This once—once more! . . .'
> (*Manfred*, II. iv. 142–8)

Emily's response to Byron was the more vivid because her reading of him coincided with her growth from girlhood to adolescence. She, too, was becoming an unsociable being. She shunned the people with whom her father's position in the parish brought her into contact, refused to teach in the Sunday school, spoke to no one in the village street on the unhappy occasions when she had to go to one of the shops alone, and steadily averted her glance when a stranger spoke to her. This aversion from ordinary social ways did not spring from misanthropy, but from her intense inner life, into which she allowed none to penetrate, from her growing awareness of the difference between her interests and other people's, and a dread of their intrusion into her privacy. Such intrusions could break the charm and snap the thread of narrative; and at this age she was furiously beset by the demon of poetry.

Milton had been Mr. Brontë's favourite poet as a boy when he learnt *Paradise Lost* by heart. On Emily, the impact of the figure of Satan was deep and lasting. The sense of thwarted power in the fallen angel, conscious of his lost rights, stirred her to admiration and sympathy. The very magnitude of Satan's demands and losses made her his champion. Satanic will-power, like Satanic vengeance, figures early in the Gondal Saga as a theme that found a ready response in her own wilful and independent character; it suited the boldness of her mind to conceive heroes in Satan's image.

Emily's were but erratic studies. From the course of reading she desultorily pursued in her formative years, the following authors left the clearest traces on her own work: Scott's poetry and novels; the poetry of Byron and Milton; and ballad poetry from both sides of the Border.

It has already been noticed that the names she gave her Gondal characters were predominantly Scottish,[1] and it cannot be overlooked that the Douglas, of 'Chevy Chase' fame—and of Scott's *Lady of the Lake*— the 'Black Douglas' of history and legend, contributed vital characteristics to Emily's 'black-browed' hero-villain of Gondal. The ballad form adopted by Emily in her earliest Gondal fragments seems a natural choice for her to have made. It suited her uncomplicated mind, laconic style, and direct primitive narration. It was not in her to beat about the bush; she went straight to the heart of any matter without preamble. Dramatic action and dialogue were her strength, as the following examples of her earliest transcribed poems show. (Their date of composition was probably considerably earlier than their date of transcription in August 1837.)

> Lord of Elbë, on Elbë hill,
> The mist is thick and the wind is chill
> And the heart of thy Friend from the dawn of day
> Has sighed for sorrow that thou went away
>
> Lord of Elbë, how pleasant to me
> The sound of thy blithesome step would be
> Rustling the heath that, only now
> Waves as the night-gusts over it blow . . .[2]

> Far away is the land of rest,
> Thousand miles are stretched between,
> Many a mountain's stormy crest,
> Many a desert void of green.

---

[1] See above, p. 21.   [2] Hatfield, 16.

Wasted, worn is the traveller;
Dark his heart and dim his eye;
Without hope or comforter,
Faltering, faint, and ready to die . . .

But yet faint not, mournful man;
Leagues on leagues are left behind
Since your sunless course began;
Then go on to toil resigned.[1]

And again:

I paused on the threshold, I turned to the sky;
I looked on the heaven and the dark mountains round;
The full moon sailed bright through that Ocean on high,
And the wind murmured past with a wild eerie sound;

And I entered the walls of my dark prison-house;
Mysterious it rose from the billowy moor . . .[2]

'. . . The breeze sings like a summer breeze
Should sing in summer skies
And tower-like rocks and tent-like trees
In mingled glory rise.

But where is he to-day, to-day?'
'O question not with me!'
'I will not, Lady; only say
Where may thy lover be?

Is he upon some distant shore
Or is he on the sea
Or is the heart thou dost adore
A faithless heart to thee? . . .'[3]

The haunting quality of ballad poetry, the incomplete, unconnected incidents of its plots, the violence of its actions, had not only an enduring influence on the poetry of Gondal but on *Wuthering Heights* itself. Multiple and conflicting as were the influences shaping that work, there can be no doubt that Emily's early and deep response to ballad poetry—and especially to such a ballad as 'The Daemon Lover'—left her dissatisfied with the models and themes of current fiction, of so much lesser power and weaker magic.

---

[1] Hatfield, 32.   [2] Hatfield, 83.   [3] Hatfield, 110.

> O where hae ye been, my long, long love,
> These seven long years and more?

asks the Catherine-like, deserted woman of her returned love.

> O I'm come to seek my former vows
> That ye promised me before

asserts the bold lover, recking nothing, any more than Heathcliff, of her
new ties as wife and mother; and bewitching her away with promises:

> I hae seven ships upon the sea,
> And the eighth brought me to land;
> With mariners and merchandise,
> And music on every hand.

Only when she has left her home and sailed with him does his true
daemonic nature appear in the final gesture that destroys them all.

> And aye as she turn'd her round about,
> Aye taller he seem'd to be;
> Until that the tops o' that gallant ship
> Nae taller were than he.

> He strack the top-mast wi' his hand,
> The fore-mast wi' his knee;
> And he brake that gallant ship in twain,
> And sank her in the sea.[1]

In *Wuthering Heights* (ch. 9) Ellen Dean sings the child Hareton asleep
with a ballad—'The Ghaist's Warning'[2] and Bessie, in *Jane Eyre*, does
the same, with 'A Long Time Ago'. The Brontës were brought up in the
oral tradition of sung ballads, thanks to Tabby, irrespective of their
reading of Percy's *Reliques*, and Scott's *Border Minstrelsy*.

At no stage in her development was Emily Brontë a student. Her diary-
paper of November 1834, written past noon, unashamedly reported that
neither she nor Anne had 'done their lessons' and that their sole wish was
'to go out to play'. When she was twenty-three she confessed to having
'a good many books on hand, but I am sorry to say that—as usual I make
small progress with any'. But she cheered herself with the reflection:
'however I have just made a new regularity paper! and I will Verb Sap—
to do great things'.[3] Inspiration did not lie in 'regularity papers' (a habit

---

[1] 'The Daemon Lover'. *The Oxford Book of Ballads*, 123–6.
[2] Scott's translation of a Danish ballad. See *Lady of the Lake*, note 49.
[3] Diary-paper, 30 July 1841.

of Mr. Brontë's, to whose favourite Latin tag she alludes) but out on the moors, ranging at will in all weathers, romping with the dog, walking and playing with Anne, arguing with Charlotte, bandying invectives with Branwell. She asked nothing more of life than to pass it in this manner, with time unlimited at her command, and books and music to refresh her mind when she was tired. Few people knew better how to relax, as Charlotte wrote of Shirley afterwards, lying on the hearthrug with a book: 'Her book has perhaps been a good one; it has refreshed, refilled, re-warmed her heart; it has set her brain astir, furnished her mind with pictures. The still parlour, the clean hearth, the window opening on the twilight sky . . . suffice to make earth an Eden, like a poem, for Shirley.'[1] This freedom, this dawn of a power to create a world to her own measure was becoming hers increasingly; she cherished it as life's greatest boon. So much the greater, therefore, the shock she experienced when, in the autumn of 1835, it was decided to send her away to school.

[1] *Shirley*, ch. 22.

CHAPTER V

'UNWILLINGLY TO SCHOOL'

THE decision was part of a general break-up of family life that was to occur that autumn. Branwell was to apply for admittance to the Academy Schools, which meant a big financial drain on his father's resources. Though the schools were free, the cost of maintaining him in London lodgings for at least three years could not be met out of his father's stipend. The old friends from Thornton rallied as on previous occasions to relieve Mr. Brontë, and Branwell's godmother, the widowed Mrs. Firth, undertook to supplement the sum needed for Branwell's maintenance. Branwell's sisters were as anxious as he could have been to improve his chances; an offer to Charlotte to go back to Miss Wooler's as a salaried teacher came most opportunely that summer, especially as it was coupled with an offer to take one of her sisters as pupil in part payment. Charlotte did not hesitate to accept and already in imagination set apart a portion of her salary to help Branwell.

There was never any hesitation about which sister should accompany her; Emily was the next in age, and the most in need of schooling, if she was, as planned, to become a teacher herself in due course. Anne could, if all went well, benefit by the same fortunate arrangement at a later date. So Mr. Brontë argued, knowing his children very little indeed. He explained all these projects to his old Thornton friend, the former Elizabeth Firth, now Mrs. Francks, wife of the Vicar of Huddersfield. The proximity to Roe Head, their former kindnesses to Charlotte while at school there, decided him to beg the Franckses to keep a watchful eye on his girls. Thus, before ever Emily entered the school, her last chances of liberty were lost to her. Writing on 6 July 1835, Mr. Brontë begged his old friends to be so kind

as to interpose with your advice and counsel in case of necessity, and if expedient to write to Miss Branwell or me if our interference should be requisite. I will charge them strictly to attend to what you may advise . . . They both have good abilities, and as far as I can judge, their principles are good also, but they are very young, and unacquainted with the ways of this delusive and ensnaring world . . . It is my design to send my son . . . to the Royal Academy of Arts in

London, and my dear little Anne I intend to keep at home for another year, under her aunt's tuition and my own.[1]

As the event proved, Mr. Brontë's fears for his daughters' exposure to the snares of 'this delusive world' would have been well transferred to his son, equally 'unacquainted with the ways of the world' and less morally prepared than they to resist temptation. The issue of the relative value of educating girls and boys would arise time and again in the Brontë family as Branwell's ability to meet the challenge of life was repeatedly disproved.

The day fixed for Charlotte's and Emily's departure, 29 July, was the eve of Emily's seventeenth birthday. '. . . Emily and I leave home on the 29th of this month,' Charlotte told Ellen Nussey,[2] 'the idea of being together consoles us somewhat, and, in truth, since I must enter a situation, "My lines have fallen in pleasant places". I both love and respect Miss Wooler.'

The halves into which the school year were then divided fell at the end of January and of July, and were broken only by two holidays, at Christmas and mid-June. This was due to the requirements of an agricultural society (few residents in rural areas did not have their own hay and corn-fields) which depended on the help of all hands—including the school-children's—to carry in the harvest. By 1 August, in those days of hotter summers, the harvest was reckoned to be in.

It was Emily's first birthday away from home. She had not been away at all for ten years and her ignorance of any other way of life than that of the withdrawn but completely free environment of the parsonage made it impossible for her to imagine what the regimen in a boarding-school was like. Had she been going to the heart of Africa she might have had a better idea of what was involved; certainly she would have preferred it to a girls' school, as promising more adventure. She had no idea as yet of the constraint put on the Young Ladies in a well-regulated seminary where every hour of every day was judiciously apportioned to some useful and instructive task. Charlotte, who had been there before, and congratulated herself on returning to so pleasant a place and to a teacher she both loved and respected, did not realize how changed her own circumstances would be in the role of teacher.

Miss Wooler had once had four sisters to help her run the school, but was understaffed now that two of them were married. It was the recent marriage of Miss Marianne Wooler to the Revd. Thomas Allbutt, Vicar of Dewsbury (where Mr. Brontë had begun his ministry in Yorkshire)

[1] Lock and Dixon, *A Man of Sorrow*, 288.
[2] CB to Ellen Nussey, 6 July 1835. *SLL*, i. 115.

that had created the vacancy which Charlotte was engaged to fill. The number of pupils had greatly grown since Charlotte's schooldays, and the amount of work required of the teachers had proportionately increased. Her position in the school was naturally a junior one, and her place was to teach the youngest girls—with whom she had the least sympathy. Emily she saw little of, and what she saw soon alarmed her. Only one benefit did they enjoy; it was the custom at that time for the boarders to share beds, and she and Emily could at least unburden their hearts to each other at night.

There was nothing in school-life to make it tolerable to Emily. She found the organized routine, the rigid timetable of work and play wholly unconducive to study. The indigestible diet of dates and facts as derived from Mangnall's *Questions*; the monotonous schoolroom hours of committing items of history, grammar, geography, or literature to memory, seemed contemptible to Emily, who liked to delve deep or not at all. To a mind like hers, used to directing its own studies, the superficiality of a school curriculum was thoroughly demoralizing.

The play hour was even more insipid; for the girls were not even inventive in their play. The urbane, civilized demeanour of Miss Wooler herself, who wished the girls to acquire polished manners as much as book learning, could not convince Emily of the need for such graces which she despised in her heart of hearts. She had far more sympathy for Catherine Earnshaw when she was a 'wild, hatless little savage' losing her shoes in the bog, climbing through one garret skylight, over the roof and down again through another skylight to join her playmate, than when she gave herself airs and was dressed in tartan silk and wore a feathered beaver.[1]

Sundays were even worse than weekdays, with the added ordeal of walking in a crocodile to church across the fields to Mirfield, where Miss Wooler's brother-in-law, the Revd. Edward Carter, conducted the services. The path across the fields down Slipper Lane was sufficiently attractive in itself because it was high and looked down over the surrounding moors and woods, the woods of Kirklees Park, and distant Huddersfield. But the country had no charm for Emily since she was not free to roam in it; it was agony to be constrained to keep in step with the pupil beside her; to her long legs, accustomed to striding over peaty ground and scrambling up rocks, these walks were galling in the extreme.

There were, in addition, the occasional obligatory visits to Huddersfield Vicarage to be endured, and the well-intentioned probing of Mrs.

[1] *Wuthering Heights*, ch. 7.

Francks into their affairs. She felt imprisoned, bound and helpless, and a deep sense of frustration was the result. The loss of Anne's companionship was an added misery. There was no one at Roe Head to whom she cared to talk—except Charlotte, of whom she saw all too little. There was absolutely no possibility of thinking about Gondal—let alone writing about it. In exchange for her boyish free Byronic world whose denizens were her equals, she was offered babies' chatter.

How Charlotte viewed the schoolgirl chatter of her charges can be read in her journals of the time.

After tea we took a long walk. I came back exhausted to the last degree for Miss Lister and Miss Marriott had been boring me with their vulgar familiar trash all the time we were out. If those girls knew how I loathed their company they would not seek mine so much as they do. The sun had set nearly a quarter of an hour before we returned and it was getting dusk. The Ladies [pupils] went into the school room to do their exercises and I crept up to the bed-room to be alone for the first time that day . . . The stream of thought, checked all day came flowing free and calm along its channel . . . the toil of the day succeeded by this moment of divine leisure acted on me like opium . . . What I imagined grew morbidly vivid. I remember I quite seemed to see with my bodily eyes a lady standing in the hall of a gentleman's house as if waiting for someone . . .[1]

Emily's need for solitude, her obsession with her imaginary world, was more acute even than Charlotte's; her distress at being severed from the sources of invention was to that extent the greater; and while Charlotte recognized the necessity of submitting to the practical demands of life, Emily saw no such necessity. She was wholly opposed to the conventional patterns of a standard education; they sickened her, spiritually and physically.

To her extremely simple tastes, even the food was unpalatable. With lack of appetite, wretched nights, and the misery of each day's constraint, her health gave way. Only Charlotte knew that what ailed her was acute homesickness.

Many years later when preparing a memoir of her sister for her publisher, Charlotte tried to explain Emily's strong revulsion from the conventional modes of life, and told the story of her schooldays with great insight:

At that period she was sent to school. Her previous life, with the exception of a single half-year, had been passed in the absolute retirement of a village parsonage, amongst the hills bordering Yorkshire and Lancashire. The scenery

[1] CB's Roe Head Journals, 26 Aug. 1836. BPM, Bonnell Coll., 98 (8), 125-6.

of these hills is not grand—it is not romantic; it is scarcely striking. Long low moors dark with heath, shut in little valleys, where a stream waters, here and there, a fringe of stunted copse. Mills and scattered cottages chase romance from these valleys; it is only higher up, deep in amongst the ridges of the moors, that Imagination can find rest for the sole of her foot; and even if she finds it there, she must be a solitude-loving raven—no gentle dove . . . My sister Emily loved the moors. Flowers brighter than the rose bloomed in the blackest of the heath for her; out of a sullen hollow in a livid hillside her mind could make an Eden. She found in the bleak solitude many and dear delights; and not the least and best loved—was liberty.

Liberty was the breath of Emily's nostrils; without it, she perished. The change from her own home to a school, and from her own very noiseless, very secluded, but unrestricted and inartificial mode of life, to one of disciplined routine (though under the kindliest auspices) was what she failed in enduring. Her nature proved here too strong for her fortitude. Every morning when she woke, the vision of home and the moors rushed on her, and darkened and saddened the day that lay before her. Nobody knew what ailed her but me—I knew only too well. In this struggle her health was quickly broken; her white face, attenuated form, and failing strength threatened rapid decline. I felt in my heart she would die, if she did not go home, and with this conviction obtained her recall.[1]

Happily, the indelible memory of Cowan Bridge made Mr. Brontë and Miss Branwell accept the evidence of Emily's illness without argument; the permission for her to return home was sent immediately.

The truth was that it was already too late to make Emily conform to the normal contemporary standards of female education; she had passed beyond them, both in maturity and inclination. For too long she had developed along lines traced exclusively by herself; her nature could not now be trained in any other direction. She was too tall, too awkward and too shy to flourish outside the environment of her choice; she had already decided that she wished to be not other than 'as God made her'.[2] The fact that her return home from Roe Head completely restored her health is proof enough that the origin of her troubles had been psychological.

The offer which Miss Wooler had made for one of Charlotte's sisters to be taken in part payment for Charlotte's services, was now transferred to Anne, and immediately on Emily's return home, Anne was sent to Roe Head in her place. The evidence of a drawing dated from Roe Head shows that she was established there by 27 October 1835. Emily had not been three months at school.

[1] Biographical Notice.
[2] See below p. 130. J. J. Green. 'The Brontë–Wheelwright Friendship', *Friends, Quarterly Examiner*, 1916.

CHAPTER VI

THE STIMULATING SINNER

It was no joyous situation she found on returning home. To begin with, she was speedily bereft of Anne who took her place at Roe Head; and it seemed no compensation at first to find Branwell there, returned ignominiously from London, with all his hopes unfulfilled.

This was reckoned a disaster by the elders of the family. Because they had built such extravagant expectations on Branwell's talents, their disappointment, Emily soon found, was out of all proportion. The true reasons for his failure could not be explained to or understood by them; he had simply found himself unequal to the strain of competing with far more capable and better qualified young men than himself. He had undergone a mental and moral collapse, as it were, within sight of his goal, and had accomplished none of the objectives for which he had gone up to London. He made no attempt to present his letters of introduction to the Secretary of the Academy, to the illustrious teachers whose pupil he might have become; without giving himself even the chance of an interview at which his work could be examined, he fled before the ordeal, a beaten man. To explain his penniless return to his father and aunt, who had financed him for a long sojourn, he had to invent tales of robbery in the coach to London;[1] whereas he had spent his small patrimony on 'little squibs of rhum' in the 'snug' of the Castle Tavern in Holborn, among the prize fighters and the artists' models whose ordinary it was, and in whose robust but kindly company he found some comfort.[2] His inability to face the realities of an academic training, and his moral deflation before the jostling London crowds, induced a feeling little short of terror, and was such a pitiable thing that he could not speak of it without inventing a score of false reasons to account for it. The bitterness of failure lay for Branwell far more in the loss of prestige at home than in a wrecked career. He never showed the same passion for painting that he did for writing. What he had done so far, from childhood upwards, had come

[1] Chadwick, 192.
[2] MS. 'History of Angria'. Brotherton Coll., Leeds Univ. Library.

without effort; when a great effort was required—an effort he felt that was beyond his powers—he simply gave in.

Though this was not Emily's case, her first confrontation with the world had been a dismal failure too. She had no hard thoughts for Branwell on this score; for his miserable experiences in London she felt nothing but sympathy; his plight provoked the stirring of a first common cause between them, which neither had ever explored before. The sight of Branwell's hollow-eyed misery as he crept about the village, trying to elude his former cronies, was pitiable indeed, strange in its novelty, appealing to every impulse in her nature. His pride was cruelly wounded, his sense of frustration intolerably acute. He had been meant for something better, so his family had always claimed, and Emily's sympathy for the wretched figure he cut in the home circle now went very deep. Every feeling that was generous in her rose in response to Branwell's misery: if she had resented his assumption of superiority over his sisters in the past this was now all forgotten. It needed the collapse of Branwell's vanity and the stirring of Emily's protective sense (the same she extended to the injured creatures on the moors) to bring these two together, and nothing could help Branwell so much as Emily's belief in him. The little world of Roe Head had sown not only seeds of rebellion in her; it had prompted her to evolve her own scale of values, in which failure or success was not judged by results, but by the ideals engaged. What mattered was not to enter academies or to win prizes, but to aim at something above and beyond attainment—a philosophic mind.

Emily could believe, as yet, that Branwell's failure was the result of his rejection of conformity, and that, given time, he would show himself superior to others. She might, at that early stage, be excused for believing in Branwell more than he merited. He had a persuasive tongue, as his friends attested, a vivid personality, enthusiasm and humour—as well as a morbid fancy. When he chose, Branwell could captivate; he was undeniably gifted (perhaps gifted in too many contradictory ways) and it is understandable that Emily's imagination was kindled by him in their youthful isolation. They were budding poets who spoke a common language, shared common tastes, held common enthusiasms, which, by their very nature, could not be communicated to the elders. And as Mr. Brontë was often out on his extended visits to the sick and sinning poor of his far-flung parish, and Miss Branwell was increasingly confined to a rigid routine in her own room, the two young people were frequently left on their own. They were free to fetch books from the Keighley or Ponden libraries, and if she had sewing to do Branwell read aloud to

Emily. *Blackwood's* was still regular reading with them, and they had other tastes in common. They liked Mrs. Radcliffe's romances, and both loved music—Emily's piano could accompany Branwell's flute. He played the organ and, if not regularly for church services, he played to please himself. To listen to him was no small pleasure for Emily either, though he was not particularly accomplished. Leyland recalled how Branwell was

acquainted with the works of the great composers . . . and although he could not perform their elaborate compositions well, he was always so excited when they were played for him by his friends that he would walk about the room with measured footsteps, his eyes raised to the ceiling, accompanying the music with his voice in an impassioned manner, and beating time with his hand on the chairs as he passed to and fro.[1]

Whatever injury his vanity had suffered, the urge to write had not been crushed in him. As Emily listened to his confident talk of contributing to *Blackwood's*, there could be no doubt that he retained plenty of mental energy. Almost immediately after his wretched return from London he set about writing a long new Angrian narrative called 'The History of Captain Henry Hastings'—a rebel whose ill-success on entering the world, whose gullibility and insignificance in women's eyes, were a penetrating self-portrait, such as he could not have attempted in paint. The history of his lamentable adventures in London, written in the character of Charles Wentworth, followed in due course, a promising sign that he was exorcising the evil fortune that had crushed him.

From 'Captain Henry Hastings' it can be judged how Branwell's failure in London lost him his father's and aunt's ready credulity. Better than the inexperienced Emily they saw through Branwell's shiftless excuses, but they also judged him too harshly. Their moral condemnation only made him reckless. In the character of his new prototype—and pseudonym— Henry Hastings, he complained of the ready censure of his conduct by those at home:

Now, with respect to the reports about my conduct, I must say one word further. It has been stated that within the last year past I have done nothing but drink and gamble and do everything that is BAD . . . I like my glass of a night, the same as another. Well, 'I am in a continual and beastly state of intoxication'. I bet a nominal guinea on the issue of our topics of daily curiosity, I am 'an abandoned gambler' and, if successful, 'an arrant swindler'.[2]

---

[1] Leyland, *The Brontë Family*, i. 119–20.
[2] 'History of Angria', fragment dated 23 Jan. 1836. BPM.

The voice of the critic he flippantly quotes is, without doubt, his father's, whose views they very accurately expressed.

What Branwell's father did not know was that he was at the same time writing with a new truthfulness and power of his lost Paradise, and of his fall from Grace. In the December immediately following his return from London, he analysed the causes of his condition in a long poem to which he gave the appropriate title 'Misery'. In these lines he harked back, for the first time, to the initial source of all his sorrows, the death of his sister Maria. Reunion in death seems the only consolation, and then the doubt whether there is a heaven, a God, a hell, shatters the hope and sends his spirit probing through futurity, to proclaim the hollowness of the old promises and to end on a note of defiance. It was all very Byronic, and at the same time pitiable. Beneath the bravado, however, Emily could see her brother wrestling with the first genuine repulse he had suffered in life; in her eyes, he had become a solitary figure battling against the injustice of established order. The subject was familiar (Byron had never treated of any other), but for the first time in her life the subject was real and she was personally and intimately involved in it. Her absolute inexperience of people, except from what she had learned from books, made her judge Branwell's predicament as an heroic one—more heroic than his moral stature warranted. The great question for her now was not when but how Branwell would rise to the occasion, and defy his contrary stars. His present failure was in her eyes a further guarantee that he would eventually come to play a distinguished role in the world.

This period of close association with Branwell lasted for two years, while Charlotte and Anne remained at school, and it was during this time that Emily's preoccupation with the theme of guilt and failure, found in her early Gondal verse, and ultimately to become one of the themes central to her thought, began to take root. Already, in the view of Augusta Geraldine Almeda, her dead lover Lord Alfred Aspin was blameless of his misdeeds.

> If thou hast sinned in this world of care,
> 'Twas but the dust of thy drear abode—
> Thy soul was pure when it entered here,
> And pure it will go again to God.[1]

During these two years Emily matured as she would never have done at school: she read and practised her music, and she must also have set herself some planned course of general study, for her next departure from home was as a teacher in a big school. She taught herself German, it is

---

[1] Hatfield, 61.

known, and had a good enough knowledge of French when she finally accompanied Charlotte to Brussels in 1842, to express herself very creditably in her first compositions. This knowledge was not gained in a few weeks.

At home Emily continued to derive immense amusement from Tabby's company in the kitchen and on the moors, and her considerable store of moorland folklore. The relationship in which they stood, of grumbling devoted servant and 'giddy' young mistress, always alert to 'raise a crack' at Tabby, was one of the happiest and healthiest in Emily's life; in due course she immortalized it in *Wuthering Heights*.

Above all, she lived in contact with a masculine mind, listened to how a man talked, studied his tastes and motives, the unworthy as well as the good; watched his passions and his responses to pleasure, noted how different they were to her own or her sisters', and recognized how seldom he acted from disinterested motives or from simple kindness, and even less from motives of duty. Now he was a grown man, there was hardly any particular in which Branwell resembled his sisters; while his pretensions were far greater than theirs, his resolution to attain his desires was immeasurably weaker. Such as he was, Emily would not judge him. She grew to accept him, like the prevailing wind ('Very dull' if it were an east wind) or any other manifestation of nature.

Her own failure at Roe Head, as Charlotte said later,[1] was a source of deep mortification to her. So deep, it would seem, as to drive her yet further away from normality, into herself; into the rebellious world of Gondal, where she found fulfilment for every failure elsewhere. If she was proved 'a misfit' at Roe Head, and later at Law Hill, she sought, and found, a natural compensation in self-identification with the outlaw society of her saga—with the anti-social ideal, in particular, of her hero—the 'dark man' of her poems, the Douglas who already prefigured Heathcliff.

Failure and defiance were the themes asserting themselves in the poems of that time. What other schoolgirl ever wrote such lines as these?

> Strong I stand, though I have borne
> Anger, hate, and bitter scorn;
> Strong I stand, and laugh to see
> How mankind have fought with me
>
> Shade of Mast'ry, I contemn
> All the puny ways of men;
> Free my heart, my spirit free;
> Beckon, and I'll follow thee.

[1] Biographical Notice.

False and foolish mortal, know,
If you scorn the world's disdain,
Your mean soul is far below
Other worms, however vain.

Thing of Dust—with boundless pride,
Dare you take me for a guide?
With the humble I will be;
Haughty men are naught to me.[1]

On 14 December 1836, Charlotte and Anne came home for the Christmas holidays. Quickly the old partnerships between the brother and the sisters were resumed. Charlotte and Branwell had not ceased corresponding on 'Angrian' matters, as though nothing were changed in his situation in her eyes by the London fiasco. He was writing more than ever, and they were not long together before he told her of his determination to make a bid at professional writing. No news could be more welcome to her, or more reviving; she hated teaching and was desperate to escape from it and resolved with Branwell to seek advice on the possibilities for both of them to earn a living as writers. On 29 December she wrote to Southey, enclosing a specimen of her poetry, while on 19 January (1837) Branwell wrote to Wordsworth. In due course, and after an unavoidable delay which Southey kindly explained in his answer, Charlotte heard from him; his verdict was wholly against her making any attempt at professional writing—not because her talent was insufficient but because she was a woman. Wordsworth never answered Branwell at all. The arrogant tone and 'ill-manners' of Branwell's letter, as Wordsworth stigmatized them to Southey, quite disgusted him.[2] Branwell should by then have become inured to the rebuffs of his correspondents, whose antipathies he had an unfortunate habit of arousing. He wrote to the editor of *Blackwood's* both before and after writing to Wordsworth, and again in the following year, pressing his services on him with such wild and extravagant conceit that the recipients could put it down to nothing short of madness.[3] Writing to *Blackwood's* on 9 January 1837, Branwell asked:

Will you still so wearisomely refuse me a word when you can neither know what you refuse nor whom you are refusing? Do you think your Magazine so perfect that no addition to its power would be either possible or desirable? Is it

---

[1] Hatfield, 35.
[2] *The Correspondence of Southey with Caroline Bowles*, ed. Dowden, 1881, 348.
[3] As Mrs. Oliphant later revealed. See her *Annals of a Publishing House* (1897), ii. 177ff.

pride which actuates you—or custom—or prejudice? Be a man, Sir! and think no more of these things. Write to me . . .

It may well be supposed that thus adjured, the editor of Blackwood's did nothing of the kind.

Disappointment was pervasive during those Christmas holidays: Charlotte, who had eagerly looked forward to a visit from Ellen Nussey, had to put her off on account of a serious accident to Tabby, who fell in the icy village street just before Christmas and broke a leg. She remained, as Charlotte wrote to Ellen several days afterwards, 'at our house in a very doubtful and dangerous state.'[1] The reference to Tabby's being 'at our house' was explained by Mrs. Gaskell years later: once she was out of danger, Miss Branwell very strongly urged that Tabby should be moved to her sister's cottage to obviate the trouble and expense of nursing her at the parsonage. Mr. Brontë only reluctantly agreed to this proposal, it being, as Mrs. Gaskell added, 'repugnant to his liberal nature'.[2] It was, however, neither Miss Branwell nor Mr. Brontë who decided the issue: Tabby's three 'childer' were adamant in rejecting any such plan; they declared that Tabby 'had tended them in their childhood, and none should tend her in her infirmity but they',[3] and they showed the elders that they meant business by going on hunger strike. To the amazement of their aunt, they sent away their meals untouched until they carried the day. Tabby remained. The gesture was characteristic of them all, but it must principally have been prompted by Emily on whom, when the holidays were over and Charlotte and Anne returned to school, the whole responsibility for nursing Tabby and taking her place in the kitchen must fall. This was exactly what happened. No regular help was at that time available (the sexton's daughters, who each in turn were later employed at the parsonage, were still too young) and as Charlotte wrote to Ellen: 'since the event we have been almost without assistance—a person has dropped in now and then to do the drudgery . . . but the whole work of the house, as well as the additional duty of nursing Tabby, falls on ourselves.' At a time when all the household bread was baked at home, and the heavy domestic washing was a weekly event in the out-house, even if occasional help was forthcoming, Emily's task was a heavy one.[4] The remarkable thing is that both then and later she showed herself a most able housekeeper.

Miss Branwell had never taken an active part in domestic affairs; she

---

[1] CB to Ellen Nussey, 29 Dec. 1836. W & S, ii. 149.
[2] Gaskell, 90.   [3] Gaskell, 109.
[4] See diary-paper of 24 Nov. 1834. BPM.

held the purse strings and ordered the meals, but the cooking and cleaning had always devolved on the servants, and in later years, on Tabby alone, with some help from her young ladies. Now Tabby was incapacitated for several months, and remained lame for the rest of her life. Indeed anyone knowing the interior of the parsonage will realize how difficult it must have been for her to get down the winding stairs to her kitchen again. All she could do, even then, was to sit by the kitchen fire, peel the potatoes and perform other easy tasks, and gird at her young mistress in her rich dialect. She was, and remained, an indomitable character, loyal, honest, uncompromising, not always easy to manage, but Emily knew perfectly how to humour her, answering her in Tabby's own racy language.

As a baker of excellent bread Emily's reputation was soon established in the village, where it won her far more respect than her reputed 'learning'. The parish clerk, invading her kitchen on church affairs, or tradesmen delivering goods, observed her at her bread-trough, kneading the dough.[1] Though awed by her silence, some of them noticed the book propped up on the kitchen table at her side, and the little scraps of paper and pencil to hand, though for what purposes they did not guess until years later they learned that she wrote, and published, poetry.

Exacting as such household tasks and the nursing of Tabby must have proved to a girl of her age, it is noticeable that she did not fall ill in consequence, as from the far less exacting drudgery of school-life. Her ability to deal so capably with practical domestic concerns (better than Charlotte, on her own confession, ever managed to do) would suggest that she found a release in them from the mental pressure of the time, which coincided with the first flowering of her poetic powers. To prove to herself and others that she was capable of doing an uncongenial task well was no doubt an added incentive. Emily was proud, and her failure at school, though condoned by an indulgent family, had not ceased to rankle with her and she would not be satisfied until that stain had been wiped out.

The experience of this time, the heavy demands on her physical energies which left her little leisure for the writing that was becoming an imperative need, brought about a fresh withdrawal into herself, a deepening of the division between the life of domestic conformity and of spiritual daring and escape. The recognition of the warring elements within herself, of her intense dissatisfaction not with her personal lot but with life itself, was at the origin of the recurring escape-theme that now found its way into her poetry:

[1] Gaskell, 109.

> I'm happiest when most away
> I can bear my soul from its home of clay
> On a windy night when the moon is bright
> And the eye can wander through worlds of light—
>
> When I am not and none beside—
> Nor earth nor sea nor cloudless sky—
> But only spirit wandering wide
> Through infinite immensity.[1]

At night, released from the toil of day, she lay on the low camp-bed under the curtainless window, her eyes fixed on the sky, and followed through the immensities of space the tracks of the stars. Her love of the radiant presences of the night, the moon, stars, and meteors, later expressed in incomparable verse, seemed to breed in her a growing dread of day, not only for the barren tasks it imposed, but for its destruction of her dreams. She was already evolving as a poet of darkness rather than of light, and shrinking from the sun as an infringement on her privacy.

> Sun, set from that evening heaven,
> Thy glad smile wins not mine;
> If light at all is given,
> O give me Cynthia's shine.[2]

On 20 June 1837, very early in the morning, the young Princess Victoria was called to the throne of England, an event whose repercussions were felt as far from the centre of government as Haworth parsonage. Emily noted it in her diary of 26 June, the only reference of its kind in all her records of family life. Emily was no declared feminist, but it was artistically satisfying to her that a woman—young, unmarried, almost her own age—should hold this unique position in the land. Long ago Emily had made Victoria a Gondal heroine. How the young Victoria would conduct herself as queen became a matter of more than passing interest.[3] The immediate question of her coronation was to have a bearing on the Gondal plot. The rival claimants to the throne of Gondal, Julius Brenzaida and his cousin Gerald Exina, were to mark the truce in their civil strife by a joint assumption of power, to which their dual coronation was to set the seal.

The presence of Anne at home for the holidays made it a doubly propitious time to plan further developments in the Gondal plot; and the

---

[1] Hatfield, 44.   [2] Hatfield, 24.
[3] See Emily's interest in the Queen's state visit to Brussels in Sept. 1843. CB to EJB. 1 Oct. 1843. W & S, i. 305.

fact that it was Branwell's birthday lent a festive and leisured air to the last-minute report written that day on Gondal and household permutations and occupations, as though all were equally urgent to Emily.

Monday evening June 26th 1837

A bit past 4 o'clock Charlotte working in Aunt's room, Branwell reading Eugene Aram to her[1]—Anne and I writing in the drawing-room—Anne a poem beginning 'Fair was the evening and brightly the sun'[2]—I Augusta Almeda's life 1st v. 1–4th page from the last—fine rather coolish thin grey cloudy but sunny day Aunt working in the little room the old nursery Papa gone out Tabby in the kitchen—The Emperors and Empresses of Gondal and Gaaldine preparing to depart from Gaaldine to Gondal to prepare for the coronation which will be on the 12th July Queen Vittoria ascended the throne this month. Northangerland in Monkey's Isle—Zamorna at Eversham. All tight and right in which condition it is to be hoped we shall all be this day 4 years at which time Charlotte will be 25 and 2 months—Branwell just 24 it being his birthday— myself 22 and 10 months and a peice Anne 21 and nearly a half I wonder where we shall be and how we shall be and what kind of a day it will be then—let us hope for the best

Emily Jane Bronte—Anne Bronte

I guess that this day 4 years we shall all be in this drawing-room comfortable I hope it may be so. Anne guesses we shall all be gone somewhere comfortable We hope it may be so indeed. [Obviously Miss Branwell put her head round the door.]

Aunt: Come Emily it's past 4 o'clock

Emily: Yes, Aunt Exit Aunt

Ann: Well, do you intend to write in the evening

Emily: Well, what think you

(We agreed to go out 1st to make sure if we got into the humour. We may stay in—)[3]

The early date announced here for the Gondal coronation was modified in due course, when the impatient chroniclers learned that coronations were not ceremonies that could be advanced with indecorous haste, and when the date of Victoria's own coronation was announced for the following year. Emily's poems, relating to King Julius's treacherous conduct on the occasion, were not written till March 1838 and remained even then unfinished.[4] This was a habit with her; poems begun and set aside were

---

[1] *Eugene Aram*, by Bulwer Lytton, was published in 1832 and figured in Keighley Mechanics' Inst. Libr.

[2] The poem is titled 'Alexander & Zenobia'—MS. at Texas Univ. Libr.

[3] Diary-paper, 26 June 1937. BPM.

[4] Hatfield, 56 and 28. The coronation of Victoria took place on 28 June 1838.

often not finished till a couple of years had passed, and the full implications of the drama had been elaborated.

It is quite evident from the straightforward description of the domestic scene in her diary-paper that Emily had no criticism of it to offer; she expressed no wish for radical changes; her detachment from her aunt's authority was both humorous and tolerant, and provided her own privacy was respected she had no complaints to make. And she saw to it that her privacy *was* guarded from all possible encroachment. The narrow slip-room over the front hall, once the nursery and former playroom for all the children, was now indisputably hers. How it looked during the twelve years of her unchallenged tenancy can be judged from the rough sketches with which she filled the corners of her diary-papers. It presents a Spartan enough scene. Across the window was her camp bed, in the left-hand wall-angle was a chest of drawers, in the centre a square of carpet; a low chair on which she sat with her writing-desk on her knees faced the window and the view beyond, and there was an oil lamp for the dark hours. It was a simple setting but the view from the window was all the luxury she required. The absence of a fireplace or any mode of heating in the room explains the necessity for the shawl in which she is wrapped in her sketches; it may also explain the hold consumption took on a constitution too long exposed to winter colds.

The influences that shaped her late teens—her brother and Tabby—were hardly those she would have received in a 'finishing school' nor in conventional home surroundings. But they did allow her special temperament the fullest freedom in which mentally and morally to expand. In such a fertile soil, it is understandable that her father's breakfast-time stories bore good fruit.

In the solitude of the moors, and of the tiny room, in long uninterrupted communings with herself, she formed a character as much in advance of her age in some aspects as it remained childish in others—this her diary-papers attest. The hermit's life of that uncomplicated household developed in her fearless questioning mind a natural bent towards metaphysical speculation.

So she passed from young girlhood suddenly, unwarned, without female companionship of her age or mentality, into the strange emotional life of poetry. The deep reserve of her nature had hitherto made the communication of experience an abortive act, one at least that left her dissatisfied, and wishful to hide her true identity under a borrowed one. Hence the elaborate scenario of Gondal behind which to screen herself even from her own recognition; hence the destruction also of most of her juvenile writing in disgust at the results achieved. Not many young poets have damned their own efforts so wholeheartedly as Emily did of a fragment scribbled down one July evening in 1836: 'I am more terrifically and idiotically and brutally STUPID than ever I was in the whole course of my incarnate existence. The above precious lines are the fruits of one hour's most agonising labour between ½ past 6 and ½ past 7 in the evening of July – 1836.'[1]

Discontent with the best she could achieve in poetry persisted. In the following August (1837) she wrote of the tears of frustration she shed

> Because I could not speak the feeling,
> The solemn joy around me stealing
> In that divine, untroubled hour.
>
> I asked myself, 'O why has heaven
> Denied the precious gift to me,
> The glorious gift to many given
> To speak their thoughts in poetry?'[2]

The fact that so much of the Gondal plot had been in existence for years, and the destinies of the major characters fixed when their creators were immature girls, makes Emily's mental development appear at this time to advance by leaps and bounds, out of all proportion to the time covered or the experience gained. Examples of the earlier Gondal poems show, from the scrupulous indication of time and place and season, that what mattered to the writer, what inspired the poem, was not what one or other of the protagonists said or did, but what the day was like, and how the earth looked, when they were born, or met, or died. Augusta's return to the lake shores where Alexander Elbë was murdered is introduced by lines that show how a genuine lyric upsurge of feeling could sweep the whole Gondal edifice out of her power, onto the plane of poetry.

> There shines the moon, at noon of night—
> Vision of glory—Dream of light!
> Holy as heaven—undimmed and pure,
> Looking down on the lonely moor— . . .
> Bright moon—dear Moon! when years have past
> My weary feet return at last—
> And still upon Lake Elnor's breast
> Thy solemn rays serenely rest
> And still the fern-leaves sighing wave
> Like mourners over Elbë's grave.[3]

[1] See C. K. Shorter, *Complete Poems of Emily Brontë* (1910), footnote to poem 'Memory'.   [2] Hatfield, 27.   [3] Hatfield, 9.

The poem sinks to banality directly the retrospective action of his hour of death is evoked.

In poem after poem, what must strike the modern reader is the poverty of the dramatic artifice in comparison with the beauty and tender observation of the natural scene. The following fragments are dated early 1837:

> Not a vapour had stained the breezeless blue,
> Not a cloud had dimmed the sun
> From the time of morning's earliest dew
> Till the summer day was done;
>
> And all as pure and all as bright
> The beam of evening died;
> And purer still its parting light
> Shone on Lake Elnor's tide. [1]

Frequently, the opening lines of a poem are all that remain, proving that it was the thing perceived that was the inspiration, not the Gondal plot. The following lines, full of foreboding as they are, have no sequel:

> Woods, you need not frown on me;
> Spectral trees, that so dolefully
> Shake your heads in the dreary sky,
> You need not mock so bitterly. [2]

Another fragment records a magical moment on the moors:

> The sun has set, and the long grass now
> Waves drearily in the evening wind;
> And the wild bird has flown from that old grey stone,
> In some warm nook a couch to find.
>
> In all the lonely landscape round
> I see no sight and hear no sound,
> Except the wind that far away
> Comes sighing o'er the heathy sea. [3]

Examples could be multiplied. It needs no commentary to recognize that the observation of nature was based on true emotion and the plot was artificially contrived.

Side by side with these uneven productions of adolescence appears a poem of genuine sombre power dated 17 May 1837, finished before she was nineteen. The sentiments, as disillusioned as any voiced by Byron, already foreshadow the creation of Heathcliff; the anti-social theme is

---

[1] Hatfield, 19.   [2] Hatfield, 6.   [3] Hatfield, 21.

recognizably Emily's own. Her mental growth during a time of apparent isolation from outside influences might appear baffling were it not for her brother's constant companionship; his experience became to some extent her own—

> I am the only being whose doom
> No tongue would ask, no eye would mourn;
> I never caused a thought of gloom,
> A smile of joy, since I was born.
>
> In secret pleasure, secret tears,
> This changeful life has slipped away,
> As friendless after eighteen years,
> As lone as on my natal day.
>
> There have been times I cannot hide,
> There have been times when this was drear,
> When my sad soul forgot its pride
> And longed for one to love me here.
>
> But those were in the early glow
> Of feelings since subdued by care;
> And they have died so long ago,
> I hardly now believe they were.
>
> First melted off the hope of youth,
> Then fancy's rainbow fast withdrew;
> And then experience told me truth
> In mortal bosoms never grew.
>
> 'Twas grief enough to think mankind
> All hollow, servile, insincere;
> But worse to trust to my own mind
> And find the same corruption there.[1]

[1] Hatfield, 11.

CHAPTER VII

LAW HILL

As Emily's diary-paper of June 1837 reported, Tabby was back in the parsonage kitchen again; Miss Branwell was at her sewing, Mr. Brontë on his parish rounds, Charlotte and Branwell reading the lately published *Eugene Aram*, and Emily and Anne planning Gondal coronations in the parlour—spoken of with exceptional formality as the 'drawing-room'. Order had, in fact, been restored to the household, disrupted ever since Tabby's accident of the previous Christmas. There was no indication of a momentous change at hand.

In early August Charlotte and Anne returned to school for the year's second 'half'. Miss Wooler had used the vacation to move her premises from Roe Head to Dewsbury Moor, an unfortunate change so far as the Brontë girls were concerned. The situation was neither so pleasant nor so healthy for Anne, who fell seriously ill before Christmas; nor so well placed for Charlotte to visit her friends, the Taylors at Gomersal, and the Nusseys at Birstall. Ellen Nussey remained inaccessible throughout that year, to Charlotte's intense chagrin, acting as housekeeper to various brothers in the south of England. Charlotte's letters to her were filled with Ellen's concerns, her own increasing over-work as Miss Wooler's deputy-head, and her tormenting religious doubts which left her neither peace, nor space in her letters, for other subjects. Of family news, they contained nothing. The suddenness, therefore, of her unheralded announcement, in a letter of 2 October 1837, that Emily had gone 'into a situation as teacher in a large school of near forty pupils near Halifax' was the more startling.

No explanation for Emily's decision to take so uncharacteristic a course remains in any Brontë record. That it was suddenly decided is evident; not only was no mention made of it in the June diary-paper, but when Anne mentioned it retrospectively four years later in her diary-paper of July 1841,[1] it was to say specifically that, together with other changes and 'diversities that had since occurred', it had not been expected or foreseen in July 1837. Two factors may have contributed to Emily's decision: according to F. A. Leyland, Branwell's later Halifax friend and fairly close confidant, Branwell 'went as usher to a boy's school in the Halifax district' that autumn. Poor Branwell, with his 'downcast smallness',[1] his quiff of carroty hair, his easy good-nature, and vulnerable nerves, was an obvious target for the boys' mischief. He made nothing of the situation, and left it after only a few months' trial, adding teaching to his growing list of failures. His engagement at a Halifax school might, as Leyland suggests, have been a reason for Emily's taking a post near him, though it is unlikely that it was the main reason. Her introduction to the Misses Patchett's school is more likely to have come about through Charlotte's intervention.

Emily was nineteen in July 1837. As they grew up, she and her sisters had no alternative but to earn their keep. Their position was wholly dependent on their father's precarious health and ability to keep his curacy and to provide a home for them. Their brother's prospects were even less promising than their own: governesses were always marketable goods, but he had neither the training nor the real ability to make a career for himself with any of the arts he loved.

One result of the proximity of Miss Wooler's new school, Heald's House, to Dewsbury, was to renew some of Charlotte's former contacts there. It had been the place of Mr. Brontë's first curacy in Yorkshire; he had had close—though not always amicable—relations with the Halliley family, whose uncontested position as leading manufacturers had earned them the nickname at one time of 'the Kings of Dewsbury'. The daughters of the Halliley family had all made good matches; one had married Mr. Brontë's Vicar, the Revd. John Buckworth; another the prosperous John Brooke, a connection of the Miss Woolers, who had gone into partnership with his father-in-law; a third had married Mr. Carter (yet another connection of the Miss Woolers); and the fourth a Mr. Jackson. When Charlotte was first a pupil at Roe Head, Leah and Maria Brooke were fellow-pupils; with them and her own particular group of the Taylor girls and Ellen Nussey, Charlotte shared her lesson-books; their names figure jointly on the flyleaves of her copies of Mangnall's *Questions*, Lindley Murray's *English Grammar*, and other text books. Since the days of their great prosperity during the war years, the Hallileys had suffered a gradual reversal of fortune and after their father's death 'Young' Halliley was declared bankrupt in 1834. Charlotte was more

[1] Leyland, *The Brontë Family*, i. 154.

touched by the misfortune of her former schoolfellows than she had been impressed by their prosperity, and wrote anxiously to Ellen Nussey on 10 November 1834 for news of the Brookes:

Can you give me any particulars respecting the failure of Halliley, Brook & Co?... Do you know whether the fortunes of Mrs. Brooke, Mrs. Duckworth, Mrs. Carter and Mrs. Jackson were in their brother's hands?... I am thus particular in my enquiries because Papa is anxious to hear the details of a matter so seriously affecting his old friends at Dewsbury, and because I cannot myself help feeling interested in a misfortune which must fall heavily on some of my late schoolfellows. Poor Leah and Maria Brooke![1]

Three years had passed since then, and in August 1837, when Charlotte and Anne returned to school, news of the prospective marriage of one of the Brooke family, Mr. Titus Senior Brooke, reached Charlotte, if not directly, at least through Miss Wooler. He was to marry a Miss Maria Patchett, a schoolmistress, who had helped her sister run a girls' boarding school at Southowram, near Halifax. Her marriage would leave her elder sister in sole charge of a large and flourishing establishment and in urgent need of help (the more so because their mother who had been living with them had recently died). What more likely than that Miss Wooler, a connection of Mr. Brooke, and a noted schoolmistress in the area, should be approached to recommend a successor, or that Miss Wooler should consult her invaluable deputy, Charlotte Brontë, on the subject? What was unpredictable was that Emily Brontë should take the vacant place. Remembering the fiasco of her former attempt at school-life and its threat to her health, Charlotte was unlikely to urge Emily to take such a course again; the idea must have originated with Emily, and have been wholly determined on by her. A wish to earn money for herself; Branwell's departure for the Halifax area; Tabby's relative restoration to health, releasing Emily from domestic duties; and, not least, the determination to prove herself capable of an effort equal to her sisters'—all these considerations would have combined to prompt Emily to take this unexpected and uncharacteristic step.

The marriage of Miss Maria Patchett and Mr. Brooke took place in her parish church at Halifax, on 21 September 1837. The officiating minister, the Revd. John Hope, who had been incumbent of St. Anne's Chapel, Southowram, since 1823, was both a close neighbour and friend of the bride. In due course he married her sister, Elizabeth,[2] and was as a result the innocent cause of the eventual closing of their school. Charlotte's

[1] *SLL*, i. 112.   [2] 27 Dec. 1842.

Law Hill, Southowram, Halifax

Ponden Hall, Stanbury

mention of Emily's arrival at Halifax in her letter of 2 October, clearly shows that her engagement at the school had been timed so that she could replace Miss Maria.

No particulars of her appointment have been preserved; it is not known whether she met her new employer or saw the school before taking up her post. Halifax is only eight miles from Haworth (Branwell used to ride over there regularly in later years), but the moorland road can be bad in autumn and winter, and the hire of the Haworth gig beyond the means of a penniless girl, except when she had actually to travel there to take up her post. Mr. Brontë used to pay Anne and Charlotte's expenses on all such occasions, but nothing has been recorded about Emily's journey from home.

The place she was going to should not have been uncongenial to her. Leyland (a Halifax man, admittedly) said she would 'find the situation of the school agreeable—besides, the air was as pure as that of Haworth, and Law Hill commanded fine views'.[1]

Law Hill was the name of Miss Patchett's house, and Leyland was right in commending its situation. It stood high up on Southowram Bank, overlooking the bowl of Halifax, surely one of the most dramatic natural sites of any town in England. Darkened as it is today by its many power stations, it must even in Emily's time have presented a Blake-like image of the conflict of Heaven and Hell in the contrast between the dark brew boiling below and the serene beauty of the encircling hills, touched as they are at dawn and sunset by an unbroken ring of light. The tower of the parish church and the blackened stone of the Piece Hall and other public buildings rising out of the smoke speak of a human power almost commensurate to nature's; Halifax is indeed no weakling of a place, and it would be surprising if its strength did not appeal to Emily. The evidence would suggest that it did.

Law Hill was not far short of 1,000 feet, comparable with Haworth in altitude, and its situation under the summit of Beacon Hill gave it commanding views in three directions of almost uninterrupted moorland ('Common' land as it was locally termed; Law Hill itself was called after the Common of Law Hill). Emily in due course became acquainted with the curious history of the house and brooded over its central theme of ingratitude and revenge. It haunted her for years till she exorcised it in the pages of *Wuthering Heights*.

To begin with, however, her attention must have been wholly taken up

---

[1] Leyland, *The Brontë Family*, i. 153.

with her new duties. The size of the school, the number of the pupils, and her own complete lack of experience made the task an overwhelming one at first. Charlotte, commenting on it to Ellen Nussey, was convinced that Emily would never stand the strain. 'My sister E. has gone as teacher in a large school of near 40 pupils near H. . . . I have had one letter from her since her departure', she wrote on 2 October. '. . . it gives an appalling account of her duties—hard labour from six in the morning until near eleven at night, with only one half-hour of exercise between. This is slavery. I fear she will never stand it.'

By those unfortunate words of Charlotte's, condemning Miss Patchett's establishment, and later published by Mrs. Gaskell,[1] such offence was given to Emily's one-time employer that, although she lived well into the 1870s (and was over eighty when she died) and preserved a lively memory and a most sprightly physique, she refused to give any information about Emily's life at Law Hill, thus depriving prospective biographers of much-needed evidence for this period of her life.[2]

It is not even known for certain how long Emily stayed at Law Hill. In the absence of her own letters and of any further family comment on her sojourn there, her reactions to the experience can only be deduced from the interior evidence of her writings. Whatever else these reveal, the context of the poems she wrote there and *Wuthering Heights* itself clearly show that her stay at Law Hill was important for her intellectual development. She gained a knowledge of people and human relationships that far surpassed the comparable experience of a year's schooling at Brussels. For all the effect that had, she might never have been abroad—her writings carry no trace of the experience. But the pages of *Wuthering Heights* are filled with memories of Law Hill and its special atmosphere.

Evidence relating to the Miss Patchetts and the place itself has been preserved. They were Halifax women, sisters of a banker in the town, with connections among professional people and the local landed gentry. Their first attempt at keeping school was at Soyland in 1822, and from there they moved to Law Hill when it fell vacant in 1825. The size of the house and the commodious outbuildings, especially the large wool-warehouse, made it eminently suitable for a boarding school—a Boarding Academy as it was listed in the directories of the town. Miss Patchett's acquaintance with three ladies among the principal families in the area—Miss Anne Lister of Shibden Hall, Miss Elizabeth Wadsworth of Holdsworth House, and Miss Caroline Walker of Walterclough Hall, Southowram—who had all attended the same fashionable Manor School in York suggests that Miss Patchett herself had been educated there. One other thing this group of ladies had in common: they all kept diaries covering approximately the same period, 1812–30 (Miss Lister alone continued hers until 1840), in which they mutually appear; Miss Patchett is mentioned more than once in Miss Lister's diary. That she had some social standing, and was well considered in the district, is apparent. All the more reason for her to be indignant about Charlotte Brontë's strictures upon herself and her school, for she prided herself on the admirable way she ran it. Though there were forty pupils, not half that number were boarders. There was room and to spare in the great gaunt house, with its five large bedrooms on the first floor and its five attics above, its spacious ground-floor reception rooms, its playgrounds and home-farm, to provide airy accommodation, civilized living, and enlightened leisure for growing girls. There was no reason why the food should have been bad, for poultry was kept and Miss Patchett was noted for her liberal way of living. Lessons were given in a large schoolroom made out of the converted warehouse which dated from the origins of the place in the previous century. The day-girls thus had no occasion to enter the house itself, but came and went by a separate door in the outer wall which communicated with the schoolroom only. The tone of the establishment can be judged from the 'accomplishments' offered by Miss Patchett, such as horse-riding. The mounting-block stands to this day in the courtyard, and the large barns and stables attest to the number of horses kept. Miss Patchett herself was a fine horsewoman and could teach her pupils by example. The school was more in the nature of a finishing school 'for the daughters of gentlemen' than a crammer for tradesmen's daughters.

Miss Patchett was a great believer in taking her pupils to concerts and museums, and accompanied them regularly to both. Halifax had much to offer in this respect, including the local Natural History Museum with its collection of rare birds. The local concerts themselves were much patronized by the ladies of the district as a social function at which to show off their latest gowns, so Miss Patchett was assiduous in attending personally. We can assume that Emily was not often privileged to take charge of the pupils on these occasions, therefore, although music was among the subjects she taught.[1]

The whole history of Law Hill and its founder is recorded in the journal

[1] The blasé Miss Caroline Walker, in whose diary there is so much information about the district, noted on 11 Dec. 1829 that she and her home circle 'went to the Concert, Miss Farrar's benefit, it was pretty well attended, but the performance was mediocre'.

of Caroline Walker, but the story was well-known in the district and must
have been part of current school gossip. Emily would have heard it either
from Miss Patchett herself, or from a member of the staff, among whom,
incidentally, was a woman named Earnshaw. Certainly Emily never forgot
the salient features of the story, nor its potentialities as the raw material
for a fiction that would complete and resolve the omissions and enigmas
of real life. Jack Sharp, the Heathcliff figure of the Walker diaries, having
brought ruin on his benefactors, was allowed to leave the district with his
wife and family and start life afresh in London. His history gave Emily
plenty to brood on.

   Walterclough Hall (a misreading of the original 'Waterclough' made
in a Will of 1582 and maintained ever after) was barely a mile from Law
Hill, and came into the Walker family in 1654. In the 1720s, the family
consisted of John Walker, his wife and four children, his two married
sisters Mrs. Ann Sharp and Mrs. Grace Stead, and two unmarried sisters,
who lived with him at the Hall. While farming his estate, his chief source
of income came from wool—which, like all men of property in the district,
he manufactured for the export market. Content with the status of manufacturer himself, he had ambitions for his sons, and bred them above his
own station. His eldest son, John, was sent to Cambridge and became a
scholarly, utterly unbusinesslike man; the second, Richard, was sent to
London to study law, but he died at the age of seventeen. With more
infatuation in hastening his own ruin even than old Mr. Earnshaw of
Wuthering Heights, Mr. Walker adopted a nephew, his sister Sharp's son
Jack, one of a large family of orphans. He brought him to Walterclough
and trained him up as his partner in the wool trade in place of his own sons.
The 'excessive indulgence' he showed Jack, who found equal favour with
his two maiden aunts at Walterclough, made him grow up so 'overbearing' that he ended by dominating the whole family, and his uncle's
business as well. Though he succeeded eventually in 'wearying' his uncle
by his ways, his hold on old Mr. Walker was so complete that he never
dared openly to resist him. The old man had to admit that 'Jack Sharp
may do without me but I cannot do without Jack Sharp.' Only one
recourse was left him; unable to dislodge the cuckoo from his nest, he took
flight himself, and leaving Jack in sole command of his business he
retired in 1758, first to Halifax and then to the neighbourhood of York,
where he eventually died in about 1771 at the age of fifty-five. Jack,
meanwhile, prospered. His uncle had endowed the business with a considerable sum, and had left him the Hall with all its fixtures and some
furniture for his use at a very low rent. Here Jack fully expected to spend

the rest of his days. The death of his uncle, however, altered matters. The legitimate heir, John Walker the second, who was still a bachelor and living in Petergate, York, not unnaturally wished to inherit his own. A pacific man, unwilling to use forceful methods, he maintained decorous relations with his cousin—and supplanter—and even visited him in a social way. On the occasion of the christening of Jack Sharp's youngest child, a girl called Dolly, the scattered Walker family, including John and his sister Mary (still in mourning for their father) and their collaterals, the Walkers of Crownest, were invited to their former home to enjoy the sumptuous hospitality provided by Jack Sharp and his wife. (She was a Miss Nicholls and had brought him no fortune.) The extravagant style in which husband and wife habitually lived had been made possible only by old Mr. Walker's money. Unfortunately for Jack Sharp, however, the christening party put an end to all this, for on that very occasion John Walker met a young lady at the church with whom he fell instantly in love, and to whom he lost no time in declaring his passion and offering his hand. The young lady, Elizabeth Waddington, whose home was in Thirsk, had a widowed and somewhat hostile mother. One of her first conditions for considering the match was to insist on a proper establishment being provided for her daughter. Elizabeth could bring her husband some property in Kent, but did not choose to live there; instead, Walterclough Hall appeared the obvious residence for the newlyweds, and John Walker was constrained to give Jack Sharp notice to quit.

The venom with which Jack Sharp received this news was soon apparent. With no legal claim to the place, he had no recourse but to leave it, but he built himself a house as close to Walterclough as he could—within a mile— on the crest of the hill, and called it Law Hill after the ground on which it stood. John Walker and his fiancée had to wait to marry until his removal there, and when he did at last leave Walterclough Jack Sharp 'acted very unhandsomely', Caroline Walker recorded in her diary, 'tearing up all the fixtures and heirlooms, stripping the house and outbuildings of everything he could possibly move'. To this despoiled habitation and heavily mort- gaged estate, John Walker—like Hindley Earnshaw of Wuthering Heights —all unknowingly brought his bride directly after their marriage at Thirsk on 11 November 1772. Elizabeth's bridesmaid, her half-sister Miss Wal- bank, accompanied them. Only two reception-rooms were 'fit for habita- tion', and 'the lodging-rooms [bedrooms] were unfit to be seen'; there was a 'great want of Table linen' and only 'a small quantity of family plate' remaining.[1] The whole place was in dire want of repairs and

[1] Walker diaries, Halifax Public Libraries.

furniture. Even so, Jack Sharp, who was directing the family wool trade from his new premises, and living in 'a very expensive manner' up at Law Hill, expected the new Mrs. Walker to accept him and his wife on equal terms, and to exchange visits. He had reckoned without Mrs. Walker. She was not only a very arrogant young woman, well educated at expensive boarding schools both at York and in Kensington Square, London, but she was frugal; it was bitter enough to her to have to furnish many of the necessities lacking in her husband's home through the sale of her Kentish property; she had no intention of trying to keep up with the Sharps, nor indeed was she prepared to tolerate their society. Sharp had two partners, his former apprentices, named Landford and Yates, whom he established in houses near his own, and with whom he and his wife maintained social relations that chiefly entailed card-playing and drinking. The new Mrs. Walker noted

with disgust the vulgar extravagance which reigned in these houses and she declined having much acquaintance with them, for with admirable prudence she considered that to be intimate with them would occasion great additional expense to her own house, and their society was not sufficiently genteel to afford her pleasure. Mr. Sharp was much hurt that she was so shy towards him, he tried every way to gain her favour, but in vain.[1]

Not content with having despoiled the rightful owner of Walterclough Hall of much of his property and possessions, Jack Sharp employed a more subtle means to revenge himself on the family of his benefactors. He laid hold of a young cousin of Mr. Walker's, a minor called Sam Stead, and apprenticed him to his own business in the worsted trade without informing Mr. Walker. The lad was not at all a promising character, and Jack Sharp soon degraded him further by indulging his taste for drink and gambling. Sam's mother, old Mr. Walker's sister, paid Jack Sharp her savings of £300 to apprentice her son, and received nothing but unkindness from him in return. The degradation of Sam, systematically undertaken by Jack Sharp, just as Heathcliff planned to degrade Hareton Earnshaw, was a complete success and caused much chagrin to the Walkers. Sam in his turn became good for nothing, and when Jack Sharp was eventually bankrupt, and Sam was charitably harboured by the family at Walterclough Hall, he paid them evil for good, just as he had learnt to do from his mentor at Law Hill. By that time, Mr. and Mrs. Walker had a family of young children, and Sam found no better employment for his time than in teaching the young heir—'who could just run about'—'to say words

[1] Walker diaries.

which he knew the boy would be corrected for'[1]—again as Heathcliff did with young Hareton. He delighted in setting all the children against each other, and 'he would go into the kitchen and make the servants dispute for his amusement'. Among the servants was the children's nurse, called Wordsworth, who became her young ladies' confidante and remained in the family for years—a parallel figure to Ellen Dean. She had many skirmishes with Sam. The manservant employed by Sharp was called Joseph.

The ruin of Jack Sharp, though inevitable, was twice staved off by the intervention of his cousin and victim John Walker. On two occasions, when his bankruptcy seemed imminent, Mr. Walker found the money to pay his debts. This he did with his wife's money from the sale of her Kent estate, but without her knowledge. She had judged from the first that 'Mr. Sharp would become a bankrupt, and condemned his mode of proceeding'.[2] Mr. Walker's own estate was in very bad shape and he could only keep the Hall going by subletting the farms on his land. Money was so tight that if his wife 'wished to go to see any amusement which happened to be at Halifax he scarcely could furnish her with a little money to go with . . . As he never fitted up the house in a way suitable for visitors to lodge in it and was always ill-provided with money to make handsome dinners,' Caroline Walker remembered, 'my mother was forced to conform to his rules as she could not bear to do anything in a shabby way'.[3] The riddle of these proceedings, of the repeated help given Jack Sharp by his injured cousin, must have perplexed Emily Brontë as it does us today, for there is no known explanation for it.

It was the American War which completed Jack Sharp's ruin. His most flourishing business was in America, where one of his own brothers, Richard Sharp, had emigrated and become his best export agent for wool. With the cessation of remittances from his American customers, Jack Sharp's main source of income dried up. He was heavily in debt to his former apprentices, Landford and Yates, and had mortgaged his houses and property to them. His troubles did not come singly: at the same time, his eldest daughter, Nancy, who had lived with an aunt in London for some time, came home with her 'character ruined'. Her lover could not be brought to make an 'honourable woman' of her, and on the pretence of regularizing her situation, and also of pursuing some personal business, Jack Sharp accompanied her up to London and never returned. In due course, his wife and the rest of his family followed him there. His death in

---

[1] Ibid.   [2] Ibid.   [3] Ibid.

London occurred some time before 1798, when his widow became residuary legatee of the estate of his cousin, Mary Simpson of Hipperholme. His own business at Law Hill, and the Walkers' interest in it, was at an end; Mr. Walker's losses were immense.

Although he was no businessman and had been harassed for so many years by Jack Sharp's misappropriations, Mr. Walker recognized that changes were occurring in the wool trade, that the old methods were becoming out of date, and on the advice of friends he eventually abandoned worsted spinning in favour of the new machinery. He built his own mill at Walterclough to take the machines, and after great initial difficulties, he prospered. His daughter recorded that 'the Mill found employment for most of the poor people in the vicinity, they soon began to improve in their appearance by having better wages, and all things proceeded tolerably well'.[1]

In 1837 when Emily Brontë arrived at Law Hill Caroline Walker was still living at Walterclough Hall. Her parents were dead by then, and her only brother also. He had proved himself a worthy pupil of Jack Sharp and Sam Stead, and had systematically drunk himself to death. Caroline carried on her diary till 1830, in which year her sister Georgiana married Edward Strangeways and settled at Walterclough with her. The diary ends in that year, perhaps because Caroline was subsequently less lonely and had more to do.

Miss Walker was not very happy about the new incumbent at the church of St. Anne's, Southowram, which she attended together with Miss Patchett and her pupils. He was Mr. John Hope, a Scotsman from Langholme with pronounced Presbyterian leanings: 'C'est un écossais,' Miss Walker noted in her diary after his first sermon, 'il est assez bien pour son état . . .' After observing that he conducted the service 'in a manner similar to the Presbyterians', and conceding that 'it had a good effect on me', her verdict was that 'I feel partial to the particular observation of the Established Church'; and, on a later occasion, she deplored the fact that Mr. Hope 'makes the service a good deal in the dissenting style' and 'is apt to give too mournful a turn to them. Religion has nothing gloomy in itself, why should it make us melancholy?'[2]

This was the preacher whose sermons Emily Brontë had to listen to when accompanying her pupils to church. It has been suggested[3] that she repaid the hours of boredom she suffered at his hands by the portrait of the Revd. Jabes Branderham in *Wuthering Heights*, who subdivided his sermon under four hundred and ninety heads. While the original of this caricature is far more likely to have been the Revd. Jabez Bunting, the dissident Methodist leader known to Mr. Brontë, and whose sermon delivered at the dedication of the new chapel at the Wesleyan Academy at Woodhouse Grove in 1833 was widely reported and doubtless commented upon at Haworth parsonage, Mr. Hope was Emily's weekly dispenser of religion. He may have been a very good man, and Emily, less frivolous than Caroline Walker, may have found his gloomy outlook admirable; but the fact remains that she had not much regard for the clergy or the conventional forms of religion. The obligatory attendance at church services (though at home she was not obliged to go) certainly gave her the opportunity to judge what they had to offer—and to develop her own personal views on the ways God should be worshipped.

It may have drawn a wry smile from Emily to learn, shortly after her return from Brussels in November 1842, that Miss Patchett had married her vicar, and had gone to live at his vicarage next to the church. The marriage took place on 27 December 1842. Mrs. Hope lived to a great old age and was remembered for her well-preserved looks and sprightly air, and abundant grey hair worn in curls long after the fashion had gone out.

To a girl of her independent character there was not much at Law Hill that could appeal to her; she once told a classroom of unruly girls that the only individual she liked in the whole establishment was the house-dog.[1] But while the humans were either vexatious, or trivial, or cruelly exacting, as Miss Patchett seemed to her to be, there were compensations to be found in the natural surroundings of the school. From the house itself, standing high on unenclosed common, she could go for long walks in the heather, and escape in spirit as well as body from the confining atmosphere of the classroom.

> What language can utter the feeling
> That rose when, in exile afar,
> On the brow of a lonely hill kneeling
> I saw the brown heath growing there.
>
> It was scattered and stunted, and told me
> That soon even that would be gone;
> It whispered, 'The grim walls enfold me;
> I have bloomed in my last summer's sun.'[2]

---

[1] Chadwick, 124.   [2] Hatfield, 91.

Whether written in retrospect, or on the spot, the lines are true to her experience at Law Hill:

> A little while, a little while,
> The noisy crowd is barred away;
> And I can sing and I can smile
> A little while I've holyday!
>
> Where wilt thou go, my harassed heart? [1]

There was only one place where she longed to go, and the poem with its evocation of home, of that 'spot 'mid barren hills / Where winter howls and driving rain', ranks amongst her most famous. As she mused in the 'naked' school-room, 'The flickering firelight died away', and in spirit she was in the 'little and the lone green lane' that opened onto the moors of home. The vision lasted less than an hour, and then her drudgery was resumed.

In the immediate vicinity of the school there was one place, however, to stimulate her imagination. About a mile and a half away as the crow flies, to the north of Law Hill under Beacon Hill, stood High Sunderland Hall, one of the most notable buildings in the district, the history and architecture of which became well-known to Emily.

Sunderlands had lived there since 1274, though the structure had been repeatedly modified. Before the Civil War, during which Abraham Sunderland, of the Inner Temple, died defending Pontefract Castle for the King, the old timber Elizabethan mansion had been surrounded in an impregnable outer shell of stone, whose ornate carvings and Latin inscriptions so much intrigued Emily Brontë. One inscription reads:

> Hic Locus odit, amat, punit, conservat, honorat
> nequitiam, pacem, crimina, jura, probos.
>
> This place hates, loves, punishes, observes, honours
> wickedness, peace, crimes, laws, virtuous persons,

and might be thought to have prompted the *leitmotif* of Emily's Wuthering Heights. For Wuthering Heights is hauntingly reminiscent of High Sunderland Hall. There is that other Latin inscription:

> Patria domus optima Coelum
> Heaven is the best country, the best home

which might again have prompted Catherine Earnshaw's rebellious cry: 'Heaven was not my home.'

[1] Hatfield, 92.

Emily certainly knew the place well and remembered its peculiarities of style and distinctive architecture when conjuring up the façade of Wuthering Heights so vividly as to transfer there the very carvings of High Sunderland Hall; those 'grotesque carvings lavished over the front, and especially about the principal door above which, among a wilderness of crumbling griffins, and shameless little boys', the date was inset. Emily's date, 1500, was, as has been pointed out, much earlier than that of High Sunderland—1579—and moreover before the time of any stone building in Yorkshire, except for churches.

The fine imposed on the Sunderlands for their loyalty to the King (£878 of the then currency) brought ruin on the family, and the Hall was forfeited to pay the costs. It was bought in 1655 by Joshua Horton. By the time Emily knew it, the owner was Mr. William Priestley, a connection of the Walkers, through whom he inherited it.

Mr. Priestley, who lived at the Hall from 1811 to 1858, was of an old Sowerby family, and a man of great culture; a lover of music, he collected and contributed many valuable scores to form a music library at Halifax parish church. It is claimed that he knew Miss Patchett, in which case her visits to his historic home may at times have been in company with some privileged pupils and even possibly her assistant teacher, Emily Brontë. But Emily's knowledge of the place would appear to be confined to the immense façade—eighty-four feet long—with its groups of mullioned windows, framed by pillars; the pillared house door on each side of which were nude carvings may have suggested the 'shameless little boys' of Wuthering Heights. The interior 'house-rooms' and panelled bedrooms she described there belong rather to the Elizabethan farmhouses around Haworth, like Ponden House and Upper Withins.

The evidence relating to Emily's stay at Law Hill is conflicting, and opinions still vary between a period of six and eighteen months. Mrs. Gaskell, who asked Ellen Nussey,[1] was told by her that it was for six months, and recorded it in her *Life* of Charlotte Brontë (p. 90). Leyland, who got his information direct from Branwell, also said it was for six months.[2] Mme Duclaux, Emily's first quasi-official biographer (1883) while giving no data at all, judges it was for two terms only. The reason why these early and presumably reliable statements were ever doubted seems to be the evidence of a Mrs. Watkinson of Huddersfield who told Mrs. Chadwick, when she was investigating the subject in the 1880s for

[1] Gaskell, *Letters*, p. 395, 9 July 1856; Ellen Nussey's letter of 22 Oct. 1856, *SLL*, i. 10.
[2] Leyland, *The Brontë Family*, i. 153.

her book *In the Footsteps of the Brontës*, that she had been a pupil of Emily's and remembered her well, and maintained that she had not been to the school before October 1838. In support of this evidence there remains the internal evidence of Emily's poems, whose nostalgic feeling was unmistakably inspired by her surroundings at Law Hill, and whose dates, inscribed on the MSS. by Emily herself, include the autumn and winter of 1838. Because of these poems, more than for any other reason, it has been increasingly assumed that Emily stayed at Law Hill for eighteen months. Emily's habits of composition, however, do not make such a deduction irrefutable. She was in the habit of scribbling down the first draft of a poem, adding to it and altering frequently before copying the final version, when she dated it, sometimes months, if not years, after the first draft. The poems of late 1838, though relating to her period at Law Hill and begun there, may have been finished at home many months later. This appears to be the solution, despite the evidence of Mrs. Watkinson. Mrs. Watkinson could well be mistaken in the date of her going to school, after the lapse of fifty years.

Emily's return home after only six months at Law Hill is confirmed, moreover, by other domestic events that year: there is her drawing of Keeper, her father's new house-dog, dated 24 April 1838, which was obviously made at home and not in a period of school holidays. Emily was at home in June when Charlotte sent her love to Ellen Nussey. On 31 July Emily would appear to have been at Bradford copying manuscripts for Branwell, who had set up a studio there, by which date, had she been returning to Law Hill, the year's second 'half' would have begun. An event that was more likely still to determine Emily to give up her post at Law Hill was Anne's return home for good at Christmas 1837, seriously ill after a neglected cold had affected her lungs. Anne's presence at home, coinciding with Branwell's departure on a fresh attempt at earning a living, would be cause enough for Emily to return there, where her usefulness could most obviously be employed. Like Charlotte, who returned to Miss Wooler's until the end of May, Emily may have given Miss Patchett until then to replace her, but the great likelihood remains that she had left Law Hill for good by the beginning of June 1838.

CHAPTER VIII

THE STERN POWER

IT is not surprising that the poems Emily wrote during her stay at Law Hill, or subsequently while still under its unhappy influence, were predominantly nostalgic in tone—like the vision of her home in the poem evoked in the cheerless schoolroom at Law Hill 'A little while, a little while / The noisy crowd are barred away'—

> There is a spot 'mid barren hills
> Where winter howls and driving rain,
> But if the dreary tempest chills
> There is a light that warms again.
>
> The house is old, the trees are bare,
> And moonless bends the misty dome
> But what on earth is half so dear,
> So longed for as the hearth of home?[1]

And this strain is more apparent still in the vision of the moors that the faded heather on Law Hill evoked in the poem: 'Loud without the wind was roaring /Through the waned autumnal sky'.

> Awaken on all my dear moorlands
> The wind in its glory and pride!
> O call me from valleys and highlands
> To walk by the hill-river's side! ...
>
> But lovelier than corn-fields all waving
> In emerald and scarlet and gold
> Are the slopes where the north-wind is raving,
> And the glens where I wandered of old.[2]

Such scenes are the recognizable settings of her home, the feelings are those of common homesickness. But already in the poetry of that period other visions are being evoked, other longings are beginning to obsess her, as the strange lines written barely a month after her arrival at Law Hill show. They tell of a moment of spiritual experience—dramatized in

[1] Hatfield, 92.   [2] Hatfield, 91.

human terms—as of a real presence breaking in upon her bondage and challenging her to surrender to its liberating power.

> I'll come when thou art saddest,
> Laid alone in the darkened room;
> When the mad day's mirth has vanished,
> And the smile of joy is banished
> From evening's chilly gloom.
>
> I'll come when the heart's real feeling
> Has entire, unbiassed sway,
> And my influence o'er thee stealing,
> Grief deepening, joy congealing,
> Shall bear thy soul away.
>
> Listen, 'tis just the hour,
> The awful time for thee;
> Dost thou not feel upon thy soul,
> A flood of strange sensations roll,
> Forerunners of a sterner power,
> Heralds of me? [1]

The theme treated here for the first time in Emily's writings was to become central in her poetry and in her development as a human being. It is of more importance than any single fact in her life, and, as such, concerns the biographer more closely than all the chronological data available about her. Its precise nature, however, escapes definition and can only fairly be analysed by close adherence to the very terms that Emily herself used in an attempt to describe it. While she had shown signs, both in conduct and in her earliest writings, of living on two planes of being through the strength of her imagination, this poem written at Law Hill shows a development in her imaginary life; whereas hitherto the creative will came from within her, the experience here relates to an external power, whose mastery—one is tempted to say whose *presence*— she recognizes as being outside herself. It was, admittedly, an effect of her immediate circumstances, the loneliness, homesickness, and frustration, which in a girl of such far-reaching imagination were powerful enough to induce a state of mind responsive to a profound spiritual experience, as though the very intensity of her longing could realize her heart's desire. The 'desire', as she repeated often enough in the future, was to be free— free from the trammels of physical existence as a first condition towards attaining complete union with 'the soul of nature', as she sometimes

[1] Hatfield, 37.

called it, with the life of the universe, or with the Absolute (a term she never used). The ecstasy once achieved, became a permanent craving that no lesser happiness could assuage.

Emily, in alien surroundings, would be more exposed than most people to 'heart-shaking reflections', as De Quincey called them in a memorable passage in the *Confessions*. On the eve of a great decision in his life—his removal to London—he found himself alone in a strange house, after midnight.

More than ever I stood upon the brink of a precipice; and the local circumstances around me deepened and intensified these reflections, impressed upon them solemnity and terror, sometimes even horror. It is all but inconceivable to men of unyielding and callous sensibilities how profoundly others find their reveries modified and overruled by the external characters of the immediate scene around them.[1]

Emily's experience at Law Hill was to be recurrent: her poetry shows that, depending chiefly on her material surroundings and on conditions of almost total solitude, it took possession of her with increasing frequency. There appears to be no indication that these visitations (as they must be called for want of a better word) occurred in childhood and left her permanently desolate by their cessation, as Charles Morgan suggested.[2] Her experiences were in fact different from those of other known mystics like Traherne, Vaughan, and Wordsworth, in this very respect: childhood had for them been the period of greatest revelation. With Emily Brontë, the contrary appears to be true: she was nineteen when at Law Hill. It was only from then on that such manifestations became the purpose and fulfilment of her life, as physical love is to other women. They were the inspiration of her poetry; without them she was only half alive, and when they ceased altogether she died.

The character of these experiences does not seem to have varied greatly, except perhaps by becoming increasingly overpowering. Her 'double vision', while often resembling Blake's, attained none of his cosmic range; it remained personal, affecting sight and hearing even, while its fullest effect was to annihilate her personality in a rapture that at times almost released her from physical life. That the rapture was not necessarily pleasurable is apparent from the early poem in which she speaks of the Visitant's 'stern power', of its appearance at the 'awful hour' of dusk. The aftermath of such visitations could be agonizing:

[1] De Quincey, *Confessions* (New University Library, 1905), 144.
[2] Charles Morgan, *Reflections in a Mirror* (1944), 132.

Oh, dreadful is the check,—intense the agony,
When the ear begins to hear and the eye begins to see;
When the pulse begins to throb, the brain to think again,
The soul to feel the flesh and the flesh to feel the chain![1]

At times she personified her visitant, as in her poem 'The Night Wind', where it speaks with the wind's voice to tell her: 'Heaven was glorious / And sleeping Earth was fair, and urges her, to come with him against her will.

> Have we not been from childhood friends?
> Have I not loved thee long?
> As long as thou hast loved the night
> Whose silence wakes my song.
>
> And when thy heart is laid at rest
> Beneath the churchyard stone
> I shall have time enough to mourn,
> And thou to be alone.[2]

At times the visitant speaks on nature's behalf, as in the poem:

> Shall earth no more inspire thee,
> Thou lonely dreamer now?
> Since passion may not fire thee
> Shall Nature cease to bow?
>
> Thy mind is ever moving
> In regions dark to thee;
> Recall its useless roving—
> Come back and dwell with me . . .
>
> I've watched thee every hour;
> I know my mighty sway,
> I know my magic power
> To drive thy griefs away.
>
> Few hearts to mortals given
> On earth so wildly pine;
> Yet none would ask a Heaven
> More like this Earth than thine.[3]

At other times, the vision is powerful enough to 'sweep the world aside', as she wrote in another poem, and to merge her being with that of the universe. She invokes the wind as a great force of nature:

[1] Hatfield, 190.   [2] Hatfield, 140.   [3] Hatfield, 147.

And thou art now a spirit pouring
Thy presence into all—
The essence of the Tempest's roaring
And of the Tempest's fall—

A universal influence
From Thine own influence free;
A principle of life, intense,
Lost to mortality.[1]

The escape Emily sought was not a mere departure from conditions she hated, like that of many romantics, but a positive attainment of ideal conditions, of that union with nature which she prayed above all to achieve, even before the deliverance of death would secure her a 'mutual immortality' with the earth she loved.[2] Incidentally, the conditions she hated were not the domestic conditions of her life, with which she was strangely at peace, but the human condition itself deprived of its spiritual dimension.[3]

With the years, if one can speak in terms of time of a girl so little bound by time and who died so young, this longing for a complete union with nature came to be accompanied by a comparable longing for a surrender of personal identity. It belonged to the darker period of her development, and was associated with her refusal to publish her works or to seek distinction of any kind.

The presence of other themes in the poems of the Law Hill period, the themes of love and guilt, has seemed less explicable to Emily's biographers, and has led some among them (Romer Wilson notably) to believe that they reflect some real experience of betrayal and passion suffered at the time. There is no evidence for this, apart from the internal evidence of the poems; and to interpret them as personal revelation is to forget, or to ignore, the Gondal framework into which, with very few exceptions, they can be fitted. Two poems:

Sleep brings no joy to me,
Remembrance never dies;
My soul is given to misery
And lives in sighs. . .[4]

and

---

[1] Hatfield, 148.   [2] Hatfield, 149.
[3] Other poems specifically dealing with this theme are Hatfield 39, 138, 144.
[4] Hatfield, 34.

> Why do I hate that lone green dell?
> Buried in moors and mountains wild,
> That is a spot I had loved too well
> Had I but seen it as a child . . .[1]

are cited among others as betraying a deep sense of guilt, but they are clearly Gondal poems and inscribed as such by the author.[2]

That Gondal should take increasing hold of Emily at twenty is but another proof of her need to escape from her actual life into a world of fantasy; but the very language of Gondal, compared with the poems of keenly felt personal experience, betrays its artificial inspiration. One has to be very careful in speaking of Emily Brontë's 'experience', since her power of imagination was such it could, and in her best work sustainedly did, equal the force of actuality.

An important Gondal poem written either at, or immediately after Law Hill, is the sensational 'Light up thy halls!', whose theme foreshadows the love-hate situation of *Wuthering Heights*. Written in language and with a passion that could entitle it to rank as a love poem, it relates the suicide of Fernando De Samara as a result of his love for Augusta, and the parting curse he lays upon her. Here is no mere echo of Byronic attitudes; in this poem, and in many shortly to be written, Emily Brontë was simply proving herself to be a genuine poet.

> Light up thy halls! 'Tis closing day;
> I'm drear and lone and far away—
> Cold blows on my breast the northwind's bitter sigh,
> And oh, my couch is bleak beneath the rainy sky!
>
> Light up thy halls—and think not of me;
> That face is absent now, thou hast hated so to see—
> Bright be thine eyes, undimmed their dazzling shine,
> For never, never more shall they encounter mine!
>
> The desert moor is dark; there is tempest in the air;
> I have breathed my only wish in one last, one burning prayer—
> A prayer that would come forth, although it lingered long,
> That set on fire my heart, but froze upon my tongue . . .
>
> Do I not see thee now? Thy black resplendent hair;
> Thy glory-beaming brow, and smile, how heavenly fair!
> Thine eyes are turned away—those eyes I would not see;
> Their dark, their deadly ray, would more than madden me.

[1] Hatfield, 60.
[2] Both poems bear the Gondal initials A. G. A. = Augusta Geraldine Almeda.

There, go, Deceiver, go! My hand is streaming wet;
My heart's blood flows to buy the blessing—To forget!
Oh could that lost heart give back, back again to thine,
One tenth part of the pain that clouds my dark decline!

Oh could I see thy lids weighed down in cheerless woe;
Too full to hide their tears, too stern to overflow;
Oh could I know thy soul with equal grief was torn,
This fate might be endured—this anguish might be borne!

How gloomy grows the night! 'Tis Gondal's wind that blows;
I shall not tread again the deep glens where it rose—
I feel it on my face—'Where, wild beast, dost thou roam?
What do we, wanderer, here, so far away from home?

I do not need thy breath to cool my death-cold brow;
But go to that far land, where she is shining now;
Tell Her my latest wish, tell Her my dreary doom;
Say that *my* pangs are past, but *Hers* are yet to come!'

Vain words—vain, frenzied thoughts! No ear can hear my call—
Lost in the vacant air my frantic curses fall—
And could she see me now, perchance her lip might smile,
Would smile in careless pride, and utter scorn the while.

And yet for all her hate, each parting glance would tell
A stronger passion breathed, burned, in this last farewell.
Unconquered in my soul the Tyrant rules me still;
Life bows to my control, but *Love* I cannot kill! [1]

Wonder has often been expressed that a girl with no experience of love should be able to describe the feelings of Heathcliff and Catherine for each other; yet, already the presentiment of such feelings is apparent in this poem, written at least seven years before *Wuthering Heights*. The only conclusion the reader of both works can reach is, either that Emily Brontë had a capacity for entering dramatically and imaginatively into feelings she had not herself experienced, or that she had, in fact, had an experience of love. With our knowledge of her intense reticence, of her absolute refusal to make contact with strangers, it is difficult for us to believe in the latter solution. Mrs. Gaskell made a very pertinent distinction in analysing the disadvantage the Brontë girls were at with strangers, women as well as men: she noted most particularly that Anne was 'shy', and Emily 'reserved', and added: 'I distinguish reserve from shyness, because I

[1] F. De Samara to A. G. A., 1 Nov. 1838. Hatfield, 85.

imagine shyness would please, if it knew how; whereas, reserve is indifferent whether it pleases or not.'[1]

Is such a girl likely to have had a love affair at Law Hill? It is extremely unlikely, yet 'love-poems' within the framework of Gondal succeeded each other fast during the year 1838.[2] So too did poems dealing with treachery, disillusionment, and revenge, powerful poems which can hardly be explained in terms of her own experience. The fact is that all Emily's views and feelings are surprising for their vehemence and intensity. To her, even the loss of the familiar flowers of home arouses a passion of grief such as most women reserve for their lovers.

> There is a spell in purple heath
> Too wildly sadly dear;
> The violet has a fragrant breath
> But fragrance will not cheer.
>
> The trees are bare, the sun is cold,
> And seldom, seldom seen;
> The heavens have lost their zone of gold
> The earth its robe of green . . .
>
> The bluebell cannot charm me now,
> The heath has lost its bloom,
> The violets in the glen below
> They yield no sweet perfume . . .
>
> For these I weep, so long divided
> Through winter's dreary day,
> In longing weep—. . .
>
> How do I yearn, how do I pine
> For the time of flowers to come,
> And turn me from that fading shine
> To mourn the fields of home.[3]

When such emotion is aroused by a flower, the language to which the writer will have recourse when her theme is tragic love is likely to be proportionately exalted. In judging Emily Brontë's 'love poems' this has to be kept in mind. Her capacity for feeling was acute, her mood inclined to be sombre; while her sources of joy were more numerous than those of an ordinary woman, they were also almost incommunicable except in poetry. All experience, with her, demanded a heightened language,

---

[1] Gaskell, 81.   [2] See Hatfield, 80, 81, 85, 86.   [3] Hatfield, 94.

whether the subject were joy or sorrow; hence the difficulty for the literal-minded reader of her works to assess the degree to which they reflected reality. Defiance and pride are at the heart of the Gondal heroes (recognizable Byronic traits), as treachery is at the heart of the heroines. Julius Brenzaida, later so bitterly lamented by Rosina in the famous elegy 'Cold in the earth', at one time the fool and slave of Geraldine, rejected her at last in terms hardly weaker than those to which readers of *Wuthering Heights* are accustomed:

> I knew not 'twas so dire a crime
> To say the word, Adieu;
> But this shall be the only time
> My slighted heart shall sue.
>
> The wild moorside, the winter morn,
> The gnarled and ancient tree—
> If in your breast they waken scorn,
> Shall wake the same in me.
>
> I can forget black eyes and brows,
> And lips of rosy charm,
> If you forget the sacred vows
> Those faithless lips could form.[1]

The vehemence of passion voiced in the poem 'Light up thy halls!' is not its only striking feature. It shows a new technical skill that comes to be the hallmark of Emily Brontë's writing, whether prose or verse: the terseness of style, the intense economy. The dying Fernando commands the winds to tell his faithless love of his suicide:

> tell her my dreary doom;
> Say that *my* pangs are past, but *Hers* are yet to come

and earlier, when he takes the decision to kill himself:

> And then I go to prove if God, at least, be true!

The fierce disillusionment of such a line might, indeed, make the Victorian reader ask what sort of experience this girl of twenty had known? In the act of killing himself, Fernando recalls Augusta's many treacheries, and finds comfort only in the thought that some day her sufferings will equal his.

> Oh could I know thy soul with equal grief was torn,
> This fate might be endured—this anguish might be borne!

[1] Hatfield, 81.

A sentiment that perfectly anticipates Catherine's in *Wuthering Heights*, saying of her husband: 'If I were only sure it would kill him! I'd kill myself directly!'

If the Gondal poems were to be literally interpreted as relating to Emily's own sentiments and experience—and indeed the defiance and rebellion expressed in many of them might legitimately be assumed to reflect her frustrating life at Law Hill—then the analogy would have to be taken to its logical conclusion and her own conduct and sentiments be related to those of the ferocious Gondal characters, whose practice of retribution on the Old Testament scale of 'an eye for an eye' was hardly in keeping with her own magnanimous character. Not much is known about the facts of Emily's life, but about her character we know a good deal. While putting animals first because of their helplessness, she was not only selfless but without self-interest in her human relations. As Ellen Nussey said, 'Her extreme reserve seemed impenetrable, yet she was intensely lovable; she invited confidence in her moral power.' When Charlotte planned to open a school with her sisters' help, she told M. Heger: 'Emily does not care much for teaching but she would look after the housekeeping and, although something of a recluse, she is too kind hearted not to do all she could for the well-being of the children. She is very generous by nature.'[1]

What the Gondal literature tells us about Emily Brontë is of the deep division in her mind; of the incompatibility between the mundane facts of her life and her aspirations. This is a common enough condition among romantic characters, which places her indisputably among the children of her age—not the Victorian age of her maturity, but the romantic age of her adolescence; the era of Byron, Beethoven, and Blake. The influences of that era were lasting, and made her the rebel and visionary she remained to the end.

As already noted, Emily's return from Law Hill can be dated by her drawing of her father's new house-dog, Keeper, on 24 April 1838 (this was not holiday-time for schools in those days) and by her presence at home when the Taylors stayed at Haworth in June.[2]

During the next four years her life underwent few outward changes. She stayed at home, the centre of her brother's and sisters' varying adventures, the fixed point around which they revolved, leading on the surface a domestic uneventful life, of increasing usefulness as Tabby's powers declined. The escape through poetry became not easier, perhaps, but more imperative, as the liberating visions crowded in and tantalized

---

[1] Letter of 24 July 1844. BM.
[2] See CB's letter of 7 June 1838. *SLL*, i. 151–2.

her with their ephemeral presence. The unfinished condition of her manuscripts is evidence of this, though the fragments are numerous.

> In dungeons dark I cannot sing,
> In sorrow's thrall 'tis hard to smile:
> What bird can soar with broken wing?
> What heart can bleed and joy the while?

Together with the terseness of style that was becoming characteristic, a feature of the poetry of this time was a growing power of stark evocation with its own peculiar immediacy:

> There are two trees in a lonely field;
> They breathe a spell to me;
> A dreary thought their dark boughs yield,
> All waving solemnly.[1]

Scenes created by insistence on a distinguishing feature, as here, and in the poem 'Geraldine, the Moon is Shining'[2] with the lover's invitation to his mistress to sit 'beneath the ancient thorn', remind us that if she had one over-riding literary model, it was the Border Ballads whose abrupt opening lines, dramatic dialogue, and natural settings so exactly suited her own needs.

> Come, sit down on this sunny stone:
> 'Tis wintry light o'er flowerless moors—
> But sit—for we are all alone
> And clear expand heaven's breathless shores.[3]

The hill-farmers became accustomed to seeing her tall figure pass up the valley towards the heights, with the great mastiff padding at her side, whose fierce devotion to Emily became something of a local legend. 'The Brontës' love of dumb creatures', Ellen Nussey learnt early in her acquaintance with the family, 'made them very sensitive of the treatment bestowed on them. For any one to offend in this respect was with them an infallible bad sign, and a blot on the disposition.'[4]

The year 1838, during the whole of which Charlotte and Anne remained at home, saw a fresh attempt by Branwell to make a living. He went to Bradford and set up on his own as a portrait painter. The venture represented another combined family operation: his aunt paid the necessary fees for further painting lessons with his former master William Robinson;

---

[1] Hatfield, 77, 67.   [2] Hatfield, 80.   [3] Hatfield, 93.   [4] *SLL*, i. 105.

and his father contacted his old friend William Morgan, Vicar of Christ Church Bradford, to find Branwell decent lodgings—and a few 'commissions' among his acquaintance, to help launch him on his new career. Always ready to serve the Brontës, William Morgan found lodgings for Branwell in his own street at no. 3 Fountain Street, Manningham Lane, sat as his first 'subject', and persuaded his friend the Vicar of Bradford, the Revd. Henry Heap, to follow suit. It was hoped that the finished portraits, which were pronounced 'good likenesses', would bring in other commissions. Eventually they hung in the gentlemen's respective church vestries.

Branwell won golden opinions with the ladies of his landlord's family—Mr. Isaac Kirby, Wine and Spirit Merchant, with premises at 33 Market Street—and was engaged to paint the portraits of husband and wife and the young niece, Margaret Hartley, who generally lived with them. Her recollections in later life of Branwell's exemplary conduct at Bradford make his eventual failure there all the sadder. Margaret Hartley remembered how he went home regularly at week-ends (he usually walked the eight miles, to save the coach money), except when Charlotte visited him once, when he took the coach home with her. Charlotte's visit to his studio was remembered by Margaret, who was struck 'by her sisterly ways', but she was 'not aware that his other sisters or his father . . . ever came to Mr. Kirby's'.[1] A visit from Emily, however, is suggested by the manuscript of Branwell's poem 'The Wanderer', now at the British Museum, which Emily fair-copied for him and dated 'Bradford July 31st 1838'.

It was a Sunday, and the fact that the previous day was her birthday might suggest that she had come over from Haworth to spend it with Branwell. Margaret Hartley's evidence that she never saw Branwell's other sisters might also show that she was away at the time of Emily's visit—and indeed, that Emily's visit was made possible by her absence.

Emily's help showed something more than what young Margaret Hartley called 'sisterly' attention; it is evidence of a sympathetic understanding of her brother, a knowledge of his needs, a sharing of his thought. The character of 'The Wanderer' is profoundly despondent, expressing a disillusionment not only with his own circumstances, but with life—with human relationships—that was very much in tune with Emily's own outlook after the experience of Law Hill. The poem showed, moreover, a self-knowledge in Branwell unallied to self-pity, that was rare in him, and gives some dignity to the work. The description of the return home of Sir

Henry Tunstal, after sixteen years' service in India, is full of a sense of moral failure, of loss of innocence, of change in heart and mind, and of the gulf separating his family from that irrevocably altered self. As in his 'Henry Hastings' narratives,[1] written after the London fiasco, Branwell is impatient here with the guileless family's exaggerated accusations of his doing 'nothing but drink and gamble', which are more likely than not to drive him to excess.

Different as Emily was from Branwell, their responses to experience were in some ways alike. The human contacts she had made at Miss Patchett's school, even more than those at Roe Head, only roused her hostility; there was nothing in the conventional adornments and accomplishments which the teachers were expected to impart and the pupils to absorb to engage her respect. Their standards were not hers; she could dismiss them from her thought as too insignificant to merit even contempt. The whole of her striving was after a state of being 'immeasurably above and beyond' them all, as Catherine Earnshaw was to say.[2]

In many respects Emily and Branwell were growing alike. They both recoiled before effort, though for different reasons. In Branwell's case, it was the result of repeated disappointments and a lack of staying power. His exorbitant expectations of happiness and success had brought him no returns. Could he have achieved his ends without effort, he would have pursued them. Emily was already beginning to doubt the value of the ends to be achieved. She had not Charlotte's ambition; she had not, even, Anne's sense of purpose. What she prized had not to be worked for, it was revealed. Her practical good sense (of which she gave constant proof in household matters, in emergencies of illness and accident, even in investing money) told her, however, that Branwell must earn his living, and be encouraged on his way. So she copied his manuscripts for him to leave him free to pursue his painting.

The Bradford experiment lasted only one year; by May 1839 Branwell was back home, no richer for the attempt but in debt all round. He was lucky in the friendship of a fellow-artist, J. H. Thompson, whom he had met in the studio of their former master, William Robinson, at Leeds, and who now undertook to finish Branwell's portraits of the Kirby family (left in part-payment with his irate landlady) and to placate their ill-will. Branwell's indignation at their claims against him was typical, but so too was the desire to give a guinea or two to the widow of William Robinson,

[1] Angrian MSS. Jan. 1837. BPM. [2] *Wuthering Heights*, ch. 15.

whose situation was pitiable. Branwell had generous impulses, but they did not include paying his just debts. The world, he wrote indignantly to Thompson on the occasion, 'is all rottenness',[1] a view he no doubt frequently aired to his sisters at home. How were they not to be affected by his outlook? Branwell's major misfortune at the time was not Mrs. Kirby's claim on him for payment, but his introduction to opium which he began using after his disappointments at Bradford and, he declared, as a result of reading De Quincey. The lax legislation of the time gave him every encouragement; he could buy it across the counter at the village druggist's, in the form of pills in 6d. packets, or as laudanum. From then on, the habit was formed. Compared with drink, he found it economical and productive of the same euphoria; effective also in deceiving his father and aunt (from whom his debts had equally to be hidden), for opium in the form of pills left no smell on the breath of the addict.

The year began unpropitiously for Branwell's sisters also. An unacceptable proposal of marriage from Ellen's brother, Henry Nussey, brought home to Charlotte their precarious financial position, with no better prospects than such wholly uncongenial proposals to look forward to. It determined her and Anne to go out as governesses in private families, despite their father's reluctance to let them go. Anne was the first to leave home, on 8 April 1839, for a post at Blake Hall, Mirfield, with the family of Mr. Joshua Ingham, J.P. Her sponsor there had been Miss Wooler's brother-in-law, the Revd. Edward Nicholl Carter, former Vicar of Mirfield. Charlotte followed her example in June when she went to the family of Mr. John Benson Sidgwick, of Stonegappe, Lothersdale, where again her sponsor was Mr. Carter who had just been appointed to the living of Lothersdale.

Emily remained at home once again alone with Branwell, more deprived of Anne's companionship than ever before, and feeling her loss acutely. The poem she wrote on the occasion was typical of her method of composition; begun as an expression of personal feeling, evoked by Anne's departure, it continued as a Gondal incident of no very defined character. It is dated 17 April 1839, just a week after Anne left home.

> From our evening fireside now,
> Merry laugh and cheerful tone,
> Smiling eye and cloudless brow,
> Mirth and music, all are flown.

[1] Letter of 24 Aug. 1839. BPM.

Yet the grass before the door
Grows as green in April rain;
And as blithely as of yore
Larks have poured their day-long strain . . .

One is absent, and for one
Cheerless, chill is our hearthstone,
One is absent, and for him
Cheeks are pale and eyes are dim.

Arthur, brother, Gondal's shore
Rested from the battle's roar—
Arthur, brother, we returned
Back to Desmond lost and mourned . . . [1]

It is not possible always to accept the Gondal interpretation for everything written under a Gondal title, nor to decide how much of any poem
was genuine Gondal plot, and how much Gondal façade, put up to
disguise the true subjects of Emily's thoughts at the time. How much in
fact did Emily's real circumstances feed her Gondal dream? There are
three poems dating from the summer of 1839 whose preoccupation with
an ill-fated man (no doubt the Black Douglas) whose early promise is
belied by his cursed manhood, point the way to the creation of Heathcliff. They prefigure even Heathcliff's 'swarthy brow' and 'iron nature',
but they must also leave the reader wondering to what extent they apply to
Branwell, or at least whether without Branwell they would ever have been
written.

The poem dated 28 April describes the writer rejoicing in the beauty of
a spring day and watching to see its benign influence act upon the companion lying by her side.

But did the sunshine even now
That bathed his stern and swarthy brow,
Oh, did it wake—I long to know—
One whisper, one sweet dream in him,
One lingering joy that years ago
Had faded—lost in distance dim?

That iron man was born like me,
And he was once an ardent boy:
He must have felt, in infancy,
The glory of a summer sky.

[1] Hatfield, 97.

Though storms untold his mind have tossed,
He cannot utterly have lost
Remembrance of his early home—
So lost that not a gleam can come; ...

Silent he sat. That stormy breast
At length, I said, has deigned to rest;
At length above that spirit flows
The waveless ocean of repose ...

Perhaps this is the destined hour
When hell shall lose its fatal power
And heaven itself shall bend above
To hail the soul redeemed by love.

Unmarked I gazed; my idle thought
Passed with the ray whose shine it caught;
One glance revealed how little care
He felt for all the beauty there ... [1]

In a further poem, dated 26 July, she imagines the grave of an unre-deemed sinner and argues the problem of judgement.

Shed no tears o'er that tomb
For there are Angels weeping ...
Is it when good men die
That sorrow wakes above?
Grieve saints when other spirits fly
To swell their choir of love?

Ah no ...
Shut from his Maker's smile
The accursed man shall be:
Compassion reigns a little while,
Revenge eternally. [2]

This is followed by an undated poem, purporting to be the reflections of Alexandria, Augusta's daughter, on the destiny of a boy, a 'Darling enthusiast', a 'holy child', who all too soon is doomed to be 'Hell-like in heart and misery'. Questioning the cause why such a change should be wrought in his 'angel brow' and his spirit's 'glorious glow', she realizes that it is the effect of

[1] Hatfield, 99.   [2] Hatfield, 111.

Relentless laws that disallow
True virtue and true joy below . . .
'Tis thus that human minds will turn,
All doomed alike to sin and mourn,
Yet all with long gaze fixed afar,
Adoring virtue's distant star.[1]

Certainly, her mood in the summer of 1839 was a despondent one, echoing very closely Branwell's view that the world was 'all rottenness'. Comparing the loveliness of the springing earth about her, to her own feelings, she wrote:

May flowers are opening
And leaves unfolding free;
There are bees in every blossom
And birds on every tree.

The sun is gladly shining,
The stream sings merrily,
And I only am pining
And all is dark to me.

O cold, cold is my heart!
It will not, cannot rise;
It feels no sympathy
With these refulgent skies . . .[2]

The moments of ecstasy, all too rare, found her increasingly capable, however, of recording them, in language so concrete and circumstantial as to refute any doubt of their veracity. In the spring of that year they were crowding in upon her.

I did not sleep; 'twas noon of day,
I saw the burning sunshine fall,
The long grass bending where I lay,
The blue sky brooding over all.

I heard the mellow hum of bees
And singing birds and sighing trees,
And far away in woody dell
The Music of the Sabbath bell.

[1] Hatfield, 112.   [2] Hatfield, 101.

I did not dream; remembrance still
Clasped round my heart its fetters chill;
But I am sure the soul is free
To leave its clay a little while,
Or how in exile misery
Could I have seen my country smile?

In English fields my limbs were laid
With English turf beneath my head;
My spirit wandered o'er that shore
Where nought but it may wonder more.

Yet if the soul can thus return
I need not and I will not mourn . . .[1]

The poem trails off into a Gondal theme; but the opening verses were what inspired its writing.

A greater awareness informs her account, in that poem, of the actual circumstances of her vision; the burning sunshine, the long grass, the sound of the church bells, all promise the possibility of the soul's escape from 'its clay a little while'. Obviously, certain conditions were more conducive than others to such raptures; the silence of the upper reaches of the moors where the long grasses stretch for miles in unbroken swathes round the pools of cotton grass and rushes, and the solitude in which she was able to empty her mind of all conscious thought. She could anticipate in such moments, the coming of her liberator. She wrote on 12 August 1839 of such an expectant hour, trying to convey the dialogue between conflicting Reason and Imagination:

How long will you remain? The midnight hour
Has tolled the last note from the minster tower.
Come, come: the fire is dead, the lamp burns low,
Your eyelids droop, a weight is on your brow.
Your cold hands hardly hold the useless pen;
Come: morn will give recovered strength again.

'No: let me linger; leave me, let me be
A little longer in this reverie.
I'm happy now, and would you tear away
My blissful dream, that never comes with day;
A vision dear, though false, for well my mind
Knows what a bitter waking waits behind?' . . .[2]

There is no evidence whatever that Emily knew or read St. John of the

[1] Hatfield, 102.   [2] Hatfield, 114.

Cross or St. Theresa of Avila or the other great Christian mystics; her language is never that of worship, nor her imagery Christian. But the degrees by which she attained her soul's release, and the agony of its recapture, are in essence the same as theirs. As has already been noticed, while the seventeenth-century English mystics wrote mainly in retrospect of ecstasies experienced in childhood, Emily's experiences grew with her growth, and were contemporary with her descriptions of them. Hence the sense of immediacy in her poems. In the poem she wrote in February 1845, 'The Philosopher', quoted below, her imagery and sense of her own divided nature is strongly reminiscent of Blake; yet once again, the probabilities are that she never read a line he wrote.

> I saw a Spirit standing, Man
> Where thou dost stand—an hour ago;
> And round his feet three rivers ran
> Of equal depth and equal flow—
>
> A Golden stream, and one like blood,
> And one like Sapphire, seemed to be,
> But where they joined their triple flood
> It tumbled in an inky sea . . . [1]

Emily suffered like Blake in unpropitious surroundings (he had his Felpham and she her Roe Head and Brussels). As she needed her moors he needed his London 'to carry on my visionary studies in London unannoyed. I may converse with my friends in Eternity, see Visions, Dream Dreams . . . there unobserved and at liberty . . .'[2]

They both had the supreme gift of perceiving the greater contained in the lesser, the ability

> To see a World in a grain of sand,
> And a Heaven in a flower,
> Hold Infinity in the palm of your hand,
> And Eternity in an hour . . .

Nevertheless, Emily formulated no complex systems of the universe as did Blake, no hierarchy of celestial and diabolical Powers controlling Man's destiny; her vision remained intensely personal and concerned the one theme only: the soul's release from its 'dungeon of clay'.

At twenty-two, Emily was already aware that her unhappiness was a result of not being able constantly to live in this other metaphysical dimension.

[1] Hatfield, 181.
[2] Letter to Thomas Butts, 25 Apr. 1803 (Keynes, *Letters of William Blake*, 1968).

CHAPTER IX

'THE MAJOR'

IN the summer of 1839 Mr. Brontë received a grant from the Curates' Aid Society which at last enabled him to keep a curate. He had met the need for one hitherto out of his own pocket, but the arrangement was unsatisfactory both for the poor curate who could not receive a living wage, and for Mr. Brontë who had to find the money. Mr. Hodgson, who had worked for him since 1836, was thankful to get a living of his own and to leave Haworth, not because he did not get on well with his parson and the villagers, but because, as he alleged, his lodgings were haunted. He maintained that an evil spirit tipped up his bed at night and played other intolerable pranks on him. He was a good friend of Branwell, who found his grievances highly diverting, and took a bet with him in order to prove his case. Branwell submitted to the conditions with much levity, but after a few hours of being shut in the room at night and repeatedly thrown out of bed by the violent manifestations, he ran shrieking from the house. The incident, vouched for by Mr. Hodgson's son in old age,[1] was typical of the region and the period, where the calendar and the customs had not caught up with nineteenth-century 'progress'. Such tales, and many others, experienced and vouched for by living witnesses, would find a ready ear in the future author of *Wuthering Heights*. Emily's contact with the world through her father and brother, the parish sexton, and the servants, provided a richer vicarious experience than Emily's sisters could enjoy in their cloistered schools and employments.

Charlotte's contempt for curates in general, as expressed in *Shirley*, had not yet taken root—for lack of much experience of the breed as yet. The year 1839 would, however, begin her initiation. In the spring she received a proposal of marriage from the Revd. Henry Nussey, Ellen's brother, whom she had met on some occasions at the Nussey home. Henry was recently appointed to a living in Sussex where he found his vicarage far too large for him—as was his parish for comfort—and decided to convert it into a school. The terms of Mr. Nussey's proposal made it quite plain that his need for Charlotte was to halve his work in the parish and the

[1] *BST*, 1898, p. 17.

school. No unnecessary expressions of unfelt attachment marred the letter's perfect practicality throughout; Charlotte could appreciate the writer's honesty, if nothing else. (She did not know, what Mr. Nussey's private diary only revealed to posterity,[1] that she was merely one of three on a list of eligible young women to whom in turn he wrote and who, it must be said to their credit, unanimously rejected him.) As a proposal, and her first one, it had its comic features (as well, no doubt, as its hurtful ones) and with her sisters, if not with Ellen who worshipped her brother, Charlotte could laugh. But the incident proved to be not such a single oddity as they might all think; before five months were out, Charlotte received a second proposal—also from a curate. The gentleman's acquaintance and courtship lasted, in the event, the space of one afternoon. The wholly comical character of this second proposal could be communicated to Ellen, and Charlotte did so lightheartedly. That she had already given some thought to the subject of marriage and of her chances was also made apparent, and what she had to say on the matter is relevant to her sisters, for their fortunes were linked with hers and they could hardly hope to do better than she could. Charlotte, however, was the only one of them to receive proposals.

Prepare for a hearty laugh! [Charlotte wrote to Ellen]. The other day Mr. Hodgson, papa's former curate now a vicar [of Colne just across the Lancashire border from Haworth] came over to spend the day with us, bringing with him his curate ... Mr. Bryce ... a young Irish clergyman from Dublin University. It was the first time we had any of us seen him but however, after the manner of his countrymen, he soon made himself at home ... At home, you know Ellen, I talk with ease, and am never shy, never weighed down and oppressed by that miserable *mauvaise honte* which torments and constrains me elsewhere. So I conversed with this Irishman and laughed at his jests, and though I saw faults in his character, excused them because of the amusement his originality afforded ...

However, when Mr. Bryce began to 'season his conversation with Hybernian flattery' towards the latter part of the evening, Charlotte saw it was time to 'draw in', and in due course the visitors went away, 'and no more was thought about them'. A few days later, however, she received a letter which proved to be a proposal of marriage 'expressed in ardent language' from the Irish curate. 'Well!' Charlotte continued, 'I have heard of love at first sight, but this beats all.' She concluded however that she was certainly doomed to be an old maid, and had been resigned to that fate since the age of twelve.[2]

[1] Now in the BM. [2] *SLL*, i. 164–5.

As Charlotte was admittedly the least attractive of the three Miss Brontës, we may ask why the proposals were made to her and never to the others. Perhaps the gentlemen assumed that as she was the eldest she was also her father's frugal housekeeper—and hence the ideal helpmeet for a poor clergyman. But even when Emily was her father's housekeeper she received no proposals. Admittedly she did not go half-way to meet strangers, as Charlotte did. Ellen Nussey has left the picture of Emily successfully eluding all unwelcome intercourse, no matter who the stranger might be. 'If Emily wanted a book she might have left in the sitting-room she would dart in again without looking at anyone, especially if any guest were present.'[1]

Such traits have to be kept in mind if the writer's sentiments, later to be so fearlessly expressed, are to be understood. The scorn with which Emily spoke of 'love'—of lovers' infirm and shallow conduct towards those they professed to love—could not have been so withering if she had not felt its total inadequacy in comparison with the ideal her early and intoxicating reading of the poets had set before her. Anything less than a Byronic passion, or a Satanic one—whether for love or power—must appear contemptible in her eyes. Charlotte's adventures were hardly likely to persuade her of the contrary.

About her first chance of knowing something of a young man other than her brother came that year with the arrival in the village of Mr. Brontë's new curate, the Revd. William Weightman. Whether because of Mr. Hodgson's ghost, or because the sexton's wife, Mrs. Brown, was in need of a lodger to supplement her limited income, Mr. Weightman lodged opposite the parsonage at the Browns' cottage, where he was conveniently at hand to attend his parson's needs, and to get a footing in the household of his family. How completely he succeeded in this objective is too well known to repeat here. For Mr. Weightman as for the parsonage circle, the intimacy which grew up between young and old (he managed Miss Branwell better than anyone else was ever known to do) was to everybody's gratification. A classical graduate from Durham, he was sufficiently well read to satisfy the old parson, and to exchange literary quotations with his daughters. He was a keen shot and could accompany Branwell with the guns.

By Christmas 1839 when Anne lost her situation at Blake Hall and joined her sisters at home, an era of light-hearted social intercourse had begun; the genial curate did not suffer from shyness himself and knew how to break through the solidest barriers of shyness in others. Early in February 1840, Ellen Nussey was invited to the parsonage, and with the addition of her very feminine and 'ladylike' presence, the scene was set for unwonted frivolities. Charlotte's unusual high spirits, her preoccupation with the curate's comings and goings, his own mercurial conduct towards the entire female population of the district, were a study, as novel as it was informative, that Emily did not neglect.

This period of light flirtation, begun by Mr. Bryce's proposal to Charlotte and continued by Mr. Weightman, made an impression on Emily which was not forgotten when she came to write *Wuthering Heights* years later. When Charlotte wrote of Mr. Weightman 'idolising the memory' of one of the objects of his pursuit, Caroline Dury, a week or so after she had left the district, she, too, ironically contributed to Emily's knowledge of life upon which she drew when writing her novel. Mr. Weightman contributed something personal in the figure of Lockwood, vain and changeable like himself, who yet made an observation of great profundity to Ellen Dean on this very subject. Contrasting the characters and conduct differentiating the men of the countryside from those of the towns, Lockwood said: 'They *do* live more in earnest, more in themselves, and less in the surface change, and frivolous external things. I could fancy a love for life here almost possible; and I was a fixed unbeliever in any love of a year's standing.'[1] But by the time Emily wrote *Wuthering Heights* and made its subject 'a love for life', she had come a long way from Mr. Weightman and his badinage, and seen the real thing in action.

Meanwhile she watched the others make fools of themselves over Mr. Weightman with some amusement. Mr. Weightman was full of plots to please them. It has been recorded to his eternal credit that, hearing that none of them had ever received a Valentine, he walked the eight miles to Bradford to post them each a highly rhetorical specimen of the kind, so that no suspicion might be entertained by Miss Branwell or Mr. Brontë from whom they came. The gesture caused an enormous sensation among the unspoilt recipients. Ellen Nussey remembered only three of the titles (there were obviously four). They were: 'Fair Ellen, Fair Ellen', 'Away fond love', and 'Soul Divine'. It is pure surmise that the last was addressed to Emily, but it certainly seems the one most appropriate. Charlotte made herself the spokesman for all four of them when she sent Mr. Weightman a reply in verse, which shows that he had not been able to keep his secret.

[1] *Wuthering Heights*, ch. 7.

> A Roland for your Oliver,
> We think you've justly earned;
> You sent us each a valentine,
> Your gift is now returned.
>
> We cannot write or talk like you;
> We're plain folks every one;
> You've played a clever jest on us,
> We thank you for the fun . . .

He was likeable, and though fickle had a generous, compassionate nature—soon perceived by Anne—that won Emily's tolerance. Ellen Nussey wrote, 'Among the curates, Mr. Weightman was her only exception for any conventional courtesy.'[1] While the fun lasted Emily neither withdrew into unsociable retirement, nor in any way damped the spirits of the friends. No talker herself, she sat with them, an amused and highly observant witness. Ellen Nussey testified years later that on the occasions of these visits to Haworth 'Emily did what we did, and never absented herself when she could avoid it.' Ellen went so far as to venture an outsider's view that 'Life at this period must have been sweet and pleasant to her.'[2] What is certain is that the creator of Joseph in *Wuthering Heights* had plenty of grim humour of her own, and amid the general enthusiasm for Mr. Weightman Emily came out with a novel interpretation of him as a highly dangerous character, that delighted him as much as it did his admirers. Emily decided that he needed watching, especially in his attentions to Miss Nussey (which indeed were very pronounced), and constituted herself Ellen's bodyguard on all their outings.

Her vigilance earned her the nickname of 'The Major' from Mr. Weightman, an attention which caused her as much quiet satisfaction as his own fancy name—'Miss Celia Amelia'—gave him. 'The Major' perfectly suited Emily, as Charlotte admitted in her portrait of her sister in *Shirley* whom she nicknamed 'Captain Keeldar' and described striding ahead with her great dog at her side and whistling a 'merry tune—very sweetly and deftly'.[3] The nickname stuck to Emily long after poor Mr. Weightman was gone; as late as October 1847 Anne was sending 'The Major's' regards in a letter to Ellen Nussey.

The Major's watchful eye, directed at Mr. Weightman perhaps half humorously, half contemptuously, was not only intended to protect Ellen Nussey, but her own sisters as well. Charlotte was by now somewhat prone to proposals, though so far of an unsatisfactory kind; and Emily was close

---

[1] *SBC*, 163.   [2] Duclaux, 70.   [3] *Shirley*, ch. 12.

enough to Anne to sense the dawning of a sentiment in her for the curate which later flowered so sadly and alone. While Ellen was supposedly Mr. Weightman's 'object', Emily was acting watch-dog on them all. The role of detached, tolerant, uncommitted spectator suited her well. It was already as if she felt immune from the follies of other girls. 'Match-making' and 'fortune-hunting' were activities of which the echoes reached her from without, and left her incredulous. The thought, mulled over in her own fastidious mind, found expression in such surprising lines for a girl to write as the following:

> Riches I hold in light esteem
> And love I laugh to scorn
> And lust of Fame was but a dream
> That vanished with the morn—
>
> And if I pray, the only prayer
> That moves my lips for me
> Is—'Leave the heart that now I bear
> And give me liberty.'[1]

Ellen survived Mr. Weightman's attentions unscathed, whether or not as a result of the vigilance of The Major.

Emily lived up to her new nickname in other ways and acted as watch-dog in a more literal sense. Mrs. Gaskell has related how, when Keeper was young and as yet untrained, he had a trick of slinking upstairs in the daytime to nap on the spotless parsonage beds. This habit was anathema to Miss Branwell and Tabby alike, and Emily was warned that if she could not control Keeper, the consequences would be dire for him. He was the first dog to be admitted to 'house' status (Ellen Nussey remarked how on her first visit to Haworth Miss Branwell allowed no 'pets' indoors) and his presence was barely tolerated now by the older ladies. The truth was they were frightened of Keeper, who had a ferocious reputation, and dared not discipline him. As Shirley explained to the trembling curates about her dog Tartar, he was of a breed that did not tolerate being 'struck or threatened with a stick';[2] he just flew at the throat of the aggressor and, bulldog-like, did not leave go. Like Tartar, Keeper loved his mistress, and was indifferent to the rest of the world; only Emily counted, and only she could control him. Knowing this, and knowing also what she risked, Emily belaboured him ferociously with her bare fists, and tamed his wild heart as no stranger could have done. The scene, witnessed by Charlotte

---

[1] Hatfield, 146.   [2] *Shirley*, ch. 15.

and Tabby, was more terrifying to the witnesses than to the performer. Emily bathed Keeper's swollen eyes and jowl after the event without regard to her own swollen hands. He loved her all the more and was wise enough to learn his lesson.[1] The incident, which concerned both Tabby and Miss Branwell, presumably occurred in 1839 before Tabby left; she did not return to the parsonage until after Miss Branwell's death.

Kindness to Keeper was the quickest way to Emily's heart, as Ellen Nussey learnt very early:

One evening, when the four friends were sitting closely round the fire in the sitting-room, Keeper forced himself in between Charlotte and Emily and mounted himself on Emily's lap; finding the space too limited for his comfort he pressed himself forward on to the guest's knees, making himself comfortable. Emily's heart was won by the unresisting endurance of the visitor, little guessing that she herself, being in close contact, was the inspiring cause of submission to Keeper's preference.[2]

Two other glimpses of the world were afforded Emily during 1840 which, in their differing ways, gave her insights into the hearts of her female contemporaries. The first instance, which concerned Mary Taylor, she introduced into *Wuthering Heights*. Mary Taylor, Charlotte's strong-minded school-friend, a radical in politics and a rebel at home, who had passionately admired and loved her father, lost him at the beginning of that year, and visited Haworth in the summer. There was a circumstance about Mary's visit that somehow came to Emily's knowledge—though Charlotte tried to keep it secret. Branwell had once loved Mary, who had not returned his love. But now the roles were reversed; Mary had grown to love Branwell and had the misfortune to show it. Branwell had no sooner understood it than he scorned her for it. Describing the circumstances to Ellen Nussey, Charlotte wrote in great confidence: 'Did I not once tell you of an instance of a relative of mine who cared for a young lady until he began to suspect that she cared more for him and then instantly conceived a sort of contempt for her? You know to whom I allude—never, as you value your ears, mention the circumstance . . .'[3]

In *Wuthering Heights* it is Lockwood who tells the tale:

While enjoying a month of fine weather at the sea-coast, I was thrown into the company of a most fascinating creature, a real goddess, in my eyes, as long as she took no notice of me. I 'Never told my love' vocally; still, if looks have language, the merest idiot might have guessed I was over head and ears; she

[1] Gaskell, 184.   [2] *SBC*, 163.   [3] 20 Nov. 1840. *SLL*, i. 195.

understood me, at last, and looked a return—the sweetest of all imaginable looks
—and what did I do? I confess it with shame—shrunk icily into myself, like a
snail, at every glance retired colder and farther; till, finally, the poor innocent
was led to doubt her own senses, and, overwhelmed with confusion at her supposed mistake, persuaded her mamma to decamp.[1]

In unaccustomed numbers visitors came to the parsonage that year.
Limited as was their outlook, they brought echoes of a way of life outside
Emily's experience which, though she might reject their standards, gave
her some insight into the way other people lived. In August, it was the
relatives of Miss Branwell, Mr. John Branwell Williams and his family,
who made the parsonage their headquarters for a week.

They reckon to be very grand folks indeed [Charlotte wrote to Ellen in some
disgust], and talk largely—I thought assumingly . . . My cousin Eliza is a young
lady intended by Nature to be a bouncing, good-looking girl; Art has trained her
to be a languishing, affected piece of goods. I would have been friendly to her,
but could get no talk except about the Low Church Evangelical Clergy, the
Millennium . . . and her own conversion.[2]

How much about human nature did Emily learn from such contacts?
All such encounters were grist to Charlotte's inventive mill (they figure in
Mr. Rochester's and Edward Crimsworth's drawing-rooms)—but what
trace of them occurs in *Wuthering Heights*? If they played no positive role
in enlarging Emily's knowledge of human nature, they certainly fed her
contempt for the social animal, whose trite conversation was meaningless
to her. Endure their presence as she must by day, the poetry written that
summer shows how she sought escape even from the thought of such
people at night. In lines in which the passion assumes the language of love,
she implores her vision to return:

> If grief for grief can touch thee,
> If answering woe for woe,
> If any ruth can melt thee,
> Come to me now!
>
> I cannot be more lonely,
> More drear I cannot be!
> My worn heart throbs so wildly
> 'Twill break for thee.

[1] *Wuthering Heights*, ch. 1.   [2] *SLL*, i. 190.

And when the world despises,
When heaven repels my prayer,
Will not mine angel comfort?
Mine idol hear?

Yes, by the tears I've poured,
By all my hours of pain,
O I shall surely win thee,
Beloved, again![1]

In one of the most perfect poems she had so far written, she describes her
frequently interrupted dialogues with the voices of Nature which, for her,
took the place of close contact with humans:

In summer's mellow midnight,
A cloudless moon shone through
Our open parlour window
And rosetrees wet with dew.

I sat in silent musing,
The soft wind waved my hair:
It told me Heaven was glorious,
And sleeping Earth was fair.

I needed not its breathing
To bring such thoughts to me,
But still it whispered lowly,
'How dark the woods will be!

The thick leaves in my murmur
Are rustling like a dream,
And all their myriad voices
Instinct with spirit seem.'

I said, 'Go, gentle singer,
Thy wooing voice is kind,
But do not think its music
Has power to reach my mind.

Play with the scented flower,
The young tree's supple bough,
And leave my human feelings
In their own course to flow.'

The wanderer would not leave me;
Its kiss grew warmer still—
'O come,' it sighed so sweetly,
'I'll win thee 'gainst thy will.

[1] Hatfield, 138.

Have we not been from childhood friends?
Have I not loved thee long?
As long as thou hast loved the night
Whose silence wakes my song.

And when thy heart is laid at rest
Beneath the churchyard stone
I shall have time enough to mourn
And thou to be alone.'[1]

The need to be alone, to communicate with the unseen, expressed in that last line, was increasingly a condition of her life—the only way in which she could find fulfilment. She was already not far from recognizing that what she sought was life-in-death, the philosophy or mood which would inform all her later poems.

After a further failure as tutor in the family of Mr. Postlethwaite at Broughton-in-Furness, Branwell set out once again from home on 1 October 1840, this time on a novel career, as new to his age as nuclear research is to this: it was as clerk to the railways, with a starting salary that compared favourably with the teaching profession. He was engaged at a Board Meeting of the Company at Manchester as 'Assistant Clerk in Charge' of the newly opened station at Sowerby Bridge, Halifax, at a salary of £75 per annum, with the prospect of a yearly rise of £10. At the end of his first six months Branwell had for him the unusual experience of learning he had given satisfaction and was promoted to Luddendenfoot Station as 'Clerk in Charge' at a starting salary of £130 per annum. In a very little while he could be earning as much as his father had ever earned. It was Emily who commented to Charlotte on this news that 'it *looked* like getting on at any rate'[2]— which showed if not scepticism at least an open mind as regards his prospects.

Both Charlotte and Anne left home again in the spring of 1841, to take up new posts as governesses in private families. Tolerable as their situations were, both girls had mortifications and frustrations to put up with; they were not willingly subjected to the will of others, even of decent employers. Though neither Charlotte nor Anne complained to their father and aunt, the old people were not unaware of their unhappiness. But the suggestion that the girls should give up their situations and start a school of their own was astounding; no such solution to their problems had ever been mooted before. Miss Branwell was prepared, moreover, to advance some of the necessary cash. The effect on Charlotte and Anne could not be in doubt: they had everything to hope for from such an arrangement, the

[1] Hatfield, 140.   [2] *SLL*, i. 208.

prospect of release from their monotonous unrewarding situations and of a worthwhile career spent in each other's company.

The most surprising feature of the school project was not Miss Branwell's willingness to advance the cash, but Emily's support of the scheme. Alone with Anne during her holidays that June, she no doubt had plenty of opportunity to realize the depths of Anne's unhappiness among strangers and to recognize that the school plan was the lesser of two evils. It meant leaving Haworth and living at some distance from the moors (the sea-coast, as Charlotte judged, was the obvious choice for a school), but it also meant there would be no more partings from Anne and Charlotte. Her decision on so important a matter is proof enough that she put her human affections before her other needs. Her views on the subject were almost immediately registered in the birthday note she wrote on 30 July 1841 for her own eyes only—and for Anne to open by their usual arrangement, four years later. Emily's feelings were, therefore, quite unforced when she wrote with optimistic enthusiasm of the plan:

A scheme is at present in agitation for setting us up in a school of our own; as yet nothing is determined, but I hope and trust it may go on and prosper and answer our highest expectations. This day four years I wonder whether we shall still be dragging on in our present condition or established to our hearts' content. Time will show. I guess that at the time appointed for the opening of this paper we, i.e. Charlotte, Anne, and I, shall be all merrily seated in our own sitting-room in some pleasant and flourishing seminary, having just gathered in for the mid-summer ladyday. Our debts will be paid off, and we shall have cash in hand to a considerable amount. Papa, aunt, and Branwell will either have been or be coming to visit us. It will be a fine warm summer evening, very different from this bleak look-out, and Anne and I will perchance slip out into the garden for a few minutes to peruse our papers. I hope either this or something better will be the case.[1]

Echoing Emily's sentiments, though less sanguine in her tone, Anne wrote from Scarborough:

This is Emily's birthday . . . I am now at Scarborough. My pupils are gone to bed and I am hastening to finish this before I follow them. We are thinking of setting up a school of our own, but nothing definite is settled about it yet, and we do not know whether we shall be able to or not. I hope we shall . . . We are now all separate and not likely to meet again for many a weary week, but we are none of us ill that I know of and all are doing something for our own livelihood except Emily, who, however, is as busy as any of us, and in reality earns her food and raiment as much as we do.[2]

[1] *SLL*, i. 216.   [2] *SLL*, i. 215–16.

Neither Charlotte nor Anne, though they went out among strangers themselves to earn their livings, ever underestimated Emily's contribution to the family's welfare. Describing their new situations that year to her former admirer and occasional correspondent still, Henry Nussey, Charlotte wrote to him: 'We are all separated now and winning our bread amongst strangers as we can—my sister Anne is near York, my brother in a situation near Halifax, I am here [Rawdon]. Emily is the only one left at home, where her usefulness and willingness make her indispensable.'[1]

The only one of the young people at home, Emily's situation was certainly not enviable. Since Tabby had retired to her sister's cottage with her lame leg, there were now no sessions to enliven Emily with the old woman's wit, her grumbling, her devotion. Twelve-year-old Martha Brown, who later remembered Emily's kindness to her as a child, was no substitute as a companion. When her father and aunt had gone to bed, Emily was left alone to her evening's vigil. Her last task of the day was to feed the animals; this was, characteristically, the one she would never delegate to others, not even to her sisters. By the summer of 1841 the number of animals kept at the parsonage had increased with the addition of a cat, 'little black Tom', two tame geese called after the queen regnant and the queen mother, 'Victoria' and 'Adelaide', and a hawk, 'Hero', which they had rescued from its abandoned nest up on the heights. Miss Branwell viewed these additions with suspicion, but bided her time before taking summary action. Whether on her account, or for its own safety, the hawk was kept in a cage. Seeing it there, keenly aware of its plight, Emily wrote the lines, dated 27 February 1841:

> And like myself lone, wholly lone,
> It sees the day's long sunshine glow;
> And like myself it makes its moan
> In unexhausted woe.
>
> Give we the hills our equal prayer:
> Earth's breezy hills and heaven's blue sea;
> We ask for nothing further here
> But our own hearts and liberty.
>
> Ah! could my hand unlock its chain,
> How gladly would I watch it soar,
> And ne'er regret and ne'er complain
> To see its shining eyes no more.

[1] *SLL*, i. 211.

But let me think that if to-day
It pines in cold captivity,
To-morrow both shall soar away,
Eternally, entirely Free.[1]

Emily's drawing of a Merlin hawk, initialled and dated 27 October
1841, cannot be proved to be of 'Hero' (she would probably have said
so if it were) and it varies only slightly from Bewick's plate;[2] it shows her
fondness, however, for the bird and her close observation of its plumage
and colouring.

The school plan was given a quite fresh and unexpected impetus by
Martha Taylor. After the death of Mr. Taylor, the young people had
dispersed and Martha had been sent to a finishing-school outside Brussels,
where Mary and her brothers joined her for the summer holidays of 1841.
From there they wrote to Charlotte Brontë about their stimulating
experiences. Their descriptions of continental life, of art galleries and old
churches, aroused in Charlotte a state of agonized longing.

I hardly know what swelled to my throat as I read her letter [she confided to
Ellen Nussey on 7 August], such a vehement impatience of restraint and steady
work; such a strong wish for wings— . . . such an earnest thirst to see, to know,
to learn; something internal seemed to expand boldly [bodily?] for a minute. I
was tantalised with the consciousness of faculties unexercised; then all collapsed,
and I despaired.[3]

The feeling, painful though it had been, taught Charlotte something.
Consulting her employers, who were sympathetic, on the best course to
follow to start a school of her own, she became convinced that if it were
not to be doomed to failure, she and her sisters must be able to offer
foreign languages; and for that purpose needed first to perfect their own
schoolgirl French and German by study abroad. 'In extreme excitement',
as she later confessed, she wrote to her aunt to beg a loan for that objective.
She had already enquired the cost of travel and the 'facilities of education'
in Brussels, prompted in everything by the Taylors.

These are advantages which would turn to vast account, when we actually
commenced a school [she wrote to Miss Branwell on 29 September 1841], and,
if Emily could share them with me, only for a single half-year, we could take a
footing in the world afterwards which we can never do now. I say Emily instead
of Anne; for Anne might take her turn at some future period, if our school

[1] Hatfield, 144.
[2] Bewick, T., *A History of British Birds*, 2 vols. 1797 and 1804.
[3] *SLL*, i. 218–19.

'Hero'. Drawing by Emily Brontë of her Merlin hawk

G. H. Lewes, by Anne Gliddon. 1840

answered. I feel certain, while I am writing, that you will see the propriety of what I say.[1]

Charlotte was right; Miss Branwell did see the good sense of her arguments, and agreed to the loan. Mr. Brontë, moreover, equally convinced by some unanswerable arguments put forward by his fiery young daughter submitted to the plan. 'Papa will perhaps think it a wild and ambitious scheme', Charlotte wrote to Miss Branwell, 'but who ever rose in the world without ambition? When he left Ireland to go to Cambridge University, he was as ambitious as I am now. I want us *all* to go on.'[2]

Here was a plan far wider in scope than the proposed school at Bridlington; and to convince Emily all at once of its advantages was not easy. Emily immediately objected to the exclusion of Anne, and wanted reassurances on her account. Miss Wooler, who was giving up teaching, had offered Charlotte the reversion of Dewsbury Moor: Emily saw the chance to benefit all three of them there and urged this plan against the Brussels one. 'Grieve not over Dewsbury Moor,' Charlotte answered her on 7 November, 'you were cut out there to all intents and purposes, so in fact was Anne; Miss Wooler would hear of neither for the first half-year. Anne seems omitted in the present plan, but if all goes right I trust she will derive her full share of benefit from it in the end. I exhort all to hope.'[3] At the same time, Charlotte did not hide from Emily that she fully intended extending their half-year abroad to a whole year, 'if all continues well and we and those at home retain good health'. The mitigating condition to get Emily's consent was that Anne should return home for good during her sisters' absence abroad. Anne was little accustomed to housekeeping, and would be left in charge of the parsonage, with the help of young Martha Brown. This was a consideration that made Charlotte ask Emily: 'How will Anne get on with Martha?' However, Anne would at least be spared a return to the Robinsons. That was the plan; and with it Emily had to be content. But before the actual departure for Brussels, the plan suffered several modifications.

To begin with, the Robinsons would not agree to let Anne go. 'She had rendered herself so valuable in her difficult situation that they entreated her to return to them, if it be but for a short time,' Charlotte told Ellen on 10 January 1842. 'I almost think she will go back, if we can get a good servant who will do all our work. We want one about forty or fifty years old, good-tempered, clean, and honest.'[4] No good servant could be found, however.

[1] *SLL*, i. 220.   [2] *SLL*, i. 221.   [3] *SLL*, i. 224.   [4] *SLL*, i. 226.

Ellen, who was expected on a final visit to Haworth before the departure for Brussels, was promised all the news when she came, and further enticed with accounts of Mr. Weightman. 'Mr. Weightman is still here, just the same as ever. I have a curiosity to see a meeting between you and him. He will be again desperately in love, I am convinced.'[1] In fact, when Ellen came, Mr. Weightman was in love with someone else; after nearly two years away, Anne on her return had completely captivated him, and, as Charlotte observed in much amusement, 'he sits opposite to Anne at Church sighing softly and looking out of the corners of his eyes to win her attention—and Anne is so quiet, her look so downcast—they are a picture.'[2] Anne's decision to return to Thorp Green when she might have stayed at home—and seen Mr. Weightman without rivals—might suggest that she was running away from him. The depth of her own feelings was already then clear to her, however, and she must have feared exposing them to his volatile attentions. Willy Weightman had many virtues—he was generous and kind and charitable—but constancy was not among them. Marriage was as yet very far from his thoughts.

Branwell, who himself had not been home for five months, was supposed by all to be doing well at Luddendenfoot; no echo of his mental and moral collapse there had yet reached his family. He was expected home to bid farewell to his sisters on the last Saturday in January.

The departure for Brussels was fixed for Tuesday, 8 February 1842. The final surprise of all had been Mr. Brontë's decision to accompany his daughters abroad. As late as 20 January they were awaiting confirmation from a French lady travelling at the same time that she would chaperone them on the journey. Mr. Brontë had, in the last weeks, shown himself active on his daughters' behalf, writing to the British Chaplain in Brussels (whose brother he had formerly known) for particulars of suitable schools. On the recommendation of the Chaplain's wife, contact with the Pensionnat Heger was established.

Monsieur Heger told Mrs. Gaskell years later that Charlotte's letter enquiring about terms had so impressed him and his wife by 'its simple earnest tone, that they had said to each other: "These are the daughters of an English pastor of moderate means, anxious to learn with an ulterior view of instructing others, and to whom the risk of additional expense is of great consequence. Let us name a specific sum, within which all expenses shall be included."'[3] They were therefore charged the fees for board and tuition of £26 per annum—650 Belgian francs—without incurring any expense for the customary extras—drawing, dancing and music, etc.

[1] 10 Jan. 1842. *SLL*, i. 227.   [2] *SLL*, i. 228.   [3] Gaskell, 146.

A week before the scheduled departure Charlotte gave Emily a Book of Common Prayer for their sojourn in a foreign land. The gift suggests not only that Charlotte was richer by her earnings than her sister, but that Emily possessed no suitable Prayer-book. It was simply inscribed in pencil: 'Emily Jane Bronte from her sister C. Bronte. Feb 1st 1842'.

While Charlotte and Emily bent under their great burden of sewing, with 'chemises, nightgowns, pocket-handkerchiefs to make besides clothes to repair' for their journey,[1] Mr. Brontë was not idle. There remains a little hand-sewn, hand-made notebook into which he copied extracts from a *Manual of French Usage* whose thoroughness testifies to his intention of enlarging the original scope of the journey. Upright and enterprising still, and always impressive in the white stock and navy blue coat that he regularly renewed from the same Cambridge tailor of his student days, Mr. Brontë could set out for the first time in his long and laborious life to enjoy a trip abroad. Had he not Mr. Weightman to take charge of the parish, and Miss Branwell to take care of his home? There was to be no question of his daughters travelling in a hole-and-corner manner; he would escort them to their destination.

Despite the completeness of the little French Manual, it was fortunate perhaps that Mary Taylor and her brother Joe—who had business interests in Belgium—were to 'squire' Mr. Brontë's party, for they had made the journey several times. On the morning of Tuesday 8 February, the Brontës left home for Leeds, where they took the 9 a.m. train scheduled to reach London, Euston Square, at 8 p.m.

[1] CB to Ellen Nussey, 20 Jan. 1842. *SLL*, i. 228.

CHAPTER X

TO SCHOOL IN BRUSSELS

THE Brussels episode, because of the powerful impression it made on Charlotte's imagination and work, is always considered in its relation to her alone, as though Emily had no part in it. Yet she stayed there nine months and was subjected to the same influences as her sister. Because they left no tangible traces on her life and work, it does not necessarily follow that they left her unchanged. What she saw and heard may not have been congenial to her, but it was all part of her experience of life. In the course of her stay she visited two capital cities and met some learned and cultured people. After her nine months in Brussels it could not be said of her that she had never left her village or had occasion to meet people other than rustics. The opportunity was given to her; what she made of it was her own choice.

Though Joe Taylor might advise on foreign customs, in London Mr. Brontë took charge. He led them to the Chapter Coffee House, in Ivy Lane, Paternoster Row, the only place he knew, and which, for its retirement and respectability and literary associations, he liked. It was a place where he was not made to feel out of his clerical depths. It was, indeed, a meeting ground for provincial clergy, where he had been recommended as a young candidate for ordination thirty-five years before. To Patrick's daughters, the far older literary associations of the place (it was already flourishing in the days of Richard Steele) and its close connections with Goldsmith and Dr. Johnson were infinitely attractive. And there was too its situation: though it was night when they arrived, they knew, as Charlotte eloquently wrote in *Villette*, that it lay within the shadow of St. Paul's. St. Paul's was their obvious first objective the next morning, as Mary Taylor recalled to Mrs. Gaskell. St. Paul's was more than the sum of its parts to the Brontës; since their childhood the idea of St. Paul's, no doubt transmitted by their father, had been an inspiration, having figured in their earliest Glasstown stories as 'St. Michael's Cathedral'.[1]

[1] Patrick Branwell Brontë, 'History of Angria', May 1836. Brotherton Coll., Leeds Univ. Libr.

The travellers had three full days for sightseeing in London; they were not taking the Ostend packet, which made only two crossings a week, till the Saturday morning.

Mary Taylor's recollections give a clear enough picture of Emily's inevitably personal reaction to everything she saw. Her priorities were the same as Charlotte's; galleries and museums were what she wished to see, but she had her own views on the masterpieces they were shown. 'Emily', wrote Mary Taylor, 'was like her in these habits of mind, but certainly never took her opinion, but always had one to offer.'[1] In the company of the Taylors, the taciturn Emily was evidently not so tongue-tied.

Before the railway between London and Dover had been completed in 1844, passengers for the cross-channel packets were picked up at London Wharf, and sailed down-river to Margate, from where the crossing took fourteen hours, and the fare varied between £5 and £6 according to the class travelled. The Brontës and the Taylors left London early on 12 February, and were in Ostend late the same night. The rule was for foreigners to stay there the night (which they did) and to be visited by the Customs and the Police the next day only. This being Sunday, however, they were unable to travel on to Brussels until the Monday morning. The railway linking the coast with the capital was completed the following year, and Charlotte made the second journey by train. Emily, however, went by diligence, a long day's journey of 145 kilometres through the Flemish landscape.

Arriving in Brussels late in the evening, they went straight to the Hotel de Hollande, 1 Rue de la Putterie, which was quite near the pensionnat Heger. In the Police Registers for Foreigners arriving in Belgium only the gentlemen of the party had to be registered; Mr. Brontë, despite his 'cloth' was registered, like Joe Taylor, as a 'Gérant d'Affaires',[2] as though the status of business man had more prestige than that of an Anglican clergyman in predominantly Catholic Belgium. Mr. Brontë's age was also entered as sixty-three, whereas he was actually sixty-five.

It was Tuesday morning, 15 February, exactly a week after they had left home, when they presented themselves at the door of Madame Heger's Pensionnat de Jeunes Filles, in the Rue d'Isabelle. They had been met at their hotel by Mr. and Mrs. Jenkins, the British Chaplain and his wife, who came to effect the introduction. Mary Taylor told Mrs. Gaskell that she and her brother Joe took leave of the others there, to go out to

[1] Gaskell, 3rd edn., 148.
[2] Registre des Étrangers 1842. Archives de l'Hotel de Ville de Bruxelles.

Koekelberg where Mary was joining Martha at school. 'We were, of course, much preoccupied', wrote Mary, 'and our prospects were gloomy.'[1] Her own intensely self-reliant and independent character resembled Emily Brontë's in that discipline was quite repellent to her. For different reasons—Mary certainly did not have a poetic temperament—they shared the gloom of submitting to the routine of school life in their mid-twenties. Neither of them had Charlotte's longing to learn, though both recognized the inevitability of earning their own livings. It was a bad moment for them both, though the Taylors were only two miles out of town and in due course Charlotte and Emily were able to visit them.

The fame of M. Heger so far exceeds that of Madame, because of Charlotte's portrayal of him in *Villette*, that it is sometimes overlooked that it was Madame who directed the Pensionnat (which she inherited from an aunt before her marriage), where Monsieur was only a visiting master. His main appointment was as professor of rhetoric and mathematics at the Boys' College next door, of which he ultimately became the Head. It was Madame, therefore, who received the new English pupils— with her customary grace and consideration for which she was well known—and who, briefly, was seen by Mr. Brontë. M. Heger he never met. On leaving his daughters at the Pensionnat, Mr. Brontë was taken by the Jenkinses to their home outside the city in the Chaussée d'Ixelles. He stayed several days with them seeing the sights of the town and visiting the Field of Waterloo, before taking final leave of his daughters, reassuring himself of their welfare, and returning home via Dunkerque and Calais.

The Pensionnat Heger was very different from the English boarding schools of which Charlotte and Emily had had experience. Its material comforts were so superior—the food excellent and liberal, the hours of study never overtaxing, the opportunities for recreation and fresh air frequent (the school had both a flower-garden and a large playground), and the sleeping accommodation both sufficiently private and hygienic— that neither girl could find anything of which to complain. In consideration of their age and natural desire for privacy, Mme Heger gave them curtained beds at the far end of the senior dormitory, where they were as removed from the other girls as in a room of their own. The vast dormitory which ran the whole length of one side of a quadrangle (the house was rebuilt on an old foundation in 1800 in the French style) had rows of high windows which overlooked the garden, and allowed plenty of fresh air to the outdoor girls they were. Their only problem on first arriving was the language difficulty, as all the lessons were given in French. But Charlotte had nothing to complain of when she sent her first report to Ellen Nussey in the following month: 'I think we have done well—we have got into a very good school—and are considerably comfortable.'[1] By May, the reservations and complaints concerned the religion of the establishment and the female staff, but still Charlotte could say:

Yet I think I am never unhappy; my present life is so delightful, so congenial to my own nature, compared with that of a governess. My time, constantly occupied, passes too rapidly. Hitherto Emily and I have had good health, and therefore we have been able to work well . . . Emily works like a horse, and she has had great difficulties to contend with, far greater than I have had. Indeed, those who come to a French school for instruction ought previously to have acquired a considerable knowledge of the French language, otherwise they will lose a great deal of time, for the course of instruction is adapted to natives and not to foreigners.[2]

There were three resident women teachers, and seven visiting masters for French, Drawing, Music, Singing, Writing, Arithmetic, German, and Dancing; of these, the principal was Madame's husband, Constantin Heger, who took the French language and literature classes. Realizing early what language difficulties the Brontës had to contend with to keep up with the others, he gave them additional private coaching. He was a man of wide culture, immense mental energy, strict moral integrity, inexhaustible benevolence, and easily exhausted patience. He lived to a great old age and achieved a national reputation as a teacher who had applied new methods with resounding success. When he died, in 1896, the Belgian press was unanimous in giving him conspicuous and highly eulogistic obituaries. In 1842, however, Charlotte and Emily Brontë were aware only that he was an irascible and exacting little man. It was to be expected that with a temperament like his, he should get on the wrong side of Emily, a girl for whom all coercion was anathema.

There is one individual of whom I have not yet spoken [Charlotte wrote to Ellen in May], M. Heger, the husband of Madame. He is a professor of rhetoric, a man of power as to mind, but very choleric and irritable in temperament; a little black being with a face that varies in expression. Sometimes he borrows the lineaments of an insane tom-cat, sometimes those of a delirious hyena; occasionally, but very seldom, he discards these perilous attractions and assumes an air not above 100 degrees removed from mild and gentlemanlike . . . Emily and he don't draw well together at all.[3]

[1] *SLL*, i. 355.   [2] *SLL*, i. 287-8.   [3] *SLL*, i. 238.

Mrs. Gaskell, who met M. Heger later, learnt from him what special methods he applied in teaching the English girls, who, being adults, he judged could be spared the grind of grammatical exercises and the learning of long vocabularies by heart. Instead, he read them passages from some masterpiece of a biographical, descriptive, poetical character, pointing out their individual qualities of style and then asking them to adopt them for an original composition of their own on a subject of their choice. Having put the plan to them, he asked their views on it, and was doubtless startled to be told flatly by Emily that she saw no good in it at all; it would crush all originality of thought and expression.[1]

M. Heger was accustomed to the deferential obedience of his young lady pupils, and the experience of hearing his teaching methods condemned by this fierce young foreigner was a novel one for him. Yet his considered verdict on Emily Brontë before they parted shows how penetrating he was in recognizing the rarity and profundity of her mind. In this encounter, where the writing of French was involved, he insisted on his suggestion being tried; and the result, of which we can still judge today from Emily's seven preserved French essays, can only be reckoned as a triumph for teacher and pupil.

Their degree of excellence naturally raises the whole question of the extent of Emily's knowledge of French when she first arrived in Brussels. Charlotte reported that Emily had many more difficulties to contend with than herself because of the language—and consequently 'worked like a horse'. Already, however, an early essay like 'Le Roi Harold avant la bataille de Hastings', dated June 1842, shows a fluency of phrase, a range of vocabulary (the use of a dictionary was not allowed) that would have been impossible to master in the four months since her arrival at the school without exceptional ability. This, of course, Emily had. But more exceptional still was the will-power she displayed in the whole of her Brussels experience. Charlotte gives the reason for Emily's resolution to conquer in this second ordeal: it was because of her 'former failures at school'.[2] The challenge of Brussels developed in Emily, not only the will to endure an alien atmosphere and the exacting routine of foreign studies, but a latent power in herself for mastery. She had none of Charlotte's ambitions or purposes in life—study was not an end in itself to her. But to overcome opposition and difficulties, to acquire a mastery over things and people— above all, a mastery over her own weaknesses—became a feature of her growing impatience with the imperfection of life. It was present in the

---

[1] Gaskell, 152.   [2] Biographical Notice.

young writer who had scribbled that note on a poem of July 1836: 'I am more terrifically and idiotically and brutally STUPID than ever I was in the whole course of my incarnate existence.'[1] And as will appear, it became the motive-power of her maturity.

The model given Emily for her essay on King Harold (and for Charlotte's similar one on Peter the Hermit) was drawn from Victor Hugo's portrait of Mirabeau, as M. Heger told Mrs. Gaskell. An historical portrait was, therefore, the subject to be treated, but what distinguishes Emily's treatment of the theme is her choice of the moment in Harold's career, the eve of the battle of Hastings, so that the interest is concentrated not on the action but on the king's state of mind and on the analysis of his feelings. Despite Emily's opposition to M. Heger's plan, her essay proved in fact to be both highly personal and characteristic and instinct with typically noble and heroic sentiments. The energy of the language, moreover, though in a foreign tongue, is all her own.

Of Emily's seven preserved French essays, all show this characteristic choice of subject and treatment; this it is that gives them a value other than a mere school-exercise, as expressing her views on a variety of subjects. Their titles are: 'Le Chat', 'Le Roi Harold avant la bataille de Hastings', 'Une Lettre' (a letter to a mother), 'Lettre d'un Frere à un Frere', 'L'Amour Filial', 'Le Papillon', 'Le Palais de la Mort'.[2]

Discontent with the way the universe is run, and not only with sinful man's share in its imperfections, was a theme that ran through this startling young woman's 'devoirs', to the considerable interest of her teacher. This was not a mere 'Protestant' approach to life, as he knew from his enlightened readings on matters heretical; it was a reasoned pessimism, based on an individual judgement. 'Man', he read in her essay on 'The Cat', 'cannot stand up to comparison with the dog; for the dog is infinitely too good.' Cats, on the other hand, share man's qualities of hypocrisy, cruelty, and ingratitude—but are less blameworthy in exercising them than Man, whose education tends exclusively towards the development of these very qualities. 'No doubt', Emily concluded, 'cats remember that they owe all their wretchedness and bad qualities to the great ancestor of the human race, for surely cats were not wicked in Eden'.[3] Watching the summer flies floating on the surface of a stream in 'Le Papillon', the writer condemned their folly in exposing themselves to the predatory urge of the fish and the diving swallows, and warned these in their turn of their own certain destruction by 'some tyrant of air or

---

[1] See above, p. 67.   [2] See Appendix.
[3] 'Le Chat', 15 May 1842. Berg Coll., New York Public Library.

water': 'Man, for his own amusement or his needs, will as certainly kill
their murderers', she argued, '. . . life only exists on a principle of destruction.' The discovery of a caterpillar at the heart of a rose made her
exclaim that the universe appeared to her at that moment a vast machine
constructed only to bring forth evil; 'I almost doubted the goodness of
God for not annihilating Man on the day of his first sin,' she wrote. The
thought had hardly been formed, when she saw a butterfly emerge from
the place where the caterpillar had been, and was silenced by the sight.
'Just as the ugly caterpillar is the origin of the glorious butterfly, so this
world is but the embryo of a New Heaven and a New Earth,' she concluded.[1] In the essay called 'L'Amour Filial', while inveighing against the
stony-heartedness of children who had to be threatened into loving their
parents, she reflected on the universal devotion of all creatures for their
young: 'The love of parents for their children is a law of Nature; the doe
does not fear the hounds when her fawn is in danger; birds rather die in
defending their fledglings, than desert their nests; in this we share a
common soul with all animals, and are children the only exceptions in
wanting this devotion to their parents?'[2]

Such philosophical reflections in schoolroom exercises were hardly what
M. Heger was accustomed to, either in his wife's Pensionnat, or in the
boys' school—the Athénée Royal—where he spent the greater part of his
days, and he discussed Emily's views with her, as he later told Mrs.
Gaskell. Disagree with him as Emily might, he was the first man she had
met outside her family circle who had any power of mind. She cannot
have been tongue-tied with him, for his lasting impression of her was of
her originality, of her latent power. He not only let her argue, but he
listened, struck more than he perhaps allowed to appear at the time, by the
extraordinary range and colour of her mind. He did not judge her on her
essays, necessarily hampered as these were by the use of a foreign tongue;
he provoked, and listened to her verbal arguments, which, however
halting, were yet the true expression of her passionately held opinions.
M. Heger had the habit of coaching pupils in his own study, where the
fumes of his 'noxious cigars', as Charlotte wrote of them in *Villette*, made
the air a palpable pall of smoke, and where, in a relaxed and genial mood
he often dropped the dictatorial tone, and came down to a pupil's level.
(With little children he was universally patient and kind, and rewarded
their efforts to learn by giving them sweets or a piece of brioche from his

---

[1] 'Le Papillon', 11 Aug. 1842, Berg Coll., New York Public Library.
[2] 'L'Amour Filial', 5 Aug 1842. BPM.

pocket.[1]) At what level he met Emily Brontë may be judged from his own percipient words to Mrs. Gaskell. He said Emily had a head for logic and a capability for argument, unusual in a man, and rare indeed in a woman. 'She should have been a man—a great navigator', he added. 'Her powerful reason would have deduced new spheres of discovery from the knowledge of the old; and her strong, imperious will would never have been daunted by opposition or difficulty; never have given way but with life.' Yet, he was aware, 'her faculty of imagination was such that, if she had written a history, her view of the scenes and characters would have been so vivid, and so powerfully expressed, and supported by such a show of argument, that it would have dominated over the reader, whatever might have been his previous opinions, or his cooler perceptions of its truth.'[2] The judgement, made after only a few months' acquaintance, and in ignorance of the circumstances of Emily's childhood, is strangely apt when one remembers Emily's earliest passion for the polar explorer, Sir Edward Parry.

M. Heger had reservations, however, about Emily's character: though he rated her genius higher than Charlotte's, he considered 'she was egotistical and exacting compared to Charlotte, who was always unselfish; and in the anxiety of the elder to make her younger sister contented, she allowed her to exercise a kind of unconscious tyranny over her'.[3] What M. Heger saw going on between the sisters could not entirely be understood by him; if Charlotte were perpetually considerate of Emily, and attempting to smooth her path, it was from a knowledge of the greater effort Emily had to make to live among strangers, and in a confined atmosphere. Charlotte was in her element (as she told Ellen Nussey) in a school; she enjoyed the discipline, she accepted the routine, since it all led to acquiring knowledge; for Emily, this was no compensation in itself— and if M. Heger had known the truth he would have realized that it was Emily who was making the greater sacrifice, and on Charlotte's account.

A weekly trial had to be undergone by the Brontë girls in the regular invitations extended to them by Mr. and Mrs. Jenkins, who expected them at their Sunday dinner-table. The Jenkins lived at the further end of the Chaussée d'Ixelles, a good hour's walk from the Pensionnat and across town. For Charlotte and Emily, deprived of their regular exercise on the moors, a long walk once a week would have been welcome, but they were not allowed to go alone; Mrs. Jenkins sent her sons, John and Edward, to escort them. The chance of an hour's freedom to look around and to

[1] Frederika Macdonald, *The Secret of Charlotte Brontë* (1914), 208, 216–17.
[2] Gaskell, 151.   [3] Ibid.

explore on their own the old streets and squares, the medieval churches and narrow byeways, was thus lost; the walk turned into a torment for the two shy creatures.

Charlotte wrote to Ellen Nussey in May that 'Brussels is a beautiful city', but as yet they had had few chances of seeing more than the aristocratic quarter round the park, and had not seen the thronging medieval streets of the commercial lower quarter of the town. Punctually every Sunday they were fetched from the Rue d'Isabelle by the young Jenkinses, who, try as they did to engage them in conversation, found themselves up against a wall of silence; nothing elicited more than monosyllables from their unwilling guests. The obligation to squire the Miss Brontës across Brussels became as disagreeable to their escorts as it was to them; and the young men urged their mother to give up inviting them. Mrs. Jenkins did what she held to be her duty; the Chaplain made a habit of inviting all British residents and the passing tourist, to his table, and the regular appearance of strange faces made the obligation to dine there an added ordeal for the Brontë girls. At last, noticing that Emily never spoke, and Charlotte, though occasionally roused to speak on subjects that interested her, sat turned away from her interlocutor as though in terror, Mrs. Jenkins decided to end what was so disagreeable to all parties, and ceased inviting them.[1]

It could be said that the history of Brussels is written in its stone, so characteristic is the architecture of the different historic influences that shaped its destinies. The Pensionnat Heger in the Rue d'Isabelle, built in 1625 and called after the last Spanish Governor of the Netherlands, lay midway between the two extreme levels of the town; the old Spanish city huddled below in the 'basse ville', and the elegant eighteenth-century quarter of the town above, laid out in the 1770s in the architectural style of Vienna under the influence of the Emperor Joseph II. With this 'Court' district the Rue d'Isabelle was directly connected by a flight of stone steps abutting onto the Rue Royale, the most fashionable street in town. It ran the whole length of the park on one side and was flanked by patrician houses and hotels on the other. The statue of General Belliard (first French ambassador to the new Belgian kingdom in 1830) marked the top of the flight of steps, and was well enough known to Charlotte Brontë to be mentioned in both her novels of Brussels life. It was a landmark for the girls returning from their rare exploratory walks to the upper town. The Rue Royale led to the king's palace and the colonnaded Place Royale

[1] Chadwick, ch. 15 et seq.

Gateway at High Sunderland. Lithograph by John Horner

The Place Royale, Brussels, in the 1840s

where Charlotte placed one of the opening incidents in *Villette*. They had
to traverse the Place Royale and pass under the little rococo arch at the
entrance to the Rue de Namur, on their way up to the Chaussée d'Ixelles
when they visited the Jenkins on Sundays. Just off the Place Royale, in an
opposite angle formed by the former Austrian Governor's palace, was the
Chapel Royal, where the Protestant community of Brussels had held its
services ever since Napoleon appropriated the little chapel to their use.
Alternating with the Huguenots, and the Lutheran services held in the
morning, the Anglican services were held at 2 p.m., the officiating minister
being the British Chaplain, the Revd. Evan Jenkins. Here, the Brontës
regularly attended. A greater contrast to Haworth church than this little
gilded and stucco chapel, with its painted ceiling and bas-relief medallions
of tumbling cherubs, cannot well be conceived. The English colony in
Brussels numbered over 2,000 at the time; many of them had settled there
after Waterloo on account of the cheap living and good schooling offered
their sons and daughters. (The widowed Mrs. Trollope, mother of
Anthony, took her family there to be educated in 1834-6.[1]) Charlotte
observed the shabby-gentility of the congregation in *The Professor*, fore-
gathering in the little ornate square after church:

Gracious goodness! why don't they dress better? [her protagonist William
Crimsworth exclaims]. My eye is yet filled with visions of the high-flounced,
slovenly, and tumbled dresses in costly silk and satin, of the large unbecoming
collars in expensive lace; of the ill-cut coats and strangely fashioned pantaloons
which every Sunday, at the English service, filled the choirs of the chapel-royal,
and after it, issuing forth into the square, came into disadvantageous contrast
with the freshly and trimly attired foreign figures hastening to attend 'salut' at
the church of Coburg.[2]

Charlotte's unwonted sartorial strictures of her compatriots' faded finery
emphasize the difference in fashions obtaining at that time between the
two sides of the Channel; she wholeheartedly approved the fresh, wash-
able textures worn by the continental ladies, and the pretty cottons worn
by the Belgian schoolgirls. She noted in *Villette* the regulation schooldress
for summer: a 'clean fresh print dress, and light straw bonnet, each made
and trimmed as the French work-woman alone can make and trim, so as
to unite the utterly unpretentious with the perfectly becoming, was the
rule of costume. Nobody flaunted in faded silk: nobody wore a second-
hand best article.'[3]

---

[1] A. Trollope, *Autobiography*, World's Classics, 23-7.
[2] *The Professor*, ch. 19. [3] *Villette*, ch. 33.

These comments on continental dress are the more interesting because Emily Brontë came in for some sharp criticism on account of her clothes from some English fellow-pupils at the Pensionnat. These were the Wheelwright girls, the five daughters of an English doctor who, like Mrs. Trollope, settled in Belgium in the summer of 1842, to recoup his finances and educate his children at low cost.

The family arrived in Brussels in May; Dr. Wheelwright took a furnished apartment at the Hotel Cluysenaer in the Rue Royale, like Mr. Home in *Villette*, and sent his girls as day-boarders to Madame Heger's school. They were Laetitia ('Tish') aged 14; Emily aged 12½; Frances aged 11; Sarah aged 8; and Julia aged 7. The parents took a great liking to Charlotte in the following year when she returned to Brussels alone, and she became a constant visitor at their flat. The friendship begun then was renewed later when the Wheelwrights returned to England and discovered Charlotte Brontë as the famous 'Currer Bell'. Replying to Clement Shorter's subsequent enquiries about their school connections with the Brontës, Laetitia wrote him the following reply:

I am afraid my recollections of Emily Brontë will not aid you much. I simply disliked her from the first; her tallish, ungainly ill-dressed figure contrasting so strongly with Charlotte's small, neat, trim person, although their dresses were alike; always answering our jokes with 'I wish to be as God made me'. She taught my three youngest sisters music for 4 months, to my annoyance, as she would only take them in play hours so as not to curtail her own school hours, naturally causing many tears to small children, the eldest 10 and the youngest 7 . . . Charlotte was so devotedly attached to her, and thought so highly of her talents.[1]

Fanny Wheelwright recalled how Emily Brontë used to 'teach her and her little sisters the piano in play-hour in the Long-room, but this they hated as they preferred the "pas-de-Geant" (the giant stride) in the playground which had four knotted ropes to hold by'. Fanny echoed her elder sister's views on the Brontës. Comparing Charlotte to another grown-up English pupil (Maria Miller) who 'despised the little girls in the school', she said of her that 'she always noticed us youngest ones very kindly and I liked her, but not Emily Brontë'. Emily was disliked because she was aloof, too reserved to mingle with the other girls, clinging to Charlotte's arm in the playground as her only protection and so debarring Charlotte from talking and walking with the others. The Wheelwrights bore her a

[1] J. J. Green, 'The Brontë–Wheelwright Friendship', *Friends' Quarterly Examiner*, 1916.

further grudge for preventing Charlotte visiting their home on a Sunday, to which she was cordially invited. In the little Wheelwrights' view, Emily was a spoil-sport, and no one would expect a different judgement from them.

From Mrs. Gaskell, however, one might have expected a different standard of judgement from the criterion of fashion she applied to Emily; but she also, like the little Wheelwrights, roundly condemned her 'insular ideas of dress'. 'Emily', she wrote, 'had taken a fancy to the fashion, ugly and preposterous even during its reign, of gigot sleeves, and persisted in wearing them long after they were "gone out". Her petticoats, too, had not a curve or a wave in them, but hung straight and long, clinging to her lank figure.'[1] Emily Brontë had not only her genius to contend with (a barrier at all times between her and the banalities of society) but she was naturally and unaffectedly in conflict with her contemporaries in matters of dress and demeanour. Her 'singularities', as Charlotte spoke of them, were conspicuous in those days, when original thought and independent manners in women were neither encouraged, nor much known. Realizing early at Roe Head how out of touch she was with the tastes and desires of her classmates, Emily gave up the attempt to understand, or to be understood by them. An arrogant attitude, perhaps, that is not easily pardoned by those it hits. That she was not antipathetic to all strangers is clear from Ellen Nussey's deep and affectionate perception of her qualities; and even in Brussels she was not without her advocates. A fellow pupil at the Pensionnat, the sixteen-year-old Louise de Bassompierre, recorded her memories of school and the Brontës many years later:

J'ai beaucoup connu les Misses Bronte lorsqu'elles sont arrivées au Pensionnat Heger; c'était je crois en 1842. Miss Charlotte avait 25 ans et moi 16; ce qui excluait toute relation d'intimité ... Elle ne se rendait pas très sympathique parmi les jeunes filles, et un jour même il y eut une petite altercation entr'elles au sujet de l'Empereur Napoleon ... Miss Emily était beaucoup moins brillante que sa soeur mais bien plus sympathique. Elle voulait se perfectionner dans l'étude du dessin et y avait acquis un veritable talent. Elle m'a donné un joli paysage signé de son nom et que j'ai gardé avec soin.[2]

The unpopular Emily was evidently moved by Louise's sympathy, and to have given her before leaving Brussels a drawing, signed and dated, was an unusual and certainly no casual offering.

Apart from these subjective observations, Emily's school-fellows tell of the energy she brought to her studies, whether in music or drawing; her

[1] Gaskell, 150-1.　　[2] BST, 1913, 28.

French essays, as has been seen, confirm she was up to the standard required by the exacting M. Heger. But more important still, she did not fall ill; and the conclusion, surprising as it is, points to the fact that she bore with the alien atmosphere of the Pensionnat better than with the comparable establishments at home. Such self-mastery had not been achieved without a struggle, however, as Charlotte later revealed when she related Emily's various experiences in schools:

> She went with me to an establishment on the Continent. The same suffering and conflict ensued, heightened by the strong recoil of her upright, heretic and English spirit from the gentle Jesuitry of the foreign and Romish system. Once more she seemed sinking, but this time she rallied through the mere force of resolution: with inward remorse and shame she looked back on her former failure, and resolved to conquer in this second ordeal. She did conquer; but the victory cost her dear. She was never happy till she carried her hard-won knowledge back to the remote English village.[1]

There was one aspect of school-life with which neither Emily nor Charlotte ever came to terms: this was the religious instruction given daily, in the form of morning prayers, and evening readings aloud from the Lives of the Saints, with which the day's activities closed. Towards the Belgians' 'idolatrous messe' the Brontës remained implacable, though the fact was they were freely exempted from all attendance at these exercises. It was the opportunity to hear French read, especially when the reader was M. Heger, that tempted them to attend the evening 'lecture'. There were occasions when they were lucky enough to hear M. Heger read from a Racine play or other great classic work instead of from the scorned hagiographical studies, and then they felt rewarded for their pains. He had spent much time in his youth learning declamation at the Comédie Française, and could powerfully inject a text with feeling and poetry.

The original plan for the Brontës to stay only a half-year in Brussels may have buoyed Emily up with the prospect of a return home by late summer; but when July arrived, Madame Heger made them a proposal which, while it delighted Charlotte, effectually put an end to Emily's hopes. The fact that she did not oppose Charlotte's wishes to accept the offer and stay another 'half' shows that the self-mastery she had won was greater even than Charlotte allowed; and that the selfishness remarked by the Wheelwrights and M. Heger was also something less.

[1] Biographical Notice.

I consider it doubtful whether I shall come home in September [Charlotte wrote to Ellen Nussey in July]. Madame Heger has made a proposal for both me and Emily to stay another half-year, offering to dismiss her English master, and take me as English teacher; also to employ Emily some part of each day in teaching music to a certain number of the pupils. For these services we are to be allowed to continue our studies in French and German, and to have board, etc., without paying for it; no salaries, however, are offered. The proposal is kind . . . I am inclined to accept it . . . I don't deny I sometimes wish to be in England, or that I have brief attacks of home-sickness; but on the whole, I have borne a very valiant heart so far; and I have been happy in Brussels, because I have always been fully occupied with the employments that I like. Emily is making rapid progress in French, German, music and drawing. Monsieur and Madame Heger begin to recognise the valuable parts of her character, under her singularities.[1]

Emily studied music with M. Chapelle, M. Heger's brother-in-law, a professor of the Conservatoire Royal of Brussels, the visiting master at the Pensionnat. The progress she made (Ellen Nussey described her later as 'amazing' in 'style, touch, and expression, like a professor absorbed heart and soul in his theme') was exceptional enough for the Hegers to decide on giving her lessons next half with the finest teacher in Belgium.[2]

The incentive of working with a really great pianist must have reconciled Emily to the new plan. The news from home told of Anne's staying even yet longer at the Robinsons. The old people were well, and if, as appears from subsequent evidence, Branwell's latest disaster was hidden from his sisters abroad, and they knew nothing of it, their conclusion was that all was for the best and Madame Heger's offer too good to refuse.

Meanwhile, the long vacation was at hand, ushered in by the usual school party, with supper and ball, held on the occasion of Madame Heger's 'Fête' day, the Ste Claire, 12 August. This was followed by the annual breaking-up on 15 August. The Brontë girls were left in the empty school with a skeleton domestic staff, the five little Wheelwright girls left in their charge while the parents made a trip up the Rhine, and two other foreign girls who could not go home. For Charlotte and Emily, the routine was not greatly altered, for they worked on their own, determined to catch up on their languages and reading, and supervised the Wheelwrights' holiday tasks.

The only difference was that they worked out of doors, in the pleasant high-walled garden that figures so significantly in *Villette* and *The Professor*. There was a large vine-covered arbour where on hot days

Madame Heger was accustomed to take the youngest class of children for their lessons, and shaded walks—out of bounds to the others in term-time because they were overlooked from the windows of the neighbouring boys' college. There were winding paths and espaliered pear trees, and rose bushes bordering the walks; it was fragrant and restful, and Charlotte deeply loved its seclusion, while kindled at the same time by the continuous hum of the city which reached there from the Rue Royale above, and the neighbouring streets where the great banking firms had their business premises. At evening, the bells of Ste Gudule, only two streets away, were borne to the Pensionnat garden, and often after the girls were in bed the music from the band in the park came through their opened dormitory windows. On summer evenings outdoor concerts were a regular feature of Brussels, given under the trees of the 'Vauxhall' enclosure in the park to a packed public. Charlotte liked it all so well that there was a danger, as Emily later wrote to Ellen Nussey, of her 'vegetating there till the age of Methusalah'. The fact was, Charlotte was far from vegetating, but was keenly absorbing the most stimulating experience of her life. The pity was she attempted to prolong it, and found the serpent in her Eden the following year.

To Emily, it all meant very little except perhaps for the satisfaction she derived from overcoming difficulties and oppositions. She did not easily concede to others the direction of her life and leisure, but having resolved to learn all she could in Brussels she bore the complete appropriation of her time with a good grace, for Charlotte's and Anne's sake, and for the great objective they shared, of opening their own school one day. Occasionally they allowed themselves a holiday, as when they visited the 'Salon' of contemporary art, which was held triennally and occurred that summer of 1842, as Charlotte's recognizable descriptions of some of the exhibits in *Villette*[1] remain to show.

At the holidays' end, Mary and Martha Taylor returned to Brussels and could report well of both Brontë girls to Ellen Nussey on 24 September 1842 '. . . Charlotte and Emily are well,' Mary wrote, 'not only in health but in mind and hope. They are content in their present position and even gay and I think they do quite right not to return to England.'[2] The occasional meetings with the Taylors, whose school in the converted Château de Koekelberg was within walking distance of town, was one of the few relaxations the Brontës allowed themselves. There was nothing artificial about the Taylors; they spoke as they felt, especially Martha, an

[1] See *Villette*, ch. 19.   [2] W & S, i. 272.

enfant terrible, whether at home or abroad. Spending the Whitsun holiday together, the Taylors and Brontës joined in a budget of news to Ellen Nussey at home, to which Charlotte added a few lines: 'we are spending the day with Mary and Martha Taylor—to us such a happy day—for one's blood requires a little warming, it gets cold with living amongst strangers . . . Mary and Martha are not changed; I have a catholic faith in them that they cannot change.'[1]

Home on a brief visit in August, Martha summoned Ellen to her brother's house in characteristic terms:

My brothers and I shall be exceedingly gratified if you, your sister Mercy, and your brothers will come to tea on [Wednesday]. Now, will you come? or will you be stupid as you were about going to Brier Hall, and if you refuse you will make me seriously angry with you, and you had better not, or I will tell all kinds of things of you to Miss Brontë. We leave here . . . Thursday next, so you must bring your letters with you [for Brussels]. I remain conditionally, yours truly Martha Taylor.[2]

Since childhood Martha had been her father's pet and had expected to have her own way in everything, and on the whole she had. She was now twenty-three. The shock to her indulgent sister and friends was the greater when she was stricken down with cholera (a very prevalent infection in Brussels) in early October 1842. Before the gravity of her condition was fully realized, Mary wrote to tell Charlotte that she was ill, and the next day being Thursday and their usual half-holiday, Charlotte walked out to Koekelberg to learn, on arriving, that Martha had died during the night.

In Charlotte's account of what happened, written later to Ellen Nussey, she refers to herself going alone to Koekelberg. But the unlikelihood of Emily remaining at the Pensionnat without her sister suggests that they went together, and that Emily, like Charlotte, saw Mary Taylor on the occasion. In view of the customs of the day, there is the further possibility that they saw the dead Martha. The question may have a bearing on a passage in *Wuthering Heights*, in which the author seems to speak from experience. It is that in which Nelly Dean watches by the dead Catherine. 'I don't know if it be a peculiarity in me,' says Nelly, 'but I am seldom otherwise than happy while watching the chamber of death, should no frenzied or despairing mourner share the duty with me.'[3]

For Emily, who was too young at the deaths of her elder sisters to register such thoughts, the dead Martha Taylor must have been one of the

[1] 26 Mar. 1842. *SLL*, i. 235.   [2] W & S, i. 271.   [3] *Wuthering Heights*, ch. 16.

first corpses she had seen. The curious reflection about 'no frenzied or despairing mourner' sharing the vigil with her, applies, if it applies to anyone, most aptly to Mary Taylor, whose courage under this and other trials was remarkable. Charlotte said when relating the incident to Ellen Nussey, 'She appears calm and serious now; no outbursts of violent emotion, no exaggeration of distress.'[1] Mary Taylor's restraint was just what would impress Emily Brontë.

The death of Martha effectually brought to an end the carefree period of the four girls' schooldays in Brussels. It could never have been the same again, even if other circumstances had not followed to change the whole situation.

Mary was fortunate in having an uncle and cousins staying in Brussels at the time. The uncle was Mr. Abraham Dixon of Gomersal (1779–1850), an engineer and inventor, who had married Mary's aunt, Laetitia Taylor. A widower by then with two grown-up sons (George and Tom) and a daughter Mary (later a friend of Charlotte Brontë's), he was living in Brussels where, like Robert Moore in *Shirley*, he was extending his foreign business connection. His objective was to sell new machinery for the manufacture of military cloth to the Belgian government. The Dixons had a furnished apartment in the Rue de la Régence, off the Place Royale, and there Mary Taylor was taken after Martha's death. To her relief and surprise, she found them most congenial. 'They are the most united, affectionate family I ever met with,' she told Ellen Nussey. 'They have taken me as one of themselves, and made me such a comfortable happy home that I should like to live here all my life.'[2]

The Taylors were dissenters, and Martha's funeral was conducted not by the Anglican Chaplain Mr. Jenkins but by the French Huguenot Pastor, Chrétien-Henri Vent, at the Chapel Royal on 14 October; the burial took place in the relatively new Protestant cemetery—le Cimetière de l'Est—outside Brussels along the Chaussée de Louvain. It was nearly three miles out, and a fortnight after the funeral Charlotte and Emily walked to visit Martha's grave there with Mary. It was the Protestant Cemetery of which Charlotte wrote later in *The Professor*[3] and referred to in *Villette*. When she was alone in Brussels the following year, Martha's grave was a regular objective of her walks.

The return from the cemetery and the evening spent with the Dixons, made so lasting an impression on Charlotte that years later hearing the rain come down in England as on that evening in Brussels, the whole scene

---

[1] *SLL*, i. 246.   [2] 30 Oct. 1842. *SLL*, i. 243.   [3] Ch. 19.

rushed back to her memory as she wrote her dirge for the death of Martha Taylor (Jessie Yorke).[1]

Mary Taylor also wrote of that evening. In a post-script to her letter to Ellen Nussey of 30 October, she said: 'Well, I have seen her and Emily. We have walked about six miles to see the cemetery and the country round it. We then spent a pleasant evening with my cousins, and in the presence of my uncle and Emily, one not speaking at all, the other once or twice.'[2]

The impression that Emily Brontë gave in a 'crowd' (there were at least three if not four Dixon gentlemen present that evening) was piquant enough for Mary Taylor to remember it months later, when all the friends were dispersed; the Brontës had gone home, and Mary herself was teaching in a German school. Ellen Nussey had written of her first meeting with the Brontës after their return home and must have commented not without surprise on Emily's 'acquirements' abroad, for Mary wrote with some humour on 16 February:

I know well how you would spend the month you talk of when Miss Brontë was with you and how you would discuss all imaginable topics and all imaginable people all day and half the night. Tell me something about Emily Brontë. I can't imagine how the newly acquired qualities can fit in, in the same head and heart that is occupied by the old ones. I imagine Emily turning over prints or 'taking wine' with any stupid pup and preserving her temper and politeness![3]

Mary Taylor finished her letter to Ellen on 1 November. The next morning, Wednesday. Charlotte and Emily received an urgent letter from home to say their aunt was gravely ill. There was no doubt of the gravity of the case, and they went at once to Madame Heger to say they must go home by the next packet. The next crossing from Ostend was on the Friday and they decided to take it, little time as it allowed them; but by the next morning's post another letter came from home to say Miss Branwell had died. Her death occurred on 29 October, and, realizing that the funeral would in any case be over before they could get home, they decided to delay their return till the Sunday's packet from Antwerp, which allowed them a longer respite in which to pack. The suddenness of the summons left them in great uncertainty of their future movements. Would they return to Brussels, where the new 'half' had barely yet begun? They had not only their own interests to consider, but their obligations towards the Hegers, who had taken them on as pupil-teachers with new responsibilities towards the school. Madame Heger had indeed got rid of her English master to give the place to Charlotte; the thought was balm to

[1] *Shirley*, 23.   [2] *SLL*, i. 243.   [3] *SLL*, i. 261.

Charlotte's troubled mind, for she longed to return to Brussels and M. Heger, for whom she had, perhaps as yet unconsciously, acquired such deep feelings. M. Heger himself came to her rescue by writing to Mr. Brontë to urge the return of both girls, or in default of both, at least of one to reap the benefits of their year's hard work. The terms in which M. Heger wrote of them shows in what an affectionate and paternal light he had come to judge them. Nothing but mutual esteem and kindness marked the parting, but while Charlotte prayed it might only be temporary, Emily had already made up her mind that, for herself, it was final.

The feeling that Emily was probably leaving for good is shown in the parting present of a book which Madame Heger gave her; and in her own gift to Louise de Bassompierre of her drawing. Encouraged by every kind assurance from both Monsieur and Madame (who followed up her verbal persuasions to Charlotte with a cordial letter addressed to her at home), Charlotte could face the parting with tolerable equanimity: if Emily was prepared to look after their father, her own chances of returning to Brussels were vastly heightened. There seemed to be no impediment to her return—unless, as she admitted later—it were in her heart and conscience.

Accompanied by Madame Heger as far as Antwerp, they took the steam packet from there on the Sunday morning, 6 November, and without stopping overnight in London, reached home on the morning of Tuesday. They had been abroad exactly nine months.

CHAPTER XI

THE VISIONARY

It was Branwell who had written to his sisters to notify them of their aunt's illness and death. The event fell hardest on him, not only because of his lifelong affection for his aunt, but because in the absence of his sisters the chief attendance on her during her fortnight's illness had devolved upon him.

He had suffered another disastrous year, being dismissed from his post with the railways in March on a charge of 'negligence' and 'defalcation' of the company's accounts. He was innocent of the worst charge[1] for which his porter, Walton, was found guilty, but as the senior in the post Branwell was held responsible, and suffered the penalty. The sum involved was not very great, £11 1s. 7d.—which was of course deducted from Branwell's last quarter's salary—but the disgrace was more than he could bear, and his return home was followed by a complete breakdown. His state of mind, as shown in his letters to his new friend Grundy, bordered on the insane.

During that summer of his deepest dejection, his best friend and most cheering companion, had been his father's curate, William Weightman, who had got him out and about again, reviving his old interest in following the guns and taking healthy exercise. The shock was all the harder to bear when Mr. Weightman contracted cholera, and died. 'I have had a long attendance at the deathbed of the Revd. William Weightman, one of my dearest friends,' Branwell wrote to Grundy on 25 October,[2] almost stupefied by his loss. Mr. Brontë visited his curate twice a day, got in a doctor and a nurse, sent for his family from Appleby, and fought for his life with every practical known method of the time, and sincerely lamented his loss when he died. He had come to regard his curate in the light of a son and spoke in his praise with tears made all the more bitter from disappointment in his own son.

There are many who for a short time can please [Mr. Brontë said in his funeral sermon on 2 October], but who soon retrograde and fall into disrepute—Mr.

[1] F. H. Grundy, *Pictures of the Past* (1879), p. 86.   [2] *SLL*, i. 242.

Weightman's character wore well; the surest proof of worth. He had, it is true, some peculiar advantages. Agreeable in person and manners, and constitutionally cheerful, his first introduction was prepossessing. But what he gained at first he did not lose afterwards. He had those qualities which enabled him rather to *gain* ground.[1]

From Anne Brontë, who had loved him, Willie Weightman was given a lasting memorial:

> Life seems more sweet that thou didst live,
> And men more true that thou wert one;
> Nothing is lost that thou didst give,
> Nothing destroyed that thou hast done.[2]

The circumstances of her own life aiding, Anne's sorrow for the death of the 'sunny curate of Haworth' deepened into a profound grief, increasing rather than diminishing over the years.

Branwell had hardly buried his poor friend, when his aunt fell ill. In the same letter of 25 October to Grundy, he wrote: 'now I am attending at the deathbed of my aunt, who has been for twenty years as my mother. I expect her to die in a few hours.'[3] Miss Branwell died on 29 October, and Branwell wrote again to his friend to say: 'I am incoherent, I fear, but I have been waking two nights witnessing such agonizing sufferings as I could not wish my worst enemy to endure.'[4]

Whatever the weaknesses of his character and constitution, Branwell never showed want of heart, and these double griefs following so swiftly on one another found him equal to the effort required of him. By the time his sisters reached home (Anne was given leave of absence too late by her employer to nurse her aunt and got home only for the funeral) he was a different being from the one who had returned disgraced early in the year, and could face them with something like a regained self-respect. His absolute poverty, which prevented him drinking or even buying opium, proved a boon to his health. He was presentable enough for Anne to decide to introduce him to the Robinsons, who were in quest of a tutor for their eleven-year-old son, Edmund, whom she had hitherto been priming in Latin.

To this emotionally-charged atmosphere Charlotte and Emily returned from Brussels on 8 November. The funeral was over (it took place on 3

---

[1] *A Funeral Sermon for the late Rev. William Weightman, M.A. preached . . . by the Rev. P. Brontë A.B. Incumbent*, Printed Halifax, 1842.
[2] Anne Brontë, 'Severed and gone', April 1847.
[3] *SLL*, i. 242.   [4] *SLL*, i. 243.

November) and the shaken household had resumed an appearance of calm. Inviting Ellen Nussey to visit them, Charlotte wrote:

Papa desires his compliments to you and says he should be very glad if you could give us your company at Haworth a little while. Can you come Friday next? I mention so early a day because Anne leaves us to return to York on Monday, and she wishes very much to see you before her departure . . . Do not fear to find us melancholy or depressed. We are all much as usual. You will see no difference from our former demeanour.[1]

Emily had her own personal and additional cause for grief—the loss of her pet hawk Hero, and of the tame geese disposed of by her aunt in her absence. Reporting on the changes that had taken place at the time, she recorded in July 1845 the acquisitions and losses among domestic pets. She wrote: 'We have got Flossy; got and lost Tiger; lost the hawk Hero, which, with the geese, was given away, and is doubtless dead, for when I came back from Brussels I inquired on all hands and could hear nothing of him . . . Keeper and Flossy are well, also the canary acquired four years since.'[2]

Anne remained at home till 29 November, and had thus three weeks with her sisters in which to deliberate on the changes in their situation brought about by their aunt's death. One of them would now be needed to keep house for their father, and there does not seem to have been any doubt that it would be Emily.

The long-term project towards which they had all been working for opening a school of their own was not allowed to lapse. Charlotte was as eager as ever to promote it, and believed that she could reconcile it with her dearest wish to return to Brussels for another year's study.

In the first shock of their aunt's death, none of them seems to have realized that they were going to inherit a small capital which could radically alter their circumstances. Only on 28 December, when Miss Branwell's Will was proved in the Probate Court of York (where Mr. Brontë and his fellow-executor Mr. George Taylor of Stanbury attended), was the full amount of Miss Branwell's legacies to her nieces known— some £1,500 to be divided between the Brontë girls and a fourth niece in Penzance, Elizabeth Jane Kingston. For the first time in their lives they thus found themselves in possession of money—some £350 each—which made their modest earnings as governesses in the past appear negligible. Miss Branwell had been both frugal and generous, living carefully in her brother-in-law's house and seldom touching her personal income of £50 per annum so as to save it for her nieces. It was more than they could ever have expected. Miss Branwell made her will in 1833, long before Branwell became a family problem, and it is wholly incorrect to say, as some biographers have asserted, that his aunt cut him out of her will for his misconduct. Miss Branwell's motives in leaving her money to her nieces exclusively were obvious enough: Branwell was expected to make his own way in life, whereas they had no prospects other than to become ill-paid governesses, and finally penurious old maids. Miss Branwell knew well enough how small were the chances of marriage for girls with no money and no looks—and estimated her nieces' prospects at their realistic worst.

The little windfall was to make no difference to their immediate plans, as both Charlotte and Anne decided, in taking up their teaching posts again, but for the unworldly Emily her aunt's legacy spelt incalculable riches, since it insured her against leaving home again.

In the hurry of the fresh departures after the Christmas holidays—Anne and Branwell to Thorp Green and Charlotte to Brussels on 27 January 1843, the onus of investing their aunt's legacies fell, ironically enough, on Emily, who had never given money a thought. In the event, she proved herself a very able business-woman, as Charlotte was the first to acknowledge later. She took shares for her sisters and herself in the York and North Midland Railway Company which had been started in 1839 by the enterprising George Hudson. It may well be that the decision to take Hudson Shares was made after consultation with Anne, for Anne was in a position to have first-hand information on the subject. Hudson's railway was a York enterprise (he was a local man, twice mayor of the city) and she could hear the views of the Robinsons and their circle on the advisability of buying shares in his booming company. At that time, before the shadow of failure fell across Hudson's multiple enterprises, the Misses Brontë might consider themselves lucky to be allotted shares then continually soaring with the rising railway mania. Emily and Anne were very content with their successful incursion into high finance, and would hear nothing of Charlotte's subsequent doubts of George Hudson's honesty when he multiplied his activities at the expense of his railway stock, and they resolutely joined the subscribers to the testimonial raised by his grateful share-holders, with a guinea apiece, the record of which still stands on the company's books. When, in 1846, Hudson's fortunes began to fluctuate, and there was a rush by shareholders to sell out, Emily and Anne stuck to their guns and would not be persuaded by the prudent Charlotte to follow the trend.

Meanwhile, the 'disinterested and energetic' Emily (as Charlotte spoke of her) was enjoying complete independence for the very first time in her life. Never had she been in unopposed control of her father's house. Replacing her aunt as his housekeeper, with only little Hannah Brown to help her, her first act was to fetch back Tabby, whose couple of years' rest had revived her sufficiently to take a modest share in the work. She was an auxiliary after Emily's own heart, vigorous of mind if not of body, and bringing to all household problems the good sense and the experience of a long life spent in useful tasks. So long as Miss Branwell lived there was no likelihood of Tabby being restored to her old position at the parsonage; but in this as in other matters of the heart, Emily and her father saw eye to eye: Tabby was reinstated—this time for good—and to the greater comfort of all. Charlotte, nostalgically writing home from Brussels, commented to her father on the new domestic arrangements, with their particular application to Emily:

You do not say anything about your health, but I hope you are well and Emily also. I am afraid she will have a good deal of hard work to do now that Hannah is gone. I am exceedingly glad to hear that you still keep Tabby—it is an act of charity to her, and I do not think it will be unrewarded, for she is very faithful, and will always serve you, when she has occasion, to the best of her abilities; besides, she will be company for Emily, who, without her—would be very lonely.[1]

The cost of postage abroad—1s. 6d. to Belgium—precluded much correspondence, and it was Charlotte in her crowded world at the Pensionnat who suffered from loneliness and begged for news of home. She complained to Branwell on 1 May:

I hear you have written a letter to me; this letter however as usual, I have never received, which I am exceedingly sorry for, as I have wished very much to hear from you. Are you sure you put the right address and that you paid the English postage, 1s. 6d. Without that, letters are never forwarded. I heard from papa a day or two since—all appears to be going on reasonably well at home— I grieve only that Emily is so solitary, but however you and Anne will soon be returning for the holidays which will cheer the house for a time.[2]

In reply to an offer from Ellen Nussey to forward a letter by hand to Brussels (by one of the Dixons going over), Emily wrote in high good humour on Monday, 22 May:

Dear Miss Nussey
    I should be wanting in common civility if I did not thank you for your kindness in letting me know of an opportunity to send postage free.

[1] CB to Mr. Brontë, 2 June 1843. W & S, i. 300.   [2] BM, Ashley MSS.

I have written as you directed, though if next Tuesday means to-morrow, I fear it will be too late to go with Mr. —— Charlotte has never mentioned a word about coming home. If you would go over for half a year, perhaps you might be able to bring her back with you, otherwise she might vegetate there till the age of Methusalah for mere lack of courage to face the voyage. All here are in good health; so was Anne according to her last account. The holidays will be here in a week or two, and then, if she be willing, I will get her to write you a proper letter, a feat that I have never performed.

With love and good wishes,

Emily J. Brontë.[1]

Anne and Branwell came home in June, bringing with them a welcome addition to the home circle: a black-and-white King Charles spaniel bitch whom they called 'Flossy'. Thenceforward, 'Flossy' appears in all the family records and was the subject of several sketches, both by Charlotte and Emily; she outlived Keeper, dying in 1854.

Branwell was giving satisfaction in his post; his employers even invited Mr. Brontë to visit Thorp Green, which he did with much gratification to himself in the early summer.

If Emily were lonely at times, there was compensation for her in the unaccustomed leisure, in the absolute mental freedom that were now hers after the turmoil and effort of the year in Brussels. Her genius needed tranquillity in which to grow. The stimuli to which she responded best were not intellectual exchanges, such as Charlotte yearned after; it was not museums, art galleries or the opportunity for higher studies that satisfied her longings; for her there was no place that liberated her mind like her boundless moors. Charlotte was already out of touch with Emily when she supposed her dejected in solitude; the poetic output of that time shows sufficiently how Emily was faring on her own.

The image of Emily longest preserved in Haworth memory was the one later reported to Mrs. Gaskell:

When at home, she took the principal part of the cooking on herself, and did all the household ironing; and after Tabby grew old and infirm, it was Emily who made all the bread for the family; and any one passing by the kitchen door, might have seen her studying German out of an open book, propped up before her, as she kneaded the dough; but no study, however interesting, interfered with the goodness of the bread, which was always light and excellent.[2]

For as far as it went, the image was true enough; Emily did all the

<hr>

[1] *SLL*, i. 265. BM, Ashley MSS.   [2] Gaskell, 90.

cooking, baking, much of the housework, all the ironing (for the house-hold washing a woman always came in from the village), and the reading-aloud to her father when his sight failed. How little such work filled her mind appears by her calling herself 'idle' in her letters to Charlotte: '*You* call yourself idle,' Charlotte answered her, 'absurd! absurd!'[1]

When Emily called herself 'idle' to her studious sister, she meant she was not pursuing any set course of study. With the school-plan ever in the background of Charlotte's thoughts it was tacitly agreed between them that Emily should continue her studies of French, German, and music. Sporadically she did all that, but hers was not a studious nature; in her diary of July 1841 she confessed to having 'a good many books on hand, but I am sorry to say that—as usual I make small progress with any. However I have just made a new regularity paper! and I will Verb Sap—to do great things.' When the next diary-paper was written in July 1845, she could report that she 'was not as idle as formerly'.

Writing of her sisters after their deaths, Charlotte said: 'Neither Emily nor Anne was learned; they had no thought of filling their pitchers at the well-spring of other minds; they always wrote from the impulse of nature, the dictates of intuition, and from such stores of observation as their limited experience had enabled them to amass.'[2]

On the subject of Emily's German studies, it is interesting to note that there appeared a series of articles in *Blackwood's Magazine* by Bulwer Lytton on 'The Poems and Ballads of Schiller'. They ran for twelve months, from September 1842 to August 1843 with copious selections in translation of his works. There can be little doubt that Emily read the articles, since one of her daily tasks was to read to her father the political comment, a duty formerly performed by Miss Branwell. The poetry of Schiller, with its ballad form and fiery substance, held obvious attractions for Emily. It was surely a kindred mind to hers which composed the allegory called 'The Sharing of the Earth', published in *Blackwood's* in September 1842, in which the riches of earth are divided out between the grasping squirarchy, the merchants, the clergy, and the kings, while the poet alone is left without a portion.

> 'Woe is me, is there nothing remaining,
>   For the son who best loves thee alone!'
> Thus to Jove went his voice in complaining,
>   As he fell at the Thunderer's throne.

[1] 1 Oct. 1843. W & S, i. 305.   [2] Biographical Notice.

'In the land of the dreams if abiding',
Quoth the God, 'Canst thou murmur to Me.
Where wert *thou* when the Earth was dividing?'
'I was', said the Poet, 'by Thee!

Mine eye by thy glory was captured—
Mine ear by thy music of bliss,
Pardon him whom *thy* world had enraptured—
He has lost all possession in this!'

'What to do?' said the God—'Earth is given!
Field, forest, and market and all!—
What say you to quarters in Heaven?
We'll admit you whenever you call!'

In Charlotte's description of Mary and Diana Rivers at their studies in *Jane Eyre*, one sees the likenesses of Emily and Anne: 'they were all delicacy and cultivation. I had nowhere seen such faces as theirs . . . I cannot call them handsome—they were too pale and grave for the word; as they each bent over a book, they looked thoughtful almost to severity.' In the flash of 'her dark and deep eye' as 'Mary' read a passage to her taste, Charlotte gave us a glimpse of her sister in the fictitious girl.[1] The atmosphere of Haworth parsonage is further evoked by the Tabby-like comments of the servant Hannah, asking her young ladies 'what good' it did them learning a foreign language.

John Greenwood, the Haworth stationer, who kept a diary of village events, was particularly devoted to Emily, and noted all her doings that came to his knowledge. He said her promptitude, firmness, and presence of mind were such that she was always relied upon by the whole household; whatever the difficulty, she was appealed to by them all, for she could always do the right thing at the right time.

On one occasion a person went to tell them that Keeper and another great powerful dog out of the village were fighting down the lane. She was in the garden at the time, and the servant went to tell her, as a matter of course, what was up. She never spoke a word, nor appeared the least at a loss what to do, but rushed at once into the kitchen, took the pepper box, and away into the lane, where she found the two savage brutes each holding the other by the throat, in deadly grip, while several other animals, who thought themselves men, were standing looking on like cowards as they were, afraid to tuch [sic] them—there they stood gaping, watching this fragile creature spring upon the beasts— seizing Keeper round the neck with one arm, while with the other hand she

---

[1] *Jane Eyre*, ch. 28.

dredges well their noses with pepper, and separating them by force of her great will, driving Keeper, that great powerful dog, before her into the house, never once noticing the men, so called, standing there thunderstruck at the deed.[1]

Between Emily and her father a new closeness grew up in the year of their isolation together. His deteriorating eye-sight made him dependent on her about the home for more than reading. It affected not only his clerical avocations, his reading and writing, but the daily discharge of his pistols over the heads of the gravestones in the churchyard. He has been made a figure of fun by his daughters' biographers for this eccentric habit so little in accordance with Victorian manners, but so much in keeping with those of the Regency to which he belonged. The habit went back to the Luddite emergency of 1812, when most clergymen in the West Riding went about armed in anticipation of riots in their parishes. Mr. Brontë was unusual in continuing the practice into peaceful times, but to the Irishman who had also seen the 'Troubles' of 1798 in his native Co. Down it still seemed perfectly natural—the more so in that his parsonage at Haworth was particularly isolated, with the moors reaching almost to his back door. To cock his pistol nightly in case of alarm, and to discharge it in the morning from his bedroom window, was a normal operation in his view for a gentleman with a pack of women to defend. As his sight failed, and the risk increased of winging some unwary parishioner crossing the churchyard at first light, Mr. Brontë realised the good sense of teaching Emily to fire, in case the need to protect the household should ever arise. Her willingness to learn may be assumed considering her imaginative girlhood among 'the fighting gentry' of Gondal. Indeed to master a pistol might be a more congenial task than learning French grammar. John Greenwood, who was witness to her prowess, recorded it in his diary:

Mr. Brontë formerly took very great pleasure in shooting—not in the way generally understood by the term, but shooting at a mark, merely for recreation. He had such unbounded confidence in his daughter Emily, knowing, as he did, her unparalleled intrepidity and firmness, that he resolved to learn her to shoot too. They used to practice with pistols. Let her be ever so busy in her domestic duties, whether in the kitchen baking bread at which she had such a dainty hand, or at her ironing, or at her studies, raped [sic] in a world of her own creating— it mattered not; if he called upon her to take a lesson, she would put all down; his tender and affectionate 'Now my dear girl, let me see how well you can shoot to-day' was irristable to her filial nature, and her most winning and musical voice would be heard to ring through the house in response, 'Yes, papa' and

[1] John Greenwood's diary; by courtesy of Mrs. Mary Preston of Haworth.

away she would run with such a hearty good will taking the board at him, and tripping like a fairy down the [sic] to the bottom of the garden, putting it in its proper position, then returning to her dear revered parent, take the pistol, which he had previously primed and loaded for her. 'Now my girl' he would say, 'take time, be steady'. 'Yes papa', she would say taking the weapon with as firm a hand, and as steady an eye as any veteran of the camp, and fire. Then she would run to fetch the board for him to see how she had succeeded. And she did get so proficient, that she was rarely far from the mark. His 'how cleverly you have done, my dear girl', was all she cared for. She knew she had gratified him, and she would return to him the pistol, saying 'load again papa,' and away she would go to the kitchen, roll another shelful of teacakes, then wiping her hands, she would return again to the garden, and call out 'I'm ready again, papa', and so they would go on until he thought she had had enough practice for that day. 'Oh!' he would exclaim, 'she is a brave and noble girl. She is my right-hand, nay the very apple of my eye!' [1]

While it is highly improbable that either Mr. Brontë or Emily spoke in precisely those terms, Greenwood, from the vantage-ground of the adjoining graveyard or even from John Brown's stonemason's yard opposite, could be witness of the comings and goings of father and daughter and of their mutual absorption in their task. To a man feeling blindness stealing upon him, she was indeed becoming his right hand as she had long been the apple of his eye.

It is a measure of the freedom Mr. Brontë allowed his children that he never obliged Emily to teach in the Sunday-school—general as the practice then was for the daughters of clergy. She did not do so even in the absence of her sisters when help would have been needed. He showed even greater tolerance in putting no pressure on her to attend church regularly. These were facts well known to the villagers of the time, and handed down by them to their descendants. Emily's appearances in the parsonage pew (the old square box-pew with seats all round) were duly noted by the observant John Greenwood, who recorded that she invariably sat in the seat with its back to the pulpit, looking straight ahead of her. Emily was not prepared to discuss the question of conventional religion with anyone, as Mary Taylor remembered,[2] probably not even with her father. But his own deep-rooted love of nature was a bond between them sufficient to bridge any divergencies of view: there was nothing in her avowed worship of the high places of nature to shock his strong Wesleyan leanings. Had not Wesley, like the Druids whose traces abide about Haworth, chosen to stand under an oak tree or in a natural arena to deliver

[1] John Greenwood's diary cf. Gaskell, 3rd edn., 140-2.
[2] See below, p. 156.

himself of his Gospel of Hope? Mr. Brontë had long ago found that he
could look 'by faith through Nature, to Nature's God'.[1] If his daughter
preferred to worship the Eternal Spirit up on the moors, he saw no evil in
it.

There Emily could escape her mortal condition, and feel at one with the
scene around her. She sought the highest points of the moors where the
heaving miles of heather and bilberry, of bracken and monolithic stones,
lay stretched below. There are two places particularly connected with
Emily Brontë on the moors, made recognizable by her descriptions of
them. One is 'Penistone Crag', as she calls it in *Wuthering Heights*, with
the 'Fairy Cave' beneath, whose local name is Ponden Kirk. At the head
of the valley, the platform of the Kirk juts out so far over the cleavage in
the hills that its shadow falls on the beck beneath; it is a high, isolated spot.
And there is the high and wide plateau of long grasses, stretching above
and beyond the Withins—Tudor farms whose interiors Emily knew well
and introduced into *Wuthering Heights*—leading towards Walshaw Dene.
There she would lie and watch the clouds, which from that altitude appear
to float below one, lulled as she described it, by all the sounds of summer
noon, with only the far-off sound of the church bells to recall her to reality.
Whatever the churchgoers might say, for her the truth was not confined
within sacred precincts:

> Let others seek its beams divine
> In cell or cloister drear;
> But I have found a fairer shrine
> And happier worship here.[2]

At these times of peculiar perception she gained a vision of the essential
oneness of life which she gradually and haltingly communicated in her
poetry. This was the experience above all others which she sought to
describe, and often found that language failed her. The conditions under
which such experiences were possible were not constant; nature, which
revealed so much at times, could not be relied upon to renew the revelation.
Even before going to Brussels, she came to realize that the magic formula
did not always work, and had to put the question squarely to herself:

> Shall Earth no more inspire thee,
> Thou lonely dreamer now? ...

---

[1] *Sermon, in Reference to an Earthquake, preached by the Rev. P. Brontë 12 Sept. 1824
in Haworth Church*, Printed Bradford, 1824.
[2] Hatfield, 137.

Thy mind is ever moving
In regions dark to thee;
Recall its useless roving—
Come back and dwell with me . . .

I've watched thee every hour;
I know my mighty sway,
I know my magic power
To drive thy griefs away.

Few hearts to mortals given
On earth so wildly pine;
Yet none would ask a Heaven
More like this Earth than thine.[1]

Her mind was already reaching forward to the spiritual discoveries of *Wuthering Heights*, and to the sense of Catherine's dream of a heaven that could offer nothing she had not known on earth.

The ideal condition for the soul's release—so hard to recapture each time it was lost—was not always denied her, as the poem, written on 13 April of that year, shows. In it, the completeness of the experience is matched by the poet's ability to express what happened; a year or two back, Emily's joy would have been unclouded. But her joy was no longer wholly independent of her human condition. Just as Keats before her was oppressed by

The weariness, the fever, and the fret
Here, where men sit and hear each other groan,

so Emily's vision of a radiant world was being marred by her growing awareness of humanity's misery. Far though she ranged in spirit, across that 'heaven of glorious spheres', her compassion bound her to earth.

How clear she shines! how quietly
I lie beneath her silver light
While Heaven and Earth are whispering me
'To-morrow wake, but dream to-night.'

Yes, Fancy, come, my Fairy love!
These throbbing temples, softly kiss;
And bend my lonely couch above
And bring me rest and bring me bliss.

[1] Hatfield, 147.

The world is going——Dark world adieu!
Grim world, go hide thee till the day;
The heart thou canst not all subdue
Must still resist if thou delay!

Thy love I will not, will not share;
Thy hatred only wakes a smile;
Thy griefs may wound—thy wrongs may tear,
But, oh, thy lies shall n'er beguile!

While gazing on the stars that glow
Above me in that stormless sea,
I long to hope that all the woe
Creation knows, is held in thee!

And this shall be my dream to-night—
I'll think the heaven of glorious spheres
Is rolling on its course of light
In endless bliss for endless years;

I'll think there's not one world above,
Far as these straining eyes can see,
Where Wisdom ever laughed at Love,
Or Virtue crouched to Infamy;

Where, writhing 'neath the strokes of Fate,
The mangled wretch was forced to smile;
To match his patience 'gainst her hate,
His heart rebellious all the while;

Where Pleasure still will lead to wrong,
And helpless Reason warn in vain;
And Truth is weak and Treachery strong,
And Joy the shortest path to Pain;

And Peace, the lethargy of grief;
And Hope, a phantom of the soul;
And Life, a labour void and brief;
And Death, the despot of the whole![1]

The note of pity struck here was new in her poetry, but from then on it constantly recurs. Looking about her she saw the human condition as a 'brotherhood of misery' whose madness daily turned into agony 'The bliss before my eyes'. Looking into herself to find the old sources of consolation, she saw the same deep division there which cleft the universe in two.

[1] Hatfield, 157.

> So stood I, in Heaven's glorious sun
> And in the glare of Hell—
> My spirit drank a mingled tone
> Of seraph's song and demon's moan—
> What my soul bore my soul alone
> Within its self may tell . . . [1]

Always, in her philosophy, division was at the root of suffering; and, inversely, joy could only be attained by a state of union between the individual and the universe.

In March 1844 she wrote a poem describing a mystical experience of which every detail is sharply defined in terms of sight, sensation, hearing, giving to the incident a factual authentic quality never before achieved in her writing.

> On a sunny brae alone I lay
> One summer afternoon . . .
> Methought the very breath I breathed
> Was full of sparks divine,
> And all my heather-couch was wreathed
> By that celestial shine.
>
> And while the wide Earth echoing rang
> To their strange minstrelsy,
> The little glittering spirits sang,
> Or seemed to sing to me . . .

The message of the 'glittering spirits' was one of jubilation; they told her that death, far from being the tragedy of life, was its one certain bliss.

> 'Let Grief distract the sufferer's breast,
> And Night obscure his way;
> They hasten him to endless rest,
> And everlasting day.
>
> To Thee the world is like a tomb,
> A desert's naked shore;
> To us, in unimagined bloom,
> It brightens more and more.
>
> And could we lift the veil and give
> One brief glimpse to thine eye
> Thou would'st rejoice for those that live,
> Because they live to die.' [2]

[1] Hatfield, 168.   [2] Hatfield, 170.

The Shelleyian symbol of the veil used here by Emily, and the whole concept of death as the fulfilment of life, and not as life's destroyer, must raise the question with readers of both poets—how much, if anything, of Shelley's work had Emily read. In 1833 Medwin's *Life of Shelley* appeared, with extracts from his poems; in S. C. Hall's anthology *The Book of Gems* published in 1838 other titles were included. Finally, despite the long opposition of Sir Timothy Shelley to *any* publication, Shelley's widow succeeded in bringing out the Complete Works in 1839. In anticipation of this, *Fraser's Magazine* for June 1838 carried a long appreciation of Shelley which Emily had the opportunity to read; *Fraser's* critic, even while deploring the 'atheism' of Shelley, paid tribute to his goodness, comparing him to Plato in being not alone 'a sublime poet, but amongst the most virtuous of men'.[1] A direct reference to Shelley was made by Charlotte in an unpublished novelette written between July and December 1839, which indicates how quickly the young Brontës had assimilated even such a work as *Prometheus*. 'However, time is advancing,' wrote Charlotte, 'and the hours, those "wild-eyed charioteers" as Shelley calls them—are driving on.'[2]

Fraser's comparison of Shelley to Plato serves to remind us of the difference in degree, if not in kind, that separated the work of the two romantic poets. While Shelley wrote on a range of subjects, social, scientific, and political which remained beyond Emily's compass, in spiritual experience they were equals. A common vision informed their work even if Shelley's Platonism derived from a long study of the Greek philosophers whilst Emily's was purely intuitive and personal. If, untaught as she was, she thought and wrote at times like Shelley, it was out of a natural sympathy: the lines quoted above could be an echo of Shelley's

> Die, If thou wouldst be with that which thou dost seek . . .
> No more let Life divide what Death can bring together . . .[3]

and again:

> Death is the veil which those that live call life;
> They sleep, and it is lifted . . .[4]

Both poets found the same image for the absolute of love: 'How beyond refuge I am thine,' wrote Shelley. 'Ah me! I am not thine; I am a part of

---

[1] *Fraser's* June 1838.
[2] 'Caroline Vernon', Harvard Univ. Library. Lines from *Prometheus Unbound*, II. 4. 132.
[3] *Adonais*, lii, liii. [4] *Prometheus Unbound*, III, iii. 113.

thee'[1]—which Emily Brontë equalled with Catherine Earnshaw's declaration: 'Whatever our souls are made of, his and mine are the same ... Nelly, I *am* Heathcliff.'[2] Parallels spring to mind between Shelley's 'Night' and Emily's 'Stars', between *Adonais* and *Epipsychidion* and Emily's 'Death that struck', between Shelley's 'Ode to the West Wind' and Emily's lines:

> And thou art now a spirit pouring
> Thy presence into all ...
>
> A universal influence
> From Thine own influence free;
> A principle of life, intense,
> Lost to mortality.[3]

And above all, between *Prometheus* and *Wuthering Heights*, in the whole concept of redemption by love.

It could be claimed that the resemblance between the two poets went beyond their philosophy; in character they were alike—both were 'tameless and swift and proud'. Both placed personal freedom above material good; both were oppressed by humanity's plight—Emily's 'Brotherhood of misery, With smiles as sad as sighs'.[4] Both sought comfort not here, but in eternity.

So long as nothing came to undermine the promise of the 'little glittering spirits' of Emily's 'Day-dream', she lived in its reflected light, often attaining to a state of rapture. How transfigured she appeared at such times has been recorded by John Greenwood, who met her one morning returning from the moors. The poor man never forgot the experience (he was something of a cripple and a chronic invalid and susceptible to kindness) because, he said, 'in her rapture' she acknowledged his greeting with a great 'sweetness of manner ... Her countenance was lit up with a divine light. Had she been holding converse with Angels, it would not have shone brighter. It appeared to me, holy, heavenly.'[5]

---

[1] *Epipsychidion*, lines 51–3.   [2] *Wuthering Heights*, ch. 9.
[3] Hatfield, 148.   [4] Hatfield, 168.
[5] John Greenwood's diary.

CHAPTER XII

'THE WORLD WITHOUT'

CHARLOTTE BRONTË later told Mrs. Gaskell that there were many touches in the portrait of Shirley that were directly taken from the character of Emily; that some incidents in the novel had their origin in fact. One of the most memorable of these is the incident of the mad dog.[1] True to character, Emily tried to befriend a lost dog hurrying up the lane 'with hanging head and lolling tongue', offered it a draught of water, and got bitten for her pains. Whether informed or not, as was Shirley, of the villagers' suspicion that the dog was mad, Emily went straight into the kitchen and branded the wound with one of Tabby's 'red-hot Italian irons'.[2] Like Shirley, she told no one what had happened till the danger was past. Such an action, in the narrow confines of the parsonage, would have been difficult when her sisters were at home; it is more likely therefore to have occurred during the year when all were away, and Mr. Brontë's failing sight made him less observant than he once had been. The action, calling for resolution of no common kind, is perfectly in character with the author of *Wuthering Heights*. Time, and her own brooding vision of the nature of things—as some of her French essays had already shown—was further strengthening and tempering her naturally daring character.

It had other sides to it, that her sister equally captured in the portrayal of Shirley. Of Shirley we read how, in a restless mood, 'a sudden thought calls her upstairs; perhaps she goes to seek some just-then-remembered old ivory-backed needlebook, or older china-topped workbox, quite un-needed, but which seems at the moment indispensable.'[3] This aspect of Emily, acting in a purposeless way at times, is the more convincing because the articles mentioned were named in Miss Branwell's will as legacies to Emily.

Like his children, Mr. Brontë was passionately fond of music. This was the time when Emily's playing on the little upright piano in his study became so intimate a language between these two silent people that when

---

[1] *Shirley*, ch. 28.   [2] Gaskell, 148.   [3] *Shirley*, ch. 22.

she was dead he could not bear its presence there, and had it carried up-stairs out of sight. Her music books show that she played Beethoven, Mozart, Haydn.

Mary Taylor spoke of Emily lying on the hearthrug 'while the other friends discussed questions of religion'; Emily's only contribution was a laconic 'that's right' when Mary claimed that it concerned merely God and oneself.[1] Ellen Nussey described Emily as habitually kneeling on the hearth, reading a book, with her arm round Keeper; both recollections are confirmed by Charlotte's picture of Shirley:

After tea Shirley reads, and she is just about as tenacious of her book as she is lax of her needle. Her study is the rug, her seat a footstool, or perhaps only the carpet. . . . The tawny and lion-like bulk of Tartar is ever stretched beside her; his negro muzzle laid on his fore-paws, straight, strong, and shapely as the limbs of an Alpine wolf. One hand of the mistress generally reposes on the loving serf's rude head, because if she takes it away he groans and is discontented.[2]

The limitations put on Mr. Brontë by his failing sight were of course increased by the long winters—worse and more lasting up in his moorland parish than down in the towns. In February (1844) he wrote to old friends and parishioners: 'I have understood that your son and heir has met with an accident. For this I am very sorry, and as soon as the snow goes away I shall do myself the pleasure of seeing how you all are. As my eyes are very weak, I cannot very well go out whilst the snow is on the ground.'[3]

Mr. Brontë's troubles seldom came singly. While the approach of blindness halted many of his activities, he found that his obligatory with-drawal from many parish duties and longer daily confinement to his home had started rumours in the village that he had taken to drink and was spending his days toping in his study, which the gossipmongers averred smelt of whisky. One of his churchwardens, another Mr. Greenwood, called with his wife to warn him of the malicious tales being spread.

The fact was that Mr. Brontë's doctor, Mr. Milligan, had prescribed an eye lotion which, with a little ill-will, could be said to smell of alcohol. Mr. Brontë had very particularly asked the doctor to sign each prescription afresh, but the 'pernicious censures of the weak—wicked—and wily—often on the alert to censure those who are wiser and better than them-selves'[4] persisted, as Mr. Brontë learnt from his churchwarden. While

---

[1] Gaskell, 140–2.   [2] *Shirley*, ch. 22.
[3] Mr. Brontë to George Taylor, Esq.; Stanbury. Lock and Dixon, *A Man of Sorrow*, 340.
[4] See his letter in *A Man of Sorrow*, 374.

his language was that of the old-world evangelicals he knew how to hit back. Writing to Mr. Greenwood on 4 October 1843, he said:

> Since you and Mrs. Greenwood called on me on a particular occasion, I have been particularly and more than ever guarded. Yet notwithstanding all I have done, even to the injury of my health, they keep propagating false reports. I mean to single out one or two of these slanderers, and to prosecute them, as the Law directs. I have lately been using a lotion for my eyes, which are very weak, and they have ascribed the smell of that to a smell of a more objectionable character. These things are hard to bear but perhaps under Providence I may live to overcome them all.[1]

Slander dies very slowly in villages, where the flavour of life is chiefly maintained by its propagation. Thus the tales of Mr. Brontë's predilection for whisky were still being bandied about in the 1880s when Mary Duclaux was investigating for her memoir of Emily Brontë: she was informed then that 'the old man, so Emily feared, acquired the habit of drinking, though not to excess, yet more than his abstemious past allowed. . . . But Emily grew afraid, alone at Haworth . . . knowing herself deficient in that controlling influence so characteristic of her elder sister. Her burden of doubt was more than she could bear. She decided to write to Charlotte.'[2]

This highly uncharacteristic conduct ascribed to the forceful Emily is contradicted by the sisters' correspondence. Emily was so far from re-calling Charlotte that she left her in doubt whether her return would be welcome to herself and their father: 'Tell me', Charlotte wrote to her on 1 October 1843, 'whether Papa really wants me very much to come home, and whether you do likewise. I have an idea that I should be of no use there—a sort of aged person upon the parish.' She had already declared that she had 'no thought of coming home just now. I lack a real pretext for doing so.'[3]

The story of Mr. Brontë's addiction to spirits only merits attention for its bearing on the reputation of the author of *Wuthering Heights*, whose first readers refused to believe it the work of a young woman on the score that its degraded characters and scenes of violence were wholly outside a woman's experience, and could not have been written without a male collaborator. Emily was not unaware of the stories going round about her father's drunkenness; nor was she uninformed of each and every of her brother's hapless falls from grace: but it is very evident that she did not send for Charlotte.

[1] *A Man of Sorrow*, 375.   [2] Duclaux, 109.   [3] W & S, i. 305.

In the event, it was not Emily but Mary Taylor who prevailed on Charlotte to go home. Mary's advice, sent from Germany, and prompted by some knowledge of Charlotte's feelings for M. Heger, came in the nick of time to save her from an emotional breakdown. Until her return Emily knew nothing of this development although intimations of her state of mind—ascribed always to 'homesickness'—appeared at intervals in her letters.

This is Sunday morning [she wrote to Emily on 1 October 1843]. They are at their idolatrous 'messe', and I am here i.e. in the réfectoire. I should like uncommonly to be in the dining-room at home, or in the kitchen or in the back-kitchen. I should like, even, to be cutting up the hash, with the Clerk and some registry people at the other table, and you standing by, watching that I put enough flour and not too much pepper, and, above all, that I save the best pieces of the leg of mutton for Tiger and Keeper, the first of which personages would be jumping about the dish and carving knife, and the latter standing like a devouring flame on the kitchen floor. To complete the picture, Tabby blowing the fire, in order to boil the potatoes to a sort of vegetable glue! Yet I have no thought of coming home just now.[1]

Far more puzzling to the unsuspecting Emily was the account of the impulse that drove Charlotte to confess herself to a Roman Catholic priest in the church of Ste Gudule. Confess herself of what, Emily might well ask? 'I think you had better not tell papa of this,' Charlotte concluded her account. 'He will not understand that it was only a freak, and will perhaps think I am going to turn Catholic.'[2]

The speed with which Charlotte acted when she had once made up her mind to leave Brussels, shows clearly enough that it was a flight. By then, the envenomed situation with Mme Heger made even the benevolent M. Heger see the wisdom of her departure; there were no scenes, no opposition to overcome this time. Charlotte wrote to Emily on 19 December to announce her decision, and to ask her as her 'banker' to send money for the journey.

Brussels, December 19th, 1843

Dear E. J.—I have taken my determination. I hope to be at home the day after New Year's Day. I have told Mme. Heger. But in order to come home I shall be obliged to draw on my cash for another £5. I have only £3. at present, and as there are several little things I should like to buy before I leave Brussels—which you know cannot be got as well in England—£3. would not suffice. Low spirits have afflicted me much lately but I hope all will be well when I get home,—

[1] W & S, i. 305. [2] SLL, i. 270-1.

above all, if I find papa and you and B. and A. well. I am not ill in body. It is only the mind which is a trifle shaken—for want of comfort.

I shall try to cheer up now.—Good-bye.   C. B.[1]

The Hegers, who were equally resolved to avoid a scandal, and to avoid hurting Charlotte's feelings, resumed towards her in those last days— outwardly at least—the cordial relations that had existed at the beginning; on 10 December she went with them to a concert (which figured years later in *Villette*), was given parting gifts of books, and a Teaching Diploma from the Athénée Royal by M. Heger. At parting, moreover he promised to send his little girls as pupils to the school she was eventually going to open, and authorized her to correspond. Much as she suffered at parting from him, she was left with the hope that the friendship would be lasting, even that she might visit Brussels again. Mme Heger scrupulously ful- filled her obligations by accompanying her to the ship, which sailed from Ostend on Tuesday 2 January 1844. Charlotte travelling non-stop reached home the next day.

Emily's year alone with her father had ended. It had brought her, with the gift of liberty and solitude, the peace in which to find herself. The new year shows her collecting her poems in two carefully kept notebooks, as if in acknowledgement of the fact that, at last, she knew the worth of what she was writing. No more unpretentious receptacles for great poetry exist than the limp-backed, wine-coloured, faintly lined notebooks (they have been compared to laundry books) in which she set about copying her verse in the cryptic writing that she had evolved. From the old much- scored notebook and from the scattered scraps of paper on which she had jotted down the lines and verses as they had come in the past, she selected those poems she intended to keep. Though the actual copying began only in February (at a time of renewed tranquillity in the house) the purpose was clearly formed before, and the final division made between her Gondal Poems which she copied into one notebook and clearly marked 'Emily Jane Brontë. GONDAL POEMS', and the poems that were not about Gondal copied into another, and whose purely personal character is thus established. Her later violent opposition to the idea of publishing the poems does not necessarily prove she never intended doing so; it only proves that she did not feel ready to do so then, and wished for time before communicating her most secret experiences to other people. The action of collecting her poems did not in fact mean that she was even ready

[1] Ibid., 274.

to show them to her sisters, but merely that she knew they were worth preserving.

Mary Visick, in her admirable study of *Wuthering Heights*,[1] has pointed out how the Gondal poems were not copied in chronological order of composition, but grouped in sequences relating to the characters and subjects of which they treated, as though Emily were already then planning some further use for her main characters in another context. The grouping defined the attitudes of the protagonists towards each other—Augusta divided in her numerous loves for the two totally dissimilar types of men, whose strongly marked traits could be said to prefigure the gentle Edgar Linton and the ruthless Heathcliff.

For a time, after Charlotte's return, the mere fact of reunion with the sisters and brother filled the house with animation; Anne and Branwell were home for the Christmas holidays, and they had a year's news to exchange. Even after Anne and Branwell returned to Thorp Green, the full nature of Charlotte's anguish did not appear. She paid a long visit to Ellen Nussey in March but looked so ill that on her return Ellen enquired anxiously after her health.

It was not until the beginning of April, when a spell of 'delightful weather' drew Charlotte and Emily out on to the moors, that the secret came out; only then did Charlotte begin to confide in Emily the tale of her sorrows.

Parting from M. Heger was not the worst of them; sooner or later she must have left Brussels to open her own school. What tormented her was his silence as time passed, and no letter came in reply to her unwise repeated appeals. She suspected her letters were intercepted by Madame; and equally feared they were disregarded by Monsieur. Whatever the cause of the silence, she could not bear it, and must write at every opportunity. It eased her heart to speak to Emily. They walked out daily on the moors 'to the great damage of our shoes, but I hope to the benefit of our health'.[2]

To Emily, Charlotte's partial confidences can have appeared not very different from Anne's; both were suffering heartbreak on account of the men they loved, and there was no cure for either. Willie Weightman was dead, and M. Heger married.

Her sisters' tragic loves were affording her insight into an as yet unexplored region of human experience. By contrast, the flirtations of the lamented Willie Weightman appeared anodyne indeed. Fresh instances of

<hr />

[1] *The Genesis of Wuthering Heights*, Hong Kong University Press, 1958.
[2] CB to Ellen Nussey, 7 Apr .1844. *SLL*, i. 279.

the levity generally brought to the subject of love were given her that year when Ellen Nussey visited the parsonage again and became, as before, the centre of conspicuous attentions from Mr. Brontë's curate, Mr. Weightman's successor, the Revd. James William Smith.

Mr. Smith's calculating courtship of Ellen Nussey in the mistaken belief that she had money once again caught the unworldly inhabitants of Haworth parsonage unprepared.

I certainly cherished a dream during your stay [Charlotte wrote to Ellen afterwards], but the dream is dissipating. Mr. Smith has not mentioned your name since you left, except once when papa said you were a nice girl, he said, 'Yes, she is a nice girl—rather quiet. I suppose she has money.' . . . I think the words speak volumes . . . Papa has two or three times expressed a fear that since Mr. Smith paid you so much attention he will perhaps have made an impression on your mind which will interfere with your comfort. I tell him I think not. . . . Still, he keeps saying that I am to write to you and dissuade you from thinking of him. I never saw papa make himself so uneasy about a thing of this kind before; he is usually very sarcastic on such subjects.[1]

Mr. Brontë's sarcasm may well have been the source of Emily's generally scornful attitude to the flirtations going on around her; they were, as yet, her only experience of what was termed 'love', experiences which were not calculated to heighten her respect for social conventions. What she had read in Byron and in the Border Ballads applied to creatures of an altogether higher and more heroic cast, far more in keeping with her own feelings of uncompromising possessiveness that brooked no half measures. Mr. Smith's obnoxious conduct eventually won him the honour of being pilloried in *Shirley*, in the character of the rampageous Irish curate Peter Augustus Malone.

The problem of the girls' future livelihood remained, with the further complication of their father's increasing blindness. To leave him now to set up a school on the east coast was no longer possible. Inactivity only heightened Charlotte's unhappiness, and she cast around to find what, in conscience, she could allow herself to do. With whom the idea originated of converting a part of the parsonage to the uses of a school has never been told, but its good sense immediately recommended it to Charlotte. Mr. Brontë's consent must, of course, have been procured, and the legacies of their aunt advanced to make it practicable. By the time the summer holidays arrived and Anne and Branwell were home once more (by 23 June), the plan was formed. Ellen Nussey, staying at the parsonage during the

[1] 5 Apr. 1844. *SLL*, i. 278-9.

first fortnight of July, was called upon to advise on the project. It was a practical proposal and no dream-fabric, and Ellen undertook to get them pupils. On the model of the Pensionnat Heger Charlotte drew up school circulars, fixing the terms and specifying the subjects to be taught, and the extras offered. It was something to do, and she threw herself energetically into it. It was also something to write about to M. Heger, an unexceptionable subject on which to consult his expertise and one with which even Madame could not find fault. Charlotte wrote to him on 24 July:

I have a plan. Our parsonage is a fairly big house—with a few alterations there would be room for five or six boarders. If I could find this number of children of good family, I would devote myself to their education. Emily does not care much for teaching, but she would look after the house-keeping and, although something of a recluse, she is too good-hearted not to do all in her power for the well-being of the children. Moreover, she is very generous.[1]

From Charlotte's reference here, and in every following reference to the school, Emily's backing seems to have been fully gained from the outset; there is no sign at this stage of her failing to give Charlotte all the support she wanted. Charlotte included her in every allusion to the venture. She wrote to Ellen Nussey on 2 October: 'I, Emily and Anne are truly obliged to you for the efforts you have made on our behalf, and if you have not been successful, you are only like ourselves. Every one wishes us well, but there are no pupils to be had. We have no present intention, however, of breaking our hearts on the subject, still less of feeling mortified at defeat.'[2] By mid-November, when it was obvious nothing could or would come of the plan that year, Charlotte wrote to Ellen again:

We have made no alterations yet in our house. It would be folly to do so while there is so little likelihood of our ever getting pupils. I fear you are giving yourself too much trouble on our account. Depend on it, if you were to persuade a mamma to bring her child to Haworth, the aspect of the place would frighten her, and she would probably take the dear girl back with her instanter. . . . We are glad that we made the attempt, and we will not be cast down because it has not succeeded.[3]

To see the change that came over Emily the following year in its right perspective, it is important to note the part she took in Charlotte's plans, and indeed in all the domestic arrangements throughout 1844. From every reference to her, she appears in the role of an alert, helpful companion.

Whatever the intensity of her life within, outwardly Emily never showed herself more conciliating, more co-operative than in the year following Charlotte's return from Brussels. She put no difficulties in the way of the school-plan; she saw its good sense, its practical possibilities. How practical Emily could be, Charlotte learnt to her surprise when, on returning to England, she heard of the way in which she had dealt with the investment of their small capital in railway stock. 'Emily has made herself mistress of the necessary degree of knowledge for conducting the matter,' Charlotte wrote to Miss Wooler on 23 April 1845,[1] 'by dint of carefully reading every paragraph and every advertisement in the newspapers that related to railroads, and as we have abstained from gambling, all mere speculative buying-in and selling-out—we have got on very decently.' When in the following year Hudson's company threatened bankruptcy and for a time the Brontës' small investments seemed in danger, Charlotte again spoke of Emily's capable management: 'Emily managed in a most handsome and able manner for me when I was at Brussels and prevented by distance from looking after my own interests . . .'[2]

After Branwell had been home for the holidays, Emily sat with Charlotte 'shirt-making' for him and 'stuck to it pretty closely' for days. She showed herself friendly and forthcoming to Ellen Nussey, and endorsed Charlotte's invitation to her to stay at the parsonage early in July. She was vitally interested in the fortunes of 'Flossy junior', the little bitch they gave Ellen to take home, and anxious at her delay in sending news of it. She was pleased with the flower-seeds Ellen sent her, and wanted to know if they were hardy or delicate, and where they should be sown, 'in warm or sheltered situations?' She read the French newspapers lent by Joe Taylor, and read them promptly, so that they could be forwarded to Ellen within five days.

Her sympathy, though silent, must have made itself felt, since Charlotte confided in her constantly about M. Heger; and only deprived herself of that 'consolation', as she wrote to him eventually, in an attempt to forget him. 'J'ai tout fait,' she wrote in November 1845, 'j'ai cherché les occupations, je me suis interdit absolument le plaisir de parler de vous—même à Emilie mais je n'ai pu vaincre ni mes regrets ni mon impatience—c'est humiliant cela—.'[3] The sense of the humiliation of not being able to conquer her feelings may well have been pointed out to her by Emily; but

[1] Allbutt Coll., Fitzwilliam Museum, Cambridge.
[2] 30 Jan. 1846. _SLL_, i. 315; Allbutt Coll., Fitzwilliam Museum, Cambridge.
[3] Heger letters, BM.

that Emily was her rock, her mainstay throughout that time, is plain to see.

How Emily saw these things can only indirectly be divined. It can never be supposed that the author of *Wuthering Heights* was impervious to the sight of her sisters' sufferings; the dependence of the lover on the beloved corresponded to her own dependence on her visions. Charlotte was going the way of Anne, whose grief for the death of Willie Weightman was bearing her down, despite her heroic efforts to hide its traces. Her life at the Robinsons, too, was devoid of all consolations; it wounded her sensitive nature, crushed her to the point of revolt. In the end flyleaf to her Prayer-book is the angry pencilled comment: 'sick of mankind and their disgusting ways', a statement which explains, if nothing else does, how 'gentle Anne' came to write *The Tenant of Wildfell Hall*. Experience was changing Anne, as no doubt Emily found each time she came home for the holidays. Life was not dealing kindly with either sister.

Charlotte's letter to M. Heger of 24 July remained unanswered. A further pretext to write offered itself when Joe Taylor went to Belgium and Charlotte wrote again on 24 October: 'For six months I have been waiting for a letter from Monsieur. . . . However, I do not complain and I shall be richly rewarded for a little sorrow if you will write a letter and give it to this gentleman—or to his sister—who will hand it to me without fail.'[1] There was no reply to this letter either. As the year drew to its close, Charlotte awaited Joe's return (Mary was due back also), convincing herself that the reply which M. Heger hesitated to commit to the post, for fear of interception by his wife, would be delivered by hand. Joe's business trip was prolonged and he went on to Switzerland; still Charlotte waited. The school-plan was definitely shelved; there was nothing else for her to think of but her sorrow. Night and day, as she wrote M. Heger in the New Year, she 'found neither rest nor peace'. When she slept, she was 'disturbed by tormenting dreams, in which I see you, always severe, always grave, always incensed against me'.[2]

No news of any kind came to cheer her. She knew that Mary Taylor was emigrating to New Zealand in the new year, and that her return to England was only to take farewell of her family and friends. Ellen Nussey left her without news for many weeks that autumn, and when it came, it was to announce that her favourite brother, George, had gone mad and was put under medical care. (He never recovered.) The atmosphere of crushing gloom surrounding Charlotte and permeating the parsonage,

---

[1] Heger letters, BM.   [2] Heger letters, BM.

has to be realized to appreciate the two major poems Emily wrote that autumn, to explain why she felt the need, at that precise time, to take her stand and make her declaration of faith. The burden of both poems can be summed up in the lines

> So hopeless is the world without
> The world within I doubly prize.

Significantly enough, the title of the poem is 'To Imagination'.

> When weary with the long day's care,
> And earthly change from pain to pain,
> And lost, and ready to despair,
> Thy kind voice calls me back again—
> O my true friend, I am not lone
> While thou canst speak with such a tone!
>
> So hopeless is the world without,
> The world within I doubly prize;
> Thy world where guile and hate and doubt
> And cold suspicion never rise;
> Where thou and I and Liberty
> Have undisputed sovereignty.
>
> What matters it that all around
> Danger and grief and darkness lie,
> If but within our bosom's bound
> We hold a bright unsullied sky,
> Warm with ten thousand mingled rays
> Of suns that know no winter days?
>
> Reason indeed may oft complain
> For Nature's sad reality,
> And tell the suffering heart how vain
> Its cherished dreams must always be;
> And Truth may rudely trample down
> The flowers of Fancy newly blown.
>
> But thou art ever there to bring
> The hovering visions back and breathe
> New glories o'er the blighted spring
> And call a lovelier life from death,
> And whisper with a voice divine
> Of real worlds as bright as thine.

> I trust not to thy phantom bliss,
> Yet still in evening's quiet hour
> With never-failing thankfulness
> I welcome thee, benignant power,
> Sure solacer of human cares,
> And brighter hope when hope despairs.[1]

Barely six weeks separated that poem from the next, written on 14 October (it remained without a title), but obviously Emily's faith had received a battering in the interval. She was in evident need of reassurance. Like an accused prisoner in the dock, she calls on her confederates to defend her choice of the life of the imagination in defiance of the real one, and even while calling on her 'God of Visions' for protection, trembles lest he should desert her. The Power, of which she had had mystic perception, was, she declared, within herself, and therefore should not fail her. The tragedy of Emily Brontë, as her last years show, did not lie in an early death or literary failure; but in the loss of her 'God of Visions', in the departure of her 'radiant angel' when she most needed him.

> O thy bright eyes must answer now
> When Reason, with a scornful brow,
> Is mocking at my overthrow;
> O thy sweet tongue must plead for me
> And tell why I have chosen thee!
>
> Stern Reason is to judgement come
> Arrayed in all her forms of gloom:
> Wilt thou my advocate be dumb?
> No, radiant angel, speak and say
> Why I did cast the world away;
>
> Why I have persevered to shun
> The common paths that others run;
> And on a strange road journeyed on
> Heedless alike of Wealth and Power—
> Of Glory's wreath and Pleasure's flower.
>
> These once indeed seemed Beings divine,
> And they perchance heard vows of mine
> And saw my offerings on their shrine—
> But careless gifts are seldom prized,
> And mine were worthily despised;

[1] Hatfield, 174.

So with a ready heart I swore
To seek their altar-stone no more;
And gave my spirit to adore
Thee, ever present, phantom thing—
My slave, my comrade, and my King!

A slave because I rule thee still;
Incline thee to my changeful will
And make thy influence good or ill—
A comrade, for by day and night
Thou art my intimate delight—

My Darling Pain that wounds and sears
And wrings a blessing out from tears
By deadening me to real cares;
And yet, a king—though prudence well
Have taught thy subject to rebel.

And am I wrong to worship where
Faith cannot doubt nor Hope despair
Since my own soul can grant my prayer?
Speak, God of Visions, plead for me
And tell why I have chosen thee![1]

In the first week of January 1845, Mary Taylor visited Haworth on her
return from Brussels; she brought neither message nor letter from M.
Heger. For three months Charlotte had waited first for Joe's return, then
for Mary's, absolutely confident that after so long a silence M. Heger
would write at last. Under the rebuff, she wrote to him immediately, on
8 January, a stinging letter in which for the first time her scorn and anger
blazed.

You will say once again that I am hysterical—that I have black thoughts, etc.
So be it, Monsieur. . . . All I know is that I cannot, that I will not, resign myself
to lose wholly the friendship of my master. I would rather suffer the greatest
physical pain than always have my heart torn by intolerable regrets. . . . Monsieur,
the poor have not need of much to sustain them—they ask only for the crumbs
that fall from the rich man's table. But if they are refused the crumbs they die of
hunger . . . I shall not re-read this letter. I send it as it is written. Nevertheless,
I have a shrewd idea that there are some people, cold and commonsensical, who
in reading it would say: 'She is talking nonsense.' I would avenge myself on such
persons in no other way than by wishing them one single day of the torments
which I have suffered for eight months. We should then see if they did not talk
nonsense also. One suffers in silence so long as one has the strength to do so, and

[1] Hatfield, 176.

when that strength gives out one speaks without too carefully measuring one's words. I wish Monsieur happiness and prosperity.[1]

In early February Charlotte went over to Hunsworth, the Taylors' home, to take leave of Mary. The meeting and the parting were intensely sad. Mary later told Mrs. Gaskell how she had urged Charlotte to leave home and seek new interests elsewhere. Charlotte agreed that she would like any change at first, as she had liked Brussels at first, that 'she thought there must be some possibility for some people of having a life of more variety and more communion with human kind, but she saw none for her.'[2] And she did not take Mary's advice. However gloomy the future might be she was resolved to face it at home.

In the blank left by Mary's departure in mid-March, in the comparisons she could not help making between Mary's adventurous life and kindling prospects and her own disappointments, Charlotte sank into a condition of hopeless lethargy. She wrote to Ellen Nussey on 24 March:

I can hardly tell you how time gets on here at Haworth. There is no event whatever to mark its progress—one day resembles another—and all have heavy, lifeless physiognomies—Sunday—baking-day and Saturday are the only ones that bear the slightest distinctive mark—meantime time wears away—I shall soon be 30—and I have done nothing yet—Sometimes I get melancholy—at the prospect before and behind me— . . . There was a time when Haworth was a very pleasant place to me, it is not so now. I feel as if we were all buried here— I long to travel, to work, to live a life of action.[3]

The failure of the school-plan not only deprived her of an occupation, but it left the future unprovided for. Obviously Charlotte and Emily talked over their financial position and came to the conclusion that they might do well to take out life annuities. As on the question of setting up a school, Charlotte applied to Miss Wooler for practical advice; Miss Wooler had done it all before them. Miss Wooler's reply brought an interesting statement on their affairs from Charlotte:

Both Emily and I thank you for the kind promptitude with which you answered my last letter and for the clear information contained in your reply. We have written to Mr. Bignold. He says the terms for female lives are very low he can offer $4\frac{1}{2}\%$ for annuities purchased at 25—and 5% for those purchased at 30. As you say—an advantage so trifling would scarcely compensate for the loss of the principal. Our rail-road investment is not threatened with immediate danger —and as we have none of us quite attained the age of thirty, we think it best to take a twelve month to consider the matter. . . . We have never hitherto consulted

---

[1] Heger letters, BM.   [2] Gaskell, 190.   [3] *SLL*, i. 291–2.

any one but you on our affairs—nor have we told any one else of the degree of success our small capital has met with, because after all, there is nothing so uncertain as rail-roads; the price of shares varies continually—and any day a small shareholder may find his funds shrunk to their original dimensions. Emily has made herself mistress of the necessary degree of knowledge for conducting the matter . . . we have got on very decently.[1]

Emily's ability on the stock-market if not vouched for by her sister Charlotte could barely be credited in the light of the poetry she was writing at that very time—yet it must not be forgotten that the commentators on *Wuthering Heights* have always rated the legal and financial dealings in the tale to be sound.

Almost uninterruptedly, from February to June, she was writing poetry of a high speculative order, the result, it would seem, less of flashes of inspiration than of long concentrated thought. At times, she ranged so far afield in uncharted regions that the return to consciousness was an agony, and the heat of the risen sun a blinding pain. Summer nights at Haworth are an interval of scented darkness, always fresh, often chill. When the temperature drops after a cloudless day, the stars are exceptionally clear and seem peculiarly close. To Emily Brontë lying on her low camp bed under the window of her narrow room, the crowded heaven of stars was an ocean of strong currents, impelling her away, a universe whose harmony was unbroken, because one spirit permeated all.

> All through the night, your glorious eyes
> Were gazing down in mine,
> And with a full heart's thankful sighs
> I blessed that watch divine!
>
> I was at peace, and drank your beams
> As they were life to me
> And revelled in my changeful dreams
> Like petrel on the sea.
>
> Thought followed thought—star followed star
> Through boundless regions on,
> While one sweet influence, near and far,
> Thrilled through and proved us one.
>
> Why did the morning rise to break
> So great, so pure a spell,
> And scorch with fire the tranquil cheek
> Where your cool radiance fell?

[1] C. B. to Miss Wooler, 23 Apr. 1845; Allbutt Coll., Fitzwilliam Museum, Cambridge.

Blood-red he rose, and arrow-straight
His fierce beams struck my brow;
The soul of Nature sprang elate,
But mine sank sad and low . . .

I turned me to the pillow then
To call back Night, and see
Your worlds of solemn light, again
Throb with my heart and me! . . .

O Stars and Dreams and Gentle Night;
O Night and Stars return!
And hide me from the hostile light
That does not warm, but burn— . . .[1]

There were few changes on the domestic scene. Having succeeded in
getting rid of the obnoxious Mr. Smith, Mr. Brontë engaged a new curate;
he was the Revd. Arthur Bell Nicholls, another graduate from Dublin,
who took up his duties in the parish on 25 May. Writing the next day to
the former Sunday-school teacher, Mr. Rand, on her father's behalf,
Charlotte said of him: 'he appears a respectable young man and reads
well.'[2]

In early June Ellen Nussey's brother Henry, recently married, was to
take up a new living at Hathersage in Derbyshire, and Ellen went to put
his house in order. Aware of Charlotte's restless state of mind, she invited
her to join her there. The opportune arrival home of Anne and Branwell
for the summer holidays made it possible for Charlotte to accept the
proposal, and she went to Derbyshire on 26 June and stayed there till 19
July. Before leaving home she learnt one satisfactory piece of news: Anne
had given notice to her employers, and had come home for good.

Causes enough had long existed to prompt Anne to leave Thorp Green,
and her decision to do so at last need not be greatly queried by her family.
She could give them a sufficient one in the conduct of the eldest Miss
Robinson, Lydia Mary, now aged twenty, whose reckless love affair with
a Scarborough actor, Henry Roxby, promised to bring ruin on her, as
indeed it shortly did. Lydia eloped on 20 October, and was cut out of her
father's will in consequence. Anne had long been unable to control her
former pupil, but still felt morally responsible for the younger girls, in a
home where their mother's influence increasingly counted for nothing.
The causes of the children's insubordination were so bound up with

[1] 14 Apr. 1845. Hatfield, 184.   [2] SBC, 439–40.

Branwell's concerns that Anne could not openly discuss them. Mr. Robinson's cash-accounts for the period show that Anne received her last month's salary on the day she left Thorp Green, 11 June, and that Branwell, whose salary was not due till 21 July (as Mr. Robinson carefully noted), was also paid that day the sum of £20. This should have been intimation enough for the dismissal to come, but Branwell had his own reasons for suppressing the knowledge of it from his family.

Charlotte went away to Hathersage in ignorance of the impending blow, and Anne continued to keep her own counsel. Too happy in her return home and the companionship of Emily to anticipate misfortune, Anne was obviously the moving spirit in a short excursion she and Emily took together just after Charlotte's departure for Hathersage. Their original plan was for an outing to Scarborough but for reasons which Charlotte could not at the time understand it was altered to York. The Robinsons were at Scarborough; much as Anne loved the place and obviously wanted Emily to see it, she could not risk meeting them. From the account of the outing written both by Emily and by Anne in their diary-notes of 30 July we can see Emily's wholehearted and carefree enjoyment of the expedition, her willing submission to Anne's direction in the whole affair, and Anne's own disillusioned state of mind. As it turned out, the journey to York was to prove about the last carefree occasion of their lives.

The excursion lasted barely three days, but in Emily's account of it, it assumed large proportions: 'Anne and I went our first long journey by ourselves together,' she wrote on her birthday, 30 July, 'in leaving home on the 30th June, Monday, sleeping at York, returning to Keighley Tuesday evening, sleeping there and walking home on Wednesday morning. Though the weather was broken we enjoyed ourselves very much, except during a few hours at Bradford.'[1] The stop at Bradford meant either duty calls on old friends of Mr. Brontë's—'Uncle Morgan' and Anne's godmother, Miss Outhwaite, who both lived in the Manningham district—or necessary shopping, which was equally abhorrent to Emily.

Ellen Nussey told Mary Duclaux years later about such a shopping expedition to Bradford at which she was present with Charlotte when Emily bought herself a gown-length:

she chose a white stuff patterned with lilac thunder and lightning, to the scarcely-concealed horror of her more sober companions. And she looked well in it; a tall, lithe creature, with a grace half-queenly, half-untamed in her sudden supple movements, wearing with picturesque negligence her ample purple-splashed skirts; her face clear and pale; her very dark and plenteous brown hair fastened up behind with a Spanish comb; her large grey-hazel eyes, now full of indolent, indulgent humour, now glimmering with hidden meanings, now quickened into flame by a flash of indignation, 'a red ray piercing the dew'.[1]

Contentment was Emily's predominant state of mind following Anne's return. This is apparent in her account of their journey, during which, she zestfully reported, they played at Gondal like two teenagers—'during our excursion we were Ronald Macalgin, Henry Angora, Juliet Augusteena, Rosabella Esmaldan, Ella and Julian Egremont, Catherine Navarre, and Cordelia Fitzaphnold, escaping from the palaces of instruction to join the Royalists who are hard driven at present by the victorious Republicans. The Gondals still flourish bright as ever.'[2] The happy mood is expressed in one of her few surviving letters. Ellen Nussey was anxious for Charlotte to prolong her visit (which had already lasted two weeks) and permission had been sought from those who would have to fill her place at home.

Dear Miss Ellen,
If you have set your heart on Charlotte staying another week she has our united consent. I for one will take everything easy on Sunday. I'm glad she is enjoying herself: let her make the most of the next seven days and return stout and hearty. Love to her and you from Anne and myself and tell her all are well at home.

Yours affectly / E. J. Brontë[3]

That the Gondals were uppermost in her mind that spring is shown by the Gondal poem written on 3 March which has long been regarded as one of the great poems in the language. It is Rosina's lament at the graveside of her dead lover, Julius Brenzaida, 'Cold in the Earth'. In terms of Gondal history, the event was fifteen years old; but what made Emily write about it at this particular time remains an enigma.

There was an influence close at hand, however, that cannot wholly be discounted: it was that of her sister Anne whose grief for her lost love seemed if anything to get worse instead of better. However hard she tried she could not hide her feelings from her sisters, and in this spring of 1845 she returned to the theme of her sad little love affair in lines that strangely foreshadow Emily's:

---

[1] Duclaux, 213.   [2] *SLL*, i. 304–5.
[3] 11 July 1845. The original letter, lent to Mrs. Gaskell by Ellen Nussey, had the signature cut away and re-copied by Mrs. G. BPM.

> Cold in the grave for years has lain
> The form it was my bliss to see,
> And only dreams can bring again,
> The darling of my heart to me.[1]

It would be unfair to Anne to make a literary comparison. What matters is that, even without Anne's experience, Emily was able to write one of the great love poems in the language. For years readers supposed it to relate to a real experience (Virginia Moore went so far as to identify the man from the pencilled title 'Love's Farewell', which Charlotte, when editing her sisters' works, gave to an earlier poem of Emily's; Miss Moore deciphered 'Love's Farewell' as 'Louis Parensell'). But the question can only be answered in terms of the two planes of being on which Emily lived—that of 'the World without' and of 'the World within'. The atmosphere of suffering and grief generated by her sisters gave Emily an insight into feelings which she would not otherwise have known; the sympathy of the creative artist supplied the rest.

R. Alcona to J. Brenzaida

> Cold in the earth, and the deep snow piled above thee!
> Far, far removed, cold in the dreary grave!
> Have I forgot, my Only Love, to love thee,
> Severed at last by Time's all-wearing wave? . . .
>
> Cold in the earth, and fifteen wild Decembers
> From those brown hills have melted into spring—
> Faithful indeed is the spirit that remembers
> After such years of change and suffering!
>
> Sweet Love of youth, forgive if I forget thee
> While the World's tide is bearing me along:
> Sterner desires and darker hopes beset me,
> Hopes which obscure but cannot do thee wrong.
>
> No other sun has lightened up my heaven;
> No other Star has ever shone for me:
> All my life's bliss from thy dear life was given—
> All my life's bliss is in the grave with thee.
>
> But when the days of golden dreams had perished
> And even Despair was powerless to destroy,
> Then did I learn how existence could be cherished,
> Strengthened and fed without the aid of joy;

---

[1] Anne Brontë, 'Night', *Brontë Poems*, ed. A. C. Benson, 1915, 294.

Then did I check the tears of useless passion,
Weaned my young soul from yearning after thine;
Sternly denied its burning wish to hasten
Down to that tomb already more than mine!

And even yet, I dare not let it languish,
Dare not indulge in Memory's rapturous pain;
Once drinking deep of that divinest anguish,
How could I seek the empty world again?[1]

The Gondal poems, for all their fictional framework, give clear indications of the fresh truths discovered by their author. Only a few months after the writing of that poem her ability to live 'without the aid of joy' would be put to the test.

In the personal poem 'How Beautiful the Earth is Still', written—or transcribed—on 2 June 1845, the theme reverts to the world of suffering mankind that had haunted Emily since the previous year, and proclaims the poet's faith in the comforting assurance of nature that even while she lives in this harsh world she will be able to escape at times.

How beautiful the Earth is still
To thee—how full of Happiness;
How little fraught with real ill
Or shadowy phantoms of distress;

How Spring can bring thee glory yet
And Summer win thee to forget
December's sullen time!
Why dost thou hold the treasure fast
Of youth's delight, when youth is past
And thou art near thy prime?

When those who were thy own compeers . . .
Have seen their morning melt in tears . . .
Blest, had they died unproved and young
Before their hearts were wildly wrung,
Poor slaves, subdued by passions strong,
A weak and helpless prey!

'Because I hoped . . .
As children hope, with trustful breast,
I waited Bliss and cherished Rest.

[1] Hatfield, 182.

'A thoughtful Spirit taught me soon
That we must long till life be done;
That every phase of earthly joy
Will always fade and always cloy—

'This I foresaw, and would not chase
The fleeting treacheries,
But with firm foot and tranquil face
Held backward from the tempting race,
Gazed o'er the sands the waves efface
To the enduring seas—

'There cast my anchor of Desire
Deep in unknown Eternity;
Nor ever let my Spirit tire
With looking for *What is to be* . . .

'Hope soothes me in the griefs I know,
She lulls my pain for others' woe
And makes me strong to undergo
What I am born to bear.

'Glad comforter, will I not brave
Unawed the darkness of the grave?
Nay, smile to hear Death's billows rave,
My Guide, sustained by thee?
The more unjust seems present fate
The more my Spirit springs elate
Strong in thy strength, to anticipate
Rewarding Destiny!'[1]

It was at this time of spiritual preparedness that the need for exceptional courage arose. Branwell, who had returned home for the holidays
in mid-July received a letter from his employer, Mr. Robinson, within
forty-eight hours, dismissing him in the most insulting terms and implying
that he had been conducting an intrigue with his wife. He was threatened
with pain of exposure if he attempted to see her or any member of the
family again.

For the Brontë family domestic peace was at an end. Branwell's collapse
was mental as well as physical. He told his friend Grundy later that he
spent 'eleven continuous nights of sleepless horror' which reduced him to

[1] Hatfield, 188.

'almost blindness'. He remained 'nine long weeks utterly shattered in body and broken down in mind'.[1] During the first days of his frenzy his family sent him away to Liverpool in the charge of John Brown, but he returned as bad as he went. It is symptomatic of Charlotte's attitude to the event that from the outset she gave Branwell no credit for an ability to mend. She saw his ruin now as inevitable.

[1] *SLL*, i. 295.

CHAPTER XIII

'THE WORLD WITHIN'

EMILY alone appeared to bear a stout heart under the pressure of calamity.

I am quite contented for myself [she wrote in her birthday-note of 30 July], not as idle as formerly, altogether as hearty, and having learnt to make most of the present and long for the future with the fidgetiness that I cannot do all I wish; seldom or never troubled with nothing to do, and merely desiring that every body could be as comfortable as myself and as undesponding and then we should have a very tolerable world of it.

In case the source of her inward contentment was not clearly enough stated, she added before closing the document: 'I have plenty of work on hands, and writing, and am altogether full of business.'[1] The drawing of herself writing with her desk on her knees, Keeper at her side, and a sleeping Flossy sprawled on the camp bed under the window, that fills the bottom corner of her page, completes the impression of contentment her words convey. Emily was no longer fighting against odds, as at Roe Head, Law Hill, or Brussels: she had no need to be in open rebellion against authority—whether it were her aunt's, or the social conventions that obliged her to dine at the Jenkins's. She was at peace with herself, having at last found what she wanted in life. No wonder she wished that the other members of the family were as 'undesponding' as herself.

In this state of heightened being, even Branwell's fall from grace appeared a curable evil to Emily; she could believe that he would 'be better and do better hereafter'. She had known him very low before, after the London fiasco; he could pull himself up again as he had done then, given goodwill all round. Emily's attitude to failure had crystallized years ago; in nature there was no such thing as success or failure, only suffering and death—and who scoffs at suffering? She could not condemn. In November 1839 she had written:

> . . . Do I despise the timid deer
> Because his limbs are fleet with fear?

[1] *SLL*, i. 304-5.

> Or would I mock the wolf's death-howl
> Because his form is gaunt and foul?
> Or hear with joy the leveret's cry
> Because it cannot bravely die?
>
> No! Then above his memory
> Let pity's heart as tender be:
> Say, 'Earth lie lightly on that breast,
> And, kind Heaven, grant that spirit rest!'[1]

Though there is no indication that the lines applied to Branwell, as some commentators have suggested (they have clearly a Gondal connotation), they fitted his case well enough. For the time being neither Emily nor Anne judged Branwell as irredeemable: both hoped he would 'do better hereafter'.

The similarity of their views does not end there: the words are an obvious echo of their father's evangelical language. Mr. Brontë was never unhopeful, despite the ruin of his son's worldly prospects; his salvation was now his dearest concern. Directly his eye-operation was over the following year, he watched over Branwell night and day, taking him into his own room to sleep, for fear of his attempting suicide, or setting the house on fire in his drunken bouts. Branwell was not wholly indifferent to his father's efforts through the long horror of such nights, and would come down in the morning muttering, as Mrs. Gaskell reported: 'He does his best, the poor old man.'[2]

For Charlotte, Branwell's disaster was the climax to the whole sequence of sorrows that had accumulated upon the family—and especially on herself—during the past year: the rupture with M. Heger, the failure of the school-plan, her father's threatening blindness, their own unprovided future. The school-plan, even had it been possible to find pupils, would have had to be abandoned.[3] Branwell's mere existence, his permanent presence in the home, a shiftless dissipated wreck, was an incubus on his sisters, preventing social intercourse or active employment of any kind. So Charlotte judged him; perhaps it was the inevitable consequence of her former devotion to her brother. 'Branwell still remains at home, and while he is here—you shall not come,' she wrote to Ellen on 4 November.[4] 'I am more confirmed in that resolution the more I know him. I wish I could say one word to you in his favour, but I cannot, therefore I will hold my tongue'.[5]

How Anne felt after the blow fell which she had so long tried to avert

---

[1] Hatfield, 123.   [2] Gaskell, 198.
[3] *SLL*, i. 308.   [4] Ibid., 311.   [5] *SBC*, 122.

while at Thorp Green, she confided to her diary-paper that July: '...
during my stay I have had some very un-pleasant and un-dreamt of experience of human nature... I for my part cannot well be flatter or older
in mind than I am now.' But her brother had endured 'much tribulation
and illness'. She, like Emily could at least still say of him: 'We hope he
will be better and do better in future.'[1]

Despite the dejection of spirits caused by her late experience, it was
Anne, strangely enough, who initiated a new move at that time which
had important consequences for her sisters. While at Thorp Green she
had written the first two parts of a novel originally called 'Passages in the
Life of an Individual', later called *Agnes Grey*. This was the first surviving
attempt of any of them to write a work of fiction based on observation and
experience.

Relating under barely concealed circumstances her life first as governess
at Blake Hall and then among the Robinsons, the truthfulness of Anne's
narration, its unexaggerated honesty in presenting incident and character,
its scrupulous self-analysis, still give it its strongest appeal today. The
sensitive, reflective nature of the author lends a charm to all her descriptions whether of landscape or of feeling; the tone throughout is elegiac
and temperate; nothing untrue to the author's experience is attempted.
It is, in fact, the first Brontë novel to describe real life as opposed to the
fantasy world of Gondal and Angria. It is very plain from Anne's diary-
note that she had outgrown Gondal. While Emily could still insist that the
Gondals were 'flourishing bright as ever', Anne recognized that, for her
part, 'The Gondals in general are not in first-rate playing condition. Will
they improve?' Her own answer was 'Never'. The experience of Thorp
Green had been too potent a disenchantment for Gondal ever to be revived. The lack of romance in real life, the waste of refined feelings, the
disillusion of tender hearts, these were subjects far more to her taste by
that time than the heroics of Gondal; to attempt the truthful delineation
of daily life became her object.

In judging her 'Passages in the Life of an Individual' as a new departure
it is important to note exactly what Anne said about their writing at the
time. When two-thirds of the book was written, she noted that 'Emily is
engaged in writing the Emperor Julius' Life. She has read some of it, and
I want very much to hear the rest.' Emily was still engrossed with the
Gondals, but though she went so far as to show some of her manuscript
poems to Anne she did not allow her to read them. To Charlotte she did
not even mention their existence. Anne obviously confided in her sisters,

[1] Anne Brontë, diary-paper 30 July 1845. Ibid., 139.

and probably read her novel to them, with notable effect when the dates of composition of *The Professor* and *Wuthering Heights* are considered. Though it would not be true to say that neither had attempted prose fiction before (for Charlotte had written several novelettes before going to Brussels and destroyed the greater part), they had not attempted a novel of contemporary life based on personal experience. Anne did just this. Her example prompted Charlotte at least to do the same. Another influence was also prompting the family's simultaneous attempt at writing fiction that autumn, and that, surprisingly enough, was Branwell.

Branwell's collapse was not yet so complete as Charlotte believed or as it became the following summer. That he was capable of some constructive work is shown by his correspondence that autumn with his Halifax friend, the sculptor J. B. Leyland. Branwell had a real regard for Leyland as a man, and admiration of his work as an artist. On 10 September he told him that he had started work on a three-volume novel—one volume of which was completed. 'I felt that I must rouse myself to attempt something while roasting daily and nightly over a slow fire—*to wile away my torment*[1] and I knew that in the present state of the publishing and reading world a Novel is the most saleable article . . .'[2]

The manuscript of the novel—'the results of years of thought'—has been preserved.[3] He called it *And the Weary are at Rest*. It was never completed, only 58 pages of it were written, and, of course, it was never published in his lifetime. A limited edition for private circulation was published by J. A. Symington in 1924. The tale contains some sharply-focused scenes of love between a married woman, Maria Thurston, and a young man who tries to seduce her under her husband's roof. As evidence of Branwell's views on marital infidelity, the book has a biographical if no artistic value. Its importance, however, as it relates to his sisters, lies in his avowed purpose in writing it to make money. From his various literary contacts (and Branwell still had some, like Macaulay, Hartley Coleridge, Edward Baines, from his Bradford days) he learnt that fiction was the most profitable form of literary hack-work at the time. He told his friend Grundy that it was at their instigation that he was writing a novel. He was never one to keep his own counsel (like Emily), and if he was writing a novel the whole household would hear of it. The point had not yet been reached when Branwell and Charlotte were no longer on speaking terms;

[1] See below, pp. 198–9, 201, for comparisons between Branwell's desperate language and the language of *Wuthering Heights*.

[2] Branwell's letters to Leyland: Brotherton Coll., Leeds Univ. Library.

[3] Berg Coll., New York Public Library.

disbelieve him as she might, Charlotte could not fail to hear his views on the profitable aspects of writing fiction. If he said nothing else worth hearing in her presence, this was something of interest to her at a time of such total deprivation. Encouraged by his sisters or not, Branwell persisted sufficiently in his course that autumn to seek publication of some of his poems in the press; through the intermediary of his friend Leyland, he sent several poems to the *Halifax Guardian* (which had formerly published pieces of his during his stay at Sowerby Bridge) which were accepted and published. The poems included: 'Penmaenmawr', 'Juan Fernandez', 'Letter from a Father in earth to his Child in the Grave'. The fact must be noted to correct the impression Charlotte later gave that the sisters' first venture into publication was a spontaneous gesture of their own; the practical aspects of publication as a means of earning money had been pointed out to them by their brother. Unhappily for him, he had neither their artistry nor their staying power. By the time they had succeeded, he was a mental ruin. According to his letter to Grundy, he had already given up the attempt to write a novel by the end of October 1845. 'I have striven to write something worthy of being read, but I really cannot do so.' [1]

In attributing the praise for their success where praise was mainly due, to the genius of Emily, Charlotte showed not only love for her sister but her own critical acumen. Her account of the discovery of Emily's notebook of poems in the late autumn of 1845 is one of the best-known and most quoted passages in Brontë literature; yet it cannot be omitted here, as it is central to any study of Emily's life and work.

The timing of the discovery has to be remembered to realize the impact it made on Charlotte, lowered in vitality as she was after two years' suffering from unrequited love; and wounded afresh in her oldest affections by Branwell's ruin. Life did not hold out many pleasing prospects as that year drew to a close, and the only certain anticipation for the New Year was Mr. Brontë's dreaded operation.

Emily, who had just finished copying out a new poem in her 'Gondal' notebook, either forgot to put it away in her desk or was called away before being able to do so. She left it open and on the desk, and there Charlotte found it. Whatever the cause of her absence, she was gone long enough for Charlotte to read all the forty-three poems it contained. Very likely this happened on 9 October 1845: Charlotte later placed the event in the late autumn of that year and it was on that day Emily copied the only poem entered since August. It was the major poem 'Julian M. and A. G. Rochelle', which contains the mystical passage

[1] W & S, ii. 65.

'Then dawns the Invisible, the Unseen its truth reveals; / My outward sense is gone, my inward essence feels.'[1] On Charlotte, who thought she knew the subject-matter of her sister's writings within the Gondal framework, and who had received no confidences from Emily on the nature of her visionary life, the effect of the poem was so electrical that it made her careless of the consequences. She saw only one thing, the greatness of her sister's mind, the splendour of her poetry. She did not see that its very quality made it intensely personal, and sacred to the writer; she did not recognize that it might not be meant for other people's eyes.

Emily's rage at her indiscretion, when she returned and discovered it, took Charlotte by surprise therefore; deeply as she had always loved Emily, well aware though she must have been of her great reticence, she could not credit the degree of anger her ill-considered action aroused. Nothing she could do would placate Emily.

Charlotte, however, had had a glimpse of hope and was not to be frustrated of it; she bided Emily's time, many days as it proved—upheld by the reviving vision of a common purpose to which the three, Emily, Anne, and herself, might turn their long-neglected talents. The prospect was too sweet to be abandoned; with enormous patience, Charlotte waited for the storm to pass over. So resolute was she, so determined to win Emily back, that even when Emily at last appeared to bend to her entreaties, she did not perceive the effects of the injury that had been done—not only to Emily, but to their mutual love. Charlotte's record of the incident was written five years later, when it was too late to undo the harm, or even to acknowledge it. By then, her sisters were dead, and all she was asked to do by their publishers was to trace the origins of their success.

One day, in the autumn of 1845, I accidentally lighted on a MS volume of verse in my sister Emily's handwriting. Of course, I was not surprised, knowing that she could and did write verse; I looked it over, and something more than surprise seized me—a deep conviction that these were not common effusions, nor at all like the poetry women generally write. I thought them condensed and terse, vigorous and genuine. To my ear, they had also a peculiar music—wild, melancholy, and elevating.

My sister Emily was not a person of demonstrative character, nor one on the recesses of whose mind and feelings even those nearest and dearest to her could, with impunity, intrude unlicensed; it took hours to reconcile her to the discovery I had made, and days to persuade her that such poems merited publication. I knew, however, that a mind like hers could not be without some latent spark of honourable ambition, and refused to be discouraged in my attempts to fan that spark to flame.

[1] Hatfield, 190, lines 81–2.

Emily Feby 23

Dear Miss Ellen,

I should be writing in common civility if I did not thank you for your kindness in letting me know of an opportunity to send "postage paid"

I have written as you directed though if "next Tuesday" means tomorrow, I fear it will be too late to go with Mr. Taylor.

Charlotte has never mentioned a word about coming home if you would go over for

Facsimile of letter in Emily Brontë's normal hand-writing

Emily Jane Brontë. ~~~~ Transcribed February 1844

Gondal Poems

A.G.A. ——————— March 6th 1837

There shines the moon, at noon of night,
Vision of glory - Dream of light!
Holy as heaven - undimmed and pure,
Looking down on the lonely moor -
And lovelier still beneath her ray
That drear moor stretches far away

Till it seems strange that aught can lie
Beyond its zone of silver sky -

Bright moon - dear moon! when years have past
My weary feet return at last -
And still upon Elnor's breast
Thy solemn rays serenely rest
And still one Fir-trees sighing wave
Like mourners over Elbä grave
And Ennë the same but Oh to see
How wildly Time has altered me!
Am I the same long years ago
Sat watching by that waterside
The light of life expiring slow
From his fair cheek and brow of pride?
Not oft these mountains feel the shine
Of such a dying ray as then,
Cast from its front of gold divine
A last smile on the breathing plain
And kissed the forest peaks of snow
That gleaming on the horizon shone
As if in summers warmest glow
Stern winter claimed a loftier throne -
And there he lay among the bloom
His rich blood dyed a deeper hue
Shuddering to feel the ghostly gloom
That coming death around him threw -

Facsimile of Emily Brontë's italic script, in which her poems were written

Meantime, my younger sister quietly produced some of her own compositions, intimating that, since Emily's had given me pleasure, I might like to look at hers. I could not but be a partial judge, yet I thought these verses, too, had a sweet sincere pathos of their own.

We had early cherished the dream of one day becoming authors. This dream, never relinquished . . . now suddenly acquired strength and consistency; it took the character of a resolve. We agreed to arrange a small selection of our poems, and, if possible, get them printed.[1]

Even in relating the incident, Charlotte could not keep out echoes of the excitement that had overcome her at the time; the plan held out a lifeline to her just when her heart had died within her; though she used the plural pronoun in her narration, it was she who was the driving force behind her sisters. Without Charlotte her sisters' works might never have been published, but it was Emily's genius which made their publication imperative. If Emily reproached her for invading her privacy, Charlotte had an unanswerable argument in the right of such poems to be read by all the world.

From Emily's subsequent contempt for the volume, her studied lack of interest in its fortunes, her references to her own contributions as mere 'rhymes', it is clear she was never reconciled to the enterprise. Charlotte confided to W. S. Williams, reader for her eventual publisher George Smith, that 'Emily never alludes to them, or, if she does, it is with scorn.'[2]

Under the circumstances it is impossible to know how far, if not pressed by Charlotte, Emily might have gone in her own good time towards accepting or even seeking publication of her finished work. Was her vehement opposition to publication a permanent attitude, or were the conditions under which publication was forced upon her what she chiefly resented?

The problems publication presented to her were not the same as for her sisters. Half her completed work was on Gondal themes, and, without explanation, the Gondal characters and dramatic sequences could not be given to the public. The names of her *dramatis personae* and of their places of origin must be eliminated and their actions presented to the world rather in the form of ballad poetry. Emily's own strict division of her work into two categories, Gondal and *other* poems, reflected her intention not to confuse what was personal in her work with what was dramatic. In so doing, she greatly simplified the task of the editor of her works and the biographer of her life; but, with the obligation to remove the Gondal signposts from her poetry, the distinctions were confused, and her life falsely

[1] Biographical Notice.   [2] W & S, ii. 256.

interpreted in the light of poems that had originally been Gondal in character, like Rosina's lament 'Cold in the Earth', which for many years was regarded as a personal statement of loss.

Far worse for her was the situation created by her purely mystical poems, which were strictly personal. To a girl with so reticent a nature, the revelation of her most secret experiences was wholly repugnant. Poems, whose existence she had never mentioned to Charlotte and barely mentioned to Anne, were now to be exposed to the judgement of strangers. In giving her unwilling consent to the deed, Emily may have counted on the incomprehension of the public, on its too great dullness to pierce the mystery at the heart of her poems; in so thinking, she was not far wrong. The press notices never once commented on the unique spiritual quality of her vision.

Finally, in judging the motives which actuated Emily in consenting to publication, two considerations must be weighed: her innermost sense of the value of what she had written; and, after all, pity for Charlotte. No one knew better than Emily how Charlotte had suffered over the last two years, how she had lost all hope and direction in consequence of her tragic love. Her world had crumbled; even work was denied her. It was not in Emily to grudge her this small measure of consolation. As her sisters must have pointed out to her, without her contribution the volume of poems stood little chance of publication.

Charlotte had no illusions about her own poems; she roundly condemned them later as 'crude' and 'rhapsodical'. It was not vanity that pushed her into publication, only the conviction that they all had it in them to produce something better later. As she said, they had 'early nourished dreams of authorship'—the *Poems* were only the beginning.

The new zest, the revived energy she put into preparing the book for publication, proved the best anodyne for her sorrows; in that, if in nothing else connected with the enterprise, Emily must have found her reward.

Charlotte never admitted to any qualms. She told Mr. Williams later that from the first moment Emily's manuscript fell by chance into her hands she had been convinced of their 'startling excellence'.[1]

The pieces are short, but they are very genuine; they stirred my heart like the sound of a trumpet when I read them alone and in secret. The deep excitement I felt forced from me the confession of the discovery I had made. I was sternly rated at first for having taken an unwarrantable liberty. This I expected for Ellis Bell is of no flexible or ordinary materials. But by dint of entreaty and reason I

[1] CB to WSW, Sept. 1848. W & S, ii. 256.

at last wrung out a reluctant consent to have 'the rhymes', as they were contemptuously termed, published . . . I know no woman that ever lived who wrote such poetry before'.[1]

Selecting the poems, balancing their rival claims for inclusion, cutting them to suit their altered status—was the work of several weeks that autumn and winter. Emily and Anne decided on twenty-one contributions each, and Charlotte on twenty. The poems were to be presented alternately, in a rotation of one by each of the three authors. While Charlotte and Anne generally gave titles to their poems, Emily hardly ever did, except by initialling the Gondal poems to indicate the characters speaking. Her personal poems had no titles. She had now, therefore, in making her choice for publication, to find them titles, and these were not always happily chosen. Of the twenty-one poems representing her work, six only were Gondal in subject, but these included some of her best, like 'Cold in the Earth', given the title 'Remembrance'; and the central section of Julian M. and A. G. Rochelle, under the title 'The Prisoner'.

Comparison between that first published text and Emily's manuscript shows several alterations in favour of more conventional readings. In the last lines of 'The Philosopher', the published text reads:

> And Conquered good, and conquering ill

which in the original manuscript read far more forcefully:

> And vanquished Good, victorious Ill
> Be lost in one repose.[2]

The question of what names the authors would assume had to be settled next. They decided against anonymity, while wishing to remain unknown. To keep their own initials was a natural wish, and they decided on a choice 'not positively masculine' with characteristic scruple. How they came by their names they never revealed, but there are some strong indications. The name Bell may have been chosen by the arrival that summer of their father's new curate, Arthur Bell Nichols. While a governess at the Sidgwicks, Charlotte had certainly heard much of their neighbour, Miss Frances Mary Richardson Currer, of Eshton Hall, Skipton, whose property touched Stonegappe, and whose library was famous throughout the north. She was one of the founder patrons of the Clergy Daughters' School, so that her name must have been doubly familiar to Charlotte. The poetess

---

[1] Ibid.
[2] Hatfield, 181. A full list of Emily's contributions to the volume is given in Appendix B.

Eliza Acton (1777–1859), who had considerable success in her day and was patronized by royalty, may have suggested Anne's pseudonym to her. There appears to be no clue to the origin of Emily's choice of name, Ellis.

To find a publisher was the main difficulty. After writing to several without receiving an answer, they applied for advice to Messrs. Chambers of Edinburgh, whose 'paternal' attitude towards writers was widely known. In the Brontë's home, *Chambers' Journal*, though a relatively new production (1843), was already a household word. Charlotte wrote about it in *Shirley* as a 'favourite periodical' of Caroline's for its 'marvellous anecdotes of animal sagacity'.[1] Charlotte would appear to be referring more particularly to *Chambers' Miscellany*, whose 1845 issues contained some notable poems, short stories, and reminiscences dealing specifically with animals. The application to Messrs. Chambers of Edinburgh for practical advice could well have been suggested by Emily, the prototype of *Shirley* and lovers of animals par excellence.

Chambers did not disappoint his admirers; he supplied them with a list of likely publishers, among them the firm of Aylott & Jones of Paternoster Row, who specialized in verse of a serious, if not pronouncedly religious character. To Messrs. Aylott & Jones, Currer Bell wrote on 28 January 1846, asking for particulars of publication and, if necessary, offering to pay the costs of production. Miss Branwell's legacies made this possible. The offer was accepted, and the manuscript despatched on 7 February. The estimated cost was £31 10s. 0d. The proof sheets came in on 10 March, and the book was out in the last week of May. The whole operation had taken exactly four months.

The correspondence was conducted throughout by Currer Bell, who signed her letters C. Brontë, and replies were addressed to C. Brontë Esq. c/o The Revd. Patrick Brontë, Haworth, Yorks. The Bells were presumed to be relatives and were referred to in the third person throughout.

After despatching the manuscripts of the poems to Aylott & Jones, Charlotte accepted an invitation to the Nusseys on 18 February. Her absence was the occasion for Emily to write one of her rare letters in reply to a note from Ellen:

Haworth, February 25th 1846
Dear Miss Nussey,—I fancy this note will be too late to decide one way or other with respect to Charlotte's stay. Yours only came this morning (Wednesday), and unless mine travels faster you will not receive it till Friday. Papa, of course, misses Charlotte, and will be glad to have her back. Anne and I ditto; but as she goes from home so seldom you may keep her a day or two longer, if your

[1] Chapter 25.

eloquence is equal to the task of persuading her—that is, if she still be with you when you get this permission. Love from Anne.—

Yours truly,

Emily J. Brontë[1]

The note reached Charlotte in time and she stayed a further week.

On 6 April 1846 (hence some weeks before the publication of the *Poems*) an important development occurred in the correspondence with Aylott & Jones; C. Brontë wrote to the firm to enquire if they would be interested in publishing a work of fiction by the Bells, and if not, whether they could recommend a likely publisher. The letter reads:

Gentlemen—C. E. & A. Bell are now preparing for the Press a work of fiction, consisting of three distinct and unconnected tales which may be published either together as a work of 3 vols. of the ordinary novel size, or separately as single vols. as shall be deemed most advisable.

It is not their intention to publish these tales on their own account.

They direct me to ask you whether you would be disposed to undertake—after having of course by due inspection of the MS. ascertained that its contents are such as to warrant an expectation of success.

An early answer will oblige as in case of your negativing the proposal—inquiry must be made of other Publishers—I am Gentlemen   Yrs. truly

C. Brontë[2]

April 6th '46

The three 'distinct and unconnected tales' were, of course, *The Professor*, *Wuthering Heights*, and *Agnes Grey*, which were already sufficiently far advanced to justify an approach to a publisher. Messrs. Aylott & Jones did not publish fiction, but they suggested a number of firms which did, and advised the Bells on the best way of presenting their MSS. when completed. The manuscript of *The Professor* is the only one of the three to have been preserved, and it shows that Charlotte finished her fair copy on 27 June; together with the two other tales, it was posted to Henry Colburn, the first publisher on their list, on 4 July.

It is necessary to note these early dates in the fortunes of the Bell novels, both because their eventual publication was so much delayed (eighteen months in the case of *Wuthering Heights* and *Agnes Grey*; *The Professor* was never published in Charlotte's lifetime) and for biographical reasons; for only by reference to these dates can the writing of *Wuthering Heights* be timed, more or less accurately. In her birthday note of 30 July 1845, Emily said that she 'had plenty of work on hands, and writing, and

[1] *SBC*, 144–5.   [2] W & S, ii. 87.

am altogether full of business'. To judge by the preserved poems of the time, she wrote nothing between 2 June, 'How beautiful the Earth is still'; and a Gondal poem in August, 'I know that tonight the wind is sighing', her business was therefore, probably, with the Emperor Julius's Life, which Anne mentioned she was then engaged on, not with *Wuthering Heights*.

Working backwards from the certain date of its despatch to Henry Colburn on 4 July 1846, and taking into account its partial completion by 6 April, the inception of the book would appear to coincide with the decision to publish the *Poems* in the autumn of 1845, a time when even Branwell, it will be remembered, was launched on a novel, and advocating fiction as the surest means to publication. This is mere supposition, and there is no evidence to support it. *Wuthering Heights*, like *Agnes Grey*, may well have been begun two or three years before, while Emily was alone with her father, and left barely begun till the resolve to attempt publication of the *Poems* revived the author's interest in it. If this was the case, hardly more than the three opening chapters can have been written, for it is hard to imagine a writer of Emily's scope stopping in full flow once Nellie Dean had begun her narration. There does appear a hesitation, a pause in intention and direction in those opening pages, as though the author were still uncertain about which way to go. The length of the work (367 pages in a modern reprint) raises the question of whether it could have been wholly written during the winter of 1845 and spring months of 1846. Emily, Charlotte witnessed later, 'never lingered over any task', and there is nothing impossible in writing a book of that length within six months; but it is not the length of *Wuthering Heights* that matters but its spiritual content. The true indication of the dating of *Wuthering Heights* can only be found by internal evidence; and here comparison with the poems is essential. In many instances, the poems of 1843–5 read like a preface to the novel. The same subjects preoccupy the author; the same themes of separation and of union, of life in death, of the oneness of all life in nature, of the indestructibility of the soul. The poems which most clearly prefigure *Wuthering Heights* are, as might be expected, those of 1844 and 1845, in which the contents and imagery are almost identical with passages in the novel. Compare, for example, the last lines in 'The Linnet in the Rocky Dells' to the final paragraph of *Wuthering Heights*. The same reflections on the impersonality of death occur: the poet says:

> The dweller in the land of Death
> Is changed and careless too.[1]

[1] Hatfield, 173.

The novelist writes: 'I . . . wondered how anyone could ever imagine unquiet slumbers for the sleepers in that quiet earth.' The poem 'Cold in the Earth' evokes the same scene and the same sentiments as the description of Heathcliff's desecration of Catherine's grave: 'The day she was buried came a fall of snow.'[1] In 'Julian M. and A. G. Rochelle' occurs the famous passage describing the liberation of the soul, in particular the lines: 'Its wings are almost free, its home, its harbour found; / Measuring the gulf it stoops and dares the final bound!'[2]

In *Wuthering Heights*, as the tale moves to its close, Nellie urges Heathcliff to rest, and he, sensing the approach of his reunion with Catherine, uses this image in his reply: '. . . You might as well bid a man struggling in the water, to rest within arm's length of the shore! I must reach it first, and then I'll rest!'[3]

On 2 January 1846 Emily wrote (or transcribed) the poem 'No Coward Soul is Mine' whose obvious affinities with *Wuthering Heights* suggest that the vision which dictated the one must equally have inspired the other. They seem, on the metaphysical plane at least, the products not only of one mind but of one time. Perhaps the very brevity of her poetic statement of faith prompted her to extend the treatment of so vast a theme, to expand it from the limitations of a poem to the dimensions of a novel. Such conscious reckoning was, to be sure, far from Emily; what she did, she did instinctively. The fact remains that there are whole passages in the novel that read like paraphrases of the poem, as a comparison of the two texts shows.

Jan. 2, 1846

> No coward soul is mine
> No trembler in the world's storm-troubled sphere
> I see Heaven's glories shine
> And Faith shines equal arming me from Fear
>
> O God within my breast
> Almighty ever-present Deity
> Life, that in me has rest
> As I Undying Life, have power in Thee
>
> Vain are the thousand creeds
> That move men's hearts, unutterably vain,
> Worthless as withered weeds
> Or idlest froth amid the boundless main

[1] Chapter 29. [2] Hatfield, 190.
[3] *Wuthering Heights*, ch. 34.

To waken doubt in one
Holding so fast by thy infinity
So surely anchored on
The steadfast rock of Immortality

With wide-embracing love
Thy spirit animates eternal years
Pervades and broods above,
Changes, sustains, dissolves, creates and rears

Though Earth and moon were gone
And suns and universes ceased to be
And thou wert left alone
Every Existence would exist in thee

There is not room for Death
Nor atom that his might could render void
Since thou art Being and Breath
And what thou art may never be destroyed. [1]

With a human love replacing the divine, Emily pursued in the novel the theme of spiritual union that can be made to triumph over the divisions of physical existence. When Ellen asks Catherine where is the obstacle to her marrying Linton, Catherine strikes her forehead and her breast and cries: '*Here*! and *here*! . . . In whichever place the soul lives—in my soul, and in my heart, I'm convinced I'm wrong.'[2] When she gives her reasons for belonging to Heathcliff she says it is not because he is handsome, but because

he is more myself than I am. Whatever our souls are made of, his and mine are the same . . . My great thought in living is himself. If all else perished, and *he* remained, I should still continue to be; and if all else remained, and he were annihilated, the universe would turn to a mighty stranger. I should not seem a part of it . . . Nelly, I *am* Heathcliff—he's always in my mind—not as a pleasure, any more than I am always a pleasure to myself—but as my own being . . . so, don't talk of our separation again.[3]

While the theme of alienation as the source of all unhappiness in life runs through Emily's earlier poems (its finest expression is to be found in 'The Philosopher'[4]) so the sense of healing by atonement is present in the maturer poems and provides the climax of *Wuthering Heights*.

Whichever way it is looked at, *Wuthering Heights* was the direct product

---

[1] Hatfield, 191. [2] *Wuthering Heights*, ch. 9.
[3] Ibid. [4] Hatfield, 181.

of Emily's poetic experience, the child of Gondal, the repository of her philosophic thought. She dedicated to its creation all her powers, as is shown by the fact that she abandoned poetry in its favour. After January 1846, until *Wuthering Heights* was finished and published (a gap of eighteen months), she wrote no more poetry. Such a conclusion is based of course on the evidence of the existing poems; Emily may, in fact, have written many more which she or Charlotte after her destroyed. But even the act of destruction would imply that she was no longer satisfied with poetry. The fact that she was writing a second novel [1] after *Wuthering Heights*, would support this argument.

Whatever reasons prompted Emily's vehement opposition to publishing her poems, she seems never to have hesitated over publishing *Wuthering Heights*; she sent it out to successive firms despite repeated rejections. (The novel, she could argue, was invention, the poems personal revelation.)

While in the act of writing it, she freely communicated its progress to her sisters, reading each new section aloud to them, just as they read their books to her. Charlotte vividly recalled that time when she wrote later of Emily's reaction to their proffered criticisms; as might be expected from so *certain* a writer, from one who doubted so little of the truth of what she wrote, she rejected their protests.

If the auditor of her work, when read in manuscript, shuddered under the grinding influence of natures so relentless and implacable, of spirits so lost and fallen; if it was complained that the mere hearing of certain vivid and fearful scenes banished sleep by night, and disturbed mental peace by day, Ellis Bell would wonder what was meant, and suspect the complainant of affectation.[2]

Judging the book not as literature but in relation to its author's life, it appears as the motivating power, the sufficient reason for living, the compensation for pain, the fulfilment of all hopes, that sustained her during a time of unprecedented crisis. While Branwell was steadily degenerating and Mr. Brontë's sight failing rapidly, the 'world within' was assuming control of Emily's life, as she had trusted it would.

By one of those strange fatalities which marked the Brontës' lives, the publication of the 'Poems by Currer, Ellis & Acton Bell', in the last week of May 1846, coincided with Branwell receiving his 'finishing stroke', as he himself put it.[3]

The death of Mr. Robinson on 26 May, the event to which Branwell had

---

[1] See Newby's letter to Ellis Bell, 15 Feb. 1848. BPM.
[2] Preface to the 1850 edition of *Wuthering Heights*.
[3] PBB to J. B. Leyland, June 1846. Brotherton Coll., Leeds Univ. Library.

looked as the only possible end to his troubles, proved to be the cruellest mockery of his hopes. Far from sending for him, Mrs. Robinson sent her coachman over to Haworth to prevent him making any attempt to see her, inventing a codicil to her husband's will which would debar her from the inheritance if she saw him again. There was, of course, no truth in the whole fabrication, as reference to the will shows today. Kept at a safe distance by the plot, Branwell was further crammed with tales of Mrs. Robinson's mental breakdown which, even were she to risk financial ruin, would effectually prevent her seeing her lover. As fully expected, Branwell believed every word of the tale brought him by the coachman, George Gooch, and the consequences were almost fatal. Mary Duclaux received the story of that unhappy day from one of the eye-witnesses of it, the barmaid of The Bull. On receiving Gooch's message to meet him at The Bull, Branwell dressed himself with care and hurried out, prepared for the summons to Thorp Green: he 'fair danced down the churchyard as if he were out of his mind; he was so fond of that woman', she reported. Instead of the summons to Thorp Green, he received the death-blow to his hopes. The shock, following on months of drinking and drug-taking, provoked a kind of fit, in which the barmaid found him hours after Gooch had gone. He was on the floor of the bar-parlour emitting a horrible sound, 'like the bleating of a calf'.[1] From that day, he was a broken man.

[1] Duclaux, 145.

CHAPTER XIV

ELLIS BELL

THE first reviews of the *Poems* appeared in the *Athenaeum* and *The Critic* for Saturday, 4 July. The date is noteworthy since it was the same day on which Charlotte wrote to the publisher, Henry Colburn, to offer the manuscripts of the finished novels. The coincidence even raises the question: had the Bells received the encouraging reviews (forwarded by their publisher) that morning, and felt heartened to take the next step towards authorship? At all events, her letter proves that the novels were finished by then. Charlotte's letter to Colburn reads:

Sir,

I request permission to send for your inspection the M.S. of a work of fiction in 3 vols—It consists of 3 tales, each occupying a volume and capable of being published together or separately, as thought most advisable.

The authors of these tales have already appeared before the public.

Should you consent to examine the work, would you, in your reply, state at what period, after transmission of the M.S. to you the authors may expect to receive your decision upon its merits.

I am, Sir,

Yours respectfully,
C. Bell

Address: Mr. Currer Bell
          Parsonage
          Haworth
          Bradford
          Yorks.

July 4th –46
Henry Colburn Esq —

Very elated must Charlotte have felt in reading the *Athenaeum* review, for it endorsed her judgement of Emily's superiority as a poet. While the reviewer singled out Emily's work, he did so primarily for 'its music', and only secondly for the author's 'power of wing' (a metaphor that should have been pleasing to Emily). Under a general title of

'Poetry for the Million', the *Poems* were noticed together with six other volumes of verse:

The second book on our list furnishes another example of a family in whom appears to run the instinct of song. It is shared, however, by the three brothers—as we suppose them to be—in very unequal proportions; requiring in the case of Acton Bell, the indulgence of affection to which we have alluded, to make it music—and rising, in that of Ellis, into an inspiration, which may yet find an audience in the outer world. A fine quaint spirit has the latter, which may have things to speak that men will be glad to hear—and an evident power of wing that may reach heights not here attempted. Take an extract from his poem 'The Philosopher':

> So said I, and still say the same;
> —Still to my Death will say—
> Three gods, within this little frame,
> Are warring night and day.
> Heaven could not hold them all, and yet
> They all are held in me;
> And must be mine till I forget
> My present entity!
> Oh! for the time, when in my breast
> Their struggles will be o'er!
> Oh, for the day, when I shall rest,
> And never suffer more!
>
> 'I saw a spirit, standing, Man,
> Where thou dost stand—an hour ago,
> And round his feet three rivers ran,
> Of equal depth, and equal flow—
> A golden stream—and one like blood;
> And one like sapphire seemed to be;
> But, where they joined their triple flood
> It tumbled in an inky sea.
>
> The spirit bent his dazzling gaze
> Down through that ocean's gloomy Night,
> Then, kindling all, with sudden blaze,
> The glad deep sparkled wide and bright—
> White as the sun, far, far more fair
> Than its divided sources were!'
>
> And even for that Spirit, Seer,
> I've watched and sought my life-time long;
> Sought him in Heaven, Hell, Earth, and Air—
> An endless search, and always wrong!

Had I but seen his glorious eye
Once light the clouds that 'wilder me,
I n'er had raised this coward cry
To cease to think, and cease to be;
I ne'er had called oblivion blest,
Nor, stretching eager hands to Death,
Implored to change for senseless rest
This sentient soul, this living breath—
Oh, let me die—that power and will
Their cruel strife may close;
And conquered good, and conquering ill
Be lost in one repose!

The reviewer on *The Critic* was struck by another aspect of the *Poems*: he wrote, 'They in whose hearts are chords strung by Nature to sympathise with the beautiful and the true, will recognise in these compositions the presence of more genius than it was supposed this utilitarian age had devoted to the loftier exercises of the intellect.' The judgement was sufficiently heartening for the Bells to ask their publisher to use it in advertising the book. For the first time, indeed, it was decided the book was worth advertising, and on 10 July Currer Bell sent a further remittance of £10 to the publisher 'to be devoted to advertisements, leaving to you to select such channels as you deem most advisable'.

The *Poems* were sent out to several periodicals, only a few of which noticed them, but it made sufficient impact on certain editors like Lockhart, for instance, to be remembered after a couple of years had passed, when the Bells came up for review again. Lockhart's comments then show the degree of curiosity that the unknown 'Bells' had aroused in the literary establishment. On 13 November 1848, he wrote to Elizabeth Rigby, one of his reviewers, to find out something about the 'fraternity'. Recalling the volume that had been sent him, he added: 'I know nothing of the writers but the common rumour is that they are brothers of the weaving order in some Lancashire town . . . If you have any friend about Manchester, it would, I suppose, be easy to learn accurately as to the position of these men.'[1]

On the subject of her newly acquired identity, Ellis Bell would remain intractable to the end. Added to the advantages which it gave her to think, speak and act as 'he' liked in print, it is obvious she felt a liking for the part; it provided her with yet another refuge from reality, like the Gondal characters she had impersonated for years, and was still, as

[1] *Letters & Journals of Lady Eastlake* (Elizabeth Rigby), i. 221-2.

recently as the trip to York, impersonating. While, in due course, Emily's sisters would discard the disguise, and readily make themselves known to sympathetic publishers, 'Ellis' resolutely remained aloof and intimated to anyone unwary enough to make approaches that 'he' had no intention of meeting the world on any terms. The longer Emily lived with Ellis Bell, the greater the freedom 'he' enjoyed. Not only on paper, but in daily life, Ellis Bell very often 'took over' when vigorous action was required.

There is no reason to suppose that the Bells were at all discouraged by the reception of their *Poems*, though on enquiring the number of copies sold after a couple of months, they were told it was exactly two. By then, they were waiting to hear the fate of their novels; as Charlotte said later 'the mere effort to succeed had given a wonderful zest to their existence . . . it must be pursued.'[1] In her case, in particular, the 'zest' was life-giving, after the heartbreak of the previous years.

They had not much time to brood over the delays of publishers, as by the first week in August it was decided to consult a specialist for Mr. Brontë's cataract. Charlotte and Emily went over to Manchester to make the necessary arrangements. (It is noteworthy that, in an emergency, Charlotte relied on the presence of the 'practical' Emily to see her through the interview with the specialist.) Manchester was the centre chosen because of the reputation of Dr. William James Wilson, head of the Manchester Institution for Curing the Diseases of the Eye, for the foundation of which he had been mainly responsible. He subsequently saw Mr. Brontë and was hopeful of success: despite Mr. Brontë's age (he was turned seventy) Dr. Wilson advised an immediate operation. The operation took place on 25 August.

Though Mr. Brontë's courage might be equal to the ordeal (the operation lasted fifteen minutes, without anaesthetic), Charlotte knew that it would also be a long trial of patience for them both afterwards. While her fortitude proved equal to his in the long weeks of his convalescence, she had one source of consolation that he had not—the writing of a new book. The story of how Charlotte received the rejected MS. of *The Professor* on the very day of her father's operation and began *Jane Eyre* forthwith[2] has entered literary history. The letter of rejection from Colburn must have been forwarded to Manchester by Emily, who, together with Anne, was equally disappointed. In her relation of their difficulties with publishers written years later, Charlotte did not mention what decisions had been taken by the Bells to deal with the situation during her absence from home;

---

[1] Biographical Notice.   [2] Duclaux, 153.

was the parcel containing the MS. to be forwarded to the next publisher
on their list, and did Emily do this while Charlotte was yet at Manchester?
The complete unworldliness of the Bells in dealing with publishers was
recalled by George Smith, of the firm of Smith, Elder & Co., the sixth to
whom Charlotte sent *The Professor*, in the *Cornhill Magazine*, December
1900: 'In July 1847, a parcel containing a MS.—The Professor—reached
our office . . . bearing the scored-out addresses of 3 or 4 other publishing
houses; showing that the parcel had been previously submitted to other
publishers. This was not calculated to prepossess in favour of the MS.'

Charlotte's constant anxiety for those left at home was almost as acute
as it was for her father. They were barely settled in Manchester when she
wrote to Ellen Nussey on 21 August: 'I wonder how poor Emily and Anne
will get on at home with Branwell—they too will have their troubles.'[1]
The reports from home could not have been very reassuring; after a
month's absence Charlotte answered Ellen's queries: 'You ask if I have
any enjoyment here; in truth I can't say I have—and I long to get home,
though, unhappily, home is not now a place of complete rest. It is sad to
think how it is disquieted by a constant phantom; or rather two—sin and
suffering; they seem to obscure the cheerfulness of day and to disturb
the comfort of evening.'[2]

Branwell believed himself a cruelly ill-used man, the victim of a
conspiracy hatched against him by the trustees and relations of Mrs.
Robinson, Archdeacon Thorpe and Mr. Evans in particular. Such feelings
were fomented by the letters of Mrs. Robinson's lady's maid, Ann Marshall
—a chief actor in the plot—and of the Robinson family doctor, Dr. Crosby,
through whom Branwell received the only direct news he could get of
Mrs. Robinson. The Doctor in fact appeared genuinely sorry for Branwell,
and had enough influence with Mrs. Robinson to present his case to her.
In the event, Dr. Crosby got himself involved further than he bargained
for, and became the intermediary through whom Mrs. Robinson sent
money to Branwell when he became destitute. Dr. Crosby sent him £20
at a time, as Branwell's afflicted family later learnt, and Charlotte confided to Ellen. (Mrs. Gaskell received the confidence direct from Charlotte,
and mentioned it in her *Life*.[3])

Far more sinister appears the role of Ann Marshall in giving a false
picture to Branwell of her mistress's supposed illness.[4] The preserved
correspondence of Mrs. Robinson with her solicitors and family at this

time show her to have been in perfect health and extremely active in looking after her own interests, chief among which were the highly profitable marriages she arranged for her daughters, and her own court-ship and final marriage with her wealthy connection, Sir Edward Dolman Scott. While Branwell rightly felt himself to be the dupe of these people, he could not know at the time that he was the dupe of Mrs. Robinson only. Believing her to be as much distracted as he was by the enforced separation, he saw enemies everywhere, even in his own home. His misery was acute; and the language in which he voiced his sufferings took on a tone the echoes of which can, significantly enough, be heard in *Wuthering Heights*.

It must be remembered that from July 1845 when Branwell was dis-missed by Mr. Robinson to his death three years later, he lived unin-terruptedly at home, in circumstances of closest intimacy with his sisters. How close were the material conditions of their home life can only be realized by a letter of Charlotte's inviting Ellen Nussey to stay after an interval of nearly two years, in March 1847; she then wrote: 'In summer and in fine weather—your visit here might be much better managed than in winter—we could get out more, be more independent of the house and of one room—Branwell has been conducting himself very badly lately.'[1]

From the autumn of 1845 to July 1846 was the period during which Emily wrote *Wuthering Heights*; and while no one reading Branwell's own diffuse and turgid prose would ever imagine him capable of writing a page of his sister's book it is also manifest that Branwell's influence bore directly on its emotional climate. From Branwell, Emily learnt more of the devastation of love, of its destructive power, than from all her sister's sorrows stoically borne. It was Branwell's frenzy of grief that showed her the potential of love as opposed to amiable flirtation, such as she had witnessed in the time of Willie Weightman and Mr. Smith, when Ellen Nussey was their object. The comparison between the two states of love was only made possible for Emily by Branwell's conduct and sufferings. It was Branwell's experience that inspired Lockwood's reflection on the quality of love to be found in the North, among the remote inhabitants of the Pennines: 'I could fancy a love for life here almost possible, and I was a fixed unbeliever in any love of a year's standing.'[2]

That Branwell's example served Emily in the portrayal of both Heath-cliff and Hindley Earnshaw is beyond doubt; both constantly speak with Branwell's accents, and Hindley acts with Branwell's gestures. When

---

[1] *SLL*, i. 347.   [2] *Wuthering Heights*, ch. 7.

Hindley pushed the point of the carving-knife between Nellie's clenched teeth in one of his drunken bouts, he was acting like Branwell who is known to have carried a carving knife about with him in the expectation of meeting Satan, as Grundy testified.[1] Heathcliff was no Branwell—far from it. He was descended straight from Gondal, but he often spoke like Branwell when he raged over his lost love, and cursed with Branwell's oaths. Emily could not have shown how a man might behave who believed himself to have been villainously used, if she had not had constantly before her the spectacle of her brother's broken heart. Branwell had always spoken like Byron; his language was extravagant, even when he was relatively tranquil. Now he spoke like a soul in hell. He was 'in torment', he wrote his friends, 'roasting at a slow fire night and day',[2] 'a martyr bound at the stake'; and he illustrated his letters with drawings depicting his immolation, or his hanging. 'My appetite is lost; my nights are dreadful, and having nothing to do makes me dwell on past scenes; on her own self, her voice, her person'. 'What I shall *do* I know not . . . I am too hard to die, and too wretched to live. My wretchedness is not about castles in the air, but about stern realities.'[3] Emily's unconscious paraphrase of these ravings is contained in one line of Heathcliff's, spoken after Catherine's death: 'I *cannot* live without my life! I *cannot* live without my soul!'[4] If in Branwell Emily saw exemplified the *idée fixe* of love, from Anne she also learnt of its treacheries. Anne had suffered at Thorp Green, and knew better than anyone how far Mrs. Robinson had enticed, and then betrayed, her brother. Anne's confidences to her sisters must be borne in mind before discrediting Branwell's statements; for she was witness of the truth. It cannot be supposed that once the story was out, and Branwell and herself returned home for good, that Anne did not confide fully in her sisters about the family at Thorp Green; and what she had to relate was not of a nature to soften Emily's anti-social outlook.

Certain scenes in *Wuthering Heights* hauntingly recall the conduct of the Robinsons. If Catherine Earnshaw's reasons for not marrying Heathcliff, whom she loved, were false, so were Mrs. Robinson's in rejecting Branwell; and if Catherine's reasons for marrying Edgar, whom she did not love, were equally false, so were Mrs. Robinson's in promoting her daughters' loveless marriages. Emily probably also heard from Anne of the elopement of the eldest Robinson girl, Lydia Mary, with the man of her choice, the Scarborough actor, Henry Roxby, to Gretna Green, and

---

[1] Grundy, F. H., *Pictures of the Past* (1879), 86-9.
[2] PBB to J. B. Leyland, June 1846, Brotherton Coll., Leeds Univ. Library.
[3] Ibid.   [4] *Wuthering Heights*, ch. 16.

of her father's 'cutting her off with a shilling' in consequence. Wilful and foolish she may have been; she was made to suffer for it for the rest of her life.[1] And so too in similar circumstances did Isabella Linton. Nor can Branwell's descriptions of Mrs. Robinson's sufferings be overlooked when reading what Emily wrote about Catherine Earnshaw's faintings and fits. After Gooch's visit to him, Branwell wrote to Leyland:

> Her coachman said that it was a pity to see her, for she was only able to kneel in her bedroom in bitter tears and prayers. She has worn herself out in attendance on him [her husband] and his conduct during the few days before his death was exceedingly mild and repentant, but that only distressed her doubly. Her conscience has helped to agonize her, and that misery I am saved from.[2]

Reporting again to Leyland after a letter from Dr. Crosby, Branwell wrote:

> I have this morning received a long, kind and faithful letter from the medical gentleman who attended Mr. R. and who has since had an interview with one whom I can never forget. . . . When he mentioned my name—she stared at him and fainted. When she recovered she in turn dwelt on her inextinguishable love for me—her horror at having been the first to delude me into wretchedness, and her agony at having been the cause of the death of her husband, who, in his last hours, bitterly repented of his treatment of her. Her sensitive mind was totally wrecked. She wandered into talking of entering a nunnery; and the Doctor fairly debars me from hope in the future. It's hard work for me dear Sir; I would bear it—but my health is so bad that the body seems as if it could not bear the mental shock. I never cared one bit about the property. I cared about herself—and always shall do. May God bless her; but I wish I had never known her![3]

For better or for worse, the effect on the inexperienced Emily of her brother's and sister's experiences was so deep and painful as permanently to colour her thoughts. Without overstraining the point, this was inevitable. Though derived from very tarnished sources, Emily accepted Branwell's tale as typical of the evils of society, and liked the world even less than before.

In estimating the harm that Branwell did to his sisters, their differing reactions to him must be taken into account. While to Charlotte he was a source of heartbreak and shame, a destroyer of domestic peace, a hindrance to all hopes of authorship, to Emily and Anne his influence was not quite so negative. They both attempted studies of Branwell in their books, and

---

[1] Robinson Papers. See Gérin, *Branwell Brontë*, 252.
[2] PBB to J. B. Leyland, June 1846.
[3] June 1846. Brotherton Coll., Leeds Univ. Library.

to do so they sought to know something more of him than his frantic gestures revealed; they tried to penetrate his mind. The effect was to leave them not unsympathetic, and hence far more vulnerable to his influence. The character of Lord Lowborough in *The Tenant of Wildfell Hall* (who resembles Branwell whereas Huntingdon does not), is analysed with perception and pity; his drug addiction is explained, the terrors to which an imaginative mind may be subject, and the nobler impulses of a once refined temperament, are charitably described.

It has already been seen how Branwell's uncontrolled passion, his desperate gestures, his apocalyptic language, had entered into the emotional climate of *Wuthering Heights*. But he was no fictional character; he was ever present in the house. In everyday life he was a permanent threat to security when stupefied by drink or drugs. While the whole family had to learn to live with the threat, in an emergency it was Emily who acted. John Greenwood related the incident of Branwell setting the curtains of his bed on fire while deeply drugged (he often stayed in bed all day), an incident that occurred after Mr. Brontë's return from Manchester. Happening to pass his open door and see the flames, Emily shot down to the kitchen for a ewer of water, before anyone else had recovered from the initial shock or been able to rouse the supine Branwell. Drenching the bedding, Emily dragged Branwell out (throwing him unceremoniously into a corner of the room), pulled the flaming curtains down and stripped and doused the bed, all with lightning speed. Her only comment when it was over, was to say: 'Don't tell Papa.'[1]

Mr. Brontë had to be told nevertheless, and it was presumably because of this incident that he took Branwell to sleep in his room.

As a result of his operation, Mr. Brontë recovered his sight well enough to take full duty unaided by mid-November, when Mr. Nicholls went on holiday. His restoration was 'a continual subject for gratitude', as Charlotte wrote to Miss Wooler, remembering his sorry state before the operation, 'when Papa's vision was wholly obscured, when he could do nothing for himself, and sat all day long in darkness and inertion. *Now* to see him walk about independently—read, write, etc., is indeed a joyful change.'[2]

Branwell's rather complacent remarks about his father, reported to Mrs. Gaskell, after nights of horror in which Mr. Brontë wrestled with him to prevent suicide—'he does his best, the poor old man'—hide a deep dread of his death which Branwell confided to his friends; his

[1] John Greenwood's diary.   [2] W & S, ii. 116.

father's death would indeed leave him destitute: 'my father cannot have long to live, and when he dies, my evening, which is already twilight, will become night', he told Leyland.[1] Branwell's acceptance of his total dependence on his father, when if he had only had the will-power to do so he could have earned his own living ,was understandably one of Charlotte's main contentions against him. But long after all the Brontë family were dead Emily's goodness to Branwell in his degradation was still village talk. Stories abounded of her waiting up at night to let him in and carry him upstairs when he was too drunk to walk. Repeated to successive biographers, they cannot all have been invention. Emily's dashes through the churchyard to tap on the side window of The Bull to warn Branwell when his father was out to fetch him home by force were witnessed by too many people to be wholly unfounded.[2] Both actions are typical of what we know of her, and significant in showing not merely Emily's attitude to her brother but the kind of man he was; a degraded man, fast degenerating into the figure of that outcast from society to whom her sympathies had gone out ever since girlhood. Pity for the wrecked life of the failure was no new theme with her; though the lines written in March 1844 were specifically for Augusta, they applied to all unfortunates, Branwell among the rest:

> How few, of all the hearts that loved,
> Are grieving for thee now!
> And why should mine, to-night, be moved
> With such a sense of woe? . . .
>
> Sometimes I seem to see thee rise,
> A glorious child again—
> All virtues beaming from thine eyes
> That ever honoured men— . . .
>
> O, fairly spread thy early sail,
> And fresh and pure and free
> Was the first impulse of the gale
> That urged life's wave for thee!
>
> Why did the pilot, too confiding,
> Dream o'er that Ocean's foam,
> And trust in Pleasure's careless guiding
> To bring his vessel home? . . .

---

[1] Brotherton Coll., Leeds Univ. Library.   [2] Duclaux, 125.

An anxious gazer from the shore,
I marked the whitening wave,
And wept above thy fate the more
Because I could not save.

It recks not now, when all is over;
But yet my heart will be
A mourner still, though friend and lover
Have both forgotten thee![1]

The situation provoked by Branwell was no new one to her imagination; the twin figures of a blighted youth and a ministering angel—a sister or a lover—had been haunting her verse in recent years. In May 1845 she was writing about 'That melancholy boy' whom no guardian angel protected, whose 'grim Fate' had never 'Smiled since he was born'. Over such a one she imagines a Seraph descending 'to weep with him' and glorying in her mission:

I, the image of light and gladness,
Saw and pitied that mournful boy,
And I swore to take his gloomy sadness,
And give to him my beamy joy . . .

Guardian angel, he lacks no longer;
Evil fortune he need not fear:
Fate is strong, but Love is stronger;
And more unsleeping than angel's care.[2]

In the month before, in April 1845, Emily was writing yet again of such a relationship, the effect of hearing a man's groan of suffering; he was grieving for his buried love. The theme, incidentally, prefigures Heathcliff's frenzy for the buried Catherine.

About his face the sunshine glows,
And in his hair the south wind blows,
And violet and wild wood-rose
Are sweetly breathing near;
Nothing without suggests dismay,
If he could force his mind away
From tracking farther, day by day,
The desert of Despair.

[1] Hatfield, 171.   [2] Hatfield, 186.

> Too truly agonized to weep,
> His eyes are motionless as sleep;
> His frequent sighs, long-drawn and deep,
> Are anguish to my ear;
> And I would soothe—but can I call
> The cold corpse from its funeral pall,
> And cause a gleam of hope to fall
> With my consoling tear? . . .

Unable to console, she implores Death to end his misery:

> Enough of storms have bowed his head:
> Grant him at last a quiet bed,
> Beside his early stricken dead—
> Even where he yearns to be![1]

The appearance of such subjects in Emily's poems even before Branwell's final collapse shows that his influence was not alone in shaping her imagination; he only emphasized and confirmed an intuitive knowledge of the tragedy of human frailty.

The more Branwell resembled her Gondal characters or appeared to do so in her vision of him, the more Emily could feel for him. It was not that she had any illusions about him—on the contrary, she saw him clearly as he was—dishonest as well as spineless. Charlotte told Ellen Nussey of an incident that occurred on her return home after a short absence at Brookroyd. Branwell was so 'stupified' as to be unable to speak; wondering how he had got the money she asked Emily, who told her: 'he got a sovereign from Papa while I have been away under the pretence of paying a pressing debt—he went immediately and changed it at a public-house—and has employed it as was to be expected—she concluded her account with saying he was a hopeless being.'[2]

As a result of her growing involvement with Branwell Emily adopted a role less and less consonant with the style and restrictions generally imposed on parsons' daughters in the nineteenth century, and a good deal closer to her own imagined world. Parsons' daughters did not generally enter pubs, even if it were only the pub yard. The figure of the outcast man succoured by the vigorous-minded girl, already taking shape in her poems and shortly to invade her whole novel, was a product of Ellis Bell's way of thinking, and of 'his' evolving mode of life. It was an attitude which bewildered Emily's first readers; the attitude of defiance towards the social,

[1] Hatfield, 185.   [2] CB to Ellen Nussey 3 Mar. 1846. *SLL*, i. 321.

and even more towards the national, traditions of the English novel was deeply disturbing when in *Wuthering Heights* she translated into fiction the exceptional circumstance of her own life. But what was real enough in life was in her view real enough for fiction. For her there had never been in any case a separation between the imagined and the real life. This is not to say that Emily attempted to portray the figure of Branwell in *Wuthering Heights* (as Anne did in *The Tenant of Wildfell Hall*), but that Branwell's presence, and Emily's acceptance of it, permeated the book.

The evidence exists that Emily was writing a second novel which although incomplete had advanced far enough for her to approach her publisher with it. The failure to finish and the likelihood that she destroyed the manuscript before her death might be explained by her growing absorption in her real as distinct from her imagined life. Branwell, as his danger increased, could have been too much for the latter. The strength of her feelings towards the weak and suffering may have supplanted all her other impulses. The question must be examined later.

On days when he was in better shape, Branwell would borrow a horse and ride to Halifax to meet Leyland; or occasionally, when Grundy was in the district, meet him by appointment. Branwell wrote to him to arrange such a meeting at Skipton at the Devonshire Arms in July 1846. To Leyland, for whom Branwell had secured some commissions for memorial tablets in Haworth, he sometimes wrote, begging for a visit. 'I wish I could see you,' he wrote in late summer, 'and, as Haworth Fair is held on Monday after the ensuing one, your presence there would gratify one of the FALLEN . . . All is yet with me clouds and darkness. I hope you have, at least, blue sky and sunshine.'[1]

The outcome of such excursions was only deeper debt for Branwell, and a worsening of his physical condition. Towards the end of the year Charlotte reported to Ellen the visit of a Sheriff's Officer to Branwell—inviting him either to pay his debts or to take a trip to York, where was the county prison. 'It is not agreeable to lose money time after time in this way but it is ten times worse to witness the shabbiness of his behaviour on such occasions', wrote Charlotte.[2]

Charlotte's deep depression that summer was not only due to Branwell; every publisher to whom the novels were sent rejected them—mostly in two curt lines. The prospect of ever succeeding with them was dwindling with each successive rebuff. The following year, on 24 March, Charlotte wrote to Ellen: 'I shall be 31 next birthday—My youth is gone like a

[1] PBB to J. B. Leyland, Oct. 1846. Brotherton Coll., Leeds Univ. Library.
[2] W & S, ii. 118.

dream—and very little use have I ever made of it—What have I done these last thirty years? Precious little.'[1]

On 12 May, Charlotte wrote again: 'Branwell is quiet now and for a good reason: he has got through the end of a considerable sum of money of which he became possessed in the spring, and consequently is obliged to restrict himself to some degree.' (This was the money supplied by Dr. Crosby.) It was hoped by then to arrange a visit from Ellen Nussey when the weather settled, and Charlotte added: 'You must expect to find him weaker in mind, and the complete rake in appearance. I have no apprehension of his being at all uncivil to you; on the contrary, he will be as smooth as oil.'[2]

For reasons unconnected with Branwell, Ellen's visit had to be postponed several times, and did not take place until the latter half of July. Before then, two events of importance to the Bells had taken place. On 16 June, hearing that no further copies of the *Poems* had been sold, the authors decided to send out some of the remainder to the major poets and critics of the day: Wordsworth, Hartley Coleridge, De Quincey, Lockhart, and Tennyson. The covering letters, all identical in text, read:

June 16th, 1847

Sir,—My relatives, Ellis and Acton Bell, and myself, heedless of the repeated warnings of various respectable publishers, have committed the rash act of printing a volume of poems.

The consequences predicted have, of course, overtaken us; our book is found to be a drug; no man needs it or heeds it. In the space of a year our publisher has disposed but of two copies, and by what painful efforts he succeeded in getting rid of these two, himself only knows.

Before transferring the edition to the trunkmakers, we have decided on distributing as presents a few copies of what we cannot sell; and beg to offer you one in acknowledgement of the pleasure and profit we have often and long derived from your works.

I am, Sir, yours very respectfully,

Currer Bell[3]

In doing this, the Bells must have felt that the end of their venture into authorship had been reached; a full year after the publication of their first book, only two copies had sold. The novels, on which they had staked their future, had gone the rounds for nearly a year also and not found a publisher. At that moment, when their hopes were at their lowest ebb, came a turn in the tide of misfortune; early in July (the date is not known)

[1] W & S, ii. 129–30.   [2] W & S, ii. 132.   [3] *SLL*, i. 329.

the last publisher to whom they had sent out the manuscripts, T. C. Newby of Mortimer Street, Cavendish Square, wrote to say that he was prepared to accept *Wuthering Heights* and *Agnes Grey* but not *The Professor*; if the authors were agreeable to publishing the two books without the third, he would draw up an agreement to that effect. Such a proposal was totally unexpected. It was no time to hesitate, however, and by 15 July Newby's offer was accepted and the now isolated *Professor* sent out once again to the next publisher on their list. It was the firm of Smith, Elder & Co. Charlotte did not hear from them till 6 August, when their decision was a negative, but a negative so full of promise as to be more welcome, Charlotte said later, than some acceptances. What Smith, Elder wanted, in place of the too-short *Professor* was a full-length three-volume novel. This Charlotte had by now, *Jane Eyre* being almost finished. By 24 August, when she sent the completed manuscript to Cornhill, Emily and Anne were receiving the first proof-sheets of *Wuthering Heights* and *Agnes Grey*.

Ellen Nussey tells of a curious, seemingly supernatural but in their altered circumstances wholly appropriate occurrence which she witnessed during her visit to Haworth that summer.[1] Ellen Nussey told Mary Duclaux of it, and it first appeared in her *Memoir of Emily Brontë*.

Once, at this time, when they were walking on the moors together a sudden change of light came into the sky. 'Look!' said Charlotte; and the four girls looked up and saw three suns shining clearly overhead. They stood a little while gazing at the beautiful parhelion; Charlotte, her friend, and Anne clustered together, Emily a little higher, standing on a heathery knoll. 'That is you,' said Ellen at last, 'you are the three suns.' 'Hush!' cried Charlotte, indignant at the too shrewd nonsense of her friend; but as Ellen, her suspicions confirmed by Charlotte's violence, lowered her eyes to the earth again, she looked a moment at Emily. She was still standing on her knoll, quiet, satisfied; and round her lips there hovered a very soft and happy smile.[2]

The occurrence of parhelions in the Haworth sky over the centuries had been noted in the old church registers, one entry in which the Brontës no doubt knew.[3] Whether the Brontës viewed the phenomenon

---

[1] Mrs. Gaskell places the visit in August, but Charlotte's fever of activity to get *Jane Eyre* finished between 6 and 24 August makes this unlikely; a gap in the correspondence in the second half of July would suggest it took place then.

[2] Duclaux, 143.

[3] In 1649, it was recorded that 'On the 25th day of February this year, being Monday, there were two suns appeared on either side of the real sun in the firmament, which made three suns in all. They were seen betwixt nine and eleven by the country people assembled

as an augury of fame, as Ellen Nussey supposed, or whether Emily's smile was for the beauty and mystery of the scene, their fortunes seemed certainly at that moment to have taken a favourable turn.

---

at the Great Fair of Cattle kept in Colne situated in the County Palatine of Lancashire.' Early in 1907, the then Rector of Haworth, the Revd. T. W. Story, recorded how he saw 'in severe winter weather an almost similar phenomenon with the addition of a brilliant ring or halo . . . It was said to be due,' he added, 'to particles of ice in the air.' T. W. Story, *Notes on the Old Haworth Church Registers*, 6.

CHAPTER XV

WUTHERING HEIGHTS

THE firm of Thomas Cautley Newby, of 172 Mortimer Street, Cavendish Square, was newly established and on the lookout for unknown talent. When Trollope's mother, the highly successful novelist, Frances Trollope, rather shamefacedly hawked her son's first manuscript round the publishing fraternity, without expectation of success (Trollope said that he 'knew she did not give him credit for the sort of cleverness necessary for such work')[1] she went to Newby with it. It was the same year that the Bells sent their manuscripts to him, and his reaction to the two applications is significant. While he undertook to publish young Trollope's book on a half-profits basis, because of Mrs. Trollope's reputation, he made the unknown Bells share the costs of production. For an edition of 300 copies of their book, they were to advance £50, which he undertook to refund when 250 copies were sold. In the event, he never refunded them anything. His methods were consistently fraudulent: having acquired the Bells' book, and sent the first proof-sheets to the authors, in August 1847, he held up production. Repeated letters from them elicited no replies. *Jane Eyre*, which was not yet finished when *Wuthering Heights* and *Agnes Grey* were accepted, was published on 16 October 1847 and selling well before Newby resumed printing. By then he realized that there was some profit to be made out of the name of Bell. He treated his authors shabbily moreover in the book's appearance; none of their corrections on the proof-sheets were made. This they found to their chagrin when in mid-December they received their complimentary copies at last. The books were bound in deep claret-coloured ribbed cloth, decorated with blind-stamped ornamentation, the titles in gold lettering on the spine. *Wuthering Heights* filled the first two volumes, *Agnes Grey* the third. Writing to her own excellent publishers on 14 December, Charlotte deplored her sisters' ill-luck: 'The books are not well got up—they abound in errors of the press . . . I feel painfully that Ellis and Acton have not had the justice at Newby's hands that I have had at those of Smith & Elder.'[2] Happy from

---

[1] Trollope, *Autobiography*, World's Classics edn., p. 64.   [2] W & S, ii. 162.

the outset with the 'gentlemanly conduct' of her own publishers, Charlotte tried repeatedly to extricate her sisters from their entanglement with the shady Newby, but in vain; Emily and Anne, despite their many disappointments, stuck to their 'rascal'—as they stuck by the Gondals and stuck to their railway investments, despite warnings of disaster. In the event, they were wrong and Charlotte was right; but they preferred to assert their independence than take advice. Charlotte's view of their danger was confirmed more than once during 1848 as Newby's methods were exposed, but nothing would induce Emily to change publishers. The growing intractability of her character was first clearly seen in this misguided loyalty to Newby; it would shortly invade every aspect of her life.

The publication of *Jane Eyre* on 16 October followed in mid-December by *Wuthering Heights* and *Agnes Grey* had the unfortunate effect of provoking more curiosity about the authors' identities than critical interest in their works. In this respect *Jane Eyre* did better than its followers. By the time *Wuthering Heights* appeared, *Jane Eyre* had been reviewed in seventeen London journals, and in seven provincial ones. The *Athenaeum* judged that it 'deserves praise and commendation to the novel reader'. Both in the high praise of Thackeray (forwarded to Charlotte by her publishers) and in G. H. Lewes's 'very lenient' review in *Fraser's Magazine* (December 1847) Currer Bell had every reason to rejoice; they started the book on its extraordinary path to success.

With the appearance of further Bell novels, a note of suspicion crept into the critics' notices. The *Athenaeum*, reviewing *Wuthering Heights* and *Agnes Grey* on 25 December 1847 in their column 'Our Literary Table', pointed the way:

Jane Eyre, it will be recollected, was edited by Mr. Currer Bell. Here are two tales so closely related in cast of thought, incident and language as to excite some curiosity. All three might be the work of one hand—but the first issued remains the best. In spite of much power and cleverness, in spite of its truth to life in the remote corners of England—Wuthering Heights is a disagreeable story. The Bells seem to affect painful and exceptional subjects—the misdeeds or oppression of tyranny, the eccentricities of 'woman's fantasy'. They do not turn away from dwelling upon those physical acts of cruelty—the contemplation of which true taste rejects . . . and if the Bells, singly or collectively, are contemplating future or frequent utterance in Fiction, let us hope that they will spare us further interiors so gloomy as the one here elaborated with such dismal minuteness. In this respect, Agnes Grey is more acceptable to us though less powerful.

The Bell novels, it can be seen, were to be judged by comparison with each other, not according to their individual merits. The suspicion of some fraud being practised by a joker giving himself three names continued to haunt the minds of critics and readers alike. It was a suspicion which the astute Newby sedulously spread. Charlotte's publishers let her know the reports that were circulating in the literary world.

Your account of the various surmises respecting the identity of the brothers Bell amused me much [she wrote them on 10 November]; were the enigma solved it would probably be found not worth the trouble of solution, but I will let it alone; it suits ourselves to remain quiet and certainly injures no one. The Reviewer who noticed the little book of poems, in the Dublin Magazine, conjectured that the soi-disant three personages were in reality but one. . . . This was an ingenious thought in the Reviewer—very original and striking, but not accurate. We are three.

The confusion regarding the Bells' identities, begun as a mere rumour, took on larger proportions by the end of the year, when allegations appeared in the press of 'trickery' and 'artifice' being used by them. Charlotte wrote to her publishers on 31 December:

I should not be ashamed to be considered the author of Wuthering Heights and Agnes Grey, but, possessing no real claim to that honour, I would rather not have it attributed to me, thereby depriving the true authors of their just meed. . . . What is meant by charges of *trickery* and *artifice* I have yet to comprehend. It is no art in me to write a tale—it is no trick in Messrs Smith & Elder to publish it. Where do the trickery and artifice lie? [1]

The answer lay with Newby. Watching the soaring sales of *Jane Eyre*, and learning from the trade that a second edition was being called for, he did not hesitate to spread the report yet further that all three Bell novels were the work of *his* author, Ellis Bell. Emily's reaction to such proceedings can be judged from Charlotte's disclaimer: 'Mr. Newby, it appears, thinks it expedient so to frame his advertisement as to favour the misapprehension. If Mr. Newby had much sagacity he would see that Ellis Bell is strong enough to stand without being propped by Currer Bell— and would have disdained what Ellis himself of all things disdains— recourse to trickery.' [2]

No methods, indeed, could be more distasteful to the uncompromising Emily; yet it was under such auspices that her book appeared. The fact has to be borne in mind when considering her reasons for finally giving up writing.

The critics did not wholly condemn or ignore *Wuthering Heights*; they simply did not understand it. The *Athenaeum* reviewer judged it a 'disagreeable story', its interiors 'gloomy', its detail 'dismal'. No other criterion was applied to its achievement till after the author's death, when Sydney Dobell recognized its quality in 1850. Even so, he credited Currer Bell with being the author. While declaring that certain pages in *Wuthering Heights* were 'the masterpiece of a poet', and that he was at a loss 'to find anywhere in modern prose . . . such wealth and economy, such apparent ease, such instinctive art',[1] he still regarded it as an immature work of Currer Bell's, written considerably before *Jane Eyre*.

The first reviewers were impressed by the 'disagreeable' quality of *Wuthering Heights*. The *Atlas* said that the 'general effect is inexpressibly painful', even while conceding that there were 'evidences in every chapter of a sort of rugged power'. 'We know nothing in the whole range of our fictitious literature which represents such shocking pictures of the worst forms of humanity.' *Wuthering Heights* was compared, unfavourably, with works—long since forgotten—of equal gloom. The 'sprawling' story, as the reviewer saw it, was only held together by the 'singleness of malignity of the presiding evil genius'. 'There is not in the entire dramatis personae a single character which is not utterly hateful or thoroughly contemptible. If you do not detest the person you despise him; and if you do not despise him you detest him with your whole heart.' The critic's sole recommendation to the bewildered readers was to remember that the scenes and characters he is called on to witness 'are placed not in a London mansion, but far from the haunts of civilized man'.[2] The *Britannia* critic fully shared this view: he supposed 'that the characters are drawn from the very lowest of life; that they are the inhabitants of an isolated and uncivilized district, or that they are of some demoniac influence'. His overall judgement was that 'as an imaginative writer the author has to learn the first principles of his art'.[3] The reviewer in *Douglas Jerrold's Weekly* felt forced to confess that *Wuthering Heights* was a book 'baffling all regular criticism'. While admitting its power he thought it 'a purposeless power'. He warned his readers that they would be shocked, 'disgusted, almost sickened by details of cruelty, inhumanity and the most diabolical hate and vengeance', but recommended it to those 'who love novelty . . . for we can promise them that they have never read anything like it before'.[4]

Ellis Bell's 'want of art' was a further complaint of the critics; *Britannia* complained that the characters 'have all the angularity of misshapen

[1] Sydney Dobell, 'Currer Bell', *The Palladium*, Sept. 1850; *BST* 1918.
[2] See E. Weir, 'Contemporary Reviews of the First Brontë Novels', *BST* 1947.
[3] Ibid.   [4] Ibid.

growth and form in this respect a striking contrast to those regular forms we are accustomed to meet with in English fiction . . . they are so new, so grotesque, so entirely without art, that they strike us as proceeding from a mind of limited experience.'[1]

It is doubtful whether Emily derived more satisfaction from her critics' rare expressions of praise (several of them allowed the book to have power and originality—*Atlas* and *Britannia* both compared its 'savage grandeur' to the style in painting of Salvator Rosa) than from their abuse; their pronouncements were in the main equally unperceptive. The *Examiner* stood apart in its willingness 'to trust an author who goes at once fearlessly into the moors and desolate places for his heroes'.[2] By the time *Wuthering Heights* had crossed the Atlantic, critical opinion had crystallized; the reviewer on the *North American Review* stigmatized the novel's hero as 'a brute-demon', and its author, though 'a man of uncommon talents', as 'dogged, brutal, and morose'.[3]

Mrs. Gaskell, who derived her information from Charlotte, spoke of Emily's sufferings from the misjudgements of the critics. Staying with Charlotte in September 1853, she wrote to a friend: 'But Emily—poor Emily—the pangs of disappointment as review after review came out about *Wuthering Heights* were terrible. Miss B. said she had no recollection of pleasure or gladness about *Jane Eyre* every such feeling was lost in seeing Emily's resolute endurance, yet knowing what she felt'.[4]

Precocious as the Brontë children were, and paramount as was the place of reading in their lives, their initiation into contemporary literature was severely one-sided. While they possessed in their father's library the works of all the major poets, and had Byron by heart at a time when other children were reciting Cowper and Wordsworth, their knowledge of contemporary prose literature was limited to the writers contributing to the Tory periodicals, *Blackwood's*, *Fraser's*, and the fashionable Annuals. Thus, they had opportunities of reading Mrs. Norton's novelettes, but not Jane Austen, as Charlotte's later correspondence with G. H. Lewes reveals. The Scottish bias in their reading through the influence of *Blackwood's* is evident even in Emily's earliest recorded sayings and doings: when asked what 'cheif' men she wanted to inhabit her dream island (the Isle of Arran incidentally) she chose Sir Walter Scott, Mr. Lockhart, and 'Johnny Lockhart'. Scott's poetry, history, and novels (in that order) were, as has been seen, the main influences of Emily's youth. Unlike Charlotte, who later caught up with Jane Austen and Dickens, it

[1] Ibid.   [2] Ibid.   [3] *BST* 1956.   [4] Gaskell, *Letters*, 247.

seems unlikely that Emily ever read either. She would barely have had time to read Thackeray, whose emergence with *Vanity Fair* in 1847 was simultaneous with her own, and preceded her death by only a year. Fiction did not reach Emily Brontë through the main Victorian stream of realism (even Bulwer Lytton whom she read subscribed to the romantic tradition). It may be doubted if she read any novels other than Scott's and those serialized in *Blackwood's* during her impressionable girlhood, and these, as reference to the old numbers show, were markedly 'Gothic' in character.

Though Joseph, Zillah, Ellen, Dr. Kenneth owe their life to her own shrewd observation of rural types, Emily might know by comparison with the characters of Scott that such beings were no figments of the imagination, unrecognizable to their human fellows, no Frankenstein's monster composed of lifeless parts. Scott gave her the yardstick by which to measure the truth of her creations. The model he set for fiction struck a deep responsive chord in her even when, all unconsciously, she exposed its fallacies in a single work of fiction of her own. Only then could it be seen how, despite the resemblances, their minds were poles apart. Although their natural settings were essential to Scott's tales, the role of nature remained in his hands largely a picturesque one. No landscape painter had a finer eye for the right placing of a ruined castle, a craggy hillside, a clump of trees. But for Emily these things were not a part of the background, they were an integral part of the human drama; they had a meaning and an intimate relationship with the actors in the drama, as they had had for Wordsworth. It could be said that while Scott was the model she unconsciously followed as a writer of fiction, she remained fundamentally a poet, with a poet's subjective eye for the significance of what she saw.

Scott was no mystic, yet he had so much of human sympathy, so much of the antiquarian's true sense of history as to enter, dramatically, into the mystic's vision, if need be, and to speak with his tongue. In the hour of his trial, torture, and death, Scott's poor Cameronian preacher, Ephraim Macbriar in *Old Mortality*, defies his judges with the words: 'Flesh and blood may shrink under the sufferings you can doom me to, and poor frail nature may shed tears or send forth cries, but I trust my soul is anchored firmly on the rock of ages'.[1] The words are biblical no doubt, but they foreshadow the substance and imagery of Emily's later lines:

> ... Vain are the thousand creeds
> That move men's hearts ...

[1] *Old Mortality*, ch. 36.

To waken doubt in one . . .
So surely anchored on
The steadfast rock of Immortality . . .[1]

Where Emily parted company from Scott as she evolved was in her attitude of defiance to Fate, and in her acceptance of Evil. There the influence was incontestably Byron's and that of the horror-school that derived from his early works. Writers like Mary Shelley, Hoffmann, James Hogg, were not content like Mrs. Radcliffe with terrifying their readers; they aimed at taking the Devil by the horns and dragging him into full view. The works of all these writers were either published or extensively reviewed in *Blackwood's*. In either case, they were sooner or later available to Emily Brontë and almost certainly read by her. A common theme runs through these tales: they are all concerned with an alien identity existing side by side with a man or woman's known identity. Mary Shelley proclaimed it in her novel *Valperga*, published in 1823 and extensively quoted in *Blackwood's* for March of that year. The plot concerned the once virtuous and gentle Castruccio who has become a tyrant of Florence, and been transformed into a monster of cruelty. One of the victims of his crimes, Beatrice of Ferrara, places the character squarely in the full romantic tradition, when she denounces him in the words: 'I shall fly you as a basilisk, and if I see you your eyes will kill me'—words that recall not only 'the basilisk charm' of Byron's *Giaour*, but the image of his successor, Heathcliff. Possessed of an evil power that she does not hesitate to attribute to the Devil, Beatrice of Ferrara expounds her theory of the universe. 'Listen to me', she cries to her deliverer from captivity, the innocent Countess of Valperga, in a scene set in dungeons very reminiscent of Gondal

while I announce to you the eternal and victorious influence of evil which circulates like air about us. . . . Are you blind that you see it not? . . . reflect on domestic life, on the strife, hatred and uncharitableness that pierces one's bosom at every turn. . . . Oh! surely God's hand is the chastening hand of a father that thus torments his children! He created man—that most wretched of slaves; oh, know you not what a wretch man is! and what a store-house of infinite pain is this much-vaunted human soul? Look into your own heart . . . or gaze on mine; I will tear it open for your inspection. There is hatred, remorse, grief—overwhelming mighty, and eternal misery. God created me; am I the work of a beneficent being?[2]

Blackwood's reviewer, quoting this passage and evidently shaken by the

---

[1] Hatfield, 191.   [2] *Blackwood's Magazine*, Mar. 1823.

overt blasphemies it contained, was torn in his judgement between admiration for 'the clever and amusing' qualities of this romance, and the consideration that it belonged 'to a *certain* school which is certainly a very modern as well as a very mischievous one, and which ought never, of all things, to have numbered ladies among its disciples'.[1]

How much attuned to such unladylike sentiments was young Emily Brontë can be seen from her poem written in May 1837

> I am the only being whose doom
> No tongue would ask, no eye would mourn

—the concluding lines of which read like a paraphrase of the *Valperga* text quoted above:

> 'Twas grief enough to think mankind
> All hollow, servile, insincere;
> But worse to trust to my own mind
> And find the same corruption there.[2]

The subject of evil-possession, however first introduced to Emily, appears to have held a singular fascination for her. It appears in the Gondal sequences long before *Wuthering Heights*, purporting to be spoken by Augusta's daughter, Alexandrina:

> I love thee, boy; for all divine,
> All full of God thy features shine.
> Darling enthusiast, holy child,
> Too good for this world's warring wild,
> Too heavenly now, but doomed to be
> Hell-like in heart and misery . . .[3]

In a later series the subject concerns a 'melancholy boy' who lacks a guardian angel, and a radiant girl-child, the

> Child of Delight! with sunbright hair
> And seablue, seadeep eyes . . .[4]

(an obvious early prototype of Catherine Earnshaw) in whom a frightening change takes place, elsewhere described.

> I'm sure I've seen these forms before
> But many springs ago;
>
> And only *he* had locks of light,
> And *she* had raven hair . . .[5]

[1] Ibid. [2] Hatfield, 11.
[3] Hatfield, 112. [4] Hatfield, 187. [5] Hatfield, 153.

A specific contribution to the novel of evil-possession was made by the German romancer, Hoffmann, as *Blackwood's* reviewer in the July issue 1824 noted of his *Devil's Elixir*. This was his idea of a *doppelgänger*, a 'visitation of another self, a double with a man's own personal appearance, who in his name, and in his likeness, commits every atrocious crime of which he would never have believed himself capable'. It was this notion that James Hogg used to such telling effect in his *Confessions of a Justified Sinner* which he published anonymously in 1824. Like *Wuthering Heights* after it, the tale is made all the more haunting by its appearance of sober reality. Set in the Edinburgh of the early eighteenth century, the circumstantial details, the unexaggerated style, the sharply drawn characters, the vivid incidents, place it incomparably above other works of this kind, and suggests more than one close analogy with *Wuthering Heights*. Here, the *doppelgänger* theme is exploited to its logical conclusion. The Devil, capable of assuming any likeness (especially that of his victims), and working through the person of the Justified Sinner of the title, induces him to commit a succession of crimes, ending with the murder of his own innocent half-brother, mother, and father. There are similarities of incident and character with *Wuthering Heights*, like the opening of the suicide's grave, the character of the sanctimonious old servant (John Barnet is a perfect Joseph), and the name of the printer, Linton. Above all, there is the figure of the 'illustrious stranger'—in power, appearance, and expression perhaps the only comparable character to Heathcliff in nineteenth-century fiction. He is, of course, the Devil, but his unsuspecting victim imagines him to be only the Emperor of Russia—between which conception and Heathcliff's 'Emperor of China' there is not so much difference.[1] The subject of the book, like *Wuthering Heights*, appears to concern an inheritance, while its true meaning concerns the possession of a soul. Such a theme could have left a deep impression on Emily, if she encountered it at an early age. While tracing the publications in *Blackwood's* known early to the Brontë children (the *Confessions* was not among these though referred to in several numbers)[2] it has to be borne in mind that Emily's own full understanding of them could only have come much later. The battered back-numbers of 'Maga', as Branwell told the editor in 1835, were 'read and re-read' in childhood'[3], and with undiminished avidity over the years. Many of the stories that belonged to Emily's childhood had made their impact on her before she ever read them for herself.

[1] *Wuthering Heights*, ch. 7.   [2] See Aug. 1823, June 1824, July 1824.
[3] PBB to the editor of *Blackwood's*, Dec. 1835. Oliphant, *Annals of a Publishing House* (1897), ii. 178.

She was an adult when *The Bridegroom of Barna* was anonymously published in *Blackwood's* for November 1840.[1] It too has obvious points in common with *Wuthering Heights*. The story concerns the tragic loves of Hugh Lawlor and Ellen Nugent, children of rival families living in Tipperary, whose guardians oppose their marriage. Ellen's brother has fought a duel with Lawlor and been injured, and Ellen herself has fallen into a 'decline'. In consideration of this, and at the dying request of the brother, her father gives way and consents to the marriage. The whole countryside is convened to the celebrations. The bridegroom and bride are described as 'a pair marked out by nature to be memorable in their generation'; he is dark and 'scowling', has a 'dark handsome face and flashing eyes'; she is fair, 'with pale gold hair, pure colourless cheek—a form light and feary-like as ever danced in a moonbeam'. The story is told by a one-armed beggar called Tom Bush to a fellow guest as they ride towards the wedding feast at Barna. During the service, which is held in the house, a storm of extraordinary violence breaks outside. At the height of the merriment within, of the dancing and feasting, Tom Bush creates an intentional disturbance and is thrown outside by Hugh Lawlor. He swears vengeance, goes four miles through the storm to find a magistrate, Major Walker (whose comfortable home seen from outside is reminiscent of Thrushcross Grange), and tells him that Lawlor is the man wanted for an old political murder. Lawlor's victim had formerly been a suitor of Ellen's. The Major sets out at once for Barna despite the storm to arrest Lawlor there and then. While the bride and groom are dancing Sir Roger de Coverley the redcoats and constables burst in, but warned by a Fortune-teller—Nance, who has always befriended the young people—Lawlor gets away to the mountains. After remaining in hiding for months, he returns one September night when Ellen's father is from home, and gains admittance to Ellen's room. A reunion in the style of Heathcliff and Catherine follows, Ellen being almost at death's door. Nance disguises herself as Lawlor to draw off the constables, while Lawlor makes his escape again. Ellen's grief, however, wears her out, and she dies. She is buried in the grounds of a distant abbey, where Lawlor comes three days after the funeral. He unburies her, clasps her in his arms as the constables, tipped off by Bush, arrive to arrest him. He manages to shoot Bush before being shot himself. He is buried in Ellen's grave, as her kindred did not venture 'to separate in death the hapless pair who in life could never be united'.[2]

[1] The author has been identified by John Hewish as Bartholomew Simmonds.
[2] *Blackwood's Magazine*, Nov. 1840.

As a result of such reading certain things understandably lodged in Emily Brontë's mind. Desecration of graves figures in *The Bridegroom of Barna* and in Hogg's *Confessions*; in *Wuthering Heights* such desecration is perfectly in character with Heathcliff. The mystery of Heathcliff's origins, which remain undivulged to the end, is altogether in keeping with the literary traditions of such a character. Byron had set the fashion with *Lara* and the *Giaour*; Hogg exploited it in the *Confessions*; Nellie Dean was still asking herself in the last chapter of *Wuthering Heights*: ' . . .where did he come from, the little dark thing, harboured by a good man to his bane?'[1] And Heathcliff's wife after two months' marriage could still credibly ask: 'Is Mr. Heathcliff a man? If so, is he mad? And if not, is he a devil?'[2]

Essential to the fiction of this genre is the insistence on the inhuman nature of the hero/villain. (There were countless others flooding the market at the time written in the wake of Charles Maturin's highly successful *Melmoth the Wanderer*, but it cannot be proved they were known to Emily.) It was a conception or convention obviously attractive to her and one which she adopted wholeheartedly to the purposes of her own plot. No occasion for emphasizing Heathcliff's animal and unearthly nature is lost. Isabella describes his 'cannibal' teeth, his 'basilisk eyes',[3] calls him 'an incarnate goblin', and concludes: 'He is not a human being and has no claim on my charity'.[4] 'A tiger or a venomous serpent', she adds, 'could not rouse terror in me equal to that which he wakens',[5] and she speaks of the 'fiend that usually looks out of his eyes'.[6] Even the rational Nellie Dean admits that 'I did not feel as if I were in the company of a creature of my own species',[7] and describes him gnashing at her and foaming at the mouth, 'like a mad dog'.[8] In the dawn after Catherine's death Nellie sees Heathcliff 'lifting up his eyes and howling not like a man, but like a savage beast'.[9] Written by Emily Brontë such a comparison held less of condemnation than of pity; it has to be judged in the context of her poem written years before, expressive of her deepest sympathies:

> Or would I mock the wolf's death-howl
> Because his form is gaunt and foul?[10]

It is, indeed, central to the conception of Heathcliff that his creator viewed him with more compassion than hate. To this end, his early ill-treatment is offered in extenuation of the ferocious man he became. Conscious that few would share such sympathies (her own sister Charlotte

---

[1] *Wuthering Heights*, ch. 34.   [2] Ibid., ch. 13.   [3] Ibid., ch. 17.
[4] Ibid.   [5] Ibid., ch. 13.   [6] Ibid., ch. 17.
[7] Ibid., ch. 15.   [8] Ibid., ch. 16.   [9] Ibid., ch. 9.   [10] Hatfield, 123.

did not) the author of *Wuthering Heights*, speaking through the medium of the sane wholesome countrywoman, Nellie Dean, bred up in local superstitions, subscribes to the popular romantic tradition of her models in her summing up of Heathcliff: as he nears his Heaven and feels himself almost within sight of 'his soul's bliss', Nellie sees him standing at the open lattice with the light falling on his face, and she starts in terror at the look she sees there: 'Those deep black eyes, that smile, and ghastly paleness! It appeared to me, not Mr. Heathcliff, but a goblin.' 'Is he a ghoul or a vampire?' Nellie asks herself, remembering that 'she had read of such hideous, incarnate demons', an admission of her acquaintance with the Gothic novel—and still more, of Emily's own.

In her Preface to the posthumous 1850 edition of *Wuthering Heights* Charlotte did not hesitate to say: 'Heathcliff stands unredeemed'. She further confirmed his affiliation with the Gothic tradition: 'we should say he was child neither of Lascar nor gipsy, but a man's shape animated by demon life—a Ghoul—an Afreet.'

The similarities in incident and character between *Wuthering Heights* and the novels of Emily's immediate predecessors and contemporaries are nevertheless only isolated phenomena: the general character of her book is quite different. One must look to her own knowledge of life, however limited it may have been, for anything like an adequate comprehension of *Wuthering Heights*. And as already mentioned in relating her school-days at Law Hill, [1] the story of the builder of the house, Jack Sharp, offers some close parallels to Emily's tale of the 'cuckoo' Heathcliff. The points of resemblance seem too close to be fortuitous.

Both tales are concerned with property, with old houses dating back to Tudor times: Wuthering Heights and Walterclough Hall. The heads of both houses, Mr. Walker and Mr. Earnshaw, adopt a boy out of the goodness of their hearts. The boy becomes 'very overbearing', as Caroline Walker put it, and supplants the legitimate heirs. Mr. Walker's death, like that of Mr. Earnshaw, brings home the rightful heir, who, like Hindley Earnshaw, arrives with his bride in a chaise and four, direct from the celebration of their marriage at Thirsk. Very pacific in character and more like Edgar Linton than Hindley Earnshaw, John Walker seeks to placate his cousin in this awkward situation, but the new Mrs. Walker demands his eviction and the restitution of her husband's rights without delay. From then on, Jack Sharp becomes increasingly malign, harasses his relatives by every conceivable means, and even obliges them to lodge for a time

---

[1] See above, ch. VII.

with relatives while he builds himself a new house within sight of Walterclough Hall. When at last the Walkers are left in full possession of their home, they find it in the most 'dilapidated condition' with 'every removable fixture and heirloom stripped from the house and out-buildings', the 'plate and linen gone', and 'the lodging-rooms unfit to be seen'.[1] One recalls the ruin wrought by Heathcliff on a comfortable gentleman's house.

Jack Sharp takes his revenge on the family of his benefactors by ruining them financially. One of the means employed is playing cards for high stakes. Caroline Walker remembered her parents as always short of money in consequence of Mr. Walker's losses to Jack Sharp and the loans which he was more or less blackmailed into making him. When Jack Sharp found that there was little more to expect from his cousin, he systemati-cally set about degrading young Sam Stead as Heathcliff degraded Hareton Earnshaw and when Sharp's own affairs fell on evil days the boy took himself off to Walterclough Hall and sought refuge with the Walkers. There he repaid the kindness he received by setting the servants by the ears and teaching the little children to swear.

What was lacking in the story recorded by Caroline Walker was the element of romance. Typical of the district and the period, the story of the Walker family concerned property, trade, an inheritance, but it was not concerned with any question of love. Emily added to the bare bones of the plot—as Shakespeare added to and transformed the old tales from which he made his plays—the children, the lovers and the landscape—and by so doing touched a prosaic plot with magic.

The creation of the children was a masterstroke. Catherine and Heath-cliff would never move us as they do had we known them merely as adults —full of faults and careless of the havoc they wrought in other peoples' lives. In the children, the seeds of their passion were sewn when they were still generous, innocent, and oppressed. Their loves provide the sufficient motive lacking in the original tale, from which all the consequences flow. Greed, ingratitude, and revenge are recognizable enough human traits, but not enough, Emily seemed to argue, to carry such a plot to its appoin-ted close and to engage our sympathies. To bear the crushing roles Emily assigned to her protagonists, they had to be immeasurably greater than the rather mean actors in the Walker diaries; they had to be, as she had long since conceived her Gondal heroes and heroines, capable of despera-tion and courage, of abandon and madness, of sin and death. Their

---

[1] Walker diaries.

pattern would not be found in the whole range of contemporary literature (unless it be in Chateaubriand's part fiction and part autobiography, *Les Mémoires d'Outre Tombe*). To find their equal, readers had to go to classical and Shakespearean drama and the epic poets; hence the perplexity of the first critics of the book who could not find by what standards to judge it.

To find children and lovers like those in *Wuthering Heights* the critics would have to turn to the only other repository of Ellis Bell's inmost thought, her as yet unpublished Gondal poems: there, the figures of children, frail girls with 'sunbright hair', and 'melancholy boys', 'doomed to be Hell-like in heart and misery', dominate the scene. The pity and vulnerability of childhood, the evanescence of its joys, the loss of its visions, were themes constantly recurring in the Gondal sequences; they were feelings no doubt keenly experienced by Emily herself as the threat to happiness that adolescence and maturity must bring; she saw it lying in wait for the growing creature like a palpable force of evil. In July 1837 she wrote:

> I saw thee, child, one summer's day
> Suddenly leave thy cheerful play,
> And in the green grass, lowly lying,
> I listened to thy mournful sighing.
>
> I knew the wish that waked that wail;
> I knew the source whence sprung those tears;
> You longed for fate to raise the veil
> That darkened over coming years ...[1]

Growing naturally out of the close ties and loves between children, the boy and girl sequences of the early Gondal fragments,[2] the figures of the doomed man and the sorrowing unfaithful woman are introduced into the later series.[3] Upon them the fate foreshadowed in the earlier poems has fallen: the 'Darling enthusiast, holy child' has suffered the 'Relentless laws that disallow/True virtue and true joy below' and become 'wrecked and lost'. The 'iron man', once 'an ardent boy' susceptible to all the beauty of the world about him and the love of home, has become 'lost to all the beauty there'. He is untouched by any feeling of remorse, and grown, indeed, incapable of such a feeling. In vain his former companion hopes that heaven may still 'hail the soul redeemed by love'; one glance at him tells her he is irredeemable. For Emily Brontë, the 'growing boy'

[1] Hatfield, 14.
[2] See Hatfield, 7, 11, 27, 64, 86.
[3] See Hatfield, 99, 111, 112, 113.

was not merely threatened with 'shades of the prison-house', with the loss of joy, but with the loss of goodness.

> O Innocence, that cannot live
> With heart-wrung anguish long—
> Dear childhood's Innocence, forgive,
> For I have done thee wrong! [1]

She saw the change produced by growth as a change inevitably for the worse; the recognition of this obtrudes itself in such a mysterious poem as that written in October 1839:

> . . . Old feelings gather fast upon me
> Like vultures round their prey.
>
> Kind were they once, and cherished,
> But cold and cheerless now;
> I would their lingering shades had perished
> When their light left my brow.
>
> 'Tis like old age pretending
> The softness of a child,
> My altered, hardened spirit bending
> To meet their fancies wild . . . [2]

Between the 'iron man' of Emily's Gondal poems, 'the accursed man shut from his Maker's smile', and Heathcliff, the resemblances are evident though it is possible that by the time she came to write *Wuthering Heights* in 1845–6 she had modified her early conception of the character in that she believed he might be redeemable by love. We can only guess that Emily's greater involvement in Branwell's tragedy, the burden of real life as it was daily impressed on her mind, affected her final judgement on art as on life. Central to her vision of redemption, as the Gondal poems show, was the sinner's returning love of earth, of beauty, of the glorious world about him. The message, though similar, was not identical with that of 'The Ancient Mariner'—it was not merely love of 'all things both great and small' that could restore the wicked man. For Emily the love that could unlock the most imprisoned heart sprang from a full communion with nature. The degree of evil in the 'iron man' is only realized by his former playmate when she sees how impervious he has become to 'all the beauty there'.[3]

Emily Brontë saw the link between innocence and nature as a condition of childhood for most people, and the loss of that link as the primal curse of man's maturity.

[1] Hatfield, 153.   [2] Hatfield, 120.   [3] Hatfield, 99.

Whatever her experience or inexperience of the nature of love, she understood that to be excluded from union with the beloved object—as the ghost-child is excluded from her old home in *Wuthering Heights* and wails at the window to be let in, or as Heathcliff is excluded from the love of Catherine—is to know despair. Heathcliff's howl to Catherine to 'haunt him in any shape'[1] rather than leave him in the abyss where he cannot find her, is the ultimate expression of the agony of love denied, which by that time Emily understood without need of a personal experience of love.

To those readers who wonder how, in those circumstances, she was able to describe the torments and jealousies of a triangular love affair, such as exists between Catherine, Heathcliff, and Edgar Linton, a clue may be furnished by further reference to Gondal where such a situation was described as existing between Augusta, Lord Alfred (the gentle Edgar-like figure), and Fernando. Augusta's lovers were numerous and their characteristics interchangeable; the Heathcliff-like attributes were not confined to Fernando, they applied to Douglas also. Already in November 1838 when she was writing 'Light up thy halls!'[2] she had imagined a state of despair in a lover that could turn his love to hate. With his last breath Fernando curses Augusta in the words:

> Oh could I know thy soul with equal grief was torn,
> This fate might be endured—this anguish might be borne!

—words and sentiments that are paralleled by Heathcliff on hearing of Catherine's death: 'May she wake in torment! . . . I pray one prayer—I repeat it till my tongue stiffens—Catherine Earnshaw, may you not rest, as long as I am living!'[3]

If, as may be argued, without the Gothic novel the figure of such a demon-lover as Heathcliff could never have been conceived, it may also be claimed that it took an Emily Brontë to transform the remote Byronic type into a tough northcountryman. In the final analysis of Emily's achievement in *Wuthering Heights*, it is perhaps the quality of nearness that she brought to the world of the Gothic novel that is her major contribution to the genre. Mary Shelley situated her demoniacs in Italy (as did Mrs. Radcliffe before her) and it was of the essence of Gothic characters to be exotic; Emily Brontë brought them home. *Wuthering Heights* is not merely a Yorkshire tale, it is through and through English. It is the weather, and the Elizabethan buildings, and the untrammelled natures of the charac-

---

[1] *Wuthering Heights*, ch. 16.   [2] Hatfield, 85.   [3] *Wuthering Heights*, ch. 16.

ters, even more than the stark English of its style, that are untranslatable into other idioms, as every translator of the book has learnt to his cost. Emily set the drama and watched it played out, within a radius of two miles of her home. She knew the places so well that she never troubled to describe them for her readers, other than by passing allusions. It was the Tudor farmstead up at Top Withins where she had known the 'stunted row of firs at the end of the house', 'the gaunt thorns stretching their limbs one way, as though craving alms of the sun'. It was the year '1801' carved over the porch of Ponden House that dated the climax of the drama for her; and the interior of Ponden, so often visited in girlhood, with its high mantelpieces and oak beams, that furnished the homes of the Lintons and Earnshaws. Without the exact relative positions of Ponden to Withins, the four miles separating Thrushcross Grange from Wuthering Heights would not have been so essential a topographical detail in the lives of the two households. Without the hollow rock towering at the head of the Ponden Valley, with its passage below and the local legends attaching to it, there would have been no 'fairy cave under Penistone Crag'[1] or 'witches' gathering elf-locks to hurt heifers' in *Wuthering Heights*. No book was more rooted in its native soil, more conditioned by the local background of its author, than *Wuthering Heights*.

To find sources and similarities in other writers' works and in the literary conventions of her day is not to lessen the originality of Emily's work; it is rather to emphasize its personal character. Even in the matter of the telling of the tale, which Emily confided for the most part to the narration of the housekeeper Nellie Dean, where it might be said Emily was following the literary trend brilliantly set by Maria Edgeworth in *Castle Rackrent* in the narrative of the steward Thady Quirk, Emily Brontë was in fact making use of a far more homely example in her own dependence on the stories of old Tabby, to whom she was indebted for much local lore. To Tabby's doric parlance she owed the homeliness of her narrative, the elimination of literary artifice, the choice of the simple epithet in place of the laboured one. Thanks to Tabby's influence, unwitting as it was, Emily chose not to write a 'Gothic romance' about 'demon lovers', but 'a cuckoo's tale'.[2]

In placing *Wuthering Heights* within the possibilities of its author's experience, it is of interest to remember, finally, that in August 1845 Branwell was sent to Liverpool in the care of John Brown after his dismissal by the Robinsons. It was the time when the first shiploads of Irish

---

[1] *Wuthering Heights*, ch. 12.   [2] *Wuthering Heights*, ch. 4.

immigrants were landing at Liverpool and dying in the cellars of the warehouses on the quays. Their images, and especially those of the children, were unforgettably depicted in the *Illustrated London News*— starving scarecrows with a few rags on them and an animal growth of black hair almost obscuring their features. The relevance of such happenings within a day's journey of Haworth (collections were made in Haworth Church for the victims of the Irish Famine) cannot be overlooked in explaining Emily's choice of Liverpool for the scene of Mr. Earnshaw's encounter with 'the gipsy brat' Heathcliff, 'dirty, ragged, black-haired', 'as dark almost as though it came from the devil'. It spoke 'some gibberish that nobody could understand', as did the children of the famine who knew nothing but Erse. Emily left her readers intentionally in doubt as to the origin of her hero—he could be the 'Emperor of China's' heir, or, as Charlotte thought, 'an Afreet, a Ghoul'. But who can say that he was not first given a being and a body by Branwell's report of starving immigrant children in the Liverpool streets? Branwell's visit to Liverpool was in August 1845; the writing of *Wuthering Heights* belongs to the autumn and winter of that year.

Starving Irish Children

Top Withens, the Elizabethan farm on the moors above Haworth, identified as the site of *Wuthering Heights*

CHAPTER XVI

'LUST OF FAME'

CHARLOTTE'S own good fortune, the speed of *Jane Eyre*'s success, the honest dealing of her publishers (she received a first payment on 10 December and a further £100 on 17 February 1848) made her feel doubly involved in her sisters' less auspicious fortunes. She had never earned so much money at one time in all her years of teaching, nor felt so justified in any of her actions as in having spurred them all on to publish. Yet it was evident from the outset, that she had fears for her sisters, not only on account of their shady publisher, but on account of the books themselves; within a week of their publication, before even the first review of *Wuthering Heights* and *Agnes Grey* appeared in the *Athenaeum*, she wrote to Mr. Williams as though she felt there were need to defend the idiosyncrasies of Ellis and the weakness of Acton Bell:

You are not far wrong in your judgement respecting Wuthering Heights and Agnes Grey. Ellis has a strong, original mind, full of strange though sombre power. When he writes poetry that power speaks in language at once condensed, elaborated, and refined, but in prose it breaks forth in scenes which shock more than they attract. Ellis will improve, however, because he knows his defects. 'Agnes Grey' is the mirror of the mind of the writer'.[1]

The disgraceful production of the books emboldened Charlotte to add: 'If Mr. Newby always does business in this way, few authors would like to have him for their publisher a second time.'[2] She was firmly convinced at that stage that Ellis and Acton would be only too glad to change publishers and come to Smith, Elder with their future books; she had as yet no inkling of the firm, if silent, resistance Ellis would oppose to any interference in his affairs, even to the damage of his own interests. The anonymity of Ellis Bell was not merely a puzzle to amuse the gossipmongers, but the decision of a very real and inflexible individual.

A second edition of *Jane Eyre* was called for before the end of the year. Charlotte's Preface to it was dated 21 December, together with a

[1] W & S, ii. 165. [2] Ibid.

dedication to Thackeray. By the middle of January the confusion of identities was being yet further exploited:

> I see [wrote Charlotte to Mr. Williams on 22 January] that I was mistaken in my idea that the *Athenaeum* and others wished to ascribe the authorship of Wuthering Heights to Currer Bell; the contrary is the case; 'Jane Eyre' is given to Ellis Bell, and Mr. Newby, it appears, thinks it expedient so to frame his advertisements as to favour the misapprehension. . . . However, Ellis, Acton and Currer care nothing for the matter personally—the Public and the Critics are welcome to confuse our identities as much as they choose; my only fear is lest Messrs Smith & Elder should in some way be annoyed with it.[1]

Wuthering Heights, despite if not because of Newby's 'trickery', was beginning to sell well, as Charlotte noted to Mr. Williams on 5 February. She noted something more, and with apprehension: Newby's continued transactions with her sisters. 'Wuthering Heights, it appears, is selling too, and consequently Mr. Newby is getting into marvellously good tune with his authors.' Charlotte did not know, as clearly emerged later, that Ellis Bell was at that very time in correspondence with Newby on the subject of his second novel; the existence of such a book was as yet unknown to her, though she was herself already engaged on *Shirley* and Anne had been hard at work on her second novel, *The Tenant of Wildfell Hall*, ever since the previous summer. Dated 15 February 1848, Newby's letter to Ellis Bell, Esq. has been preserved. It reads:

> Dear Sir—I am much obliged by your kind note and shall have much pleasure in making arrangements for your next novel. I would not hurry its completion for I think you are quite right not to let it go before the world until well satisfied with it, for much depends on your next work, if it be an improvement on your first you will have established yourself as a first-rate novelist, but if it fall short the critics will be too apt to say that you have expended your talent in your first novel. I shall therefore have pleasure in accepting it upon the understanding that its completion be at your own time . . .[2]

In offering Newby her second novel, Emily was clearly acting against Charlotte's advice. A new sense of her powerlessness to influence her sister in her role of Ellis appears in Charlotte's letters to her publishers, in which she no longer makes definite affirmations respecting Ellis, but speaks with diffidence of 'his' reactions to her views. The change, though subtle, is notable. Emily was no longer accepting Charlotte's view of things, not even on the subjects that had formerly united them. On 15

[1] *SLL.*, i. 389.   [2] Now in the BPM.

February, writing to thank Mr. Williams for a suggestion that the Bells should visit London with a view to seeing something of the 'great world', Charlotte told him:

> I should much—very much—like to take that quiet view of the 'great world' you allude to, but I have as yet won no right to give myself such a treat; it must be for some future day—Ellis, I imagine, would soon turn aside from that spectacle in disgust. I do not think he admits it as his creed that 'the proper study of mankind is man'—at least not the artificial man of cities. In some points I consider Ellis somewhat of a theorist now and then he broaches Ideas which strike my sense as much more daring and original than practical; his reason may be in advance of mine, but certainly it often travels a different road . . .

And then Charlotte added an amazing judgement on her sister's literary abilities: 'I should say Ellis will not be seen in his full strength till he is seen as an essayist.'[1]

In the face of the achievement of *Wuthering Heights* and of the *Poems*, on what basis could such an assumption be made? On Emily's French essays? Already in her letter of 21 December, Charlotte had contrasted Ellis Bell's poetry with her fiction, with evident preference for the poems; in asserting then that 'Ellis will improve' Ellis's brother author was taking much on himself by covertly admitting need of improvement.

If such was Charlotte's undisguised opinion of Emily's achievement, and the basis of her recommendations to her sister, little wonder that the intractable Ellis was perceptibly losing confidence in Charlotte. Very firmly Ellis refused Smith Elder's offers to act on his and Acton's behalf for any future work they had in preparation. The situation placed Charlotte in an awkward dilemma: how to explain their intransigence without offending her kind publishers? She wrote to the head of the firm, George Smith, on 17 February 1848, to acknowledge a further remittance of £100 on the sales of *Jane Eyre*:

> Your conduct to me has been such that you cannot doubt my relatives would have been most happy, had it been in their power to avail themselves of your proposal respecting the publication of their future works, but their present engagements with Mr. Newby are such as to prevent their consulting freely their own inclinations and interests . . . For my own part, I peculiarly regret this circumstance.[2]

No agreement did, as yet, bind Emily, even if the advanced state of Anne's second book had led to a further agreement being entered into with Newby; so far Newby had paid neither author anything. He might

[1] W & S, ii. 189.   [2] W & S, ii. 190.

well fear to lose both of them, and in the case of *The Tenant of Wildfell Hall* he offered Anne better terms: she was not to contribute towards costs of production, but to receive £25 on delivery of the manuscript and a further £25 on the sale of the first 250 copies. Compared to Smith Elder's terms, these were pitiable, and Emily was obviously wrong to persist in dealing with Newby. She was acting so contrary to her own and Anne's interests as to raise the question of her motives; it was not merely a question of acknowledging herself wrong, but of admitting Charlotte to be right; an admission which it appears she found too hard to make at that time. Until Newby actually announced *The Tenant* late in June, Charlotte did not reveal its existence to her own publishers. Then it was too late to hide the fact from them, and she wrote on 22 June: 'Newby has announced a new work by Acton Bell. The advertisement has, as usual, a certain tricky turn in its wording which I do not admire.' *The Tenant of Wildfell Hall* proved a success; it was well received by the critics, and Newby advertised it by a mixture of quotations from the reviews of the first Bell novels, especially those of *Jane Eyre* and *Wuthering Heights*. Among 'Opinions of the Press ON MR. BELL'S FIRST NOVEL' advertised on the flyleaf of the book, were excerpts from the *Athenaeum* ('All three books might be the work of one hand'), the *Spectator* ('The work bears affinity to Jane Eyre'), from *Britannia* ('The work is strangely original. It reminds us of Jane Eyre'), from Douglas Jerrold, ('It is like Jane Eyre'), etc. The *Athenaeum* in its review of the new book, 8 July 1848, could genuinely play Mr. Newby's game, and comment on its resemblance to the earlier novels:

The three Bells, as we took occasion to observe when reviewing Wuthering Heights, ring in a chime so harmonious as to prove that they have issued from the same mould. The resemblance borne by their novels to each other is curious ... In respect to one point, however, we cannot remain silent: The Bells must be warned against their fancy for dwelling upon what is disagreeable ... Were the metal of this Bell foundry of baser quality than it is, it would be lost time to point out flaws and take exceptions. As matters stand, our hints may not be without their use to future 'castings'; nor will they be unpalatable, seeing that they are followed by our honest recommendation of 'Wildfell Hall' as the most interesting novel which we have read for a month past.

Well might Mr. Newby hug himself for having kept on good terms with his authors, of whose future such journals as the *Athenaeum* had no doubt.

The occasion for making a hit with their new publication came too easily to hand to leave unexploited. Entering into negotiations with the firm of Harper Brothers of New York, for an American edition of *Wildfell*

Hall, Newby presented it to them as a new work by Currer Bell, the author of *Jane Eyre*; he went so far as to assert that, to the best of his knowledge, all the Bell novels were the work of Currer, the highly successful author of *Jane Eyre*.

It so happened that Smith, Elder had already entered into a firm agreement with Harper's to give them Currer Bell's next novel (*Shirley*). The news of Newby's negotiations with Harper's naturally startled George Smith. It put him into a very disagreeable situation, and he wrote off to Haworth to say, in the most tactful way, that he 'would be glad to be in a position to contradict the statement', adding, at the same time, that he was quite sure 'Mr. Newby's statement was untrue'.[1]

The game of confused identities was amusing up to a point; but to allow Newby's latest trick to pass unchallenged would, Charlotte felt, impugn the honour of the Bells, and of course of Messrs. Smith, Elder. There was only one way to resolve the matter, by proving that Currer and Acton Bell were two distinct persons, writing separate works, dealing with different publishers. The decision to go up to London to show themselves to their publishers was taken at lightning speed, with Anne's full concurrence. Mr. Smith's letter reached Charlotte on Friday, 7 July; she and Anne took the night-train from Keighley that day and reached London early the next morning.

There was no need, as it happened, for Emily to accompany them. Ellis Bell was not involved in Newby's latest fraud, and could still hope for complete anonymity. In the haste of her sisters' departure, nothing definite was said respecting Ellis's position or wishes in the matter. But in the little *coup de théâtre* of the Bells' entry at the Cornhill office, Charlotte was put off her guard. She arrived bearing Mr. Smith's letter in her outstretched hand, explanations followed, there was the warmth and kindness of both the young Mr. Smith and the elderly Mr. Williams. It was a moment of relief after considerable strain. Charlotte betrayed to the attentive gentlemen the existence of three Bells and named their real names. As she confessed later, the words had hardly passed her lips when she regretted them; she knew how much the disclosure of her secret would be resented by Emily.

No record remains of Anne's confrontation with Newby, but he can hardly have been prepared for the frail-looking young woman who entered his shop. Whether or not she unflinchingly expressed her views on her rights and his duties, as she later did in the preface to the second edition

[1] *Cornhill Magazine*, Dec. 1900.

of *Wildfell Hall*, Mr. Newby was unashamedly pursuing his former course with the Bells before the year was out.

It is worth noting that Newby did not confine his trickery to unknown provincial authors; after the Bells, George Eliot was his victim, and she had the opportunity to expose his practices some ten years after Acton Bell. By then, his conduct had been pilloried by Mrs. Gaskell.[1] George Eliot wrote to *The Times* on 30 November 1859:

Sir / Mr. Newby the publisher, in issuing a work under the title of *Adam Bede, Junior*, has not only made use of my title, but has so worded his advertisements as to lead many persons into the belief that I am the author of his so-called 'sequel'. The extent to which this belief has spread urges me to come forward with a public statement that I have nothing whatever to do with the work in question, or with Mr. Newby.

I am not the first writer who has had to suffer from this publisher's method of trading. The readers of Currer Bell's life will remember a very unpleasant illustration of it.
I am, etc...[2]

Newby's answer to this well-merited correction is a masterly demonstration of how to elude disagreeable facts and gives some notion of the man with whom the Bells had to deal. He wrote in *The Times* of 5 December 1859:

I published all the novels of Ellis and Acton Bell. No disagreement ever took place between these ladies and me, and long after the publication of *Jane Eyre*, Miss Anne Bronte brought me a book, *The Tenant of Wildfell Hall*, which I, published in due course ...

Charlotte and Anne returned home on Tuesday, 11 July, laden with books, some of them gifts from Mr. Smith. For Emily they had chosen Tennyson's recently published *The Princess*. Once recovered from the exhaustion and excitement of the journey they were eager to share their experiences with their sister.

Emily had always been a willing and attentive listener, as Charlotte once recalled in a letter to Mr. Williams:

Emily would never go into any sort of society herself, and whenever I went I could on my return communicate to her a pleasure that suited her, by giving the distinct faithful impression of each scene I had witnessed. When pressed to go she would sometimes say: 'What is the use? Charlotte will bring it home to me.' And indeed I delighted to please her thus.[3]

---

[1] Gaskell, 247. See also Gaskell, *Letters*, 418.
[2] G. Haight, *George Eliot* (1968), p. 314.   [3] CB to WSW, 19 Nov. 1849. *SBC*, 161.

Of that particular journey to London, Charlotte later wrote, 'in what dear companionship I again and again narrated all that had been seen, heard, and uttered in that visit'.[1]

But there was one incident Charlotte wished she had not reported to Emily: it was her inadvertent confession of their identities. It was necessary in the case of Currer and Acton Bell, but it was not strictly necessary in the case of Ellis, as Ellis all too quickly perceived. Another scene of almost comparable anger to that which accompanied the discovery of her poems followed Charlotte's unhappy avowal. The disclosure was bitterly resented by Emily; her mood was so implacable that a warning letter had to be sent to London. The date of Charlotte's letter to Mr. Williams, 31 July, shows how long Emily's resentment lasted. It cannot have been pleasant for Charlotte to have to write:

Permit me to caution you not to speak of sisters when you write to me. I mean, do not use the word in the plural. Ellis Bell will not endure to be alluded to under any other appellation than the nom de plume. I committed a grand error in betraying his identity to you and Mr. Smith. It was inadvertent—the words 'we are three sisters' escaped me before I was aware. I regretted the avowal the moment I had made it; I regret it bitterly now, for I find it is against every feeling and intention of Ellis Bell.[2]

Charlotte's compliance with Emily's unreasonable demands is some indication of the rift opening up between them on the subject of their authorship. After Charlotte's initial indiscretion of reading Emily's manuscript without her consent, Emily showed herself intransigent towards every proposal that Charlotte put forward for their mutual benefit, as in the matter of their publishers. While in London, Charlotte and Anne had gone into the history of their *Poems* with Mr. Smith, which resulted in his offering to buy them back from Aylott & Jones and publish them under his own imprint: it was a business proposition that could only benefit the Bells. Emily was not to be enticed; she disclaimed all interest in the matter. As Charlotte had to write to Mr. Williams in early September, when the reprint was already under way: 'The author never alludes to them; or if she does, it is with scorn.'[3]

To explain this strange aversion—for Emily must have known the quality of her own work—something more than her deep resentment at Charlotte for forcing her into publication would appear necessary; and to judge from Emily's attitude towards Branwell throughout this period, one cannot rule out the possibility that she resented his being excluded from

[1] Ibid.   [2] W & S, ii. 241.   [3] W & S, ii. 256.

their venture into print. The truth is that Branwell had several poems to his credit published in the *Halifax Guardian* that were quite as good as Anne's and markedly better than Charlotte's; a contribution from him would not have brought discredit on the Bell's volume of *Poems*. If he was excluded, there is no doubt it was because of Charlotte. 'My unhappy brother', she wrote after his death, 'never knew what his sisters had done in literature—he was not aware that they had ever published a line. We could not tell him of our efforts for fear of causing him too deep a pang of remorse for his own time misspent, and talents misapplied.'[1] At the very time his sisters were preparing their volume for the press, in the spring of 1846, Branwell was deploring his lost chances: on 28 April 1846 he wrote to his friend Leyland: 'I have materials for a respectably sized volume, and if I were in London personally I might perhaps try Henry Moxon— a patronizer of the sons of rhyme. As I know that, while here, I might send a MS to London and say good-bye to it, I feel it folly to feed the flames of a printer's fire.'[2]

Charlotte's exclusion of Branwell from his sisters' literary success, and from family life, caused Emily to withdraw only further into herself. It was inevitable perhaps in view of her growing involvement in her brother's tragedy which only deepened with his decline and death. The more Charlotte sought to isolate Branwell, and at the same time promote her own and her sisters' interests, the more she lost touch with Emily. Bewildered and wounded by this first rift in a lifetime of mutual devotion, she sought to explain and excuse Emily's attitude towards her 'rhymes' to her publisher. The puzzled admission of Emily's contempt prompted a fresh appraisal of her sister's genius and of her character, which at that juncture and to a partial stranger is the more revealing. Charlotte had not hidden from Mr. Williams her doubts and criticisms respecting *Wuthering Heights*; in giving him now her considered views on her sister's poetry it was as if she were in effect saying: 'My sister Emily is an incomparable poet but I am not certain what she is as a novelist.' What she said was:

I know no woman that ever lived who wrote such poetry before. Condensed energy, clearness, finish—strange, strong pathos are their characteristics; utterly different from the weak diffusiveness, the laboured yet most feeble wordiness, which dilute the writings of even very popular poetesses. This is my deliberate and quite impartial opinion, to which I should hold if all the critics in the periodical press held a different one, as I should to the supremacy of Thackeray in fiction.[3]

[1] W & S, ii. 262.　　　[2] W & S, ii. 92.　　　[3] W & S, ii. 256.

Much dissatisfied as Charlotte was with her own contributions to *Poems*, her eagerness to see them reprinted could argue a very disinterested wish to display the genius of Ellis Bell to greater advantage than in *Wuthering Heights*. Such a view, if known to Emily, would do little to appease her growing contempt for critical opinion. Ellis, as Charlotte described him in her letter to Mr. Williams, was of 'no flexible or ordinary materials'.[1]

Charlotte's repeated cautions in her letters to Mr. Williams not to mention Emily or to refer to any confidences she might make about Ellis, show plainly enough how much she feared to offend Emily's susceptibilities. When illness yet further removed her from Emily's confidence, Charlotte's trials became a martyrdom. Then, crushed with the weight of her fears for Emily's life, she had still to deny herself the sympathy she craved even from strangers to help her face the ordeal.

The tie of sister is near and dear indeed, and I think a certain harshness in her powerful and peculiar character only makes me cling to her more. But this is all family egotism—please excuse it, and, above all, never allude to it, or to the name Emily when you write to me. I do not always show your letters, but I never withhold them when they are inquired after.[2]

Charlotte's preoccupation with Emily at this time was not due simply to Emily's difficult conduct; it was also because she was trying to portray her sister in *Shirley*. She was studying her as never before, and if the result appears unconvincing in the light of Emily's own works, it is a measure of Charlotte's love that she should attempt such a portrait. In fact, if Charlotte had not confided in Mrs. Gaskell the attempt might not have been recognized as such. The circumstances of the young, beautiful, and spoilt heiress, in surroundings of luxury and idleness, were so alien to the way of life of the ascetic and stoical Emily—irrespective of the quality of her mind—that at first sight the idea seems ludicrous and but for Charlotte's admission would be set aside. How could Charlotte, having read her sister's poems, hope to convey the mind of their writer in *Shirley*? The attempt to create a sparkling, happy Emily not when she was young and carefree but at that precise time of growing stress and sadness, makes the reader wonder whether there were not a measure of compensation, of wishful thinking in the portrait, as if the author were pursuing a vanishing ideal that she needed to believe had once existed. As it is, only that portion of the book that was written before Emily died can claim to be an impartial portrayal of her personality and temperament. (The break in composition came at chapter 23, after the prolonged analysis of Shirley's mystic

[1] Ibid.   [2] CB to WSW, 2 Nov. 1848. W & S, ii. 269.

response to nature in chapter 22.) The resumed portrait of a much-loved and lost sister suffers from the author's inability to detach herself sufficiently from her subject; the character loses direction and goes to bits. The resemblances between Emily and Shirley that can be recognized are largely superficial, concerned with externals—like being called 'Captain Keeldar' and looking like 'a grave but gay little Cavalier'; the dog Tartar; the whistling despite the governesses' rebukes; the incident of the mad dog; the physical likeness. Shirley loves Nature and Poetry, she will not tolerate coercion, she is generous and passionate and compassionate, and at dusk can see visions and dream dreams.

> If Shirley were not an indolent, a reckless, an ignorant being, she would take a pen at such moments; or at least while the recollection of such moments was yet fresh on her spirit; she would seize, she would fix the apparition, tell the vision revealed . . . But indolent she is, reckless she is, and most ignorant, for she does not know her dreams are rare—her feelings peculiar—she does not know, has never known, and will die without knowing, the full value of the spring whose bright fresh bubbling in her heart keeps it green.[1]

This is, surely, a strange appraisal of the real situation existing between the sisters, and from which Charlotte was, at that very time, suffering. Nobody knew better than Emily the rarity of her dreams, though she was refusing to communicate them. Even in her role as novelist, Charlotte was pleading with her to do so.

As 1848 advanced, and the re-issues of their successful works, and the publication of their new ones, occupied Charlotte and Anne, Emily as resolutely withdrew, not only from the race to fame, but from authorship. Of the new work she had mentioned to Newby in February nothing more is heard. How far it advanced will never be known. The conditions that had made the writing of *Wuthering Heights* possible no longer existed, either within herself or in her home.

Her hostility to the public was not likely to be placated by each fresh pronouncement of the press condemning her achievement—even when the critics praised it was for the wrong reasons. And Newby's dishonesty could only disgust her upright spirit. She had not seen much of the world, but she had seen enough to dislike its conventions. What greater criticism of this world could she have made than by writing such a book as *Wuthering Heights*, and to what greater extent could the world have confirmed her judgement than by misjudging her work? Between Emily and the conventional world there seemed to be nothing in common, and had she

---

[1] *Shirley*, ch. 22.

contemplated any compromise it would not have been by following Charlotte's advice. In her Preface to the posthumous edition of *Wuthering Heights* and *Agnes Grey*, Charlotte did not hide her reservations about either sister's work: she had not only tried to dissuade Anne from writing *The Tenant of Wildfell Hall* but urged Emily to omit certain scenes from *Wuthering Heights*. Both attempts were in vain. The fact had to be faced that the sisters no longer saw eye to eye on their work. Writing of *Wildfell Hall* Charlotte told her publishers: 'I consider the subject unfortunately chosen—it was one the author was not qualified to handle at once vigorously and truthfully.' Nothing would ever make Charlotte change her mind on this point. 'The choice of subject was an entire mistake... Nothing less congruous with the writer's nature could be conceived. The motives which dictated this choice were pure, but, I think, slightly morbid... When reasoned with on the subject, she regarded such reasonings as a temptation to self-indulgence. She must be honest; she must not varnish, soften, or conceal.'[1] When Charlotte's own publisher eventually suggested a posthumous edition of *Wildfell Hall*, Charlotte gave her final verdict against it: 'Wildfell Hall,' she then wrote to Mr. Williams, 'it hardly appears to me desirable to preserve.'[2]

Anne's sense of responsibility towards Branwell, which prompted the writing of *Wildfell Hall*, could not be shared by either Charlotte or Emily, who had not been instrumental in procuring his engagement at Thorp Green. She had only herself to blame for not sufficiently assessing Branwell's weakness of character in the face of temptation. Of her own experiences with the Robinsons, she wrote on returning home, that they had been 'very unpleasant and undreamt of'.[3] In *Wildfell Hall* she wrote with passion of the faulty education given boys that did not adequately prepare them to resist evil; if it had not been for Branwell's ignorance of such a society as that of Thorp Green, his ready credence in the deception of a woman like Mrs. Robinson, he would not, Anne thought, have wrecked his life and become a confirmed drunkard. In her sense of guilt, she felt it her duty, as Charlotte said, 'to reproduce every detail as a warning to others'.[4]

To all his associates, whether friends like Leyland and Grundy, or passing acquaintances like Searle Phillips the journalist, Branwell invariably attributed the root-cause of his misery to his family's treatment of him. According to the evidence of Mrs. Chadwick,[5] Charlotte did not speak to Branwell for weeks at a time. (This is far more likely than the statement of Mary Duclaux, that she never spoke to him for two years.) To Searle

---

[1] Biographical Notice.   [2] 5 Sept. 1850. W & S, iii, 156.
[3] Diary-paper, 30 July 1845.   [4] Biographical Notice.   [5] Chadwick, 361.

Phillips, whom Branwell met at the Bull where they made a night of it, he is alleged to have said: 'Why could they not give me some credit when I was trying to be good?'[1]

Branwell was a prey to the terrors that preceded his attacks of delirium tremens, and remained sometimes without sleep for weeks on end. In June 1848 he was threatened with arrest for debt by the landlord of a Halifax pub. Such material disasters roused him for a time to the consciousness of his physical condition; he suffered from the knowledge of the irretrievable loss of his powers and ambitions, which he could analyse at times with painful clarity. 'Noble writings, works of art, music or poetry now, instead of rousing my imagination,' he wrote to Leyland, 'cause a whirlwind of blighting sorrow that sweeps over my mind with unspeakable dreariness, and if I sit down and try to write, all ideas that used to come clothed in sunlight now press round me in funeral black.'[2]

By the end of July it was apparent, as Charlotte wrote to Ellen, that 'his constitution seems shattered. Papa, and sometimes all of us, have sad nights with him, he sleeps most of the day, and consequently will lie awake at night.'[3]

The pitiable subterfuges to which Branwell had recourse to procure the gin and the opium by which he lived, can be seen in the note scribbled one Sunday morning to his confederate the sexton:

Sunday, Noon

Dear John—I shall feel very much obliged to you if you can contrive to get me Five pence worth of Gin in a proper measure. Should it be speedily got I could perhaps take it from you or Billy at the lane top, or, what would be quite as well, sent out for, to you. I anxiously ask the favour because I know the good it will do me. *Punctually* at Half-past Nine in the morning you will be paid the 5d out of a shilling given me then.—Yours, P. B. B.[4]

His growing weakness and extreme emaciation were such that, on calling at the sexton's house one weekday, Mrs. Brown and her daughters laughed at him for wearing his father's coat. The coat was his own but it hung on him like a rag on a scarecrow. Tabitha Brown,[5] one of the sexton's six daughters who took their turns at helping 't'parson's' household, never forgot the occasion, because two days later Branwell was dead.

He had only one day's illness, and even that was not recognized as preluding the end; he often had days in bed, feeling too shattered to make the effort to dress. It was Saturday, and the only difference from the other

---

[1] Duclaux, 148. [2] W & S, ii. 124.
[3] W & S, ii. 240. [4] W & S, ii. 224. [5] Chadwick, 360.

occasions was in his changed behaviour; as they all remembered later, he appeared altered towards them. 'His mind had undergone the peculiar change which frequently precedes death', Charlotte wrote later. 'Two days previously the calm of better feelings filled it. A return of natural affection marked his last moments. . . . his demeanour, his language, his sentiments were all singularly altered and softened . . . within half an hour of his decease he seemed unconscious of danger.'[1] On the Sunday morning, as John Brown was about to set off to ring the Church bells for morning prayer, Branwell had only time to call out to him 'John! I'm dying!' for the family to be fetched. Mr. Brontë had the comfort of hearing his son distinctly say 'Amen' to the prayers he poured out at his bedside.[2]

The effect of so sudden a parting did not only aggravate the family's natural grief, but it heightened the sense of Branwell's ruin. He died at thirty-one, completely burnt out in body and mind. Once the chief hope and admiration of his family, his failure would now be the single memorable feature of his life. 'Nothing remains of him but a memory of errors and sufferings', wrote Charlotte. 'There is such a bitterness of pity for his life and death, such a yearning for the emptiness of his whole existence as I cannot describe.'[3] Later she wrote, 'Till the last hour comes, we never know how much we can forgive, pity, regret a near relation. All his vices were and are nothing now—we remember only his woes.'[4]

The shock brought on a sharp attack of jaundice, and directly after the funeral Charlotte had to go to bed for several days. It was something more than a physical collapse, and this, obviously, her sisters realized. They gave her not only care but comfort, judging her need of consolation to be greater than theirs. Writing to Mr. Williams on 6 October Charlotte said: 'The doctor has told me not to expect too rapid a restoration to health; but to-day I certainly feel better. I am thankful to say my Father has hitherto stood the storm well, and so have my *dear* sisters to whose untiring care and kindness I am chiefly indebted for my present state of convalescence.'[5]

Such evidence is important in view of the events to come. Emily, as always, seemed to stand up to calamity with something like superhuman endurance. While Anne's delicacy had been a recognized condition 'from early childhood', as Charlotte said, Emily's physical strength had never been called in doubt; she was the strong one of the family.

Branwell died on Sunday 24 September, and was buried the following Thursday. The service, like all the Brontë funerals before it, was conducted

[1] *SLL*, i. 456–7.   [2] Leyland, *The Brontë Family*, ii. 279.
[3] W & S, ii. 261.   [4] W & S, ii. 264.   [5] W & S, ii. 263.

by his father's oldest and most faithful friend, the Revd. William Morgan, Vicar of Christchurch, Bradford, who had baptised most of the Brontë children, and stood godfather to Maria. Their uncle by marriage, he had been an object of fun to them in their childhood, for his 'prosy ways' and Welsh accent, and it may be that something incongruous in the figure of so fat and jovial a man at a family funeral decided Charlotte against allowing him to conduct the next one.

It was the custom then, and still is now, for Haworth funerals to be followed by a 'Funeral Service' on the Sunday following the interment. Branwell's was held on 1 October. The date is memorable for being the last day Emily went out.

CHAPTER XVII

THE 'HIDDEN GHOST'

THE death of Branwell, in so far as it removed the ghastly spectre of 'suffering and sin' from the home, might be expected to bring relief to his much-tried family when the first shock was past. Charlotte, who had most consistently condemned his conduct, was also the most affected by his end; the signs of his returning old affection, of his contrition for what he had brought on them all, wrung her heart with the revived feelings of what Branwell had once been to her. A few days after his death she wrote to Mr. Williams, voicing the general view of the family: 'I felt as I had never felt before that there was peace and forgiveness for him in Heaven.' For Mr. Brontë, Charlotte and Anne, there was great consolation to be drawn from this belief: 'Had his sins been scarlet in their dye—I believe now they are white as wool—He is at rest—and that comforts us all—long before he quitted this world Life had no happiness for him.'[1]

What Emily felt in the presence of death she had written in *Wuthering Heights*; and while her faith in everlasting life was usually as strong as that of any of her family, there was one important point of difference: she did not recognize the need for forgiveness of the departed soul in order that it might enter into its eternity of joy.

I don't know if it is a peculiarity in me [says Ellen Dean watching by the dead Catherine], but I am seldom otherwise than happy while watching in the chamber of death, should no frenzied or despairing mourner share the duty with me. I see a repose that neither earth nor hell can break; and I feel an assurance of the endless and shadowless hereafter—the Eternity they have entered—where life is boundless in its duration, and love in its sympathy, and joy in its fulness.[2]

Emily derived no consolation from the hope that Branwell's 'sins' were now 'as white as wool', and that his death was a mercy both for him and his family. She suffered for his suffering, and saw in his death only the destructive power of love. She was aware that people who die for love need not be admirable people.

[1] W & S, ii. 263.   [2] *Wuthering Heights*, ch. 16.

The student of her life has repeatedly to be reminded that the records—even the simplest family records of Emily's views and words on the death of Branwell—have been carefully obliterated; whether by herself or by her heartbroken sisters after she was gone, the evidence of those last months of her life has been destroyed. In their absence and in default of any yardstick by which to measure her feelings and motives at a time of intense family feeling, the only conclusion to be drawn is that there was motive for their destruction.

To Martha Brown and her sisters, loyal servants of the Brontë family, there never appeared to be any doubt that Emily died of grief for her brother. She was taken ill after his funeral and was dead within three months. It was as simple as that. 'They were all well when Mr. Branwell was buried,' Martha told Mrs. Gaskell, 'but Miss Emily broke down the next week. We saw she was ill, but she would never own it, never would have a doctor near her, never would breakfast in bed.'[1]

Emily Brontë was a complex character and anything suggesting over-simplification must be viewed with suspicion. Grief might not have had the same meaning for Martha as it had for Emily. She might not miss Branwell nor long for his presence (equally she might do both), but what may have grieved her to the point of death was the injustice of his lot, the pathos of his love, which she had more opportunity than the others to recognize as the deathly thing it proved. For the lasting pity of it all there was no consolation.

Obviously Emily did not die of grief alone—the tragedy of Branwell's end was bound up with many vital issues that affected her life in its most secret sources. She could not see Branwell die without brooding over the whole purpose of life. She had early learnt by her failure at Roe Head and by Branwell's failure in London, that success had nothing to do with that purpose, and the extreme price Branwell had paid for his many failures bore no relation to her very strong sense of justice. 'She held that mercy and forgiveness are the divinest attributes of the Great Being who made both man and woman', Charlotte wrote of her after her death.[2] And it has also to be remembered that Emily's greatest quality, again according to Charlotte, was generosity. In the end, she gave Branwell everything she had to give, not, perhaps, because he was Branwell, or her brother, but because he was a human being and broken-hearted.

Her fatal illness was brought on by a cold caught at Branwell's funeral service. Though systematically neglected by her own wish, the illness

[1] Gaskell, *Letters*, 246; Duclaux, 223.
[2] Preface to 1850 edition of *Wuthering Heights*.

would not in itself sufficiently explain her rapid decline if her spiritual resistance had not at the same time been undermined. It has to be remembered that until the dramatic succession of family deaths from tuberculosis, which began with Branwell's in September 1848 and ended with Anne's in May 1849, no trace of weakness had ever been suspected in Emily. While Anne had been a chronic sufferer from asthma and bronchitis from childhood, and Branwell undermined his normal good health by his excesses, Emily was never known to ail. The first mention in the family correspondence of her suffering from the common flu-cold was as late as January 1848 when Anne wrote to Ellen Nussey to say: 'We are all cut up by this cruel east wind, most of us, i.e. Charlotte, Emily and I have had the influenza or a bad cold instead, twice over within the space of a few weeks. Papa has had it once. Tabby has escaped it altogether.'[1] Emily's flu was the normal effect of a general local epidemic, and occasioned no more concern afterwards. The only illness that had seemed to bring Emily near to death in the course of her thirty years had been the illness that sent her home from Roe Head; and that turned out to be purely psycho-somatic, induced by intense unhappiness. That is worth remembering when considering the illness to which she eventually succumbed.

She had accomplished so much in the two preceding years. In the autumn of 1845 she was the only member of the family to accept Branwell's disgrace with anything like philosophic calm. Within twelve months she produced *Wuthering Heights*, which followed a two-year period of sustained poetic output. Emily was, clearly, in fullest possession of her powers, and such creativity might only be the prelude to a succession of great works to come. Instead, in 1848 almost everything stopped.

No single cause can be said to have brought about so great a change, but it seems likely that second only to the loss of Branwell was the revulsion she felt for publishing her work. It was not only the initial violation of her privacy that she resented when Charlotte discovered her poems and urged their publication; it was the succeeding and successive encroachments upon her peace of mind that clashed with all her chosen modes of living. Publication meant that other wills were imposed upon hers, that she was asked to sacrifice total independence and to conform to values which she despised. The artifice of authorship, as compared with the truth of the imagined life of her creation, with the visions that had fed her, lowered its value in her eyes and its unimportance was constantly being confirmed by the uninspired pronouncements of the critics in London.

The pursuit of something so alien to Emily as fame would, moreover,

[1] 26 Jan. 1848. BPM.

be rendered even more meaningless as it coincided with each phase of Branwell's fitful decline. Yet this was the ineluctable condition under which the poems and novels appeared. The daily spectacle of failure, personified in her brother, as he crept in and out of the house on his pitiable shifts, after fivepenny 'squibs of gin' or sixpenny packets of opium pills, could never reconcile Emily to success, even had she achieved it.

She had shown herself practical enough in managing her sisters' and her own small investments, but the making of money was certainly no incentive for her. The 'pursuit of Fame', as it set up a feverish atmosphere of competition and excitement in the home, repelled rather than stimulated her. And as it also meant excluding Branwell from any share in his sisters' good fortunes this alone would have turned her against it. On the evidence of Branwell's friends, Grundy and Searle Philipps, Emily discussed her writing with Branwell, even if she made no use of his comments. It was not advice she was seeking, but a lifeline she was throwing to a castaway.

Charlotte fully believed that Branwell never knew 'his sisters had ever published a line',[1] and sought to keep the knowledge from him from compassion—'for fear of causing him too deep a pang of remorse for his own time misspent'. It is hard to credit this considering the confined space of the parsonage. Branwell is reported (by some rather unreliable witnesses[2]) to have bragged of writing the opening chapters of *Wuthering Heights*, a fatuous enough claim, yet one that shows knowledge of his sisters' works. Indeed, he certainly advised Charlotte to send a stamped addressed envelope for a reply with her manuscript; he had for years written to editors of the literary reviews and knew the ropes. Whatever he suspected in his more lucid moments, he certainly felt, as he reported to his friends, the misery of his family's neglect. Emily appears to have seen his case with perfect lucidity; he could not benefit by any renunciation of hers, he was beyond rescuing, but she refused to abandon him.

The true nature of their exceptional relationship has to be visualized in terms of the physical conditions of their home. She was not his wife, but she had to serve him as only a loyal partner can do when the normal barriers of common civility have broken down. What he communicated to her on those dreary nights when she waited up for him, were not merely the ravings of a drunken sot, the hallucinations of a maniac, but a profound disgust with the whole human condition. Nothing is more eloquent of the gulf fixed between reality and the dream of her life, of the evil

[1] W & S, ii. 262.   [2] William Dearden, *Halifax Guardian*, 15 June 1867.

Branwell was causing her, than to compare the lines she wrote in October 1845, shortly after his return home, and the actual experience that was habitually to be hers in the ensuing years. The lines are among her most famous: they describe those magical moments when, lost to all material perception, she looked out on the night, expecting her 'messenger of Hope'.

> The little lamp burns straight, its rays shoot strong & far;
> I trim it well to be the Wanderer's guiding star ...
> A messenger of Hope comes every night to me,
> And offers, for short life, eternal liberty.[1]

In place of her 'messenger of Hope', of the 'angel' who 'nightly tracks that waste of winter snow', it was her brother who came stumbling drunkenly up Church lane. It was Branwell who was lighted by the 'little lamp' she trimmed so well (the actual lamp can still be seen in Emily's old home). The household hours were early by immutable routine, and Emily's own inclinations nocturnal. Branwell must be got in and the house locked up without their father knowing at what time he returned. (He might bear the brunt of the rest of the night with Branwell threatening murder in his room.) To anyone knowing the interior of the parsonage, with its resounding stone-flagged entrance hall, the winding stone stairs, the narrow upper landing onto which all the bedroom doors opened—the effort required of her was beyond most women's physical powers. It is not to diminish that effort to say that it did not often happen (happily Branwell could only drink when he had money) but it was extended over a period of three years which did not fail to leave their mark on her. By the time Branwell died, she was a shadow: within a week she was taken ill.

The effect on her of Branwell's degradation was to poison every source of life—above all, the life of imagination that had made her a poet. Such a conclusion seems inescapable from the total suspension of all creative work during 1848. Even allowing for the destruction of possible manuscripts, either by Emily herself or Charlotte after her death, the absence of any work 'meriting' preservation is ominous, and argues the extinction in her of the ability to write. The manuscript of the new novel, advanced enough in February for the author to approach her publisher about it, disappeared with the rest; it was judged not worth pursuing. The want of encouragement from the critics has been advanced as a cause for her giving up writing. Writers of the calibre of Emily Brontë, who do not write for money or success, or even for appreciation, are not so lightly put down

[1] Hatfield, 190.

by the incomprehension of their readers. Emily had written poetry and prose (though none of the latter has been preserved) from adolescence, without dependence on encouragement or other incentive than her own will; her criterion was her own judgement, and however seldom she satisfied that, to write was a condition of life for her. The opinion of others could not arrest the upsurge of so strong an instinct. Her life of imagination —the 'God within her breast'—had always been lived apart. By 1846, on 2 January, when she wrote her Credo, she had discovered, as she believed, that the life within her was invulnerable, not to be touched by Time or alteration, indestructible even by death.[1] This proclamation of her faith marks the high-water mark of Emily's spiritual progression from the visionary girl who received fleeting glimpses of eternity to the assured mystic who believed she had attained to as complete a union with the soul of the universe—the 'Eternal Heart' she once called it[2]—as temporal life allowed. Only death could bestow the crown of everlasting Life. Such a state, once perceived, could, surely, never be lost again.

The tragic evidence of Emily's last year of life points however to a very different outcome; her faith was disproved, her visions ceased to come.

It might be argued that by 1848 Emily had nothing further to say, that her explorations into the life of the spirit had ended with *Wuthering Heights* and the preserved poems. Perhaps the truth must be faced that there were no further voyages to make; M. Heger's navigator had crossed her last sea. Most inhibiting of all perhaps had been the act of publication itself. For in a girl of such singular reticence, to be exposed to the world, even to the sympathetic eyes of Mr. Smith and Mr. Williams, was an appalling experience. Emily's conduct, as related by Charlotte, was one of untamed indifferent incivility, noticeably different from her former obliging and considerate conduct towards her sisters when the school plan was debated. Fear of exposure might well be strong enough to frustrate the will to write; such a reaction on the part of an intensely shy girl would not be unnatural. The evidence of Charlotte's numerous excuses for Ellis Bell's unsociable conduct partially corroborates this. But even such a rejection of human contacts would not account for what appears to have been the complete cessation of the poetic experience. Emily had written, during the last ten years at least, for herself alone; one would have thought that, had the inspiration been there, nothing could have broken her of the habit.

Fragments of two versions of the same poem—'Why Ask to know the Date, the Clime'—remain as her total poetic output for the period from

[1] See above, p. 189.   [2] Hatfield, 192.

September 1846 to May 1848. In a similar period of eighteen months, September 1843 to May 1845, she had written twenty-one poems, which included some of her best. The solitude she enjoyed during the simultaneous absence from home of Charlotte, Anne, and Branwell during 1843 and 1844, was no doubt conducive to the writing of poetry, but all of *Wuthering Heights* was probably written while the whole family was at home, between October 1845 and June 1846. Material conditions, such as want of space in which to write, seem not to have affected her; her own drawing of herself writing in her little room with her desk on her knees, is confirmed by the evidence of the servants who noticed her and Anne taking their desks into the garden during the summer of 1847 and early settling under the currant bushes to write.[1] No material difficulties would have prevented her writing—if the will to write had remained. Emily's absolute refusal to co-operate further in the publishing projects of the Bells must be seen as part of a general withdrawal into herself that marked the periods immediately preceding and following the death of Branwell. When the reprint of the *Poems* came out late in October, the reviews were as unsatisfactory as those for the first edition, and Charlotte's wounded comments show how deeply she felt the fresh insult to Ellis's genius. Acknowledging the *Standard of Freedom* and the *Morning Herald* sent by Smith, Elder on 2 November, she wrote: 'As critiques, I should have thought more of them had they more fully recognized Ellis Bell's merits; but the lovers of abstract poetry are few in number.'[2] 'Blind is he as a bat, insensate as any stone, to the merits of Ellis', she cried over the reviewer in the *Spectator*.[3] Ellis, if she glanced through such notices, could only have felt justified in turning her back on them all.

Barely a month after Branwell's death she did not even answer when spoken to. Uncommunicative she had always been, as though afraid 'of revealing herself', as Ellen Nussey had early noted. Even when pleased, her utmost expression of thanks had often been no more than a smile (one of those rare smiles that, Ellen Nussey again, thought were 'something to remember through life'). But whereas formerly Charlotte had spoken and written freely on behalf of Anne and Emily, an increasing scrupulousness is observable in her reports on Emily as though she really feared to 'exceed her commission'. Thanking Ellen for the box of gifts for the household sent on her last return from Brookroyd in September 1847, she wrote: 'Emily is just now sitting on the floor of the bedroom where I am

---

[1] Chadwick, 311.
[2] CB to WSW, 2 Nov. 1848. *SBC*, 150.
[3] CB to WSW, 16 Nov. 1848. *SLL*, i. 462.

writing, looking at her apples. She smiled when I gave them and the collar to her as your presents, with an expression at once well pleased and slightly surprised.'[1] When George Smith suggested sending down to Haworth parcels of books from Cornhill—not as gifts but as loans—Charlotte thankfully accepted them on behalf of all the family, and added: 'the loan of the books is indeed well-timed; no more acceptable benefit could have been conferred on my dear sister Emily, who is at present too ill to occupy herself . . . with anything but reading. She smiled when I told her Mr. Smith was going to send some more books—she was pleased'.[2]

By then, the final and alarming stage of Emily's withdrawal into herself had been reached. The severe cold and cough had, to the horror of the family, been recognized as 'inflammation of the lungs' by 2 November. Her illness, its relentless progress, the emaciation, the fever, the shortness of breath, the pain in the side, all confirmed the family's terrors of worse to come. In the face of this physical reality they were naturally less inclined than posterity is to reflect upon her spiritual condition.

In the great poem written in October 1845—published in 1846 as 'The Prisoner'—Emily gave to the jailor those haunting lines:

> And I am rough and rude, yet not more rough to see
> Than is the hidden ghost which has its home in me! . . .

The sense of the separateness of the spirit immured inside the body here becomes a visual reality, an inescapable condition of human nature from which the sensitive and the insensitive have to suffer alike.

The subject treated was not a new one for Emily; she had invented stories about prisoners immured in dungeons all her life, ever since the time of the children's games in the parsonage cellars; it was one of her favourite symbols, a regular Gondal theme. In this very poem the rescuing party strays in the crypts, and only after long and idle wandering through the vaults, comes on the prisoner confined behind triple walls. The prisoner had reached a condition of near-silence; counting on her weakness, her jailor expected no resistance, and was incredulous to hear her speak. And when she spoke it was with defiance, to reveal her certainty of deliverance, through the nightly visitations of a 'messenger of Hope', who came to her 'with western winds, with evening's wandering airs, / With that clear dusk of heaven that brings the thickest stars'—the condition, in short, that had always been the most propitious to Emily's own spiritual release.

[1] W & S, ii. 143.   [2] 7 Nov. 1848. W & S, ii. 271.

To the modern reader seeking to discover what happened to Emily Brontë in her last months, such a state of imprisonment appears to have become her own condition. The way out was lost, and her cell was inaccessible to would-be rescuers. Her almost total silence and unresponsiveness to outside contacts completed her isolation. Seeking to penetrate that isolation, all that her family could do was to repeat, as Charlotte did in letter after letter: 'I *do* wish I knew her state of mind . . . I wish I knew her feelings more clearly . . . but she will not give an explanation of her feelings.'[1]

What explanation could Emily give, except that she was immured and could not get out? that she was waiting for her 'messenger of Hope', and that he had ceased to come?

[1] W & S, ii. 289.

CHAPTER XVIII

'THE FINAL BOUND'

THE last months of Emily's life would not clarify the enigma; never had she been so enigmatical before. It is her conduct during that period, known to readers of Charlotte's letters and of Mrs. Gaskell's *Life*, that has been allowed to characterize her whole existence, though in truth it was highly uncharacteristic of her. Charlotte had often felt that Emily's 'peculiarities' needed explaining and apologizing for to strangers, but between the sisters there had never or seldom been dissension of any kind. Now, for the first time in their long and close union, Emily acted in direct opposition to Charlotte's dearest wishes. The history of those last weeks is one bewildered cry from Charlotte at Emily's incomprehensible and unprecedented conduct. Emily, whom she thought she knew, had become a stranger to her.

'Emily's reserved nature occasions me great uneasiness of mind,' Charlotte wrote to Ellen Nussey on 29 October: 'It is useless to question her; you get no answers. It is still more useless to recommend remedies; they are never adopted.'[1]

I would fain hope that Emily is a little better this evening [she confided in Mr. Williams on 2 November], but it is difficult to ascertain this. She is a real stoic in illness, she neither seeks nor will accept sympathy. To put any question, to offer any aid, is to annoy; she will not yield a step before pain or sickness till forced; not one of her ordinary avocations will she voluntarily renounce. You must look on and see her do what she is unfit to do, and not dare to say a word.[2]

By 23 November Charlotte had to admit to Ellen Nussey 'the terrible event of her loss as possible, and even probable'. Even so, 'she resolutely refuses to see a doctor; she will not give an explanation of her feelings, she will scarcely allow her illness to be alluded to'.[3] Never had Charlotte realized so acutely how precious Emily was to her as during that time of agonizing suspense. 'When she is ill there is no sunshine in the world for me,' she confessed to Mr. Williams on 2 November. 'The tie of sister is near and dear indeed, and I think a certain harshness in her powerful

[1] W & S, ii. 268. [2] W & S, ii. 269. [3] W & S, ii. 288.

and peculiar character only makes me cling to her more.'[1] 'Emily seems the nearest thing to my heart in this world,'[2] she told Ellen Nussey when referring to the terrible possibility of losing her. By the end of the month, despite the fearful pace of the illness, Charlotte wrote again to Ellen: 'I hope still—for I *must* hope—she is dear to me as life . . . The attack was, I believe in the first place, inflammation of the lungs; it ought to have been met promptly in time, but she would take no care, use no means'; and while conceding that Emily 'was too intractable', Charlotte bewailed her helplessness not only to nurse her sister properly, but to understand her motives. 'I *do* wish I knew her state of mind and feelings more clearly.'[3]

Charlotte had never expressed positive criticism of Emily; she had been her apologist all their lives. Now she was forced into a complaint that concerned more than Emily's hostility to doctors: it concerned Emily's character. Replying to a letter of advice from Mr. Williams, she wrote on 22 November:

I put your most friendly letter into Emily's hands as soon as I had myself perused it, taking care, however, not to say a word in favour of homeopathy— that would not have answered. It is best usually to leave her to form her own judgement, and *especially* not to advocate the side you wish her to favour; if you do, she is sure to lean in the opposite direction, and ten to one will argue herself into non-compliance. Hitherto she has refused medicine, rejected medical advice; no reasoning, no entreaty, has availed to induce her to see a physician. After reading your letter she said, 'Mr. Williams' intention was kind and good, but he was under a delusion: Homeopathy was only another form of quackery.' Yet she may reconsider this opinion and come to a different conclusion; her second thoughts are often the best.[4]

Charlotte was forced again to make a similar complaint on 7 December: 'Would that my sister added to her many great qualities the humble one of tractability! I have again and again incurred her displeasure by urging the necessity of seeking advice, and I fear I must yet incur it again and again. Let me leave the subject. I have no right thus to make you a sharer in our sorrow.'[5]

There was probably little that anyone could have done to save her, even if Emily had wished to save herself. Her dying state was soon apparent to all. 'I believe if you were to see her,' Charlotte told Ellen on 23 November, 'your impression would be that there is no hope.' Mr. Brontë was 'very despondent about her', Charlotte told Mr. Williams on 7 December:

[1] W & S, ii. 269.   [2] W & S, ii. 288.
[3] W & S, ii. 289.   [4] W & S, ii. 287.   [5] W & S, ii. 290.

he 'shakes his head and speaks of others of our family once similarly afflicted, for whom he likewise persisted in hoping against hope, and who are now removed where hope and fear fluctuate no more'.[1]

Did Emily wish to die? We cannot know. But if, as appears all too probable from the signs of her sorrow, her visions had deserted her, her pursuit of them beyond death could explain her rejection of life. As her poems had always shown, Emily had divided views on death. At one time it appeared to her as the most desirable consummation that existence had to offer; the little 'glittering spirits' of 'The Day Dream' told her that she should 'rejoice for those that live,/ Because they live to die'.[2] 'The Prisoner' welcomes the vision that penetrates her dungeon in whatever guise it comes—'robed in fires of Hell, or bright with heavenly shine', for the one sufficient reason that: 'If it but herald Death, the vision is divine.'[3]

Catherine Earnshaw, on her deathbed, voiced her longing to be gone 'into that glorious world, and to be always there, not seeing it dimly through tears, and yearning for it through the walls of an aching heart; but really with it, and in it'.[4] Yet Catherine Earnshaw had also very different views on death as the great deceiver. Dreaming that she was in Heaven, she cried her heart out to be back on earth because she discovered that after all, 'heaven did not seem to be my home; and the angels were so angry that they flung me out, into the middle of the heath on the top of Wuthering Heights, where I woke sobbing for joy.'[5]

The dread of losing the assured beauty of the earth and joy of living in it in exchange for a doubtful immortality was a very real fear that Emily had faced more than once in her poems. She wrote in May 1841:

> . . . Few hearts to mortals given
> On Earth so wildly pine;
> Yet none would ask a Heaven
> More like this Earth than thine . . .[6]

Yet again, another doubt had troubled her: watching the imperturbable cycle of the year with a heart that was wrung by the annual holocaust of life, she was impressed with the impersonality of nature, and the apparent indifference of the dead. What would it profit her to join them? she had asked on many occasions. The mourner standing by the grave of Augusta where the wild deer browsed and the wild birds raised their brood, and the linnet and the moor-lark sang their hearts out, realized that no sorrow,

---

[1] W & S, ii. 290.   [2] Hatfield, 170.   [3] Hatfield, 190.
[4] *Wuthering Heights*, ch. 15.   [5] Ibid., ch. 9.   [6] Hatfield, 147.

however deep, could reach the dead; like the earth about her, Augusta had become indifferent too.

> The Dweller in the land of Death
> Is changed and careless too.

> And if their eyes should watch and weep
> Till sorrow's source were dry,
> She would not, in her tranquil sleep,
> Return a single sigh . . .[1]

A year and a half divided that poem from the previous one—'In the earth, the earth, thou shalt be laid'—and yet the burden was the same: the oblivion and indifference of the dead.

> Farewell, then, all that love,
> All that deep sympathy:
> Sleep on; heaven laughs above,
> Earth never misses thee.[2]

Then again, Emily had considered death as an obliterating force, doing away with all distinctions of personality, all conflicting elements that tear the human heart, that level up even such total opposites as Good and Evil. Such obliteration of identity had seemed to her at times the only desirable end:

> O for the time when I shall sleep
> Without identity,
> And never care how rain may steep
> Or snow may cover me! . . .

> O let me die, that power and will
> Their cruel strife may close,
> And vanquished Good, victorious Ill
> Be lost in one repose.[3]

In strong contrast to such a philosophy stands the whole conception of *Wuthering Heights*, where faith in the reunion of parted spirits is essential to the plot. As it was the latest in composition and also the most completely integrated of all her systems of belief, it may be said to represent her final and strongest faith. It is contemporaneous with 'No Coward soul is Mine'. Challenged by Ellen Deane whether he were not afraid of death after such a life as he had led, Heathcliff burst out with the great secret by which he lived, the certainty of Catherine's immortality, of her invisible though constant presence which he believed Death would suddenly illumine:

[1] Hatfield, 173.   [2] Hatfield, 163.   [3] Hatfield, 181.

as certainly as you perceive the approach to some substantial body in the dark though it cannot be discerned, so certainly I felt Cathy was there, not under me, but on the earth . . . I felt her by me—I could *almost* see her, and yet I could not! I ought to have sweat blood then, from the anguish of my yearning, from the fervour of my supplications to have but one glimpse!

On the eve of his death, he has almost attained that vision. 'I have a single wish,' he told Ellen, 'and my whole being and faculties are yearning to attain it. They have yearned towards it so long, and so unwaveringly, that I'm convinced it *will* be reached—and *soon*—because it has devoured my existence—I am swallowed up in the anticipation of its fulfilment.'[1]

Such passion in pursuit of a lost love, such lyric power lent to a fictional character, made Emily's early readers suppose it must be the echo of a personal experience, and seek to identify a lover in her life. The lover, as the whole body of her writing attests, was the visionary power that first blessed and then abandoned her.

> What I love shall come like visitant of air,
> Safe in secret power from lurking human snare;
> Who loves me, no word of mine shall e'er betray,
> Though for faith unstained my life must forfeit pay.
>
> Burn then, little lamp; glimmer straight and clear—
> Hush! a rustling wing stirs, methinks, the air;
> He for whom I wait, thus ever comes to me;
> Strange Power! I trust thy might; trust thou my constancy.[2]

The loves of Catherine Earnshaw and Heathcliff are but the allegory of such a spiritual passion, as the *Paradiso* and the *Inferno* are of Heaven and Hell. The writing of *Wuthering Heights*, in a state of intense spiritual awareness, was both an exploration and a proclamation of the truth towards which Emily had been reaching for years. It did not seem to admit a further trace of doubt or disbelief in the author. And yet the evidence tends to show that the absolute assurance of that achievement was lost to Emily in her last months. Therein, and not in her early death, lies the tragedy of her life. Therein, it might be said, in the loss of her liberty to transcend the material world, as she had done in vision after vision, lay the real cause of her wish to die.

There was another factor at the time that would carry the greatest weight with Emily: Anne's rapidly declining health. Anne's delicacy had

---

[1] *Wuthering Heights*, ch. 33.   [2] Hatfield, 190.

been a chronic condition with which the family had learnt to live for years, but her deterioration that autumn could not be overlooked, as Charlotte admitted to Ellen Nussey. Barely recovered from her own attack of jaundice following Branwell's death, Charlotte wrote on 29 October: 'I feel much more uneasy about my sisters than myself just now. Emily's cold and cough are very obstinate ... Nor can I shut my eyes to Anne's great delicacy of constitution.'[1] Anne had never wanted for medical care in her illnesses and had doubtless been prescribed for by the family doctor called in to attend Charlotte in her jaundice. Some of the violence of Emily's contempt for 'poisoning doctors' can perhaps be attributed to Dr. Wheelhouse's failure to arrest the progress of Anne's tuberculosis. By the New Year when Mr. Brontë called in the lung specialist, Dr. Teale from Leeds, Anne's case was pronounced beyond cure. The prospect of life without Anne was another unspeakable menace that Emily had to face.

Her world was narrowing about her. As winter set in, her horizon was confined to the view framed in the Georgian window panes of the parsonage parlour; the church tower and the Jacobean chimneystacks of the sharply slanting roofs of the old houses down the village street were all she could see of the free world that had once been her kingdom. The dogs had now to be exercised by Mr. Nicholls, who showed himself a true friend to the family—he was already in love with Charlotte. To Emily, every day that she was shut away from the moors was a living death, an entombment. The love of earth was the overruling passion of her life; to be cut off from it—as she had been once before when at school—dealt a mortal blow to the sources of her being. It was the longing for complete communion with the earth she loved that had made a poet of her; every passing grief had found consolation in that hope:

> How beautiful the Earth is still
> To thee—how full of Happiness;
> How little fraught with real ill
> Or shadowy phantoms of distress;
>
> How Spring can bring thee glory yet
> And Summer win thee to forget
> December's sullen time! ...[2]

As Emily listened to Anne coughing, and the 'poisoning doctors' brought no ease to her sufferings, it was easy to despair. To someone with her beliefs, the loss of faith was a matter of life and death. By whatever name she recognized the 'strange power' in which she trusted, 'God of

[1] W & S, ii, 267-8. [2] Hatfield, 188.

Visions', 'the God within my breast', 'messenger of Hope', 'Guide', 'Comforter', it is evident that she looked on that power as a force within herself, of whose permanence she had no doubt.

> And am I wrong to worship where
> Faith cannot doubt nor Hope despair,
> Since my own soul can grant my prayer?
> Speak, God of Visions, plead for me
> And tell why I have chosen thee![1]

To anyone so self-sufficient as Emily, there seemed no need to seek assurance of a faith elsewhere than in her own breast. The God she worshipped dwelt there, and she in Him.

> . . . O God within my breast
> Almighty ever-present Deity
> Life, that in me has rest
> As I Undying Life, have power in Thee . . .[2]

It can be argued that such a creed contained more of intellectual arrogance than of humility; and this accords well with her conception of the 'tragic hero'—a conception based on the exercise of power and will, on whose strength she had always relied—not to dominate others, but herself. Blake, in words reminiscent of Emily Brontë's, wrote in a letter of 12 April 1827—his last year of life—that 'The Real Man, The Imagination which Liveth for Ever', was 'stronger and stronger as this Foolish Body decays'.[3] So it was with Emily.

While physically she perished [Charlotte testified], mentally she grew stronger than we had yet known her. Day by day, when I saw with what a front she met suffering, I looked on her with an anguish of wonder and love. I have never seen anything like it; but, indeed, I have never seen her parallel in anything. . . . The awful point was, that while full of ruth for others, on herself she had no pity; the spirit was inexorable to the flesh; from the trembling hand, the unnerved limbs, the faded eyes, the same service was extracted as they had rendered in health. To stand by and witness this, and not dare to remonstrate, was a pain no words can render.[4]

On 9 December, unable to bear the sight of Emily's suffering any longer, Charlotte wrote to the homeopathic specialist—Dr. Epps—on Mr. Williams's recommendation,[5] and gave him an account of Emily's symptoms. She did so without Emily's knowledge, of course. The features of her illness that she judged most necessary for the doctor to know were

---

[1] Hatfield, 176.   [2] Hatfield, 91.   [3] *Complete Writings*, ed. Keynes (1966), 878.
[4] Biographical Notice.   [5] W & S, ii. 292.

Emily's great emaciation, her breathlessness after any movement, her racing pulse (which she had once allowed them to take), her exhausting cough. She had never consented to lie in bed a single day, but, as Charlotte reported: 'she sits up from 7 in the morning till 10 at night'. Her sleep, of which her sisters could only judge by the periods of silence from the paroxysms of coughing as she still slept alone in her tiny room, 'seemed tolerably good'. Telling the doctor how she had rejected all medical care, Charlotte gave as the reason Emily's insistence 'that Nature should be left to take her own course'. A significant detail in the report was Charlotte's judgement that Emily had 'hitherto enjoyed pretty good health, though she has never looked strong, and the family constitution is not supposed to be robust'.[1]

Emily refused even to try the prescription Dr. Epps sent.

In baffled silence, as she waited the return of the 'strange power' that had never failed her yet, Emily's physical sufferings were intensified by her spirit's yearning. Exercised as yet over purely immaterial forces, her victorious will-power proved ineffectual against such physical odds as were leagued against her now. There is something of the animal at bay in her fiercely defensive mood, as she barricaded herself behind a wall of silence, inaccessible to human influence.

To-day, as Emily appeared a little better [Charlotte had written to Mr. Williams on 22 November], I thought the Review[2] would amuse her, so I read it aloud to her and Anne. As I sat between them at our quiet but now somewhat melancholy fireside, I studied the two ferocious authors. Ellis the 'man of uncommon parts, but dogged, brutal, and morose', sat leaning back in his easy chair drawing his impeded breath as he best could, and looking, alas! piteously pale and wasted; it is not his wont to laugh, but he smiled half amused and half in scorn as he listened. Acton was sewing, no emotion ever stirs him to loquacity, so he only smiled too, dropping at the same time a single word of calm amazement to hear his character so darkly portrayed. I wonder what the reviewer would have thought of his own sagacity could he have beheld the pair as I did.[3]

Martha Brown, both the youngest and the strongest member of the household, told Emily's biographer, Mary Duclaux, of an incident that occurred on Emily's last evening. It was Monday, 18 December, and Emily rose to go to the kitchen as usual to feed the dogs. She had never allowed anybody to deputize for her in this office. As Charlotte had teased her years before when writing from Brussels, Emily always kept the 'best

[1] W & S, ii. 292.
[2] For the text of the review in *North American Review* of the Bell Novels, see 'Novels of the Season', Oct. 1848. *BST*, 1956.　　　[3] *SLL*, i. 464-.

bits of the mutton' for them. She could only walk slowly now, as Martha remembered, and carried in her 'thin hands' an apronful of broken meat and bread. In the flagged passage, a fierce gust of wind from the front or back doors of the house, struck her against the wall. She reeled where she stood and almost fell. Even so, she refused the proffered hands stretched out to help her and insisted on giving the animals their meal.

Later that evening, Charlotte told Mr. Williams afterwards, she thought to entertain Emily by reading aloud from one of the books sent from Cornhill. Mr. Williams had suffered from a near-breakdown earlier in the year and had found Emerson's Essays—just published in England—a great solace on his enforced holiday. He sent the book to Haworth with a strong recommendation to Charlotte. She did not entirely share his enthusiasms, and perceived that they were 'of mixed gold and clay'; nevertheless, there was matter in them to appeal to Emily she judged, and began to read aloud to her. 'I read till I found she was not listening—I thought to recommence next day,' Charlotte told Mr. Williams. 'Next day, the first glance at her face told me what would happen before night-fall.'[1]

The following morning Charlotte hurried out onto the moors in the hope of finding a last sprig of heather for Emily. Mrs. Gaskell, to whom she related the incident, wrote of it afterwards: 'I remember Miss Brontë's shiver at recalling the pang she felt when, after having searched in the little hollows and sheltered crevices of the moors for a lingering spray of heather—just one spray, however withered—to take in to Emily, she saw that the flower was not recognised by the dim and indifferent eyes.'[2]

Emily had got up as usual, 'and she dying all the time', Martha remembered, 'the rattle in her throat while she would dress herself; and neither Miss Brontë nor I dared offer to help her.'[3] The story of Emily's comb, made famous by Mary Duclaux, may perhaps be apocryphal. She related how Emily sat combing her hair by her bedroom fire and dropped it into the grate from sheer weakness, and then called to Martha Brown to pick it up for her. Emily's bedroom never had any fireplace, and though she might be supposed to dress before the fire in her sisters' neighbouring room, her appeal for help to Martha does not agree with Martha's own statement that Emily would not allow either her or Charlotte to help her dress.

Emily went downstairs to the parlour as usual and went through the motions of taking up a piece of sewing. Charlotte, who had not written to Ellen Nussey for ten days, got out her desk and wrote:

[1] CB to WSW, 25 June 1849. W & S, ii. 348.
[2] Gaskell, 257.   [3] Gaskell, Letters, 246.

Tuesday,

Dear Ellen—I should have written to you before, if I had had one word of hope to say; but I had not. She grows daily weaker. The physician's opinion was expressed too obscurely to be of use. He sent some medicine which she would not take. Moments as dark as these I have never known. I pray for God's support to us all. Hitherto He has granted it. Yours faithfully—[1]

About noon Emily was visibly worse and her sisters urged her to go to bed. The only concession she would make was to lie down on the sofa— the black horsehair sofa that can still be seen today. Her last audible words, spoken in compassion for her sisters no doubt, were 'If you'll send for a doctor I'll see him now', and before he could come, she was gone. It was just two o'clock in the afternoon.

Dr. Wheelhouse, who had recently attended each member of the family with the exception of Emily, could not declare that he had been 'present at the death'; he could only certify that he had been 'in attendance', which was not strictly true, and declare the cause of death to be due to 'Consumption—2 months' duration'. He thus confirmed the quite recent origin of Emily's illness, a fact that made her determined self-neglect only the more heartrending to her family.

They carried Emily upstairs and put her on the camp bed in the little front room. Keeper howled outside her door, not for one day or days, but for many weeks.[2]

William Wood, Tabby's nephew, the village carpenter, was sent for to make the coffin. In recording the measurements, he said he had never in all his experience made so narrow a shell for an adult; it was 5 feet 7 inches by 16 inches.

It was Mr. Nicholls who conducted the funeral, which took place on Friday, 22 December. In those days there was a gate in the end wall of the parsonage garden, opening into the churchyard, through which the incumbent and his family used to walk to church. On this occasion, the order of their going was remembered by generations of the villagers; behind the coffin walked Mr. Brontë with Keeper, who at Mr. Brontë's wish stayed at the head of the little procession and entered the family box-pew with them, where he remained throughout the service. After them walked Charlotte and Anne, and behind them Tabby, an old woman of seventy-eight, and Martha.

Emily suffers no more from pain or weakness now [Charlotte wrote the next day to Ellen Nussey]. She will never suffer more in this world. She is gone, after a hard, short conflict. She died on *Tuesday*, the very day I wrote to you. I

[1] W & S, ii. 293.   [2] Gaskell, 259.

thought it very possible she might be with us still for weeks; and a few hours afterwards she was in eternity. Yes; there is no more Emily in time or on earth now. Yesterday we put her poor, wasted, mortal frame quietly under the church pavement. We are very calm at present. Why should we be otherwise? The anguish of seeing her suffer is over; the spectacle of the pains of death is gone by; the funeral day is past. We feel she is at peace.[1]

In the many, many references Charlotte made later to her sister's death, it was the one certainty she clung to, the one consolation she could find, that Emily was now at peace:

The loss is ours—not hers, and some sad comfort I take, as I hear the wind blow and feel the cutting keenness of the frost, in knowing that the elements bring her no more suffering—their severity cannot reach her grave—her fever is quieted, her restlessness soothed, her deep, hollow cough is hushed for ever; we do not hear it in the night nor listen for it in the morning; we have not the conflict of the strangely strong spirit and the fragile frame before us—relentless conflict—once seen, never to be forgotten . . . I will only say, sweet is rest after labour and calm after tempest, and repeat again and again that Emily knows that now.[2]

But, dwell on it as she might, Charlotte could not appease her sorrow nor silence her doubts.

The possibility that Emily wished to die was a thought beyond her acceptance; it was too intolerable for her to admit. She repeated over and over again to herself and to others, that Emily had been happy, that Emily was reluctant to go. 'I cannot forget Emily's death-day,' she wrote four months later to Ellen Nussey, 'it comes a more fixed—a darker, a more frequently recurring idea in my mind than ever; it was very terrible, she was torn conscious reluctant though resolute out of a happy life. But it will not do to dwell on these things.'[3]

But the wish to die had been supremely expressed three years before; Emily had envisaged death as an act of daring that could be freely accomplished, given a boldness of mind commensurate to the deed.

> . . . Glad comforter, will I not brave
> Unawed the darkness of the grave?
> Nay, smile to hear Death's billows rave,
> My Guide, sustained by thee?
> The more unjust seems present fate
> The more my Spirit springs elate
> Strong in thy strength, to anticipate
> Rewarding Destiny![4]

[1] W & S, ii. 294.   [2] CB to WSW, 25 Dec. 1848. W & S, ii. 295.
[3] W & S, ii, 324.   [4] Hatfield, 188.

Barely five months after Emily, Anne died at Scarborough. In the frequent comparisons Charlotte made between her sisters' deaths, she said much that, by implication, could illumine Emily's. Announcing Anne's death to Mr. Williams, she wrote to him on 4 June 1849:

She died . . . thankful for release from a suffering life . . . Her quiet, Christian death did not rend my heart as Emily's stern simple, undemonstrative end did. I let Anne go to God, and felt He had a right to her. I could hardly let Emily go. I wanted to hold her back then, and I want her back now. Anne, from her childhood, seemed preparing for an early death. Emily's spirit seemed strong enough to bear her to fulness of years.[1]

By implication, Emily's death was not Christian, it was *not* resigned. It was 'resolute' and 'undemonstrative'.

Reverting again to Anne's death, Charlotte said a little later:

My sister died happily, nothing dark . . . overclouded her hour of dissolution— the doctor—a stranger—who was called in—wondered at her fixed tranquillity of spirit and settled longing to be gone . . . it but half consoles to remember this calm—there is piercing pain in it. Anne had had enough of life such as it was—in her twenty-eighth year she laid it down as a burden. I hardly know whether it is sadder to think of that than of Emily turning her dying eyes reluctantly from the pleasant sun.[2]

Repeatedly, Charlotte spoke of Emily's death as striking her down 'in the fulness of life', 'the prime of life', 'in a time of promise'—as tearing her 'out of a happy life', as though there had been no loss of joy or power in Emily's last year. Stranger still, Charlotte spoke of Emily as 'rooted up in the prime of her days, in the promise of her powers—like a tree in full bearing—struck at the root'. Yet Charlotte could produce no evidence to prove her point.

When the question arose, two years later, of publishing the posthumous works of Ellis and Acton Bell, Charlotte did not deny that some manuscripts had been left.

It would not be difficult to compile a volume out of the papers left by my sisters, had I, in making the selection, dismissed from my consideration the scruples and the wishes of those whose written thoughts these papers held. But this was impossible; an influence, stronger than could be exercised by any motive of expediency, necessarily regulated the selection. I have, then, culled from the mass only a little poem here and there. The whole makes but a tiny nosegay, and the colour and perfume of the flowers are not such as fit them for festal uses.

It has already been said that my sisters wrote much in childhood and girlhood. Usually, it seems a sort of injustice to expose in print the crude thoughts of the unripe mind, the rude efforts of the unpractised hand; yet I venture to give three little poems of my sister Emily's, written in her sixteenth year, because they illustrate a point in her character.[1]

The poems to which Charlotte alluded were 'Loud Without the Wind Roaring', 'A Little While, a Little While', and 'The Blue Bell is the Sweetest Flower'. As can be seen, the poems making up this posthumous selection were predominantly youthful in character and added nothing to the quality of Ellis Bell's achievement; more important still, no work later than 'No Coward Soul is Mine' was included.

From her ambiguous reference to the remaining manuscripts, it must be supposed that Charlotte judged them either of a character unlikely to enhance her sisters' reputation, or too personal to publish. She said so clearly as regards Anne in the Memoir prefixed to her poems: 'In looking over my sister Anne's papers, I find mournful evidence that religious feeling had been to her but too much like what it was to Cowper', and added that 'their effect . . . would be too distressing, were it not combated by the certain knowledge that in her last moments this tyranny of a too tender conscience was overcome'. Of Emily Charlotte said nothing so revealing, either of the nature of her posthumous papers, or of her last moments, though it may readily be believed that if it had been possible to speak as openly about Emily, she would have done so. 'The lovers of abstract poetry are few,' Charlotte had said, and had Emily's remaining manuscripts been such as the world might see and understand Charlotte would certainly not have prevented their publication. The act of destruction of any, even a handful of Emily's writings, must have been acutely painful to her. Yet she preferred it to exposing her sister to the further incomprehension of the public. The importance of the gesture is only realized when it is remembered that no such consideration had deterred Charlotte from urging the publication of Emily's earlier poems—however much opposed to it Emily herself had been.

In obliterating the last vestiges of her sister's genius, Charlotte was as active as ever Emily herself could wish in safeguarding her privacy. Charlotte acted perhaps on orders received before her sister's death. The total absence of letters between Emily and her family is as significant as the absence of literary remains. (Ellen Nussey alone preserved those

[1] Biographical Notice.

addressed to her.[1]) There must also have been many more diary-letters exchanged between Emily and Anne than have come to light. Interpret Emily to the world as Charlotte constantly attempted to do, she did not allow the authentic voice of Emily to be heard, except in the already published works.

After Emily's funeral, Charlotte begged Ellen Nussey to stay with her awhile. 'Try to come,' she wrote her on 23 December; 'I never so much needed the consolation of a friend's presence. Pleasure, of course, there will be none for you in the visit, except what your kind heart would teach you to find in doing good to others.'[2]

During that visit, the secret of the Bells' authorship was at last confided to Ellen, and she was given a copy of *Wuthering Heights*. After her departure, she offered to send it back, not realizing, till reassured by Charlotte, that it was for her to keep.[3] The incident, following so soon after Emily's death, shows how the anonymity, so fiercely guarded before, had above all been at the instigation and on the insistence of Emily. Within a week of her funeral it was decided by the remaining Bells that no secret need now surround her identity. The world could make what it would of *Wuthering Heights*.

Intensely as Charlotte guarded her sister's image, softening here, palliating there some harsher trait, some more than usually uncompromising opinion, speaking of her with adoration not unmixed with awe, she never dared reveal the source of her sister's strength, the origin of her imaginative power. On all the many occasions she spoke or wrote of Emily, she never once admitted that she was a mystic[4] who had had exceptional spiritual experiences. And yet, Charlotte's very silence on the crucial subject of Emily's visionary life confirms the need for silence that her destruction of Emily's papers indicated. Not only in deference to Emily's wishes but for fear of the incomprehension and condemnation of the conventional society about them, she withheld the most important single fact about her sister, whose genius she had been the first to recognize. She even conceded, to placate opinion, that the creation of such a character as Heathcliff needed apology. Joan of Arc was forced to deny her Voices, and in nineteenth-century England Currer Bell felt obliged to make concessions to the Establishment to protect her sister's good name against possible charges of paganism. Emily's originality of conduct could

---

[1] Only two of these have been preserved, at BM and BPM. The text of a third, dated 25 Feb. 1846, was published by Wise & Symington, but its present location is unknown.

[2] *SLL*, ii. 16.   [3] W & S, ii. 303.

[4] Cf. Walter Allen, *The English Novel*, p. 194, for the modern acceptance of this 'central fact about Emily Brontë'.

not be hidden (she made no concessions to the world in manners, habits, dress) but the nature of her beliefs, had they been frankly admitted, could not have escaped the charge of pride and irreligion. Had her sister expressed her deepest spiritual experiences in recognizable Christian imagery Charlotte's task would have been less baffling. But how explain to a hide-bound generation that Emily had revelations of a spiritual life animating nature, of which she believed herself a part? that she regarded her material life as a fatal severance from the universal soul to which she yearned to be reunited? that she saw death as a deliverance *not* from a private grief, or as an evasion from an intolerable reality, but as the ultimate crown of life by which alone her 'spirit's bliss' could be attained? To *will* her own death was an act of daring that could not be admitted to others without condign reprobation. A clergyman's daughter should know her duty better than to hold direct communion with God.

Thus, a conspiracy of silence was created round the one sensational circumstance of Emily's life, the outward circumstances of which were quite unremarkable. Those who cherished her realized that the truth about her was too transcendental to express, except in parables.

From among her sister's literary remains, Charlotte published only eighteen pieces in the posthumous 1850 edition of her works. Eight of these were drawn from Emily's manuscript notebook dated 'February 1844', and nine from the companion 'Gondal' manuscript; none of the poems was written, therefore, during Emily's last four years. One undated poem, alone, may belong to a later period, and have been chosen by Charlotte for its supreme expression of Emily's faith—in the Heaven of her desiring, the Heaven whose landscape most resembled her earthly home.[1]

> Often rebuked, yet always back returning
> To those first feelings that were born with me,
> And leaving busy chase of wealth and learning
> For idle dreams of things which cannot be:
>
> To-day, I will seek not the shadowy region;
> Its unsustaining vastness waxes drear;
> And visions rising, legion after legion,
> Bring the unreal world too strangely near.
>
> I'll walk, but not in old heroic traces,
> And not in paths of high morality,
> And not among the half-distinguished faces,
> The clouded forms of long-past history.

[1] See Hatfield, pp. 4-5, 255.

I'll walk where my own nature would be leading:
It vexes me to choose another guide:
Where the grey flocks in ferny glens are feeding;
Where the wild wind blows on the mountain side.

What have these lonely mountains worth revealing?
More glory and more grief than I can tell:
The earth that wakes *one* human heart to feeling
Can centre both the worlds of Heaven and Hell.

APPENDIX A

EMILY BRONTË'S FRENCH DEVOIRS

1. *Le Chat*. Signed and dated, 'Emily J. Brontë, Mai 15 1842'.
   Present location, Berg Collection, New York Public Library.

2. *Portrait: Le Roi Harold avant la Bataille de Hastings*. Signed and dated, 'Emily J. Brontë, Juin 1842'.
   MS. in very poor condition. Present location, BPM Haworth.

3. *Lettre. Ma chère Maman*. Signed and dated, 'Emily Brontë, 26 Juillet 1842'.
   Present location, BPM, Haworth.

4. *L'Amour Filial*. Signed and dated, 'Emily J. Brontë, 5 Aout 1842'.
   Present location, BPM Haworth.

5. *Lettre d'un Frère à un Frère*. Signed and dated, 'Emily J. Brontë, 5 Aout 1842'.
   Present location, University of Texas Library.

6. *Le Papillon*. Signed and dated, 'Emily J. Brontë, Le 11 Aout 1842'.
   Present location, New York Public Library.

7. *Le Palais de la Mort*. Signed and dated, 'Emily J. Brontë, le 18 Octobre 1842'.
   Present location, BPM Haworth.

Nos. 2, 3, and 5 were corrected by M. Heger; his corrections are printed in small italic type. The others were apparently not corrected.

1. Emily J. Brontë   Mai 15 1842

Le Chat

Je puis dire avec sincerité que j'aime les chats; aussi je vais rendre des très bonnes raisons, pourquoi ceux qui les haïssent, ont tort.

Un chat est un animal qui a plus des sentiments humaines que presque tout autre être. Nous ne pouvons soutenir une comparaison avec le chien, il est infiniment trop bon: mais le chat, encore qu'il diffère en quelques points physiques, est extrêmement semblable à nous en disposition.

Il peut être des gens, en verité, qui diraient que cette ressemblance ne lui approche qu'aux hommes les plus méchants, qu'elle est bornée à son excès d'hypocrisie, de cruauté, et d'ingratitude; vices détestables dans notre race et également odieux en celle des chats.

Sans disputer les limites que ces individus mettent à notre affinité, je réponds, que si l'hypocrisie, la cruauté, et l'ingratitude sont exclusivement la propriété des méchants, cette classe renferme tout le monde: notre éducation développe une de ces qualites en grande perfection, les autres fleurissent sans soins, et loin de les condamner, nous regardons tous les trois, avec beaucoup de complaisance. Un chat, pour son intérêt propre cache quelque-fois sa misanthropie sous une apparence de douceur très aimable; au lieu d'arracher ce qu'il désire de la main de son maitre il s'approche d'un air caressant, frotte sa jolie petite tête contre lui, et avance une patte dont la touche est douce comme le duvet. Lorsqu'il est venu à bout, il reprend son caractère de Timon, et cette finesse est nommé l'hypocrisie en lui, en nous-mêmes, nous lui donnons un autre nom, c'est la politesse et celui qui ne l'employait pas pour déguiser ses vrais sentiments serait bientot chassé de société.

"Mais", dit quelque dame délicate, qui a meurtri une demi-douzaine de bichons par pure affection, "le chat est une bête si cruelle, il ne se contente pas de tuer sa proie, il la tourmente avant sa mort; vous ne pouvez faire cette accusation contre nous." A peu près Madame, monsieur, votre mari, par exemple, aime beaucoup la chasse; mais les renards étant rares dans sa terre, il n'aurait pas le moyen de prendre cette amusement souvent, s'il ne ménageait pas ses materiaux. Ainsi, lorsqu'il a couru un animal à son dernier soupir, il le tire des gueules des chiens, et le réserve pour souffrir encore deux ou trois fois la même infliction, terminant finalement en la mort. Vous evitez vous-même un spectacle sanglant, parce qu'il blesse vos faibles nerfs, mais j'ai vous vue embrasser avec transport votre enfant, quand il vient vous montrer un beau papillon écrasé entre ses cruels petits doigts; et, à ce moment, j'ai voulu bien avoir un chat, avec la queue d'un rat demi englouti, pendant de sa bouche, a présenter comme l'image, la vraie copie, de votre ange; vous ne pourriez refuser de le baiser, et s'il nous égratignait tous deux en revanche, tant mieux, les petits garçons sont assez liables à reconnaitre ainsi, les caresses de leurs amis, et la ressemblance serait plus parfaite.

L'ingratitude des chats est un autre nom pour la penétration. Ils savent estimer nos faveurs à leur juste prix, parce qu'ils devinent les motifs qui nous poussent de leur donner, et si ces motifs puissent quelquefois être bons, sans doute ils se souviennent toujours, qu'ils doivent toutes leurs misères et toutes leurs mauvaises qualités au grand aïeul du genre humain, car assurément, le chat n'était pas méchant en Paradis.

Emily J. Brontë   Juin 1842

Portrait : Le Roi Harold avant la Bataille de Hastings

ces hommes
Parmi tous ceux réunis ce soir sur le champ de bataille, qui demain serait la scène d'une catastrophe si grande, on pouvait facilement distinguer le roi, non par sa parure et sa suite, mais par sa figure et son maintien.

Il se promenait un peu éloigné du camp sur une éminence qui lui donnait une ample vue de la plaine où son armée s'étendait comme un océan de tous côtes jusqu'à l'horizon, qui reluisait des feux de l'ennemi.

jusqu'au camp ennemi

Quand il portait ses regards vers ce dernier spectacle, quand il songeait que
son territoire
c'était sur sa terre que les usurpateurs se reposaient, et que c'étaient ses forets
alimentaient les feux de leurs bivouacs   *vallée*
qui fournissaient leurs flammes, quand il baissait les yeux sur la campagne en
bas, quand il contemplait les longues lignes de ses troupes qu'il savait être aussi
braves que nombreuses, aussi fidèles que braves, quand il pensait à sa puissance
et à la justice de sa cause, une expression sublime illuminait son pale visage, il ne
pouvait imaginer la défaite.

C'est qu'alors Harold réunissait en lui-même toute l'énergie, le pouvoir, toutes
les espérances d'une nation. Alors, il n'était plus un roi, il était un héros. La
situation l'avait transformé; en paix il aurait été sans doute comme presque tous
inoffensive et paisible   *confiné*
les autres princes assis sur un tranquille trone, un miserable enseveli dans son
fut
palais, abimé en plaisirs, trompé par les flatteries, sachant, pourvu qu'il ne soit
pas tout a fait imbécile, que de tout son peuple il était l'homme le moins libre
(qu'il est une créature qui n'ose pas agir, qui n'ose guère penser par elle-meme.)
d'égarer   *en*
Que tous ceux qui l'environnent tachent d'embrouiller son âme dans un laby-
de ceux qui l'entourent
rinthe de folies et de vices; qui c'est l'intérêt universel d'aveugler ses yeux, que
sa main ne peut se mouvoir sans être dirigé et que son corps est un vrai prison-
nier, ayant son royaume pour prison et ses sujets pour gardes.

Harold, sur le champ de bataille, sans palais, sans ministres, sans courtisans,
sans faste, sans luxe, n'ayant que le ciel de sa patrie au dessus de lui, et sous ses
pieds cette terre qu'il tient de ses ancêtres, et qu'il n'abandonnera qu'avec la vie;
Harold, entouré de coeurs dévoués, qui lui ont confié leur sureté, leur liberté
et leur existence — quelle différence! —— Visible aux hommes comme à son
Créateur l'ame divine brille dans ses yeux —— Une multitude de passions
humaines y éveillant en meme temps, sont exaltées, sanctifiées, presque déifiées.
Son courage n'a pas de témérité, sa fierté n'a pas d'arrogance, cette indignation
n'a pas injustice, cette assurance n'a pas de présomption. Il est intérieurement
convaincu qu'aucun pouvoir mortel ne l'abattera. La Mort, seule, peut emporter
la victoire de ses armes, et Harold est pret a s'incliner? devant elle, parceque
la touche de cette main est au héros comme le geolier qui lui rendait la
était
liberté, serait à l'esclave.

3. Emily Brontë   26 Juillet 1842

Lettre

Ma chère Maman,

Il me semble bien longtemps depuis que je vous aie vue, et trop longtemps
aussi que je n'aie pas reçu de vos nouvelles. Si vous étiez malade, on m'écrirait;
cela me rassure un peu   *a*
je ne crains pas cela, mais je crains que vous songiez moins souvent de votre fille

il me faut ici, dans mon exil,   que de   pour
dans son absence; dernièrement je suis attristée par de très petites choses, et à
m'attrister   et à l'idée qu'on m'oublie   me   ici
cette idée surtout,/je ne puis m'empêcher de pleurer. On/dit que ma santé est
faible, et on m'a fait garder ma chamber et quitter mes études et mes compagnes;
aussi
c'est peut-être/pour cette raison, que je suis si triste, parce qu'il est bien en-
seule   isolé   à ne
nuyeux d'être enfermée toute la journée dans un appartement solitaire, où je n'ai
sinon
rien à faire, du matin jusqu'au soir, que de rêver et d'ecouter, de temps en temps,
a
les cris joyeux des autres enfants, qui jouent et rient sans songer de moi.
de rentrer   tous
Il me tarde d'etre chez nous, encore une fois, et de voir la maison et les
ceux
personnes que j'aime tant. *Si* Au moins vous pouviez venir ici, je crois que votre
rendrait joie et santé.   si dans
seule présence me guerirait. Venez donc, chère Maman; et pardonnez/cette
je   venez j'ai à
lettre, elle ne parle que de moi, mais moi,/vous parler de bien d'autres choses.

Votre fille dévouée

N.B. Aucune marque de souvenir pr papa – c'est une faute. C. Heger.

4. Emily J. Brontë   5 Août 1842

L'Amour Filial

"Tu honoreras ton père et ta mère si tu veux vivre." C'est par un tel commandement que Dieu nous donne une connaissance de la bassesse de notre race, de ce
qu'elle parait à ses yeux, pour remplir le plus doux, le plus saint de tous les
devoirs — il lui faut une menace; c'est par peur qu'il faut forcer la maniacque à
bénir elle-même. Dans cette commandement est caché un reproche plus amer
qu'aucune accusation ouverte ne puisse renfermer, une charge contre nous,
d'aveuglement entier ou d'ingratitude infernale.

Les parents aiment leurs enfants, c'est un principe de la nature; la daim ne
craint pas les chiens lorsque son petit est en danger, l'oiseau meurt sur son nid;
cet instinct est une particule de l'âme divine que nous partageons avec tout
animal qui existe, et Dieu n-a-t-il pas mis dans le coeur de l'enfant un pareil sentiment? Quelque chose vraiment il y a et cependant la voix tonnante leur crie:
"Honorez vos parents ou vous mourerez!" Or, ce commandement n'est pas
donné, cette menace n'est pas ajouté pour rien: il peut être des hommes qui
méprisent leur bonheur, leur devoir et leur Dieu à ce point que l'étincelle de feu
céleste s'éteint dans leur sein, et les laisse un chaos moral sans lumière et sans
ordre, une transfiguration hideuse de l'image dans laquelle ils étaient créés.

Ces monstres, l'âme virtueuse est portée d'éviter avec horreur. C'est un instinct
juste, nous devons les éviter, mais ne les maudissez pas; pourquoi ajouter notre
malédiction à celle de Dieu? Plutôt plaignez, plutôt pleurez leur condition. C'est
qu'ils n'aient jamais pensé de ce que leurs parents ont fait pour eux. C'est que la

mémoire de leurs jeunes ans ne leur a jamais rappelé les espérances et l'affection de ce père qu'ils désobéissent et les longues heures de patiente souffrance, les soins, les larmes la dévotion infatigable de cette mère qu'il tuait par la plus cruelle des morts, tournant en poison l'amour illimité qui doit être la nourriture de sa malheureuse viellesse.

L'heure viendra quand la conscience s'éveillera, alors il aura une rétribution terrible ; quel médiateur plaidera alors pour le criminel ? C'est Dieu, qui l'accuse ; Quelle puissance sauvera le misérable ? C'est Dieu qui le condamne. Il a rejeté le bonheur dans la vie mortelle pour s'assurer des tourments dans la vie éternel. Que les anges, et les hommes pleurent son sort — il était leur frère.

5.   Emily J. Brontë   5 Août 1842

Lettre d'un Frère a un Frère

Mon frère,

venue d'outre-tombe

une lettre (recue) de moi sera pour vous comme une lettre recue du tombeau.

années   *lentement*

Dix longs ans, dix ans de souffrance, de travail et de changements se sont passes depuis nous partimes de la maison de notre père, irrités l'un contre l'autre

nous   *années*   *éteint en moi*

et/vouant une séparation éternelle. Ces ans ont dissipé/bien des espérances, (á mon egard) ils *m*'ont apporté bien des douleurs, mais au mileu de tout, je conservais caché dans mon coeur ce voeu, né de la colère et nourri de l'orgueil.

maints

J'ai traversé l'océan, j'ai voyagé dans plusieurs pays, j'ai été le plus pauvre des pauvres, malade parmi des étrangers, sans pouvoir offrir le travail de mes mains en

du   *Parfois,*

échange pour le pain que je mangeais. Aussi, j'ai joui des richesses et de tous les

qui s'achètent,

plaisirs qu'elles puissent fournir au possesseur ; mais toujours seul, toujours sans

pour

ami ; assez de me flatter, mais personne de m'aimer. Cependant je ne songeais

à

jamais de me reconciler avec vous ; je ne désirais pas de goûter encore cette

ce doux et calme

ancienne concorde d'ames (qui formait le) bonheur de notre enfance, ou si la pensée me venait quelquefois je la chassais bientôt comme une faiblesse indigne et dégradante.

Enfin mon corps et mon esprit étaient fatigués d'errer ; ma barque (était)

de tant de tempêtes

ébranlée des tempêtes, il se tardait d'être au port. Je formai la résolution de

avaient   *voulais revoir*   *natale*

finir mes jours où ils s'étaient commencés et je (/dirigai mon cours vers) la terre/

maternelle

et la maison/si longtemps abandonnées.

par

Hier soir je suis arrivé aux vielles portes du parc ; c'était une nuit orageuse et versante de pluie, mais à travers l'obscurité je distinguais de loin la lumière des

    projètant   *pâles*   *la porte était*

fenêtres qui lancait de longs rayons entre les rameaux des arbres; et me guidant

   entreouverte;   *silencieux;*

a la porte, j'y entrai: tout était tranquille, en dedans je traversai la salle, le cor-
ridor, les antichambres, sans rencontrer aucune personne et me trouvai enfin

                               commune   *autrefois, et alors se ravivaient en moi mille*

dans la bibliothèque, notre propre retraite,/ le lieu consacré à tant de souvenirs

               n'a   *à*

qu'un siècle d'éloignement ne put effacer. Pendant je contemplais par la lumière

    foyer   *ées*

douteuse du feu, les tableaux sur les murs, les rangs de livres au dessous et tous

                               ent

les objets familiers qui m'entouraitnt, quelquechose se remuait dans la chambre.
C'etait un grand chien qui s'éleva d'un coin et s'approchait pour examiner

                               me le

l'étranger, il ne trouva pas un étranger, il me reconnut et/il témoigna sa recon-
naissance par des caresses les plus expressives; mais moi, je le repoussai,

                                et cruelle victoire du

parcequ'il etait le vôtre. Pardonnez, Edouard, a ce dernier/acte du tyran qui

 mauvais   *fait taire*   *coeur;*

avait usurpé si longtemps la place de/la nature dans mon sein; l'instant après je

        j'etais

fut à genoux priant et pleurant et abjurant mon inimitié pour jamais. Je me

   presque

couchai/heureux, je m'éveille triste; peutêtre que mon repentir vienne trop tard,
peutêtre que votre coeur soit plus endurci que le mien. mais mon frère était

                               mestorts

autrefois toujours le dernier à se fâcher et le premier à oublier une injure, Edouard

     ta

viens m'assurer que votre nature n'est pas changée — n'écris pas mais viens.

. Emily J. Brontë   Le 11 Août 1842

Le Papillon

Dans une de ces dispositions de l'âme où chacun se trouve quelquefois, lorsque
le monde de l'imagination souffre un hiver qui flétrit toute sa végétation; lorsque
la lumière de la vie semble s'éteindre et l'existence devient un désert stérile où
nous errons, exposés à toutes les tempêtes qui soufflent sous le ciel, sans es-
pérance ni de repos ni d'abri — dans une de ces humeurs noires, je me prom-
enais un soir sur les confines d'une forêt. C'était en été le soleil brillait encore
haut dans l'occident et l'air retentissait des chants d'oiseaux: tout paraissait
heureux, mais pour moi, ce n'était qu'une apparence. Je m'assis au pied d'un
vieux chêne, parmi les rameaux duquel, le rossignol venait de commencer
ses vêpres. "Pauvre fou", je me dis, "est-ce pour guider la balle à ton sien (sic)
ou l'enfant à tes petits que tu chantes si haut et si clair? Tais cette mélodie
mal à–propos, blottis toi sur ton nid; demain, peutêtre, il sera vide. Mais
pourquoi m'adresser à toi seul? la création entière est également insensée.
Voilà, ces mouches jouant au dessus du ruisseau, des hirondelles et des poissons

en diminuent le nombre chaque minute: ceux-ci deviendront, en leur tour, la proie de quelque tyron de l'air ou de l'eau: et l'homme pour son amusement ou pour ses besoins, tuera leurs meurtriers. La nature est un problème inexplicable, elle existe sur un principe de destruction; il faut que tout être soit l'instrument infatigable de mort aux autres, ou qu'il cesse de vivre lui-même; et cependant, nous célébrons le jour de notre naissance, et nous louons Dieu d'avoir entré un tel monde. Pendant mon soliloque je cueillis une fleur à mes côtés, elle était belle et fraîchement épanouie mais une laide chenille s'était cachée parmi les pétales et déjà elles se ridaient et se fanaient. "Triste image de la terre et de ses habitants!" récriai-je, "ce ver ne vit que de nuire à la plante qui le protège: pourquoi était-il créé et pourquoi l'homme était-il créé? Il tourmente, il tue, il dévore; il souffre, se meurt, est dévoré — voila toute son histoire. C'est vrai qu'il y a un ciel pour le saint, mais le saint laisse assez de misère ici bas de l'attrister même devant le trône de Dieu."

Je jetai la fleur à terre; en ce moment l'univers me paraissait une vaste machine construite seulement pour produire le mal. Je doutais presque de la bonté de Dieu, dans ce qu'il n'anéantit pas l'homme sur le jour du premier péché. "Le monde aurai dû être détruit," je dis, "écrasé comme j'écrase ce reptile qui n'a rien fait pendant sa vie que rendre tout ce qu'il touche aussi dégoutant que lui-même." Je n'eus guère oté mon pied du pauvre insecte lorsque, comme un ange censeur envoyé du ciel, voltigeait à travers les arbres un papillon aux grandes ailes de luisant or et de pourpre: il ne brillait qu'un moment devant mes yeux, puis, remontant parmi les feuilles, il s'évanouit dans la hauteur de la voute azurée. Je fus muette, mais une voix intérieure me dit "Que la créature ne juge pas son Créateur, voilà un symbole du monde à venir. Comme la laide chenille est l'origine du splendide papillon, ainsi ce globe est l'embrion d'un nouveau ciel et d'une nouvelle terre dont la beauté la plus pauvre excédera infiniment ton imagination mortelle et quand tu verras le résultat magnifique de ce qui te semble maintenant si basse combien mépriseras tu ta présomption aveugle, en accusant Omiscience qu'elle n'avait pas fait périr la nature dans son enfance.

Dieu est le dieu de justice et de miséricorde; puis assurément, chaque peine qu'il inflige sur ses créatures, soient elles humaines ou animales, raisonables (sic) ou irraisonables, chaque souffrance de notre malheureuse nature n'est qu'une semence de cette moisson divine qui sera resemblés (sic) quand le péché ayant dépensé sa dernière goutte de venin, la Mort ayant laché son dernier trait tous deux expireront sur le bucher d'un univers en flammes et laisseront leurs anciennes victimes à un empire éternel de bonheur et de Gloire —

7. Emily J. Brontë   Le 18 octobre 42
Le Palais de la Mort

Autrefois, lorsque les hommes étaient en petit nombre, la Mort vivait frugalement et ménageait ses moyens; son unique ministre était alors la vieilesse, qui gardait la porte de son palais et introduisait de temps en temps une victime solitaire pour apaiser la faim de sa maitresse: cette abstinence était bientôt récompensée; la proie de sa majesté s'augmentait prodigieusement et la Vieillesse commençait à trouver qu'elle avait trop à faire.

Il était à cette époque que la Mort se décida à changer sa manière de vivre, à appointer des agents nouveaux et de prendre un premier ministre. Le jour fixé pour la nomination le silence du sombre palais fut rompu par l'arrivé des candidats de tous côtes, les voûtes, les chanbres et les galeries résonnaient du bruit des pas qui allaient et venaient, comme si les ossements qui jonchaient leur pavé s'étaient subitement réanimés et la Mort, regardant du haut de son trône, sourit hidieusement de voir quelles multitudes accouraient à lui servir.

Parmi les premiers venus on voyait la Colère et la Vengeance qui allèrent se mettre en face de sa Majesté, en disputant hautement sur la justice de leurs droits particuliers; L'Envie et la Trahison prirent leurs stations derrière dans l'ombre; la Famine et la Peste, assistés par leurs compagnons la Paresse et l'Avarice obtinrent des places très commodes parmi la foule et jetèrent un regard méprisant sur les autres hôtes; cependant elles se trouvèrent forcées à céder quand l'Ambition et le Fanatisme paraissaient; les cortèges de ces deux personnages emplissaient la salle de conseil et ils demandèrent imperieusement une audience prompte.

"Je ne doute pas", dit la première, "que votre majesté sera juste dans sa décision mais à quoi consumer le temps en vaines contestations quand un coup-d'oeil suffira à déterminer celle qui est seule digne de l'office en question? Quels sont tous ces prétendants qui assiègent votre trône? Que pensent ils faire dans votre service? Le plus habile parmi eux n'est pas plus capable de gouverner votre empire qu'un soldat qui n'a d'autre qualité que son courage, de commander une armée. Ils savent frapper une victime ici et une autre là, ils savent attraper la faible proie, les hommes sur lesquels votre signe est visible depuis leur naissance et ce sont les limites de leur utilité; tandis que moi, je menerai à vos portes l'élite de la race; ceux qui sont plus éloignés de votre pouvoir; je les moissonerai dans leur fleur et vous les offrirai par troupes à la fois. Puis j'ai tant de moyens; il n'est pas le glaive seul qui gagne mes victoires; j'ai d'autres agents, des alliés secrets mais puissants; le Fanatisme lui-meme n'est qu'un instrument que j'emploierai à me servir."

En entendant ces mots le Fanatisme secoua sa tête sauvage et levant vers la Mort un oeil brulant de feu de la manie il commença: "Je sais que cette glorieuse sera aise d'emprunter mes armes et de marcher sous mes ensignes, mais est cela une raison qu'elle présume a se comparer avec moi? Non seulement je serai puissant comme elle à renverser les états et à desoler les royaumes, mais j'en-trerai dans les familles j'opposerai le fils au père, la fille à la mere; inspirés par moi l'ami fidèle deviendrai un ennemi mortel, la femme trahira son mari, le domestique son maître; nul sentiment ne peut me resister; je traverserai le terre (sic) sous les lumières du ciel et les couronnes seront comme des pierres sous mes pieds. Quant aux autres candidats ils sont pas dignes d'attention; la Colère est irraisonnable; la vengeance est partiale; la Famine peut être vaincue par l'industrie; la Peste est capricieuse. Votre premier ministre doit être quelqu'un qui est toujours près des hommes et les possède; décidez donc entre l'Ambition et moi, nous sommes les seuls sur lesquels votre choix peut hésiter."

Le Fanatisme se tut, et sa Majesté semblait balancer en doute entre ces deux rivaux lorsque la portes (sic) de la salle s'ouvrit et il y entra une personne devant laquelle tout le monde recula en étonnement car elle avait une figure qui paraissait rayonner de joie et de santé, son pas était leger comme un zephyr et la Mort elle-même semblait inquiete à sa première approche; cependant elle se rassura bientôt; "Vous me connaissez" lui dit l'étrangère, "je viens plus tarde que les autres mais je sais que ma cause est sûre Quelqu'uns de mes rivaux sont formidables j'avoue et il est possible que je sois surpassée par plusieurs en faits éclatants qui attirent l'admiration du vulgaire, mais j'ai une amie devant laquelle toute cette assemblée sera forcée à succomber; elle se nomme la Civilization: en quelques années elle viendra habiter cette terre avec nous et chaque siècle augmentera son pouvoir. A la fin elle détournera l'Ambition de votre service; elle jetera sur la colère le frein de la loi; elle arrachera les armes des mains du Fanatisme; elle chassera la Famine parmi les sauvages: moi seule j'agrandirai et fleurirai sous son règne, la puissance de tous les autres expirera avec leurs partisans: la mienne existera lorsque même je suis morte. Si une fois je fais connaissance avec le père mon influence s'étendra au fils et avant que les hommes s'unissent pour me bannir de leur societé j'aurai changé toute leur nature et rendue l'espèce entière une plus facile proie à votre majesté, si effectivement en effet, que la Vieillesse aura presque un sinecure et votre palais sera gorgé de victimes."

"Ne parlez plus", dit la Mort descendant de son trone et embrassant l'Intempérance (c'est ainsi que l'étrangère s'appelait) "il suffit que je vous connais; pour les autres j'ai des offices lucratifs et importants, ils seront tous mes ministres, mais à vous seule est reservé l'honneur d'être mon vice-roi."

APPENDIX B

TITLES OF EMILY BRONTË'S POEMS PUBLISHED IN JOINT VOLUME OF *POEMS* WITH HER SISTERS, 1846

1. *Faith and Despondency* (Hatfield 177)   6 November 1844
   'The winter wind is loud and wild'
   (Gondal poem)

2. *Stars* (Hatfield 184)   14 April 1845
   'Ah! Why, because the dazzling sun'

3. *The Philosopher* (Hatfield 181)   3 February 1845
   'Enough of thought, Philosopher'

4. *Remembrance* (Hatfield 182)   3 March 1845
   'Cold in the earth'
   (Gondal poem)

5. *A Death-Scene* (Hatfield 180)   2 December 1844
   'O Day! he cannot die'
   (Gondal poem)

6. *Song* (Hatfield 173)   1 May 1844
   'The linnet in the rocky dells'
   (Gondal poem)

7. *Anticipation* (Hatfield 188)   2 June 1845
   'How beautiful the earth is still'

8. *The Prisoner* (Hatfield 190)   9 October 1845
   'In the dungeon-crypts'
   (Gondal poem)

9. *Hope* (Hatfield 165)   18 December 1843
   'Hope was but a timid friend'

10. *A Day Dream* (Hatfield 170)   5 March 1844
    On a sunny brae alone I lay'

11. *To Imagination* (Hatfield 174)   3 September 1844
    'When weary with the long day's care'

12. *How clear she shines*! (Hatfield 157)   13 April 1843
    'How clear she shines! how quietly'

13. *Sympathy* (Hatfield 122)   no date
    'There should be no despair for you'

14. *Plead for me* (Hatfield 176)   14 October 1844
    'Oh, thy bright eyes must answer now'

15. *Self-Interrogation* (Hatfield 155)   23 October 1842–
    'The evening passes fast away'   6 February 1843

16. *Death* (Hatfield 183)   10 April 1845
    'Death that struck when I was most confiding'

17. *Stanzas to—*(Hatfield 123)   14 November 1839
    'Well, some may hate, and some may scorn'
    (Gondal poem)

18. *Honour's Martyr* (Hatfield 179)   21 November 1844
    'The moon is full this winter night'
    (Gondal poem)

19. *Stanzas* (Hatfield 136)   4 May 1840
    'I'll not weep that thou art going to leave me'

20. *My Comforter* (Hatfield 168)   10 February 1844
    'Well hast thou spoken—and yet not taught'

21. *The Old Stoic* (Hatfield 146)   1 March 1844
    'Riches I hold in light esteem'

APPENDIX C

The degree of Anne's participation in the creation of Gondal may be judged from two lists in her hand-writing preserved at the BPM. One is of Gondal characters (14 men and 12 women) which includes such major figures in the Saga as *Gerald Exina*, *Alexandria Zenobia Hybernia*, *Henry Sophona*, *Lucia Angora*, names whose incidence recurs in the Gondal poetry and chronicles of the girls' maturity. Thus, in their joint diary-paper of 26 June 1837 (see p. 65) there is reference to Anne writing a poem beginning: 'Fair was the evening and brightly the sun'—a poem whose protagonists are Alexander Hybernia and Zenobia. In Emily's diary-paper of July 1845 she mentions Anne 'writing a book on *Henry Sophona*'. *Gerald Exina* is, of course, one of the chief characters running through Emily's Gondal poems. There exists, also, a list of Gondal place-names in Anne's writing, inserted alphabetically in the index of the girls' geography book—Goldsmith's *Grammar of General Geography* (1823)—from which we learn that *Gondal* 'is a large Island in the North Pacific' divided into four kingdoms—Gondal, Angora, Alcona, Exina'. *Gaaldine*, 'a large island newly discovered in the South Pacific' which is divided into six kingdoms—Alexandria, Almedore, Elseraden, Ula, Zelona, Zedora', names which persist throughout the Gondal writings. The inclusion of the 'newly discovered' Gaaldine in this list would indicate 1834 as the date of its writing, as the girls' diary-paper of 23 November 1834 announced 'the Gondals are discovering the interior of Gaaldine' (see p. 39). From Anne's list of place-names, as the poetry of both girls reveals, were derived the titles of many of the characters, such as: Augusta Geraldine *Almeda*, Rosina *Ancona*, Julius Brenzaida of *Almedore*, Gerald *Exina*, etc. Topography is, indeed, a strong element in the Gondal poems of both sisters. Emily wrote of 'The Fall of *Zelona*' (Hatfield 156), of the *Gaaldine Prison Caves* (Hatfield 133), of *Regina* (Hatfield 13), of *A Farewell to Alexandria* (Hatfield 108), of *Zedora's* strand and *Ula's* Eden sky (Hatfield 141) many years after Anne's list was first drawn up, thus confirming the enduring character of their collaboration.

BIBLIOGRAPHY

I: ORIGINAL MSS. AND OFFICIAL DOCUMENTS

The MS. poems, diary-papers, original French essays, drawings, one holograph letter, music-albums, personal relics, account-books, etc. of Emily Jane Brontë. Brontë Parsonage Museum, Haworth.

MS. poems, 'Gondal' and other poems. Smith Bequest, British Museum (Add. MS. 43,483).

French essays. Miriam Stark Library, Texas University Library; Berg Collection, New York Public Library.

MS. poems and letters of Anne Brontë. Brontë Parsonage Museum.

Angrian MSS., poems and letters (to J. Thompson) of Patrick Branwell Brontë. Brontë Parsonage Museum and British Museum.

Angrian MSS., Young Men's Magazines, letters, and poems of Charlotte Brontë. Brontë Parsonage Museum.

MS. letters of Charlotte Brontë to M. Heger. BM, Add. MS. 38,732 A, B, C, D.

MS. letters of Charlotte Brontë to Miss Wooler. Allbutt Bequest, Fitzwilliam Museum Library, Cambridge.

Angrian MSS., and letters of Patrick Branwell Brontë to J. B. Leyland. Brotherton Library, University of Leeds.

MS. letters of Charlotte Brontë to Mrs. Gaskell. Manchester University Library.

MS. letters of the Revd. Patrick Brontë. Brontë Parsonage Museum.

Diaries of Elizabeth Firth, 1812–25, 1829. Sheffield University Library.

Diaries and family records of Caroline Walker, 1772–1804, 1796–1830. Halifax Public Library.

Diary of John Greenwood of Haworth. Privately owned.

Registers of the Clergy Daughters' School, 1824–5. Casterton School, Lancashire.

Parish registers of St. James's Church, Thornton, Yorkshire

Parish registers of St. Michael and All Angels' Church, Haworth.

The Heaton Records—catalogue of the library of Ponden House. Cartwright Memorial Hall, Bradford.

II: WORKS BY THE BRONTËS: PUBLISHED TEXTS

Poems by Currer, Ellis and Acton Bell, London, Aylott & Jones, 1846.

Jane Eyre: an Autobiography, by Currer Bell, London, Smith, Elder, 1847

Wuthering Heights: A Novel, by Ellis Bell, with *Agnes Grey*, by Acton Bell, 3 vols., London, T. C. Newby, 1847.

The Tenant of Wildfell Hall, by Acton Bell, 3 vols., London, T. C. Newby, 1848.

Shirley, by Currer Bell, 3 vols., London, Smith, Elder, 1849.

Wuthering Heights and Agnes Grey, by Ellis and Acton Bell. A new edition with a Biographical Notice of the authors, a selection from their literary remains, and a Preface by Currer Bell, London, Smith, Elder, 1850.

Wuthering Heights, Haworth edn., intr. by Mrs. Humphry Ward, 1899.

The Odes of Horace, Book I, translated by Patrick Branwell Brontë, ed. John Drinkwater, privately printed, 1923.

And the Weary are at Rest, by Patrick Branwell Brontë, ed. C. K. Shorter, privately printed, 1924.

The Twelve Adventurers and Other Stories, by Charlotte Brontë, ed. C. W. Hatfield, London, 1925.

The Complete Poems of Emily Jane and Anne Brontë, ed. Wise and Symington, Oxford, Shakespeare Head, 1934.

The Miscellaneous and Unpublished Writings of Charlotte and Patrick Branwell Brontë, ed. Wise and Symington, Oxford, Shakespeare Head, 1934.

The Poems of Charlotte and Patrick Branwell Brontë, ed. Wise and Symington, Oxford, Shakespeare Head, 1934.

The Complete Poems of Emily Jane Brontë, edited from the manuscripts by C. W. Hatfield, New York, Columbia University Press, 1941.

III: PUBLISHED WORKS ON THE BRONTËS

In chronological order of publication

1850   DOBELL, SYDNEY, 'Currer Bell', *The Palladium*, Sept. 1850, repr. in *BST*, 1918.

1857   GASKELL, E., *Life of Charlotte Brontë*, 2 vols., London, Smith, Elder; 3rd edition, Sept. 1857.

1871   NUSSEY, ELLEN, 'Reminiscences of Charlotte Brontë', *Scribner's Magazine*, May 1871; repr. in *BST*, 1899.

1877   WEMYSS REID, T., *Charlotte Brontë, A Monograph*, London, Macmillan.

1879   GRUNDY, F. H., *Pictures of the Past*, London, Griffin and Farrar.

1883   DUCLAUX-ROBINSON, MARY, *Emily Brontë*, Eminent Women Series, London, Allen.

1886   LEYLAND, F. A., *The Brontë Family, with Special Reference to Patrick Branwell Brontë*, 2 vols., London, Hurst and Blackett.

1887   BIRRELL, A., *Life of Charlotte Brontë*, London, Walter Scott.

1893 WRIGHT, DR. W., *The Brontës in Ireland*, London, Hodder and Stoughton.

1894 MACDONALD, FREDERIKA: 'The Brontës in Brussels', *Woman at Home*, July.

1896 SHORTER, C. K., *Charlotte Brontë and Her Circle*, London, Hodder and Stoughton; repr. as *The Brontës and their Circle*, London, Dent, 1914.

1897 MACKAY, ANGUS M., *The Brontës: Fact and Fiction*, London, Service and Paton.

1898 MAETERLINCK, MAURICE, *La Sagesse et la Destinée*, Paris, E. Fasquelle.

1905 SHORTER, C. K., *Charlotte Brontë and her Sisters*, London, Hodder and Stoughton.

1908 SHORTER, C. K., *The Brontës: Life and Letters*, 2 vols., London, Hodder and Stoughton.

1910 DIMNET, ABBÉE, *Les Soeurs Brontë*, Paris; transl. L. M. Sill, London, Cape, 1927.

1912 SINCLAIR, MAY, *The Three Brontës*, London, Hutchinson.

1913 SPURGEON, CAROLINE, *Mysticism in English Literature*, Cambridge University Press.

1914 CHADWICK, ELLIS, *In the Footsteps of the Brontës*, London, Pitman.

1914 MACDONALD, FREDERIKA, *The Secret of Charlotte Brontë*, London, T. C. and E. C. Jack.

1916 GREEN, J. J., 'The Brontë-Wheelwright Friendship', *Friends' Quarterly Examiner*, Nov.

1919 SPIELMANN, M. H., *The Inner History of the Brontë–Heger Letters*, London, Chapman and Hall.

1923 HOPE-DODDS, M., 'Gondalland', *Modern Language Review*, Jan.; cont. Oct. 1926.

1925 WOOLF, VIRGINIA, 'Jane Eyre and Wuthering Heights', *The Common Reader*, London, Hogarth Press.

1926 READ, HERBERT, 'The Nature of Metaphysical Poetry', *Reason and Romanticism: Essays in Literary Criticism*, London, Faber and Gwyer.

1928 WILSON, ROMER, *All Alone, the Life and Private History of Emily Jane Brontë*, London, Chatto.

1929 SIMPSON, CHARLES, *Emily Brontë*, London, Country Life.

1933 WILLIS, IRENE C., *The Brontës*, London, Duckworth; Duckworth Paperbacks, 1957.

1934 CECIL, LORD DAVID, *Early Victorian Novelists*, London, Constable.

1935 HARRISON, G. ELSIE, *Methodist Good Companions*, London, Epworth.

1936 MOORE, VIRGINIA, *The Life and Eager Death of Emily Brontë*, London, Rich and Cowan.

1936 WILLIS, IRENE C., *The Authorship of Wuthering Heights*, London, Hogarth Press.

1937 HARRISON, G. ELSIE, *Haworth Parsonage: a Study of Wesley and the Brontës*, London, Epworth.

1938 MOTT, JOAN, and BROWN, HELEN, *Gondal Poems*, Oxford, Blackwell.

1939 BROWN, HELEN, 'The influence of Byron on Emily Brontë', *Mod. Lang. Rev.*, July.

1941 RATCHFORD, F. E., *The Brontës' Web of Childhood*, New York, Columbia Univ. Press.

1944 MORGAN, CHARLES, *Reflections in a Mirror*, London, Macmillan.

1945 HINCKLEY, LAURA, *The Brontës: Charlotte and Emily*, London, Hammond.

1947 BENTLEY, PHYLLIS, *The Brontës*, London, Home and Van Thal.

1948 RAYMOND, ERNEST, *In the Steps of the Brontës*, London, Rich and Cowan.

1948 HARRISON, G. ELSIE, *The Clue to the Brontës*, London, Methuen.

1950 DEBÛ-BRIDEL, J., *Le Secret d'Emilie Brontë*, Paris.

1952–3 LEAVIS, F. R., 'Reality and Sincerity: Notes in the Analysis of Poetry', *Scrutiny*, XIX.

1953 SPARK, MURIEL, and STANFORD, DEREK, *Emily Brontë, Her Life and Work*, London, Owen.

1954 TILLOTSON, KATHLEEN, *The Novels of the Eighteen-Forties*, Oxford, Clarendon Press.

1954 ALLEN, WALTER, *The English Novel*, London, Phoenix House.

1955 BLONDEL, JACQUES, *Emily Brontë, Expérience Spirituelle et Création Poétique*, Clermont Ferrand, Presses Universitaires de France.

1958 PADEN, W. D., *An Investigation of Gondal*, New York, Bookman Associates.

1958 VISICK, MARY, *The Genesis of Wuthering Heights*, Hong Kong University Press.

1959 GÉRIN, W., *Anne Brontë, a Biography*, London, Nelson.

1961 GÉRIN, W., *Branwell Brontë, a Biography*, London, Nelson.

1961 BLONDEL, J., 'Nouveaux Regards sur Emily Brontë', *Annales de la Faculté des Lettres d'Aix*, 35.

1965 LOCK, J., and DIXON, W. T., *A Man of Sorrow: the Life, Letters and Times of the Revd. Patrick Brontë*, London, Nelson.

1967 GÉRIN, W., *Charlotte Brontë, the Evolution of Genius*, Oxford, Clarendon Press.

1969 HEWISH, J., *Emily Brontë, A Critical and Biographical Study*, London, Macmillan.

1969 BENTLEY, PHYLLIS, *The Brontës and their World*, London, Thames and Hudson.

IV: TRANSACTIONS OF THE BRONTË SOCIETY

1900 FOTHERINGHAM, J., 'The Work of Emily Brontë'.

1901 HALDANE, R. B., 'Emily Brontë's Place in Literature'.

1902 SUTCLIFFE, H., 'The Spirit of the Moors'.

1905 WARD, Mrs. HUMPHRY, 'Prefaces of *Wuthering Heights*'.

1912 VAUGHAN, C. E., 'Charlotte and Emily Brontë, a Contrast and Comparison'.

1918 DOBELL, SYDNEY, 'Currer Bell' (reprinted from *The Palladium*, 1850).

1921 HOPEWELL, D., 'Cowan Bridge'.

1922 WOOD, B., 'The Influence of the Moorland on Charlotte and Emily Brontë'.

1924 ABERCROMBIE, L., 'The Brontës Today'.

1924 HANSON, T. W., 'The Local Colour of *Wuthering Heights*'.

1929 MACKERETH, J. A., 'The Greatness of Emily Brontë'.

1932 EDGERLEY, C. M.,'Emily Brontë, a National Portrait Vindicated'.

1937 BULLOCK, F. A., 'The Genius of Emily Brontë'.

1938 BROWN, HELEN, and MOTT, JOAN, 'The Gondal Saga'.

1942 RATCHFORD, F. E., 'The Correct Text of Emily's Poems: Hatfield's Edition'.

1945 OLSEN, T., 'The Weary are at Rest: A Reconsideration of Branwell Brontë'.

1946 WEIR, E. M., 'Cowan Bridge: New Light on Old Documents'.

1947 WEIR, E. M., 'Contemporary Reviews of the First Brontë Novels'.

1948 DOBSON, M. A., 'Was Emily Brontë a Mystic?'

1949 ANDREWS, W. L., 'The Centenary of Emily Brontë's Death'.

1950 MIDGLEY, W., 'Sunshine on Haworth Moors'.

1950 WHONE, C., 'Where the Brontës borrowed Books'.

1951 BARKER, Sir E., 'The Inspiration of Emily Brontë'.

1951 PRESTON, A. H., 'John Greenwood and the Brontës'.

1952 COOPER, D. J., 'The Romantics and Emily Brontë'.

1953 HAWKES, J., 'Emily Brontë in the Natural Scene'.

1954 WEST, R., 'The Role of Fantasy in the Work of the Brontës'.

1955 HUGUENIN, C. A., 'Bronteana at Princeton University'.

1955 CHARLIER, G., 'Brussels Life in *Villette*'.

1956 FIELDING, K. J., 'The Brontës and the *North American Review*'.

1957 LEWIS, C. DAY, 'The Poetry of Emily Brontë'.

1957 ORAM, E., 'Emily Brontë and F. D. Maurice'.

1958 ARNOLD, H. H., 'The Reminiscences of Emma Huidekoper Cortazzo'.

1964 FRIESNER, D. N., 'Ellis Bell and Israfel'.

1964 NELSON, J. G., 'First American Reviews of the Works of the Brontës'.

1965 HARTLEY, L. P., 'Emily Brontë in Gondal and Gaaldine'.

1966 WADDINGTON-FEATHER, J. J., 'Emily Brontë's Use of Dialect in *Wuthering Heights*'.

1966 BRACCO, E. J., 'Emily Brontë's Second Novel'.

1967 MAXWELL, J. C., 'Emily Brontë's "The Palace of Death"'.

1968 DREW, D. P., 'Emily Brontë and Emily Dickinson as Mystic Poets'.

1968 LANE, M., 'Emily Brontë in a Cold Climate'.

V: TOPOGRAPHICAL WORKS

DEARDEN, WILLIAM, *Yorkshire Notes and Queries*, 1890.

KEIGHLEY, WILLIAM, *Keighley, Past and Present*, Keighley, A. Hey, 1879.

SCRUTON, WILLIAM,
Pen and Pencil Pictures of Old Bradford, Bradford, Brear and Co., 1889.
Brontë Files, 1894.
Thornton and the Brontës, Bradford, J. Dale and Co., 1898.

STORY, T. W., *Notes on the Old Haworth Church Registers*, 1909.

STUART, J. A. ERSKINE, *The Brontë Country*, London, Longmans, 1888.

TURNER, J. HORSFALL, *Haworth, Past and Present*, Brighouse, 1879.

TURNER, WHITELEY, 'A Springtime Saunter Round and About Brontëland', *The Halifax Courier*, 1913.

VI: OTHER WORKS CITED

BEWICK, THOMAS, *A History of British Birds*, 2 vols., Newcastle, 1797, 1804.

BLAKE, *Complete Writings*, ed. G. Keynes, Oxford 1966 (Oxford Standard Authors).

BUNTING, *The Life of Jabez Bunting*, by his son T. P. Bunting, London 1887.

BYRON, *Manfred; Cain; Lara; The Corsair; Childe Harold's Pilgrimage*.

Chamber's Miscellany, 1844-7.

CRAGG, G., *Grimshaw of Haworth*, 1947.

CROXALL, SAMUEL, *Aesop's Fables*, 1722.

DE QUINCEY, THOMAS, *Confessions of an English Opium Eater* (1822); New University Library, 1905.

EASTLAKE, *The Letters and Journals of Lady Elizabeth Eastlake*, ed. by her nephew Charles Eastlake Smith, London, Murray, 1895.

EDGEWORTH, MARIA, *Castle Rackrent* (1800), ed. G. Watson, Oxford, 1964.

EMERSON, R. W., *Essays*, London, 1848.

GALLAND, *The Arabian Nights' Entertainment*, London, 1787.

GASKELL, Mrs. E., *Letters*, ed. Chapple and Pollard, Manchester University Press, 1966.

HAIGHT, G., *George Eliot*, Oxford, Clarendon Press, 1968.

284 BIBLIOGRAPHY

HOFFMAN, E. H. A., *Elixire des Teufels*, (1815–16); translation, *The Devil's Elixir*, published in *Blackwood's Magazine*, 1824.

HOGG, JAMES (the Ettrick Shepherd), *The Private Memoirs and Confessions of a Justified Sinner* (1824), ed. J. Carey, Oxford, 1969.

MOORE, THOMAS, *Life of Lord Byron*, 1832.

——, *Journals and Letters of Lord Byron*, 1833.

MORELL, Sir CHARLES, *Tales of the Genii*, London, 1764.

OLIPHANT, Mrs., *Annals of a Publishing House : William Blackwood and his Sons*, Edinburgh and London, Blackwood, 1897.

PERCY, THOMAS, *Reliques of Ancient English Poetry*, 1765.

ROLT, L. T. C., *George and Robert Stephenson*, London, Longman, 1960.

SCOTT, Sir WALTER, *Tales of a Grandfather*, 1828; *The Lady of the Lake*; *Rob Roy*; *Old Mortality* ; *Waverley*.

SHELLEY, MARY, *Valperga*, published in *Blackwood's Magazine*, 1823.

SHELLEY, PERCY, BYSSHE, *Poetical Works*, ed. Hutchinson, Oxford 1943 (Oxford Standard Authors).

SIMMONDS, BARTHOLOMEW, *The Bridegroom of Barna*, published in *Blackwood's Magazine*, 1840.

SOUTHEY, ROBERT, *The Correspondence of Robert Southey with Caroline Bowles*, ed. E. Dowden, Dublin, 1881.

TROLLOPE, ANTHONY, *Autobiography*, 1883; World's Classics edn., 1947.

INDEX

AB = Anne Brontë
CB = Charlotte Brontë
BB = Branwell Brontë
EB = Emily Brontë
WH = Wuthering Heights